T0275150

About the Author

CORETTA SCOTT KING was an American civil rights activist, international human rights champion, author, the wife of Martin Luther King Jr., and the mother of four. Born in 1927 in Heiberger, Alabama, King died in 2006 in Rosarito Beach, Mexico.

About the Reverend

REVEREND DR. BARBARA REYNOLDS is an ordained minister, a columnist, and the author of five books, including *Out of Hell & Living Well: Healing from the Inside Out.* She was a longtime editorial board member of *USA Today*, won an SCLC Drum Major for Justice Award in 1987, and was inducted into the Board of Preachers at the 29th Annual Martin Luther King Jr. International College of Ministers and Laity at Morehouse College in 2014. For more information, please visit www.drbarbarareynolds.com.

Also by Coretta Scott King

My Life with Martin Luther King, Jr.

Additional Praise for *Coretta: My Life, My Love, My Legacy*

One of *The Washington Post*'s Books to Read of the Year
A *New York Times Book Review* Editors' Choice
A *USA Today* New and Noteworthy Book
A *Read It Forward* Favorite Reads Pick
A *Parade* Magazine Pick

"This memoir shows Coretta Scott King . . . as a leader in her own right, as a dedicated pacifist, as a persistent adherent to principles of nonviolence, as a gritty fighter for her husband's legacy, as a mother. . . . A great and inspirational read . . . This book put steel in my spine."
—Julianne Malveaux, *New Pittsburgh Courier*

"This book is distinctly Coretta's story. . . . Living with terror is the thread that runs through [it.] This is a tale of church assaults before Dylann Roof, of cattle prods before there were tasers, of nooses before there were chokeholds, of COINTELPRO before there was Breitbart, of voter suppression before anyone bothered to deny it. . . . Nonviolence, she reiterates, is not a matter of passively accepting whatever happens. It is active. It is a practice. As her husband preached: 'Justice is really love in calculation.' . . . There is unusual inspiration in that mien. The larger, more ecumenical meaning of Coretta Scott King's life, love, and legacy may be found in the peace-lending power, needed now as never before."
—Patricia J. Williams, *The New York Times Book Review*

"Eloquent . . . Inspirational . . . King's life's work, relayed in this rich retelling, provides a possible blueprint—and a beacon."   —*USA Today*

"The full life story of the civil rights activist and humanitarian is much more than just Dr. Martin Luther King Jr.'s wife. . . . It is her commitment to bettering the world that will keep her story alive in our hearts."
—*Ebony*

"The portrait that emerges here is of a woman of tremendous faith, resilience, and pride. . . . By the time she died, she'd fought for a lifetime of causes." —*New York Post*

"An important heroine in her own right, Coretta Scott King's story is mesmerizing." —*Read It Forward*

"Gracious, elegant . . . A touching memoir from an important figure in the civil rights movement." —*Kirkus Reviews*

"In [*Coretta*], legendary journalist Barbara Reynolds reveals never-before-told aspects of Mrs. King's life. . . . We learn of the brilliant mind and courageous spirit behind the enigmatic figure." —*Essence*

"A spiritual narrative with God as a frequent directing presence . . . 'In reading this memoir, I hope somehow you see Coretta,' King confides in the introduction. One does." —*Publishers Weekly*

"This account of family, faith, and activism . . . is told so genuinely that it leaves the impression of having heard the words directly from the late activist. . . . Highly recommended." —*Library Journal* (starred review)

"King was undoubtedly a singular woman, and readers will be struck by just how strongly her exceedingly compelling story resonates today. She was much more than just the woman behind the man, and now, in the most eloquent of language, she proves that truth once and for all to generations of readers who will embrace her all over again."
—*Booklist* (starred review)

Coretta

Coretta

My Life, My Love, My Legacy

Coretta Scott King

With the Reverend Dr. Barbara Reynolds

PICADOR   HENRY HOLT AND COMPANY   NEW YORK

picadorusa.com • picadorbookroom.tumblr.com
twitter.com/picadorusa • facebook.com/picadorusa

Picador® is a U.S. registered trademark and is used by Macmillan Publishing Group, LLC, under license from Pan Books Limited.

For book club information, please visit facebook.com/picadorbookclub or email marketing@picadorusa.com.

Maya Angelou interview used with permission by Caged Bird Legacy, LLC.

All photographs, unless otherwise credited, are used courtesy of the Estate of Coretta Scott King.

Designed by Meryl Sussman Levavi

The Library of Congress has cataloged the Henry Holt and Company edition as follows:

Names: King, Coretta Scott, 1927–2006, author.
Title: My Life, My Love, My Legacy / Coretta Scott King ; as told to the Rev. Dr. Barbara Reynolds.
Description: New York : Henry Holt and Company, 2017.
Identifiers: LCCN 2016039557 | ISBN 9781627795982 (hardcover) | ISBN 9781627795999 (ebook)
Subjects: LCSH: King, Coretta Scott, 1927–2006. | King, Martin Luther, Jr., 1929–1968. | Civil rights workers—United States—Biography. | African American women—Biography. | Social reformers—United States—Biography. | Spouses of clergy—United States—Biography. | Widows—United States—Biography | Baptist women—United States—Biography. | Christian women—United States—Biography.
Classification: LCC E185.97.K47 A3 2017 | DDC 323.092 B
LC record available at https://lccn.loc.gov/2016039557

Picador Paperback ISBN 978-1-250-15993-9

Our books may be purchased in bulk for promotional, educational, or business use. Please contact your local bookseller or the Macmillan Corporate and Premium Sales Department at 1-800-221-7945, extension 5442, or by email at MacmillanSpecialMarkets@macmillan.com.

First published by Henry Holt and Company, LLC, as *My Life, My Love, My Legacy*

First Picador Edition: February 2018

D 11

Contents

Coretta

Introduction

THERE IS A Mrs. King. There is also Coretta. How one became detached from the other remains a mystery to me.

Most people who have followed my career from afar, or even given me a second thought, know me as Mrs. King: the wife of, the widow of, the mother of, the leader of. Makes me sound like the attachments that come with my vacuum cleaner. In one sense, I don't mind that at all. I'm proud to have been a wife, a single parent, and a leader. But I am more than a label. I am also Coretta.

Isn't it time you know the integrated, holistic woman: one spirit, one soul, one destiny?

In reading this memoir, I hope somehow you see *Coretta*.

As I reflect upon the chapters of my life, peering into the margins and fine print as well as at the boldly illuminated headlines, I am simply amazed. I was born on April 27, 1927, in Heiberger, Alabama, at a time and in a place where everything I would eventually become was impossible even to imagine.

Who could have dreamed that a little girl who began life as a part-time hired hand picking cotton for two dollars a week in the piercing hot sun would rise to a position that allowed her to help pick U.S. mayors, congresspersons, and even presidents? Or that in the 1950s and 1960s, when a woman's place (and sometimes her imprisonment) was clearly defined as the home, I would be both an avowed homemaker and a liberated feminist? That I would be able to help build a human rights movement while also raising four beautiful children? And by no means did I dare think as a child that I could ever help create a more humane environment for African Americans: from my earliest childhood, whites regularly terrorized our family, and it was not a crime. In the 1940s and '50s, one dared not dream of equality under the law. We could not sleep in our beds without fear of being burned out by white vigilantes. We could not walk in the front door of an ice-cream parlor without being shooed to the back. We had to step off the sidewalk and lower our eyes when a white person approached. This is the narrow door I entered as a young girl. It is not the same door from which I will exit.

The movement did not only lift blacks. It elevated the entire nation toward a place of true respect, love, and justice that transcends race, color, or creed. I call that place the Beloved Community. The road to the Beloved Community is the road of nonviolence. The roadblocks are hate and prejudice. We are not there yet. But there are more doors open than ever before. We stand on the cusp of a new day, one brimming with possibilities that once lived only in the restricted passageways of our dreams.

In my teen years, I spent a lot of time trying to discover who I was. I used to look at myself in the mirror and ponder why I had been placed on this planet. Sometimes I would grow nervous; it was as though I could perceive myself as another human being, someone much larger than a little country girl sitting on a bench in the backwoods of Alabama. I used to go out in the woods and sit for hours, thinking and meditating. Rodin's statue had nothing on me. I imagined myself seated next to the proverbial man in the moon, blasting off to adventures far past Heiberger. At thirteen, that was the only way I could transcend the small space I occupied. My mind left home long before I packed my physical bags.

I hope that now, in some way, you will know this Coretta.

Of course, while my memoir is about me, it is about Martin, too. Our lives were too inseparable to be perforated. Cutting us one from the other would leave a jagged edge. Yet, I did have a life after Martin, just as I had a life before Martin. I have a purpose. I have a mission, and I have carried it out on the world stage.

To discover what you're called to do with your life, I believe you have to be connected to God, to that divine force in your life, and that you have to continue to pray for direction. I did that. My life careened down roads I had never imagined traveling. I took on tasks requiring skills and wisdom I didn't have until circumstances demanded them. All this kept me on my knees, calling on God. Over the years, as I prayed for strength, I felt a sense of relief. I was doing God's work, I knew, and He would take care of me and my family. That didn't mean that nothing bad would ever happen. It didn't mean that at all. But pain is the price some people have to pay, and death can be a redeeming voice; it can promote change and advance the work of God's kingdom. I came to understand all this in the early days of the Montgomery movement. And the understanding I found then has never left me: I had a divine calling on my life, a charge, a challenge to serve not just black people, but all oppressed humankind. That calling will be with me to the end.

As my life unfolded, I saw a pattern. My value system formed and was strengthened through pain and sacrifice—not through talking the talk but by walking the walk in the line of fire. In Montgomery, Alabama, during the famous Bus Boycott, I came to understand what I was made of, what pressures I could withstand without breaking or running away. I was not a crystal figurine, fragile and fearful. If I had been breakable, I would have been a major distraction to Martin. His concern for my safety and that of our children would have prevented him from being able to stand in the line of fire. Instead, he soon found that I could be trusted when facing trouble.

When I look back on the harassment we endured, on the persecution of my husband and the threats to our lives, I am still amazed at what lies within me. We cannot know how far we can soar until we are tested. Strangely enough, I actually become stronger in crises. I didn't understand that until I found myself in the midst of a tsunami. During that time in Montgomery, I felt an inner strength; it told me that, if necessary, I could do it again. And again.

Did Martin ever understand how deep my inner calling was? I don't think so. It transcended even our marriage, and he sometimes struggled to capture its essence. Once, when we were talking about the importance of ensuring that our children receive a proper amount of attention from their parents, he blurted out, "You see, I am called, and you are not."

I said to him, "You know, I've always felt that I have a call on my life, too. I have been called by God to do something, too, and I have to do it."

Generally, Martin was very encouraging, and there were times when he was frustrated with himself, too; he wanted to be a father who was very involved in the lives of his children, but the movement required so much of his time. In any case, our debates about how best to take care of our children did not disturb me, because I knew exactly where he was coming from. We felt a similar pull, a similar pressure from God. I was married to Martin, but I was even more married to the movement and its mission of helping to create a Beloved Community of compassion, justice, and nonviolence.

Was my path a lonely one? Yes, at times. You do not lose your husband, who is also your best friend, and not feel lonely. But I was never alone. I had my mother and father, my mother-in-law and father-in-law, my sister and brother, my sisters-in-law, my nieces and nephews, my four wonderful children, and the King Center, which I envisioned as the West Point of nonviolence, and often thought of as my fifth child. I also felt the warm embrace of that great crowd of witnesses, those yet unborn, who will live their best lives beyond limits because we dared to struggle, to put our lives on the line, to make America and the world a better place.

When I understood the places I could enter and the heights I could travel, I felt as though I were bringing many of you with me. The doors I entered were locked when I arrived, but through faith and pressure, they opened. Some of you have already walked through. The lessons I learned as a lobbyist, a teacher, an organizer, and, most of all, as a single parent felt teachable by the very fact that I was not missing in action in the midst of crisis.

WHAT DID IT take to stay on the civil rights battlefield after Martin was assassinated? I never knew if the same hate that killed my husband would claim my life or the lives of my four children. For years, I've endured death threats. There were bomb threats when I traveled. I had to vacate buildings, get off airplanes, and choose alternate forms of transportation.

You never knew the stresses and strains I underwent as a woman in a male-dominated culture, because I didn't complain. Nor did I break.

You never knew what it felt like to live in a fishbowl, to know that my conversations and whereabouts were constantly monitored by the government—so much so that Martin and I learned to talk in code.

There was much I had to learn to do in the course of my life, and I did not have a blueprint. I could not call upon Martin as Martin had called upon me. I made mistakes, but I pray those will be charged to lack of understanding and not to malicious intent. I learned how to lobby, how to advance human rights through the political system, from city councils to state houses to Congress to the White House itself.

Through these struggles and these learnings, I hope you will see Coretta.

The Mrs. King you might have heard about cares about thousands around the world, and the thousands yet unborn; Coretta cares about people, one person at a time. Over the years, when I heard about problems involving staff members or neighbors or church colleagues, I got personally involved. I brought gifts. To be a problem solver for those who were too easily dismissed, I called city council reps, mayors, housing departments. I called to stop eviction notices, to help students get into college. I called to recommend good people for good jobs. I was accused of being a micromanager, and I have to admit that in many cases I was that and more.

I suppose Coretta the person never received much attention because I always found it difficult to talk about myself. If I talked about interactions with people in which I was trying to make a difference in their lives one person at a time, I felt it might create the impression that these acts of kindness were staged for the media. So I kept those personal kinds of things to myself.

But now is the time to share the story I have wanted to tell for so long. In my first book, *My Life with Martin Luther King, Jr.*, my focus was on my husband, a man who paid the ultimate price for his commitment to creating a better world. At that time, I felt very strongly that the book had to be about Martin. Now I am turning the page.

Now I think it is time you knew Coretta.

Coretta Scott King
Atlanta, Georgia

———— ✿ ————

ONE

We Don't Have Time to Cry

O N THANKSGIVING NIGHT 1942, when I was fifteen years old, white racists burned our house to the ground. It was the home I was born in, as were my older sister, Edythe, and my younger brother, Obie Leonard. My father, Obadiah (Obie), had built it with his own hands in 1920, on my grandfather's land. The house was simple and plain, but we felt fortunate to have it. We knew scores of black share-croppers around us who were not living on their own land, and some of their homes were little more than shacks.

Shortly before bedtime, my parents smelled smoke. In what seemed like minutes, fire whipped through our home. Running for their lives, my parents grabbed my brother, Obie, and made it through the doorway, collapsing onto the grass. My mother's wails pierced my daddy's heart. They had escaped the flames with little more than the clothes on their backs. Edythe and I were away, rehearsing for a performance with the school choir. We returned to find that many of our prized possessions (clothes, family albums, our beautiful furniture, and our prized Victrola with the Bessie Smith record collection) were gone. Nothing was left of them but red coals and a dull glob of black vinyl.

Our father hushed our cries and shook us from our misery. "We don't have time to cry," he told us. He led us in prayer and told us to give thanks because we still had our lives. He even made us say we forgave those who had destroyed our home. I repeated the words to please my father, but I am not sure I really meant them.

I was only fifteen, but I was not naïve. In our little backwoods town of Heiberger, Alabama, terrorist acts at the hands of men and women with hate in their hearts were never far from me. They came with the territory. And we had few ways to get help or justice. We had no phone to call for help, but even if we had, I knew no fire trucks would have come. Nor would police or laws have protected us. In the eyes of whites, we were a black family of "nobodies" living in a place that was not a real town, a mere post office address twelve miles from rural Marion, Alabama—the middle of nowhere.

Ours was the same cruel reality with which blacks living throughout the South were all too familiar. In 1857 the notorious *Dred Scott* decision had affirmed that blacks "had no rights which the white man was bound to respect." In 1942, the *Dred Scott* decision was still the law of the land. White supremacy reigned; antebellum laws protected the white man's way of life and made ours miserable. Not only did *Dred Scott* hover over us like a menacing vulture, but the 1896 *Plessy v. Ferguson* Supreme Court decision engraved inequality in stone under the guise of "separate but equal" provisions. All forms of democracy were beyond our reach, including our vote, won briefly after Reconstruction following the Civil War, but circumvented through grandfather clauses, poll taxes, and outright tyranny.

A 1940 study on voting practices concluded that black disenfranchisement was nearly universal in the Deep South. In Alabama, as in Georgia, Florida, Mississippi, South Carolina, and Louisiana, no more than 2.5 percent of Negroes of voting age cast ballots in the 1940 presidential race. In Marion, near where I lived, and the surrounding countryside of Perry County, there were about 1,000 whites and 2,000 blacks, but as late as 1955 only about 150 black people were registered to vote.

As if the laws weren't oppressive enough, legal restrictions were backed up by the Ku Klux Klan and mob rule. Between 1882 and 1946, there were about 3,400 lynchings in the South. One of them was of my great-uncle, who had been accused of dating a white woman, although his "crime" was never proven. Proof was unnecessary. All that was needed were innuendo and rumor. Whispers were enough to spark mob rule.

One day a white woman showed up on my aunt's doorstep calling out, "Come look!" What my aunt saw, or so the story goes, was her husband hanging from a sycamore tree. His body was so riddled with bullets that it looked as though it had been used for target practice.

When my family had our brush with evil the night of the fire, I saw the awful face of hate clearly, although the perpetrators were never identified. I could not see any rational reason or purpose for our being burned out of our home. But when I look back at it through the lens of time, I see those awful charred embers as preparation. That night, I witnessed faith in action. I did not see fear in my father's eyes. In fact, the very next day, he exhibited nerves of steel. He went to work like nothing had happened, no doubt looking into the faces of those who had done this horrible thing. He would not give the terrorists the satisfaction of knowing their evil acts could bend or break him.

Our burned-out home served as a primer, a prelude, an introduction. The postcard from hell was my first taste of evil, the kind that shows up at your door in such a way that you can never forget its smell, its taste, its sting. That kind of ugliness would not remain in the shadows of that dark country night; no, it would follow me for the rest of my days.

Fortunately, I learned early how to live with fear for the people I loved. As I would go on to face my own fiery trials, I sought to obtain that same kind of internal fortitude that my dad exemplified. He had the ability to deny people with ugly agendas the power to chase him from his mission. When fear rushed in, I learned how to hear my heart racing, but refused to allow my feelings to sway me,

That resilience came from my family. It flowed through our bloodline. Before I was married to Martin and became a King, I was a proud Scott, shaped by my mother's discernment and my father's strength. Knowing what I know now, if I could have chosen parents, I would have chosen exactly the ones God selected for me: a hardworking, faithful, courageous father and a loving, nurturing, farsighted mother.

My father was one of the most fearless men I've ever met. The racial pressure on him was relentless, but it never broke him. Growing up, he provided me with incredible examples of courage. He stood at only about five feet seven inches, but he was a powerhouse. Curiously enough, he was resented because he was a hard worker and independent. He believed in rising before the sun, and would always tell us kids, "Get up early even if you don't do anything but sit down, so you won't be lazy." By 4:00 a.m., hours before daybreak, he would begin to haul lumber. He was the only black man around who had a truck, which he used to transport logs. He also cut hair, collected and sold scrap iron, and did other odd jobs to pick up extra income.

It seemed like my father was always being threatened, especially when he hauled his lumber to the train station. The whites, who were angry because he was in competition with them, would lie in wait, stop him on the road, pull out their guns, and curse him, calling him every name they could think of. He told us he never took his eyes off them. "If you look a white man straight in the eyes, he can't harm you," he said. When he was threatened, the other black men who worked with him were so frightened they would disappear into the woods, leaving my dad alone. But he never ran. If he had, they might have shot him in the back.

At some point, in the face of these constant threats, he began carrying a gun. Now, my daddy wouldn't have killed a soul, but he placed the gun in the glove compartment of his truck, which he left open so that anyone could see he had it. He wasn't trying to intimidate his attackers. He was just letting them know he wasn't unarmed. Once, I overheard him telling Mother, "I don't know if I'll get back tonight because they just might kill me." Every time we heard a car coming, and it wasn't my dad's, my sister and I would tremble. We thought it was somebody coming to tell us our dad had been killed.

AFTER THE FIRE, we stayed in my maternal grandfather and grandmother's house until my father found a home to rent. It was an old house, an old unpainted house, about four rooms and a big porch across the front and a well in back. Eventually, my father saved money to buy some land and build a new home. He also saved enough money to do something unheard-of for a black man trying to survive in the mid-1940s. After years of hauling timber, saving his meager funds, and dodging racial threats, he decided to make the giant leap to owning his own lumber mill. He even employed a white man to oversee the day's work. This courageous and history-making move by the grandson of a slave in the backwoods of

Alabama only fueled the hateful intentions of the local whites, who were determined to keep black men subservient.

My father had owned the sawmill for about two weeks when a logger came to him and asked to buy it. When my father refused, the logger threatened him, saying, "Well, it'll never do you any good." The next Monday, when my father arrived at his sawmill, the inevitable had happened: the mill had been burned to the ground.

But that didn't stop him. He was a determined man. In 1946, he started a grocery store in the building next to the new home he had built. This time the whites allowed it to survive, and that little country store shone with a spirit of compassion. Soon he was able to add a one-pump gas station and automobile services (oil change, air for tires, and so on). Both blacks and whites patronized the store, buying groceries—often on credit, which went unpaid. Or Dad would lend folks money out of his pocket. Sometimes the borrowers would pay a little on their accounts, and he would let them charge a bigger portion. When he died in 1998, shortly before turning one hundred, the amount people owed him for groceries and loans over a span of forty years added up to hundreds of thousands of dollars. He never let the mounting debt worry him.

Unlike my father, who generally blamed conditions rather than people for the way blacks were treated, my mother, Bernice McMurry Scott, was more resentful of the racist people around us. "You just can't trust whites," she would say. In later years, she did develop friendships with whites, which was only natural, since her mother, Mollie McMurry, my grandmother, was part Irish. My mother was fair skinned, with high cheekbones and straight black hair. Usually she wore her hair in two braids that reached almost to her waist; she looked like an American Indian, as she took after her father, Martin McMurry, who was part Native American. She had a pioneering spirit, which went against the grain not only for what whites expected of Negro women, but for what Negro men expected as well. In the 1920s she was the first black woman in our community to drive a car. Later, she learned how to drive a truck, and eventually, a school bus converted from a truck. She was also quite musically inclined, singing solos and playing the piano at church on Sundays, and I credit her for my musical abilities.

My mother had a sweet disposition, but she was a no-nonsense kind of person. She did not gossip about people. Down on the farm with nothing much to do, some folks made it their habit to visit with one another and talk about other people's business. Mother had an expression: "Seldom visits make long friends." In other words, friendships will be longer lasting if you don't go visiting much. When you do, there's the tendency toward idle gossip and the potential to have conflicts and to fall out.

Years later, when Martin and I moved to Montgomery, he used to ask me, "Why don't you go visit some of the members or some of the women in the church?" I would tell him, "I'm perfectly satisfied to be home. I enjoy being by myself," while my mother's words echoed in my head. *Seldom visits make long friends.*

My mother, who lived to be ninety-two, was a good judge of people, too. She had what they call discernment. She loved to help others and was very compassionate, but she needed to know people, and she didn't warm up to you until she knew you. She had to look you over and feel you out. Once she felt that you were okay, she would do anything in the world for you. I must admit, I'm a lot like her. I've never warmed up to people quickly. Once I feel comfortable, though, I'm very open. Unfortunately, this quality has often been interpreted as aloofness—just like with my mother. Because she had a fair complexion, people thought she was stuck up. But she was not arrogant, and neither am I. She just believed in minding her own business—though she was always there when you needed her, and was a very giving person when you got to know her. She was not about to let people take advantage of her, however, and I am a lot like that, too.

A day came when I had to ask my mother the same questions every black child asked sooner or later: "Why am I treated differently? Why do whites hate us so?" My mother answered in much the same way black mothers have answered for generations.

"You are just as good as anyone else," she said. "You get an education. Then you won't have to be kicked around."

The value of education was a constant drumbeat from my mother, and I cannot remember a time when I didn't know I was going to college. After all, my mother said I would. Despite the fact that, unfortunately, for most blacks in the South, education was virtually out of reach when I was growing up. Where we lived in Perry County, free education did not exist for blacks beyond the sixth grade. And while whites attended school for nine months a year, in general, blacks were entitled to go for only three months. Mother had a fourth-grade education, and Father made it through one year of high school before deficient funds forced him to quit. Nevertheless, both of them had high ideals for their children, and they prayed that a way would open for us to achieve the educational goals they had been denied.

My mother, who sounded like the feminists of today even in the 1950s, would stress, "If you get an education and try to be somebody, you won't have to depend on anyone—not even a man." My mother married my father when she was seventeen. I believe she wished she had not married so young. I remember her saying, "I never was a child. I've been a woman all my life." That was not the kind of life she wanted for me and my sister. If and when we married, she wanted us to be more than "just" a wife. When her sister, who attended Tuskegee Institute, the college started by Booker T. Washington, talked about the excitement of college, you could almost see the wheels turning in my mother's head.

It was radical for my mother to have such thoughts in those days. At that time, the ideal husband took care of his wife as if she were his property. She was assigned to the home and to child rearing. I was intrigued by the thought that, as a woman, I could have my own goals that went beyond merely being dependent on a man—though I did want to marry and have children.

As exciting as it was to think I could aspire to something beyond cooking and cleaning the house, I absorbed the derogatory examples I saw of how women and blacks were treated, and I wondered how all that could change. I saw white children riding yellow-checkered buses to their school, yet, in all kinds of weather, we black children walked three miles to our one-room schoolhouse and three miles back home. Somehow the driver of the white children would manage to steer the bus so that it kicked dust in our faces or slopped mud on our clothes, to the delight of his passengers, who often cheered as he sped by us.

I attended elementary school before the 1954 *Brown v. Board of Education* suit knocked down *Plessy v. Ferguson*, which sanctioned "separate but equal" education. Our education was not designed to be equal to that of the white students; it was meant to keep us separate and isolated from resources, so that we remained on the bottom rung. When I realized how inferior our little one-room schoolhouse was to the school attended by whites, I resented them. Though I never set foot in it, the whites' elementary school was in a nice brick building with all sorts of equipment. In ours, we had no labs, no library, and only a few books, most of which were tattered and out-of-date. More than a hundred children in grades one through six were crammed into one big room. While the whites received books for free, we had to pay for ours, and most of us couldn't afford them. Though our resources were inferior, however, our teachers were superior. They loved us and expected us to excel, as did our parents.

As strange as it may seem, despite the terrifying instances of white hate and the pervasiveness of racism, most of my childhood was happy. My parents provided a nurturing environment, and most of the people in our all-black community were kinfolk. And I had siblings (Edythe, older than me by two years, and Obie, younger by three) whom I adored. Edythe was the bookworm. Obie was the fixer who could repair anything. I was the doer, a workaholic always looking for a project.

As children, we didn't have money for store-bought games or toys, so we fashioned our own. One of our favorite pastimes was swinging. We would take an old tire, attach a rope to it, tie it to a tree, and that would be our swing. We also climbed trees and played Little Sally Walker. There were other things we wanted to do, but we had to accept that we just could not do them. There were no recreation facilities for black children. Marion had a swimming pool, but blacks were not allowed to use it. I tried to learn to swim in a pond instead, and almost drowned. The experience was so frightening that I never learned to swim as an adult; I never grew past it, and it affected me deeply.

Still, I felt secure growing up surrounded by kin (cousins and all my half-uncles and half-aunts from Grandfather Scott's second marriage) in the close-knit community of Marion's North Perry County. Marion, first called Muckle Ridge, had been renamed in honor of Gen. Francis Marion, the "Swamp Fox," hero of the American Revolution. Whites took pride in the fact that a Marion schoolteacher designed the first Confederate flag and the Confederate uniform.

None of that much mattered to blacks. We took pride in knowing that our all-black community represented three generations of black ownership. My grandfather Jeff Scott and my grandmother Cora owned three hundred acres of land, which produced pine timber for sale and vegetables of every kind, and which fed our family and provided leftovers for others. More than anything else, this tradition of landownership helped to instill in us racial pride, self-respect, and dignity. We were self-reliant, as reliant as any black could be in the racist South.

Our grandfathers hoped that they could pass on to future generations this legacy of land ownership. In many ways, their wishes were realized. The Scotts still own hundreds of acres of land in Alabama, land that I farmed as a girl.

From age six, when I was barely able to hold a hoe, I worked our fields. We raised corn, peas, potatoes, and garden vegetables. We also had hogs, chickens, and cows. Edythe and I both had to milk a cow every day. Not only did we milk them, but we'd take them to the pasture and bring them back in the evening. Sometimes we had to go to the pasture late at night to get the cows. There would be no moon, and it'd be so dark you couldn't see your feet before you. Sometimes the cows weren't at the gate, and we'd have to keep calling them until we heard their bells tinkling. Only then would we know where to find them, and we would run after them. Most always, we were barefoot, so we ran, praying all the way that we wouldn't step on a snake.

When the Depression deepened in the late 1930s, and I was about ten years old, my sister and I began working as hired hands, picking cotton. Oh Lord, I chopped and picked plenty of cotton to help pay for our schooling. We would be picked up before the crack of dawn and taken to the fields, which were quite a distance away. We'd work from sunup to sundown, sometimes to earn only sixty cents a day, though that was good money in the Depression years.

They'd always have a white male overseer to keep us working. The overseer would be ahead of us, trying to make everybody catch up with him. I was always competitive, so I kept up, and he bragged about me, saying, "Whenever I needed help, I would come straight to Obie Scott's house and get it." In an effort to keep Edythe from getting behind, I would often hoe her row, then come back to mine.

The sun was scalding hot, and I'd be so tired at the end of the twelve-hour days that I would nearly drop, but I was proud of my cotton-picking skills because my abilities furthered our hopes of getting an education. I had to pick a hundred pounds of cotton to get sixty cents; later, it got to be as much as a dollar for a hundred pounds. Once, I picked 209 pounds in a day and received $2.09, a tidy sum back then.

When Edythe finished her elementary education at Crossroads School, our family pooled the money we earned to help her go to the Hale County Training School. Because of the lack of educational opportunities in our community, my daddy had to pay for her room and board away from home in the town of Greensboro, Alabama. Yet, I never heard anyone complain. My mother always said that we were going to get an education, even if she had to sacrifice to the point where she had only one dress to wear.

The fact that Edythe was going to continue her schooling made me even more confident that I would, too. My mother's determination that I get an education made me understand that there was something wonderful awaiting me. If that weren't the case, why would she continue to be so insistent on my being prepared? I may not have known exactly where I was going, but I was excited about getting there. *Somewhere.* I would think of Judy Garland singing about a place somewhere over the rainbow. I kept looking and hoping that my somewhere would come.

A deeply religious child, I placed my faith in God to provide answers and a path. I would ponder His awesome work; how He had put the universe, the planets, and the galaxies together; and yet, He hadn't forgotten about me down on the farm. I would rock back and forth, count the stars, listen to the wind rustle around the pine cones, and wonder who I was, why I was on the planet, and where my place was in such a grand display of celestial artistry. In relationship to all I could see, would my life be like a pinpoint, a windmill, a shooting star, or a blade of grass to be trampled underfoot? Isolated, in the rural South, black, and female, I didn't see much to suggest that I could have a bright future—except for my parents' coaching. Most of the signals I received from the outside world were red lights warning me to stop, to back up my dreams. At the same time, I felt an inner self in motion; she was excited and ready to go, but where? I didn't know.

I used to sit at the mirror for hours, staring, trying to figure out who I was. Why am I here? I know God made me, but why? I would stare for so long and my mind would wander so far away that I grew frightened. Sometimes I felt I was looking at another person. It was like I wanted answers and I wasn't getting them fast enough, so my imagination, my mind, would take off without me. I was quite good at dream-walking.

When I was a child, church was the center of my social life. I can't remember a time when I didn't go to services at Mount Tabor AME Zion, about four miles from our home. Most people walked the distance barefoot because they didn't want to get their Sunday shoes dirty. Some of the men carried a rag, which they would slap across their leather shoes to give them luster when they neared the church. From my child's eye, Mount Tabor was a huge white frame structure unspoiled even by its cracking and peeling white paint. It was heated by a pot-bellied stove. Kerosene lamps provided the light.

Both my grandfathers were church leaders. Grandfather Scott would often open the Sunday school service by singing a hymn or leading a prayer. Grandfather McMurry, who had a fine baritone voice, would "line the hymns," setting the pitch for the choir to join in.

While I had hopes and dreams, I also had fears that sometimes kept me awake at night. At Mount Tabor, the preachers talked a lot about sin, damnation, and hell. These fired-up sermons kept me on edge. I was afraid of committing sins that would condemn me to burn in hell instead of joining God in that mysterious heaven hidden beyond the clouds. When I was ten, I heard about a lady who was on her deathbed; she had been forgiven by God for everything but cutting her hair. My mother had cut my hair, and for a spell, I was obsessed with the idea that cutting my hair might send me to hell. (Even after I was married, I didn't like to cut my hair, though I don't believe that childhood obsession was the reason. It was Martin. He used to say, "Corrie, that's your trademark. Don't cut your hair.")

When the older folks thought it was about time for children to join the church, they would send us to the mourners' bench. One night, when I was about ten, we were having a revival; every night, the preacher was preaching up a storm. During the revival, I was told to sit on that bench, where the sisters of the church would mourn and pray over me until they were satisfied that I had religion. They kept telling me I was going to hell because I was so mean. I didn't think I was mean, although I would fight a lot. I guess I was pretty straitlaced, and I thought I was right about everything. When anybody disagreed with me, I would haul off and sock them. I was very strong, and I could beat up both my sister and brother. But I didn't know how they knew all that at church. Maybe God had told them, I thought, and I cried out of shame. The more I cried, the more they mourned and prayed. Everything became so intense and emotional that I thought I felt something, and I stood up and joined the Church.

It was there at Mount Tabor AME Zion that my love of music and my future career were born. Edythe and I would often sing duets, and by the time I was fifteen, I was directing the choir and leading such songs as "Does Jesus Care?" ("Yes, my Jesus cares / Yes, my Jesus cares"). The song was sung softly and somberly. Our church was not what you would call a "shouting church"; we left that to the more emotional Baptists.

As a faithful teenager, it was hard for me to reconcile the lessons of Christian living I learned in church with the way whites who also called themselves Christians behaved toward us. Sometimes our father would take us to town on Saturdays, where we were greeted by Whites Only signs and made to go to the back door to get a sandwich. When we bought ice cream, we had to wait until all the whites had been served. No matter what flavor I asked for, the druggist would usually give me vanilla—served at the back door. Such treatment made me question whether my skin color was something I could rub off, since it seemed to be the cause of the problem. But church was an escape and a sanctuary from these daily degradations, and it sustained our faith that the Red Sea would be parted and opportunities would await us on the other side.

IT IS OFTEN said that the soul attracts that which it secretly harbors. Mother and I continued to harbor a vision, not out of desperation but out of faith, that I would get the chance to continue my education. Then an opportunity opened that pushed me closer to an understanding of my purpose. Mother figured out a way to send me to Lincoln Normal School, a semi-private high school founded by former slaves and supported by the American Missionary Association in Marion. She sent both me and Edythe there. The AMA, an antislavery society founded by Congregational ministers and laypersons in 1846, provided some of the best education for blacks in the South. Lincoln's faculty was mixed (half white, half black), and most were from the North. The white faculty treated the Negro students with love. They were dedicated. For that very reason, most of the white townspeople in Marion despised the teachers and delighted in calling them "nigger lovers."

There were no dormitories at Lincoln during the years that I attended, and to drive back and forth from Marion to Lincoln each day would have been too burdensome, so I had to stay with other families to be able to attend the school. That was fine with me. I was quite excited to enroll, and felt nurtured and embraced in Lincoln's halls, though when I tried to take a job doing housework for a white woman in Marion to supplement my parents' stipend, she expected me to be docile, to scrape and bow and use the back door. Her requests made me feel unworthy. To consent to her demands would have meant that I agreed with her negative assessment of me. I was not then, or ever, the submissive, subservient type. That job didn't last.

Regardless of these challenges, at Lincoln I knew I was being shaped for my destiny. This shaping was not the work of human hands, but suggested a divine intervention. I had been plucked from the middle of nowhere, where I was surrounded by islands of hostility, and placed in an environment of enlightenment. White teachers saw worth in me. In time, I saw past the terrible symbols of burning crosses, hateful words, and malicious intent and discovered that there were real, loving people under a skin color that so often meant trouble or heartache for our community. My white teachers laughed, cried, went to church, and attended county fairs. Underneath the skin—the skin that had been so foreboding to me—were people with good hearts and fair minds. It was important for me to understand this. As a child who had seen mostly the worst behavior of whites, it was critical for me to see a better side, and I feel now that these early contacts were divine connections. They reached me before the meanness that I had seen could create cement walls of enmity within my soul.

Inside the protective walls of Lincoln, my horizons were expanded. I began to understand more about being connected to a larger society and to people outside my community. Despite the reaction of the townspeople, the devotion of the dedicated faculty was richly rewarded by the harvest they produced. A study conducted by the late Horace Mann Bond in the 1950s found that the largest number of blacks with PhDs in the nation had roots right there in Perry County, of which Marion was a part. Another illustration of the school's influence was revealed at the twenty-fifth reunion of the Lincoln Class of 1943, at which the assembled graduates discovered that all their children who were old enough were either attending college or had completed four years of education at an institution of higher learning. This was Lincoln's influence.

It's also interesting that three major civil rights leaders, Martin Luther King Jr., Ralph D. Abernathy, and Andrew Young, married women from Perry County, two of whom attended Lincoln. Jean Childs, who was three grades behind me at Lincoln, graduated from Manchester College in Indiana, became a special education teacher, and married Young. Juanita Jones from Uniontown, Alabama, attended Selma University, a prestigious K–12 boarding school for "Negro" children, and graduated from Tennessee State University. She became a teacher and married Ralph Abernathy.

Many of the faculty impressed me, showing me the kind of person I wanted to become, but one of them in particular, my music teacher, Miss Olive J. Williams, a Howard University graduate, became my first role model outside of my family. She played the piano, directed the chorus, and taught us Beginning Voice and Music Appreciation. She had us singing Handel's *Messiah*, which was unusual for a high school in the South in that era. As we went through the vocal exercises, she also taught us posture and good diction, and introduced me to the world of classical music and composers like Bach, Beethoven, Mozart, and Chopin. Before seventh grade, I had never heard classical music. Upon hearing it, I loved it. We learned of the great concert performers of the day, some of whom were black. There was world-famous baritone Paul Robeson. There was Marian Anderson, the world's greatest contralto; and Roland Hayes, one of the great tenors. Learning about them made me dare to dream that I, too, could become a concert artist.

Quakers also served on the staff at Lincoln, and they started introducing us to peace activists. I met the great pacifist and peace activist Bayard Rustin, who would later play a key role with my husband and me in the civil rights movement—right there in ninth grade. At Lincoln, he addressed the student assembly and spoke about India's struggle for independence from the British Empire through the power of nonviolence. He told us how the British beat the Indians to a pulp, but in the end the Indians won their independence without firing a single shot. In a climate so punctuated by violence, I was fascinated by Rustin's lecture on how conflict could be resolved without war or bloodshed. I pondered the idea and filed it away in my memory.

Lincoln presented a ray of hope for me. Still, this was a small island in a vast sea of racial hostility; it was not enough. Like so many blacks, I knew I had to migrate from the South. I needed a place to chase my dream, a dream that didn't have a name or a shape, but that awaited me nonetheless. It was like a pull, a gentle tug with a sharp edge of urgency. I had to escape, to get out of Alabama.

Thousands of blacks had left before me, either chased out by the tyranny of white folks or led by visions of a better life in a northern promised land. Shortly before my birth, the steady flow of migration began. Southern blacks deserted their marginal farms and sharecropping in droves. By 1923, nearly five hundred thousand blacks had resettled in the North. In 1930, one Negro out of every five lived above the Mason-Dixon line. After World War II another three million left. Some were like my uncle, army sergeant Jasper Scott, who became embittered when he saw that German POWs were treated with more respect than black native sons. After fighting in the war, returning to the South briefly, and working with my father, he moved to Cleveland rather than fight another war at home with southern whites. The South was losing not only its farming class, but also the so-called Talented Tenth, those black men and women who sought higher education and resources to improve their lives and the lives of others.

My escape route opened up through Lincoln. My sister, Edythe, sang alto with a musical group called the Lincoln School Little Chorus. Lincoln faculty members (and, later, good friends of Edythe's and mine) Frances and Cecil Thomas arranged for the chorus to go on tour, and one of the stopping points was Antioch College, in Yellow Springs, Ohio. Obviously the chorus impressed Antioch such that two years later, when the college decided to open its doors wider to blacks by granting a limited number of scholarships, Antioch officials contacted Lincoln to request its two top students. Edythe, who was valedictorian, applied and was accepted. After passing a test, she received a letter offering her a full scholarship, tuition plus room and board. So, in the summer of 1943, Edythe became, for a time, the only black student at Antioch College. She wrote me glowing letters about the respect she received there, so after graduating as valedictorian of my class, I, too, applied, and was accepted in 1945.

And so it was that one of my mother's lifelong dreams for me, as well as my own, was coming true: I was going to college.

———— ❀ ————

TWO

A Sense of Belonging

BEFORE I WENT to college, I knew I would have to live and compete in a world with people different from myself. I wanted to be able to hold my own with people everywhere. To do this, I needed a broad-based liberal arts education. For me, Antioch was the answer. Founded in 1852, the college was a pioneer in multicultural living and education. It prided itself on being a laboratory for democracy. It was among the first nonsectarian educational institutions in the United States, among the first coeducational colleges in the nation to offer equivalent opportunities to both men and women, and among the first to appoint a woman to its faculty and its Board of Trustees. It was also among the first to offer African Americans equal educational opportunities.

At Antioch, I expanded the worldview I had begun to develop at Lincoln. The school had a strong sense of community, a spirit of mutual admiration for others. There was a sense of belonging. And its emphasis on being your "brother's keeper" and giving service to humankind captivated me. My horizons expanded there as I met people of all different races, cultures, and religions. I had two white roommates, which would have been unthinkable in the South. We got along and found it to be a good experience. With them and other close friends, I began building on the good experiences I had had with whites in Marion, and I remembered my father saying, even during the worst times, "There are still some good white folks." First at Lincoln, now at Antioch, I was broadening my understanding of whites and coming to see them as people like anybody else, in need of the same basic principles: love, understanding, and respect.

At Antioch, we were exposed to Judaism, Islam, Buddhism, Hinduism, and many other different religions and cultures. Nurtured by this diverse, pro-peace environment, I began to dream of a world in which all kinds of people would be welcome and could live in peace and harmony. Years later, a label would be attached to this vision: the Beloved Community, where love and trust triumph over fear and hatred. The term is most often attributed to the American philosopher Josiah Royce.

To me, the Beloved Community is a spiritual bond that claims the energies and commitment of a diverse group of people who desire to serve a cause larger than themselves. The Beloved Community is fueled by unconditional love, feels like family, and transcends race, religion, and class. At Antioch, long before I could explain it, I began to put flesh on the skeleton of my thinking about such an ideal, and the education I received and the connections I made prepared me, more than anything else, to be a part of one of the greatest human rights movements of the twentieth century.

This is not to say that there were not some bumps and bruises along the way, but the hard knocks prepare one for leadership as much as the soft landings. For one, I had to do a lot of remedial work because I had not had the proper preparation in elementary school to high school. And I had to learn how to concentrate. I didn't know how to study. As a freshman, I had to look up virtually every other word in my textbooks because my vocabulary was very limited. I hadn't been challenged enough. Now I struggled to catch up. It was very difficult, but in time I did catch up, and here I saw the vision of what I could become.

I also came rather quickly to realize that the North was not some sort of racial utopia, and that there would still be prejudice and ignorance to face. I learned that Edythe had left some of the negatives out of her letters to me, for fear that I wouldn't come to Antioch. I came to empathize with her as one of the only blacks. Any black who has been a pioneer, breaking the color line in any corporate, government, or educational position, will know what I mean. Students and faculty considered Edythe an expert in race relations. She was expected to know all about anything that happened to anyone anywhere in black America, and to have answers. Whites wouldn't want to have normal conversations with her. They just wanted to discuss "the Negro problem" morning, noon, and night. This became a burden. Also, while Edythe was tall and attractive, with that striking Native American look from our mother's side of the family, none of the white guys had the courage to formally ask her out.

While Edythe's Antioch experience was far from perfect, it didn't sour her on higher education. She transferred from Antioch in her final year, graduated from Ohio State in 1949, received a master's in English from Columbia University and, later, an MFA in theater from Boston University. In 1954 she married Arthur Bagley, a graduate of Cheyney University who received his doctorate in education from the University of Maryland. Years later, Edythe joined the faculty of Cheyney, where she founded the theater arts major. She retired in 1996, as associate professor of fine arts in the department of English; Arthur was the chair of the industrial arts department.

When I arrived at Antioch, I saw some of the difficulties Edythe had experienced. What irritated me especially was the ability of some whites to accept me only as long as they could separate me from my race. People would say ignorant things like "Well, you're so different from the rest of them," as if they actually knew the eleven million "rest of them." Often people asked me, "Why aren't there more blacks at Antioch?" The questioner's tone usually suggested it was our fault for not being there in larger numbers, giving no consideration to the economic barriers or institutional racism that had been blocking blacks from gaining a quality education since the days of slavery.

I also faced a painful scenario when it came to my love life, when in my junior year I had my first experience with interracial dating, something that never could have happened back home in the South, where miscegenation was outlawed and punishable by imprisonment. Even in the North, the practice was ahead of its time. The Antioch student body was virtually all white. In my class, there were only a few black students, so there was an unspoken expectation that I would date a certain black guy. My Cupid friends had selected a nice young black man to be my date, but I resented their matchmaking. In retrospect, I see that it would have been nice at least to have gone out with him. He was Leon Higginbotham

Jr. (now deceased), who became one of the first blacks appointed to the federal bench.

I chose, however, to date one of the Jewish guys, Walter Rybeck, a fourth-year student from Wheeling, West Virginia, and my piano accompanist. We dated for about two years, doing fun things together like bird watching and attending folk festivals. We became rather serious about each other and discussed marriage, but I wanted a career, and he was concerned about the racial and religious identity of our children. Would they be half-Jewish, half-Christian, half-black, half-white? We were stymied at the thought of the many barriers we would have to cross.

We soon had an experience that would answer our nagging questions about whether we could be happy together as an interracial couple. On Tuesday, November 9, 1948, I made my singing debut at Second Baptist Church in Springfield, Ohio, with Walter as my accompanist. The performance, publicized in several local papers such as the *Xenia Gazette*, was well attended, with more than one hundred people in the audience. Still beaming from our success after the concert, Walter and I attended a folk dancing festival in Wheeling, West Virginia. Walt got out of the car to place a phone call to his parents, asking them to meet us at a certain restaurant in town. When he got back in the car, I had one question: "What about me?" He paused, searching for words. It had not even dawned on him that I would not be allowed to eat at the restaurant he'd selected. When his parents arrived, we ate somewhere else, but the experience depressed me and marred the weekend. It gave us a powerful glimpse of what an interracial marriage would be like and the challenges we'd face if we stayed together. One of us would be welcome somewhere; the other would not be. One would be associated with what was right with the world; the other with what was wrong. All of it was too much baggage for us to carry, and so we broke up.

Bruised from that heartbreak, I distracted myself with my studies, but racism also challenged me in my degree path. I was the first black person to major in elementary education at Antioch, with a minor in voice. In order to meet all the requirements of my major, however, I had to teach for a year in the Antioch private elementary school and for a year in the Yellow Springs, Ohio, public school system. Because there were no black teachers in the Yellow Springs public school system, I was deprived of my right to teach there. When I took my concern to the supervisor of student teaching, she did not support my right to teach in the local school system. This disappointed me deeply. Instead, she suggested I travel nine miles from Antioch to teach in a segregated school in Xenia, Ohio. Her rationale was that God did not intend the races to mix. When I took the issue to the president of Antioch, he didn't support me, either. Later, I learned that he had a black dog named Nigger.

In the end, I was given two options: go to Xenia and teach in a segregated school system, or teach another year at the Antioch school. I refused to go to Xenia. I'd left Alabama to be free of segregation.

I appealed to the local school board, but that failed. I tried to rally the students to my cause, and after that failed, I appealed to Antioch College's administration, writing:

> My precious time and money have been spent for a commodity which I never received only because my skin color happened to be darker. No matter how one might try to explain why the school board and the superintendent refused to let me teach in the Yellow Springs Public School, these explanations turn out to be none other than rationalizations and the cold fact is that I was rejected because I happened to be the wrong color. This kind of injustice which I experienced is mild compared to what Negroes are facing all of the time in our society. Do you then wonder why America as a leader among nations in the world cannot command more respect among the common people who make up the majority of the citizens of the world? Her inner corruption cannot long persist without backfiring.

In the end, I had no choice but to do another year of practice teaching in the Antioch private school to qualify for my Ohio teaching certificate. This incident left me terribly disappointed, but I refused to allow it to interfere with my determination to excel. The experience also fed my inward yearning to involve myself in something bigger. This was the first time I stood up publicly against discrimination, and I found that I rather liked making waves and being a catalyst for change. And the experience only deepened my resolve to continue the struggle blacks had always fought, which was for inclusion and respect. I knew that I would be black the rest of my life, so I could not back down or remain silent in the face of the injustice I would inevitably face.

At the time, leaving my particular protest aside, Antioch bubbled with student activism, and I plunged right in, becoming active in the Antioch NAACP, a race relations committee, and a civil liberties committee, as well as with the peace movement, an organized group that aimed to bring about peace in the world. Having just lived through World War II, in which about sixty million lives were lost, peace activists wanted an end to wars. They refused to be drafted, based on their conscience. Students like me formed a coalition around the peace activists, to give them support and to send a message to the powers that be. I began to consider myself a pacifist. Pacifism felt right to me; it accorded with what I had been taught as a Christian: to love thy neighbor as thyself.

I was also active in Henry Wallace's Progressive Party, which had a student chapter at Antioch, and two of my favorite professors, Walter Anderson and Dr. Oliver S. Loud, were officers in the Ohio branch. For a long time, I avoided talking about my Progressive Party affiliation; the party was often accused of having links to communism, and I did not want to besmirch my reputation. Later, with the battle J. Edgar Hoover was waging against my husband, I didn't want that past affiliation to become a noose around Martin's neck. But in 1948, I went to the party's national convention in Philadelphia as a student delegate. Its platform sought to end segregation, support voting rights for blacks, and provide national health insurance. That year, the Progressive Party won more than one million votes in the national election.

Our local chapter convention was held in Columbus, Ohio. Paul Robeson, one of my greatest heroes, spoke, and Professor Anderson gave me the opportunity to appear on a program with him. Robeson had a lot in common with Martin. Widely remembered for his starring role in Eugene O'Neill's *The Emperor Jones* and his performance of Shakespeare's Othello, Paul was a hero to blacks because he stood up for their rights. The poor guy was harassed by the FBI (just like Martin) until his death in 1976. I was so impressed with him at our meeting and flattered that he liked my singing. Such a gifted man finding talent in me was great encouragement. After watching Robeson's performance, I tucked it away in my memory. It would provide inspiration years later. When I began giving my freedom concerts to raise funds for the movement, I patterned my concerts after his performances. He would give a political commentary before he sang, so that's what I did. I would talk about the struggle, the movement. I would narrate and sing, alternating parts of the story with a song.

At Antioch, I also began to question organized religions and to experiment with kinds of worship that were different from what I had experienced at my little country church back home. I wondered if I would continue my religious expression through Methodism (AME Zion), Congregationalism, or Unitarianism—or even become a Quaker. I had come under the strong influence of the Quakers at both Lincoln and Antioch; historically, they were zealous advocates for abolition, equal rights for women, and peace issues. I used to sit quietly in the chapel at Antioch and try to deepen my relationship with God in the Quaker way. The Quakers would sit and wait for hours for the Holy Spirit to move them. The process is like meditating and communing with the Spirit. Whoever is moved gets up and says what's in his or her heart. If you feel like singing, you sing. There is no choir, so if you feel like joining in, you do, but there is no formalized worship. The Quakers also believe in an uncluttered life and living simply, without a lot of materialism.

This aligned with the philosophy my mother had passed on to me, which emphasized that material things were not important and that education was a prime value. She had urged us to get an education first; if we wanted clothes, cars, and other things, we would then be able to afford them. She used to say, "Clothes don't make you. It's the way you carry yourselves that makes you important." In this way, my experience with the Quaker influence at Antioch only deepened my family values.

Finally, after six largely wonderful years, full of enlightenment and self-discovery, it was time for my chapter at Antioch to come to a close. But what would be next for me? Again, I relied on my faith to show me the path forward, and on what I've come to think of as guardian angels.

Two beloved mentors, close friends, and role models, my faculty counselors, Mrs. Jessie Treichler and Walter Anderson, helped me through Antioch and prepared me for the great leap forward, to follow my passion for classical music born in childhood and nurtured in college, and to pursue training at a music conservatory. Dr. Anderson, the college's sole African American faculty member, headed the music department. He was remarkably gifted and could entertain the students by playing bebop, or glide just as gracefully into a Mozart sonata. Through his counsel, I applied to five of the best music schools in the country, including Juilliard in New York City and the New England Conservatory in Boston. Although I was always interested in Juilliard, I received an early acceptance to the New England Conservatory and decided to go there. I thought it would be less expensive and stressful than New York City.

So, in September 1951, it was time to put Antioch behind me and head to blue blood country. There I would follow my passion to study music, and there a certain suitor would come calling, a call that would change the entire course of my life.

———— ✵ ————

THREE

I Have Something to Offer

NINETEEN FIFTY-ONE WAS such an extraordinary year. I felt as if I had blasted through that moonlit sky in Heiberger and touched the hem of heaven. My life, one of picking cotton and milking cows in the Deep South, was now consumed with singing classical music as a student at the New England Conservatory of Music in Boston. I was fulfilling my dream of becoming a concert singer. I imagined that one day I would study in Europe and debut at the Metropolitan Opera. These were the desires of my heart. They would only be a stepping-stone, though, because I had never looked at my career as just being onstage. I wanted something more meaningful. I felt in my heart that I had to make a contribution to serve others, through music, but also in other ways I had yet to discover.

So it was with a great deal of promise and passion that I set off for the New England Conservatory, but it wasn't always, especially initially, an easy course. The main problem was that I had no money to continue my education. I agonized over asking my parents, but decided against it; I wanted them to enjoy the fruits of their labor instead of financing my dreams. Through my friend and adviser from Antioch, Jessie Treichler, I applied to more than a dozen places for scholarships. One, the Jessie Smith Noyes Foundation, sent an encouraging reply that although its grants were already awarded for the current year, if someone dropped out or chose not to reapply, then the foundation would award me a scholarship. In retrospect, that promise was as thin as a tea leaf, but in my youthful zeal, I found it solid enough to take off for Boston.

I arrived with fifteen dollars to my name, which I soon learned would not take me far. I had a place to stay and breakfast daily, thanks to Mrs. Treichler, who had written to a contributor to the Antioch Interracial Scholarship Fund asking for help. I stayed in a five-floor rooming house on Beacon Hill, a lily-white section of Boston. I was the only black student in my building. For seven dollars a week, I had a roof over my head, but I had to get a job to buy food and take care of the rest of my expenses. My money was running out too fast. What was I going to eat? The day before my money ran out completely, dinner consisted of peanut butter, crackers, and an apple. The next day I only had thirty cents for a round-trip subway ride.

Then, seemingly out of nowhere, help came from Mrs. Bertha Wormley, a person I had met only once, through a mutual friend. During a phone call, she asked if I needed anything. Instead of answering immediately, I paused and cradled the phone, not wanting to lay myself bare and admit that I was broke. I was proud and embarrassed, but I could not hold back my feelings of desperation. I blurted out my troubles. To her ears it must have sounded like torrents of pain, because she quickly arranged for me to meet her where she worked, at the Massachusetts State House, around the corner from where I lived. When I arrived, she handed me a sealed envelope.

After I left for school, I opened it on the subway. What joy! It contained fifteen dollars. It was such a help in my dire situation that tears coated my face. The kindness of this virtual stranger served to reinforce my belief that there is no situation in which we can find ourselves where God won't send help. Mrs. Wormley shared the spirit of many blacks of that day; she wanted to be a link in the chain that prepared the next generation. Where would we be without the Mrs. Wormleys of the world?

In order to pay for my room and board, the landlord permitted me to clean three rooms on the fifth floor and to wash and iron the linens. I scrubbed the floors on my hands and knees. Because of my meager funds, however, I had to find other sources of income, which led me to part-time work with a mail-order company. It was hard work, but I was used to that. I had worked hard all my life.

Now, with a goal clearly fixed in my mind, I sang as I scrubbed. I may have been on my knees, but in my spirit I was onstage, sending my arias leaping through the concert halls. At those moments, I never felt like a scrubwoman. I felt more like a performer, playing a role that was ushering me into the fulfillment of a cherished dream.

In my second semester, my financial lot improved—but for very ironic reasons. Thanks to the 1896 Supreme Court ruling of *Plessy v. Ferguson*, which made it illegal for blacks and whites to eat together in public, ride public transportation together, share water fountains, or, of course, go to the same schools, the State of Alabama, in order to maintain that ridiculous caste system, had to go through the motions of setting up "separate but equal" educational facilities. Alabama thus gave financial aid to black students who went out of state to get the professional graduate training only white colleges and universities provided. This aided the state's goal of keeping its schools segregated. Regardless of the motivations, I enjoyed spending Alabama's money after all the hard work my family had invested in Alabama soil.

Overall, I was extremely happy. I was studying voice with Madame Marie Sundelius, a golden age Swedish American Metropolitan Opera soprano. I was also making a contribution to improving society. In Yellow Springs, Ohio, I had challenged segregated teaching assignments. Now I saw myself adding color to the overwhelmingly white concert performing arts scene. Eagerly, I looked ahead at the ground I could cover; I saw myself as a concert singer, paving the way for other blacks. As I looked at my new experiences, I felt something exciting stirring within me. It felt good trying to make a difference. I was gaining a sense of how to create a life of meaning. Granted, I had tasted only small slices of success in that area, but it was fulfilling to know that my appetite for creating change was not something nebulous or ethereal. Things really could change if you prayed about it, were determined, and worked to achieve your dreams. Although I had a gentle manner, I was beginning to suspect that I had a warrior's spirit. I was not the kind of person who was content leaving hurt or harm unchanged.

I was settled into what I thought would be my life's work, thriving and happy, when one afternoon in my second semester at the conservatory, I got a call from my classmate Mary Powell, a Spelman graduate. "Coretta," she said, "have you heard of Martin Luther King Jr.?"

When I conceded that I hadn't, she went on to tell me about this impressive young man she had met. He was a promising minister ordained in his father's church, Ebenezer Baptist in Atlanta, who was working on his PhD at Boston University's School of Theology. She told me what a great orator he was and how popular he was in Boston's black church circles.

It was clear that Mary was playing matchmaker, but from what I was hearing, I was not that interested in a meeting. At the mention of his being a minister, a mental picture flashed through my mind: someone narrow-minded, black-suited, and boring, whereas I wanted to meet someone who was exciting. I didn't want to be a minister's wife and subject my family to living in a parsonage. (You know how everybody talks about the pastor's children.) Besides, as a good Methodist, my style of worship was much quieter than that of the more emotional "shouting Baptists." I didn't know if I could make that great a leap of faith.

Mary went on to tell me that Martin Luther King Jr. had confided in her that he was on the verge of becoming cynical. "I have met quite a few girls here," he told Mary. "But none that I am particularly fond of. Aren't there any nice, attractive young ladies that you might know?"

After Mary described me, his interest was piqued. He pressed her into giving him my number, which I believe she, happy to be a matchmaker, was secretly delighted to do. Soon after I spoke with Mary, Martin called and introduced himself. On the telephone, we chatted for several minutes, and then he said something I thought strange, considering the short time we had talked.

"You know, every Napoleon has his Waterloo. I'm like Napoleon. I'm at my Waterloo, and I'm on my knees. I'd like to meet you and talk some more. When can I see you?"

"What do you mean?" I asked.

He said, "Well, any time you have."

"Perhaps lunch on Thursday," I said.

"That's fine. I'll come over and pick you up. I have a green fifty-one

Chevy that usually takes ten minutes to make the trip from Boston U. to the conservatory, but I will do it in seven."

With interest but not any special anticipation, I waited for Martin outside the conservatory two days later, a cold January day. Under my tightly buttoned coat, I wore a light blue suit. When the green Chevy pulled to the curb, my first thoughts reaffirmed what I had anticipated: he was too short and he didn't look that impressive. He looked like a boy when I had expected a grown man. (I later learned that he always wore a mustache, which made him look older, but had shaved it off because he was pledging the Alpha Phi Alpha fraternity.)

We drove a few blocks to Sharaf's Restaurant, on Massachusetts Avenue. As we talked about our different schools over lunch, I felt his stare. He examined me carefully; his eyes moved across my face, lingering on my hair. I found him easy to talk to, and we chatted about everything, from questions of war and peace to racial and economic justice. Martin seemed impressed that I was knowledgeable about subjects other than my chosen field of study in music. In turn, I felt he was a man of substance, not like I had envisioned. In fact, the longer we talked, the taller he grew in stature and the more mature he became in my eyes. As he was driving me home, we stopped at a light and he turned to me.

"You know something?"

"What?" I asked.

"You have everything I have ever wanted in a wife. There are only four things, and you have them all."

"How can you say that?" I replied in disbelief.

"I can tell," he said. "The four things that I'm looking for are character, intelligence, personality, and beauty. And you have them all. When can I see you again?"

I was shocked into silence. What was I hearing? A man I had just met face-to-face a few hours ago seemed to be hinting at matrimony. I stared at him, trying to determine if he was joking with me, if his expression would fade into a big smile and he would offer some kind of disclaimer. But he was intensely serious. Martin showed every sign of someone falling in love at first sight. I was certainly flattered by his attention, and he impressed me as a man on a mission, on an urgent assignment, who knew exactly what he wanted and wanted to rush on. But for me, it was an over-load, too much to handle at one time.

Back in my room that night, sleep was impossible. I tossed and turned as I thought about Martin. I tested myself as if I were cramming for a final exam. What did I really feel about this man, Martin Luther King Jr.? My goal was clearly established: I had come to the conservatory to become a concert artist. Music was my first love, and I didn't want anything to get in the way. I didn't want to be in love, not now. Besides, I had thought myself in love before and later found out I had made a mistake. Could I afford that same mistake again? But even though I felt as though venturing farther might put my career in jeopardy, my heart told me I clearly had to see Martin again.

The next day, he called, and I found I was excited at the sound of his voice. We chatted, and he asked me for a date on Saturday. I had a tentative date for that afternoon, but I told him I would let him know if that fell through. Sure enough, it did, so when Martin called me midafternoon on Saturday, I agreed that he could take me to a party.

When we walked in the door, girls swooned over him, and he seemed to bask in their admiration. In a bit of self-flattery, he told me, "You know, women are hero-worshipers." Their fawning behavior over Martin, my date, certainly heightened my interest. For someone only five foot seven and twenty-two years old, his personality was such that all the girls seemed to look up to him. Here he was, one of the most eligible bachelors in Boston, and he had taken me to the party as his girlfriend. Virtually every woman in the place would have traded places with me gladly.

But the question remained: Would I move out of the way and let them have him, or would I take him as seriously as he was apparently taking me?

Again that night, after the party, he talked about marriage. And again I tried to keep a level head. This time when he took me home and walked me to the door, we embraced, and for the first time I felt that here is a man I really could fall in love with, if I could just let myself.

In our subsequent dates, Martin proved so much fun to be with. He was a great tease and a good dancer; he could do everything from the jitterbug to the waltz (though after he became a pastor, we had to give up dancing). He loved concert music, too, and early in our courtship he took me to a concert by the great pianist Arthur Rubinstein at Boston's Symphony Hall. I was touched that Martin, who knew how much music meant to me, would think of such a perfect date.

The more I was with Martin, the less I could find not to like about him. There was no question that he was compassionate, held deep moral convictions, and sincerely wanted to change the conditions of the less fortunate. The more I thought about it, the more I realized that these qualities were far more important to me than his age or height, and I chastised myself for initially making these quibbles so important in my assessment of him.

It was clear that in some way he wanted to take the abstract, ethereal concepts floating in his head and apply them to concretely change the oppressive state of black America. In his discussions of Karl Marx, for example, he always analyzed Marx within the context of what was best for America's poor. He told me, "Communism or capitalism. Each holds a partial answer, but neither the whole truth. I could never be a Communist. My father is a capitalist, but I could not be that, either. I think a society based on making all the money you can and ignoring people's needs is wrong. I don't want to have a lot of money and own a lot of things."

As he continued to talk, he seemed to fit nicely into the political scene and sensibility I had embraced at Antioch, where we were all out to save the world. This is so wonderful, I thought, to meet a man who is really serious about changing society. Martin's love of Gandhi and his dedication to Jesus Christ captivated me, and I eagerly listened to his ideas about how to weave the views of both into a philosophy of nonviolence that would achieve social justice.

Later on, during the movement, Martin often told me that Christ furnished the motivation and inspiration and Gandhi furnished the technique for social change. As he explained it: "Gandhi was probably one of the first persons in history to lift the love ethic of Jesus above mere interaction between individuals to a powerful and effective social and collective transformation."

From my Sunday school studies and activist days at Antioch, I had developed core beliefs about the principles of Christ and Gandhi. I took very seriously the words, "Thou shalt not kill," one of the Ten Commandments. I felt it was a sin to kill and that war hardly ever justified it.

When Martin and I were tossing around ideas, I saw that my views were more global and pacifist, while his were more focused on direct action to change the oppressive structures of black America. At that time, that difference seemed inconsequential, but one day it would mean that I would become an earlier critic of the Vietnam War than Martin, and would help persuade him to call for a halt to the bombing.

I remember thinking how desperately black America needed a plan for social transformation, but we were only college kids tossing around ideas. Who would have thought that the ideas we discussed as young students would one day evolve into a systematic action plan that would change the circumstance and lives of black Americans, the South, the nation, and many parts of the world?

What impressed me most about Martin was his integrity and how he himself told me about "the other woman," so to speak. He had been dating a young lady back in Atlanta rather seriously. My friend Mary Powell had already told me about her, but it was so comforting to hear Martin's confession from his own lips. His honesty was the quality that touched my heart most deeply. I felt he was trustworthy. From the very beginning of our relationship, he was the kind of man who could not keep a secret. If he did something wrong, no matter how big or small, he was so tortured by his conscience that he was miserable until he discussed it and asked forgiveness. He was constantly examining himself to see if there was any sin that had crept into his life. Was he being selfish? Was his commitment as total as it should be? Had he been insensitive? Had he overlooked someone who had done something nice? He was always looking for a sin to clean up, starting with sins in himself.

As our courtship continued, we talked at length about values, morals, and philosophy, and it was clear on all the important things that Martin and I basically agreed; the other issues we felt could be worked out. As we talked about marriage, Martin made it clear that "A man should be able to take care of his wife, and she should not work." This was the fifties, when it was the norm for men to stake their manhood on their ability to provide for their households. Men worked; wives stayed at home. But in my view, that was such a waste of a woman's creativity, talent, and energy. "If a woman wanted to work, she should be able to do so," I countered. That said, it became clear that Martin wanted a stay-at-home wife who was intelligent and well educated, but who would be a homemaker and a mother of his children.

Martin explained that it was his quest to become pastor of a large black Baptist church in the South. He wanted to know if I could adjust to the rigors of the life of a pastor's wife. He wanted to know how well I could relate to women who were uneducated and unsophisticated. I reminded him that I had been born on a farm and that the most important woman in my life was my mother, who had only a fourth-grade education. Nevertheless, she had enough common sense to run circles around some people I knew who had PhDs.

That said, I understood Martin's concerns. I carried myself in the ladylike fashion that I had learned from my mother, who always behaved with great dignity. In the South, since black women were so disrespected by whites, our response was to push our shoulders back, keep our heads high, and walk with dignity, looking as if we had oil wells in our backyard. Moreover, I was not on a traditional career track for a black woman. As a budding concert singer, poise and decorum were tools of the art; unfortunately, they could be mistaken for stiffness or for trying to be a prima donna. However, as someone from the rural South who grew up without many cultural advantages, I never had any problem identifying with my heritage. I knew that no matter how far I climbed, I could never forget my origins or look down on anybody.

Though Martin continued to press the issue of marriage, I still resisted a relationship, harboring nagging concerns about what would happen to my own sense of mission if I married. At one point, my own desire to minister to the needs of the less fortunate prompted me to feel that I might be called by God to preach. In this situation, as usual, I relied on God, engaging in serious prayer and meditation to help me settle a matter I felt strongly about in my heart. I couldn't involve my whole heart until I got a strong signal from God. There was also the issue that Martin's dad, whom Martin loved and respected very much, wanted him to marry the girl back home, even as Martin told him, "I am going to select my own wife. I know the kind of wife I need."

Then, in early May, several months after Martin and I met, I had a dream that helped bring clarity. In the dream, Martin's father, whom I had never met, was smiling at me, and I had this overwhelming sense that he approved of me. When I woke up, I felt as if weights had dropped off my back. I felt this was a miraculous sign, urging me to open myself to a serious relationship with Martin. Finally, I realized I had begun to fall in love with him.

Then came a letter from my sister, Edythe, where she wrote, "Coretta, don't be silly, girl. You know how difficult it is to find intelligent, stable, well-adjusted men. You won't have your career as you dreamed it, but you will have your career." Moreover, I had finally realized that I wanted to have love in my life as well as a family. I understood that having a career without a family and true love would not make me happy.

There was also the advice I got from my good friend Frances Lucas, whom I had met at the Friendly Inn Settlement House in Cleveland as a second-year student on a cooperative work experience from Antioch College. Fran was a graduate student doing fieldwork at Friendly Inn. Now a New Yorker, Fran knew Martin; she and Martin's sister, Christine, used to stay at the YWCA in New York City while they were doing graduate work. When I told Fran about Martin's proposal, she confirmed what I already felt: "You two are ideally suited. Remember how you were so solid in your desire to be a catalyst for social change that you would talk to me way into the night, until I fell asleep? You are both serious thinkers. Both of you are compassionate."

She understood that I didn't want to marry someone so soon after meeting him. In those days, you didn't do that. But Fran encouraged me, saying, "Martin would be fortunate to marry you, because you're the kind of girl that would be more than a housewife to Martin. You could manage the house, the children, and his affairs. Your background and your experience in the North will give you a broader understanding of the circles Martin will have to travel in."

All this feedback from people I loved and trusted further cemented my decision, but there was still another hurdle: meeting Martin's family.

That June, I was going home to see my parents in Alabama. Martin asked if I would stop in Atlanta to meet his family. (I had already met his sister, Christine.) To test him, to see just how important it was that I meet his family, I told him that I didn't think I could come to Atlanta. He was very upset and snapped at me, "If you don't want to come, just forget it. Forget the whole thing."

Hmm, I thought. A good sign. He really wants me to meet his parents. He really cares.

The train that went from Boston to Alabama went through Atlanta; a stopover would not be out of my way. Besides, if I were considering marrying Martin, I needed to know as much as possible about his church and family, so I consented.

During my first meeting with his family, they treated me cordially. Martin and his mother met me at the train station. Alberta, whom everyone affectionately called Mama King, was a short, stocky, fashionably dressed woman. She took my hand, greeting me politely. We went to Martin's family home, a lovely yellow brick house on one of black Atlanta's most fashionable streets. Mary Powell, the classmate who had played matchmaker between me and Martin, was home for summer vacation, and I spent the night at her house.

The next day, we joined the King family at Ebenezer Baptist Church, where three generations of Kings had pastored: Reverend A.D. Williams, Martin's grandfather; Daddy King, Martin's father; and Martin himself, who had already taken over some responsibilities as associate pastor. There was also A.D., Martin's brother, a minister. Sitting next to him was his pretty wife, Naomi, who was also from Alabama. The church, which seated 750, was a handsome building on Auburn Avenue, a major artery in the cultural, economic, and political life of black Atlantans. The unpretentious interior was finished in off-white with polished gold-tone woodwork. There were lovely stained-glass windows. Behind the pulpit, the white-robed choir sat on tiers of seats.

So this is the King family, I thought as I leaned into the pew.

I had done my homework on the Kings, and over the years I would continue filling in the missing pieces. Daddy King was the second of ten children, born to sharecroppers James and Delia King in 1899 on a plantation called Stockbridge, a few miles outside Atlanta. At first I thought that since Martin hailed from a great line of preachers, someone in the family must have had the forethought to name him after the great German theologian Martin Luther. But that was not the case. As a boy, Martin Sr. was actually called Mike because of his mother's insistence that she had named him after Michael, the archangel. With the same intensity, his father, James, insisted that he be named Martin Luther after two of *his* brothers. Since it was uncommon for blacks to have birth certificates, which could have settled the issue, as a compromise, he was always called Mike. At the request of his dying father, "Mike" took out the necessary legal papers to have his name changed (as well as the name of his first-born, Martin Luther King Jr., who was also called Mike). From then on, he was officially Martin Luther King Sr., or, within the family, Daddy King.

Growing up, Daddy King spent a lot of time plowing behind a mule, so much so that school chums teased him about smelling like one. "I may smell like a mule, but I don't think like one," he retorted. That smell that seemed to follow him, however, made him very shy around the ladies. Daddy King had a miserable childhood because of the family's extreme poverty, and because his father often drowned his troubles in alcohol. Daddy King saw his father get cheated out of his meager earnings at the plantation store, saw whites beat black people unmercifully and even hang one man from a tree.

When Daddy King was a child, a white man stripped him naked and beat him for not giving him a pail of water Daddy King was carrying home to his mother. When his mother, Delia, heard about the incident, she made him promise not to tell his father, fearing he would kill the white man and bring retribution down on the entire community. But far from letting the matter drop, she picked up a club, found the man, and beat him herself. In time, the story did get around, and James King went after the white man with a gun; the Kings had to go into hiding until the controversy blew over.

James King used to regularly beat Mike's mother, especially after Saturday night binges. After one such episode, Daddy King became so furious he wrestled his father to the floor. Although James King apologized to his son the next day, Daddy King had had enough. At fourteen, he took off for Atlanta with nothing but the clothes on his back, his only pair of shoes slung over his shoulder. In Atlanta, he worked odd jobs, from mechanic to railroad fireman, before returning home for a few years. At eighteen, he left home for Atlanta again. This time he worked in a tire plant and loading bales of cotton and driving a truck. He felt a strong pull to the ministry. Answering the call, he became pastor of two small churches and attended high school at night to earn his diploma. Eventually he graduated from Morehouse College with a bachelor's degree in theology. He also met and married Alberta, the daughter of the Rev. Adam Daniel Williams and Jennie Celeste Parks Williams.

Rev. Adam Daniel Williams, born just before the Emancipation Proclamation was signed in 1863, had literally come up from slavery. Williams took over Ebenezer in 1894, building it into one of the biggest, most prestigious black churches in the city. A strong civil rights leader, Williams helped force Atlanta to build Booker T. Washington High School, the city's first high school for blacks. In 1927, Daddy King became assistant pastor of his father-in-law's church.

In the spring of 1931, Dr. Williams died suddenly, on his thirty-seventh pastoral anniversary. In the fall, the congregation called Reverend King to pastor the church. Like Williams, Daddy King had become a civil rights leader and was active in the NAACP. He also became a founding director of the Negro bank Citizens Trust, and amassed interests in other businesses, carving out for himself a respectable place in Atlanta's black middle-class society.

As I sat in church that June day, I fretted as my mind took off, rehearsing my fears. Despite my dream, Daddy King might not like me. Could Daddy King change Martin's mind? I thought. What if my parents didn't like Martin? How would I react to that? What if I didn't feel comfortable with their church? These questions weighed heavily on my mind. Overall, it was a pleasant and welcoming visit, but as I left to go spend the summer with my own family, I still didn't know exactly where I stood or if Martin and I had his family's full blessing.

That fall, Martin and I returned to Boston to continue school. Our courtship and love for each other had grown stronger. Martin and his friend Philip Lenud had conveniently found an apartment near the conservatory. One day Edythe, who had come to visit me, and I stopped over at their flat, and Martin asked if I could cook. Actually, I could "burn," as they say. From age fourteen, I had learned to take over a kitchen and turn out fried chicken, collard greens, and sweet potato pies, all the down-home fare that southerners are noted for. So I set out to show Martin my stuff, cooking my specialty, banana pudding, and Martin's favorite cabbage dish, smothered in bacon; my sister prepared Creole-style pork chops, and we added corn bread. After Martin and Philip dined suffi-ciently, Martin said teasingly, "Well, you've passed the test." Though I did not like his choice of words, I was pleased that he appreciated my culi-nary skills.

Finally, in November, the moment of truth arrived. Martin's father and mother came to visit him in Boston. They could see how serious Martin was about me. He was not seeing any other girls, and he had asked me to come by every day while his parents were in town. Martin wanted his parents to see that I was the only girl around him. But Daddy King had other ideas.

One afternoon at Martin's apartment, things came to a head. Daddy King began talking about the Atlanta girls. "I don't understand my son. He's gone out with some of the finest, most beautiful, intelligent girls from fine families. Those girls have so much to offer."

I tried to hold my peace, but feeling my temperature rising, I shot back, "I have something to offer, too."

Daddy King didn't seem to hear me; he continued talking about the other girls Martin had dated. Martin's stillness and lack of response to his father irked me as much as Daddy King's overlooking my fine quali-ties, which certainly matched those of the women he was praising so highly. Martin sat, not saying a word, grinning like an embarrassed schoolboy. He did not want to challenge his father any more than he had already done. I waited, wondering why Martin wasn't saying anything, why he wasn't defending me.

Without saying anything to his father, Martin rose, went into the room where his mother was, and said, "Coretta is going to be my wife."

As Martin drove me home that night, he seemed disappointed that I hadn't made a better impression on his father. I expressed my angst that his father had disregarded my feelings by talking about those other girls in Atlanta.

Two days later, however, I learned that I had made a better impres-sion than I thought. During dinner, Daddy King slammed his hand down on the table and said, "You two are courting real hard. It is best that you get married."

Only later did I find out what a sense of humor Daddy King had. Each time I would perform at a concert or excel in some way, he would remind me of what I had told him. He would say, "Coretta, I have something to offer, too." These lines would produce much riotous laughter. By then, I, too, could join in the fun. Later I would learn how Martin's sister, Christine, had beat the drum for me, and how Daddy King was impressed that his little granddaughter Alveda was so fond of me. She had nicknamed me Coco.

When Martin went home for Christmas, he discussed with his parents our plans to marry. They suggested we announce our engagement around Easter in the only black newspaper in Atlanta, the *Atlanta Daily World*. We would be married in June, after the school year ended.

As I hashed and rehashed my decision, I thought about what Edythe, who was very fond of Martin, had said. *You won't have your career as you dreamed it, but you will have your career.*

With that in mind, I decided to switch my major at the conservatory from performing arts to music education, with a voice major and a minor in violin. This way, wherever Martin and I lived, I could supplement our income by teaching.

One year and four months after we met, on June 18, 1953, Daddy King married Martin and me on the lawn of my parents' home in Marion, the one that they had built to replace the house that was burned to the ground. A.D. was best man, and Edythe was maid of honor. A.D.'s daughter Alveda was the flower girl. I decided to forgo a white formal gown, and instead wore a pastel blue, waltz-length dress.

Although the wedding was small by Atlanta standards, it was one of the biggest weddings ever held in my hometown. All of the King family came from Atlanta, along with some of the deacons and trustees of Ebenezer Church. None of the Kings, not even Martin, had ever met my parents, and I was concerned about whether they would form a favorable impression of our home in the country. My knowledge of Martin and his family should have allayed such feelings, but I suppose all brides have apprehensions. I didn't want to look like I was trying to "impress" the Kings; at the same time, I wanted all of us to be hospitable and get along. I shouldn't have worried. As soon as Martin walked in the door, smiling, said hello, and kissed my mother, the ice was broken.

I had made up my mind that I wanted the traditional language about "obeying" and submitting to my husband deleted from our marriage vows. The language made me feel too much like an indentured servant. I was worried that this break with tradition, which I later learned was quite revolutionary in the fifties, would anger either Daddy King, Martin, or both. To my surprise, neither one objected. Daddy King didn't object because he understood that the times were changing and young people were thinking differently. Martin didn't object because his view of women was more progressive than that of most men of his generation.

Because there were no hotels that accommodated blacks in the South, we spent our wedding night in the home of a friend, who happened to be an undertaker. Throughout our marriage, Martin would sometimes jokingly reminisce about this: "Honey, do you remember we spent our honeymoon at a funeral parlor?"

———— ❈ ————

FOUR

A Brave Soldier

A S MUCH AS one can feel relaxed in the aftermath of hateful, threatening phone calls, on the evening of January 30, 1956, in the little house where we lived in Montgomery, Alabama, I was in a happy mood. It was about 9:30 at night, and I was comfortable in my bathrobe, chatting with my church friend Mary Lucy Williams in the front room. My infant daughter, Yolanda (we called her Yoki), was asleep in her crib in the back room.

Suddenly, coming from the front porch, I heard a sound: a heavy thump and a rolling noise. I yelled to Mary, "Something's hit the house; run to the back!"

Before we could get halfway through the next room, a bomb exploded on the porch. The thunderous blast shattered the door and the window glass, leaving behind a cloud of putrid white smoke. It was the loudest explosion I had ever heard. The noise frightened my baby, who awoke, crying. I ran and gathered her in my arms. I gasped, calling out, "Oh, my Lord," as I saw the damage the bomb had unleashed. Broken glass and pieces of wood were piled across the floors. We choked on the smoke that clogged the air.

As we crept toward the front of the house to see if anyone was outside, we saw a big hole in the front wall and the porch hanging half off.

The chair and sofa where Mary and I had been sitting was torn to pieces; even the pictures on the walls had been shaken loose.

I heard the doorbell ring, and for a moment I panicked. Were the perpetrators returning to kill us? I worried about what to do with my baby: How could I protect her?

A concerned voice came through the front door: "Is anybody hurt?"

I went to the door and let in my neighbors. They were astonished and angered by the devastating sight of the broken windows, the hole in the concrete floor, and the split porch. I picked up the phone to call the police, but quickly put the receiver back down. From my childhood in Marion, I knew better. Instead, I thanked God that we were yet alive. If we had remained at the front of the house when we heard the noise, we might have died. A few feet had spared our lives.

Since the Montgomery Bus Boycott had begun one month before, we had experienced a barrage of harassing phone calls, including one particularly frightening caller who told Martin that if he didn't leave town in three days they were going to bomb the house and kill our baby and me. Even so, I convinced myself that the call was an empty threat. When people call you up and tell you they're going to do something, they're probably not going to do it, I reasoned. They are just trying to scare you. But tonight I realized just how deadly real those threats could be.

Long minutes passed before I could calm my nerves enough to call First Baptist Church, where Ralph Abernathy pastored and where Martin, who had recently been appointed leader of the movement, was speaking at a mass meeting about the boycott. I let them know that our house had been bombed and asked them to find Martin.

I hung up, reminding myself of the need to stay calm, even as it was clear that anger and violence against those boycotting the city buses was escalating. Ever since hundreds of black maids, butlers, teachers, and preachers refused to board the buses that denigrated us as less than human, as the whites saw that we could not be intimidated, scared off, or bought off, the level of hostility had intensified. Young white ruffians would drive through black neighborhoods squirting urine on the faces, hair, suits, and dresses of any black person they could find. Adults and children would sometimes have to double back home to clean off the filth before they could proceed to school or work. The urine tossed from cars was humiliating, but that was the tip of the iceberg in terms of the violent intimidation. Crosses were being burned around town. Bricks were being thrown from windows, resulting in sprains and concussions. One well-known amateur boxer was stomped by a carload of white men, who accosted him as he walked along the street.

While I had dismissed the angry phone calls that came to our home night and day, Martin had calculated the possible outcome more clearly and insisted that a church member sit with Yoki and me whenever he was out. I was thankful that Mary was with me when the bomb hit our house.

Seeing the glass and feeling the explosion was my wake-up call. I was shocked into a new reality: the perpetrators would do anything, even commit murder, to stop us. It sank in again: if there had been more dynamite or if we had been closer to the explosion, Mary, my daughter, and I would have been killed. I had to be realistic, to stop and think about my own life and the life of my child.

Soon, Martin rushed home from his meeting. By that time, an angry crowd had gathered outside; it was growing by the moment, and our house was so full of people that Martin had trouble getting in. The mayor and the police commissioner had also arrived; the police nervously held the crowd back.

Martin had been assured that Yoki and I were all right, but he was surprised to find me so calm. Gently, he told me, "Why don't you get dressed, darling?" I was still wearing my house robe, and he wanted me to join him on the porch to hear him address the crowd outside.

I lagged behind a moment to answer the phone. I wished I hadn't. It was a raging female voice: "I'm sorry we didn't kill all you bastards."

Martin had a textbook understanding of the Christian-Gandhian principles of nonviolence. We often debated the difference between passivism and creative nonviolence. But that night, as I joined him on the porch in the heat of the crisis, with pain and anguish all around, I saw that he was no longer the student. He was the practitioner, making the theories come alive as he spoke. This was his first test. His home had just been bombed, his wife and child could have been killed, yet he told the crowd very calmly that we were all right, and he asked them to go home. He had been told that a few of the men gathered there were armed with everything from broken bottles to pistols. "I want you to go home and put down your weapons," he said. "We cannot solve this problem with retaliatory violence. Remember the words of Jesus: 'He who lives by the sword dies by the sword.' We must love our white brothers, no matter what they do to us."

Going further still, he said, "This movement will not stop, because God is with this movement. Go home with that glowing faith and radiant assurance."

The atmosphere was so rife with tension that if a black man had tripped over a white man, it could have set off a riot. And if there had been a riot, Montgomery and the boycott would have turned into a dim memory, most likely recorded as the actions of out-of-control blacks with no mention of what had contributed to the violence.

As soon as our parents heard about the bombing, they sprang into action. Early the next day, my father and Daddy King made the drive from their respective homes to Montgomery. They were on a mission with one thing on their minds: to save our lives, to take us home. After the bombing, Martin, Yoki, and I went to stay with Mr. and Mrs. Joseph T. Brooks, both of whom were well-respected musicians in church circles. Martin's sister, Christine, and his brother, A.D., drove up to their house along with our fathers.

My father made me very nervous, pacing the floor as he tried to convince us to abandon Montgomery. And Daddy King's booming voice seemed to explode as he laid out the potential danger ahead. "Come on back to Atlanta. I need you at Ebenezer. It is better to be a live hero than a dead dog."

Martin shook his head and stood his ground, looking like a little kid before his father.

"I think you need to step back and let someone else lead for a while, because they are after you," my father told Martin. "I will take Coretta and the baby home for a while until things cool off."

It took a lot for me to stand my ground as well. "I will not be returning home," I said. "I would not be happy if I left. I am going to stay here with Martin."

As I heard the flow of words streaming from my mouth, I felt as if I had an ear to my soul. The more I spoke, the stronger I felt. I had watched my father confront terrorism as a child. I was not new to the forces of hate and evil, but I had never been in a situation in which I had to make a personal commitment, to put my body on the line, to know my life could be taken from me. I had never faced my own test of endurance. At the age of twenty-eight, I had no idea what I would do, given a choice like this: to face and endure some of the worst acts of physical hatred or to run away. But in that moment I summoned a resolve. I knew what I needed to do, what my heart called me to do: stay.

Daddy King did not give up easily. He walked the floor and preached to us through the night and until daybreak. By morning, we were all exhausted, but Martin and I dug in our heels and refused to leave.

The next morning, after we had finished breakfast and our parents had left, Martin told me, "Corrie, you are a brave soldier. I don't know what I would do without you."

Hearing those words from him kept me motivated to be the best friend and wife I could ever conceive of being to Martin. He needed me. In fact, I truly believe that if I had packed up and left Montgomery that night, Martin would have left with me. And if that had happened, one can only wonder: Would Montgomery have birthed a movement that would electrify the world?

Later, Martin would write of me, "A wife can either make or break a husband. My wife was always stronger than I was through the struggle. . . . In the darkest moments, she always brought the light of hope. I am convinced if I had not had a wife with the fortitude, strength and calmness of Corrie, I could not have withstood the ordeals and tensions surrounding the movement."

The night of the bombing, I began to understand how much it meant to Martin to have a wife who was strong. And that's really when I made my commitment to go all the way. I remember it clearly. I remember how I felt. Inside my chest, I had this nervousness. Strangely enough, though, while I was nervous and torn between decisions, I was not afraid. There is a difference. I had known fear. I don't think any black person growing up in the Deep South escaped the reality that a black person's life could be taken by whites without any consequences. Yet, that night, fear mixed with the faith I had known from childhood. In Montgomery, when tragedy hit, when I was tested, I found that the fear had left. It had been overcome by faith.

I thought of Yoki. My baby. Love keeps you moving forward. I had no fear in Montgomery not only because of the spiritual strength I had found there, but because of the unity and solidarity of the people. The Bible says that perfect love casts out all fear. I began to see love in action: how brave, how courageous black people were; how, in the midst of such terror, they could stand up and demand a better future, for themselves, for their children.

While our parents were worrying themselves to death about us, Martin and I felt secure. After the bombing, I also came to the conclusion that I was stronger in a crisis. I didn't panic or fall apart. I might get upset if the house is junky, but when there is a crisis, some mechanism inside me is set off; my mind kicks into high speed and starts racing toward solutions. Panic comes when you don't see a way out. I was learning that even in the midst of terror, there is always a way out. I had been taught, and have come to believe in, the words of the gospel song: "God will make a way out of no way."

AS NEWLYWEDS IN Boston, Martin and I had been like two schoolkids, playful and in love. We would go to Revere Beach amusement park, where Martin enjoyed the hair-raising roller coaster. He roller-skated with his friend Philip Lenud, the two laughing and roughhousing until they were ready to drop. Once, when my rather serious mother was visiting and went with us to the park, she joked, "Martin, you know you act like you are about four years old."

Most portraits of Martin depict him as so intense, serene, and cerebral; you would not think, reading them, that he did everyday, normal things. But Martin was a prankster, a person who could bring fun into our lives and see the humor in the worst situations.

Also, in Boston, and until events in Montgomery swept us up in their wake, Martin was quite the househusband. He was so secure about his manhood that he didn't equate helping me with housework as detracting from his masculinity. While he was researching his dissertation and I was finishing up at the conservatory, he was wonderful about helping with chores, and he didn't mind wearing an apron, often telling himself that it made him look manly. Martin did all the heavy cleaning, even the laundry. He would cook one night a week, usually Thursdays, and was proud of his culinary skills. Depending on how he felt, he would cook smothered cabbage and fried chicken. He could also cook turnip greens with ham hocks and corn bread.

Six months into our marriage, however, in January 1954, Martin accepted an invitation to preach at the Dexter Avenue Baptist Church in Montgomery, which was looking for someone to replace Dr. Vernon Johns, a fiery and fearless minister, who was retiring. Martin's sermon topic was "The Three Dimensions of a Complete Life." He made such a tremendous impression that, a month later, he was invited to assume the pastorate.

Having completed most of his work for his PhD in systematic theology from Boston University, Martin had any number of churches interested in offering him pastorates, particularly in Massachusetts and New York, but he felt his calling was in the South, which brought him closer to his family in Atlanta.

I was not thrilled about leaving Boston and heading south. I would have preferred to move someplace at least more progressive, like Atlanta. After all, Montgomery was only eighty miles from Heiberger, the town where I grew up, and I thought I knew all too well what to expect from the city, once the capital of the Confederacy and one of the most racist places in America.

Selfishly, perhaps, I wanted to participate for a while longer in the richer cultural life open to blacks in the North, where there was a wealth of opportunities for me to further my musical career. I was also concerned about raising children under the bonds of segregation. And having lived for so long in Antioch's Yellow Springs, Ohio, and in Boston, I knew what it was to ride anywhere you wanted on the subways and buses, to have quality friendships with whites, and not to have to move off the sidewalk when they walked by. If we returned, I feared that my will would be compressed and subjugated, that a body that knew what it meant to be free would be confined. The more we talked, the more I heard the shackles forming around my legs.

But in the end, our going south was never an issue. I had wanted to go later rather than sooner, but during our courtship Martin had prepared me in advance and let me know his intentions. So, regardless of my private concerns, on September 1, 1954, we officially moved into the parsonage at Dexter Baptist Church, where Martin began his first assignment as a full-time pastor, and I pressed on, ready to assume my role as a First Lady and pastor's wife.

When we moved, I told Martin, "I will make myself happy in Montgomery. You perfect your preaching and improve yourself in the ministry, and I will learn to be a good minister's wife"—which I did. I taught Sunday school and sang in the choir, using my formal musical training to make it one of the finest choirs in Montgomery. I also had the opportunity to appear in concert in several churches and at gatherings in surrounding towns, such as Shiloh Baptist Church in Brunswick, Georgia. Meanwhile, Martin divided his efforts between completing his dissertation and performing his church duties, rising daily at five-thirty to write and returning to it late at night. The remainder of the day was given over to church work: visiting the sick, officiating at marriages and funerals, and of course preparing the Sunday sermon.

Despite my intentions to carve out a low-key role as a pastor's wife, my role quickly evolved into more of a collaborative partnership with Martin. I began typing, listening, critiquing, and helping him prepare his sermons, something I continued to do throughout our married life. He would start his preparation around Monday. By Saturday, he would have the sermon written out word for word, and he would memorize it. He had a photographic memory, so he would go to the pulpit on Sunday and preach without notes. But in preparing the sermons, he would sometimes give me the subject matter and say, "Now what would you call my first point?" Of course I would think of something. Sometimes he would incorporate my suggestion into his sermon. Then he would rephrase it and go on to the next two points. Most of his sermons were three-point sermons. I felt very much involved in what he was doing.

As I worked with Martin's sermons and watched him preach, I grew to understand that he had the hand of God upon him. Before he mounted the sacred desk (the pulpit), he stood in the presence of God. Martin's sermons did much more than present a catchy title, a nice theme, or a message perfect in syntax and elocution. He spoke prophetically, bringing into existence images and a destiny we had not seen or lived before. It was his calling to help usher in the age of a new Negro, someone with starch in his or her backbone, someone with concern for others, regardless of the obstacles. Unlike sermons by the preachers I heard growing up, Martin's sermons were not escapist. They did not call upon the listeners to look for salvation of their souls while their minds and bodies experienced the agony of disrespect and the terror of trying to live as less than what the Bible says they were, persons "made in the image of God."

One of his sermons, "Loving Your Enemies," was built on many private discussions we had about Gandhian nonviolence and the power of Jesus's love to change minds, hearts, and behavior. Martin had to teach this concept, pound away at it continually and consistently, because nonviolence had to become a habit, a way of life for a people who would be commissioned to stand unarmed before terrorists with guns and bombs.

As I listened to Martin, I had to gird myself with the sense of his reasoning. In the beginning, I don't think I was as committed to nonviolence as he was. I was committed to pacifism, which means not cooperating with evil, but I was not ready to confront violence head-on with nonviolence, as Martin conceptualized. I had to grow into that. I don't believe any of us is born with an innate ability to effectively respond to violent situations nonviolently. Too often, we respond by doing nothing at all, and resign ourselves to live with oppression, which is wrong because, as Martin said, "non-cooperation with evil is as much a moral obligation as cooperation with good." Or we meet violence with violence, creating more social problems and leaving a bitter legacy for the next generations. Martin's ideology demanded that we confront violence in faith and love, which sometimes means moving directly into the line of fire. That is a call to pick up the Cross of Jesus, to follow Him and be prepared to die.

In Martin's sermons, I saw how he prepared the congregation for a time when they would have to act upon the words he was instilling in their souls. In one sermon, he preached that "the way to be integrated with yourself is to be sure that you meet every situation of life with an abounding love. Never hate, because it ends up in tragic, neurotic responses. . . . There is a final reason I think that Jesus says, 'Love your enemies.' It is this: that love has within it a redemptive power. And there is a power there that eventually transforms individuals. That's why Jesus says 'Love your enemies.' Because if you hate your enemies, you have no way to redeem and to transform [them]. . . . Even though they're mistreating you . . . keep on loving them . . . just keep loving them and they can't stand it too long. Oh, they react in many ways in the beginning. They react with guilt feelings and sometimes they'll hate you a little more at the transition period, but just keep loving them. And by the power of love, they will break down under the load. That's love, you see. It is redemptive, and this is why Jesus says love. There is something about love that builds you up and is creative. There is something about hate that tears down and is destructive. So love your enemies."

It was incredibly affirming to see Martin excelling in his role as pastor. In addition to this, and to being welcomed into a vibrant church community, our move to Montgomery was made more enjoyable because of the friendship we formed with Ralph Abernathy and his wife, Juanita. Ralph had come to hear Martin preach at Ebenezer in Atlanta when he, Ralph, was a graduate student at Atlanta University. When Martin was considering coming to Dexter, he called Ralph, a passionate preacher on social justice, who at the time had moved on to pastor First Baptist Church in Montgomery. Once we moved to Montgomery, the Abernathys invited us to dinner. A friendship took off from there.

That spring, as we continued to settle into our lives in Montgomery, two wonderful things happened. After years of intensive study, Martin was awarded his PhD in systematic theology from Boston University, and I discovered I was pregnant. It seemed our lives were becoming complete. We both had our degrees, and we were starting a family. Martin had always said he wanted eight children. After thinking it over, I offered a compromise of four. We were on our way.

During my pregnancy, Martin was particularly attentive. As many first-time parents do, we worried that something could go wrong, but on November 17, 1955, our little girl, Yolanda ("Yoki") Denise, was born. She was a big, healthy baby, weighing nine pounds, eleven and one-half ounces. Martin had wanted a son, but he was just as elated to have a daughter. She was born in St. Jude's Hospital, a Catholic institution that was the only hospital in Montgomery where blacks were treated with a modicum of respect. St. Jude's kept blacks and whites segregated unless the hospital became overcrowded. Then the racial ban was disregarded, and babies could take their first breath as equals—at least for a moment.

In the segregated South, there was something about giving birth, especially for the first time, that tore at your heart, forcing you to confront painful realities. You want to protect your children, to keep them from having to experience the same hardships you've suffered. Somehow you want the muck and mire cleaned up, so they won't be forced to slush through it. As I held my baby Yoki, so tiny and vulnerable, so beautiful, I reflected on some of my yesterdays and wondered aloud if those same harsh realities awaited her. One day, when she was walking to school in her nice clean dress with matching ribbons, would yellow school buses filled with jeering white children maliciously splash mud on her little dress, as they had done to mine? In their ignorance, would the whites hurl vile names at her? My little girl! How could I protect her from the evils of inhumanity?

My private thoughts about the birth of my firstborn were a soliloquy, spoken to no one but God. Yet it appeared that God must have been listening. In less than two weeks, a seamstress and NAACP secretary named Rosa Parks refused to move to the back of the bus, and we began a movement that would become our life's work. Soon, answers would come to the very questions pouring out of my soul—and not only answers. God appeared to have appointed Martin and me, and those who would answer the call, to become the messengers.

———— ❀ ————

FIVE

Time Itself Was Ready

NOTHING HAPPENS IN a vacuum, and especially not the Montgomery Bus Boycott. Not only did Mrs. Parks, my husband, and all the other protagonists have to be in place, but the social and atmospheric forces had to be right. There had been a shift in the political landscape, a buildup of climatic changes, almost like the moments before a rainstorm, when you can sense the thunder and smell the chill before the lightning flash. From afar, we heard the thunder rolling in.

There was the case of *Brown v. Board of Education* in Topeka, Kansas. Through the hard work of the NAACP Legal Defense Fund, headed by Thurgood Marshall, and the appointment of Justice Earl Warren to the Supreme Court, virtually fifty years of legal degradation ended in 1954, when the Court reversed its ancient, unworkable opinion that "separate but equal" educational facilities met the requirements of the Fourteenth Amendment to the Constitution. Marshall's team put in thousands of hours of legwork, wearing out shoe leather and making financial sacrifices, traveling and interviewing, to prove to white folks what black folks had always known: imposed segregation by the majority falls unequally and tyrannically upon the minority.

Finally, it seemed as though the Court, if not on our side, could at least understand the injustices and indignities perpetrated on black Americans in America, their homeland. After a blackout of more than fifty years, it appeared that the highest court was once again on the side of justice. A breath of freedom was stirring in the land. Although, for a while, it looked like nothing different was happening in Montgomery, at least there was an upsurge of hope. Maybe, just maybe, blacks were not to be locked into degradation forever.

Then, on December 1, 1955, the quiet and dignified Rosa Parks, a forty-two-year-old seamstress who had been trained at the Highlander Folk School in Tennessee, a training ground for labor organizers, was arrested when she refused the driver's request to move to the back of the bus. The response from the black community was disciplined outrage, demonstrated by an unprecedented 381-day boycott.

But the question in my mind as I looked back over the years was: Why then?

There had been other women arrested before Mrs. Parks. For example, in March 1955, fifteen-year-old Claudette Colvin refused to give up her seat to a white passenger. The enraged driver called a policeman. Several showed up, and the officers ordered Colvin to get up. When she refused, they dragged her kicking and screaming hysterically off the bus, and she was carted off to jail, where she was charged with misconduct and resisting arrest. Her case was widely discussed in black circles. At that time, Martin served on a committee that protested to the city and bus company officials. The committee was received politely, but nothing happened.

Further, the jailing of Mrs. Parks, who was also a volunteer secretary for the Montgomery chapter of the NAACP, was hardly one of the worst abuses by the buses, whose brutal segregated system had existed for half a century. Documented reports by the Women's Political Council (WPC), a group of politically active black women that had been working for change since the 1940s, showed hundreds of complaints against the bus company. There had been a mother who boarded a bus with two small infants in her arms. Since there were no whites on the bus, she placed the two babies on the empty front seat while she searched in her purse for a dime. The horrified driver demanded that the "black dirty brats" be removed from the seat reserved for whites; to back up his demand, he lunged the bus forward with such a terrific jerk that the infants were thrown into the aisle. In another instance, a mentally defective but harmless black man was severely beaten by a bus driver for walking in front of a bus. In 1952 an intoxicated black man argued with a bus driver over whether he had put a dime into the slot. When the police came upon the scene, they shot and killed the man as he climbed off the bus. The authorities ruled the shooting of the unarmed black man "justifiable homicide."

In fact, the northern-owned Montgomery Bus Line was the most potent, degrading symbol of southern segregation in the town. Although 70 percent of its passengers were black, the system was operated so as to make blacks feel less than human. Imagine what it was like to get on a Montgomery bus with your children.

Not only had there been worse atrocities than the Parks incident, but other leaders had challenged the bus company. Rev. Vernon Johns called on blacks to confront them. When no one would take the dare, Johns stopped riding. It was a long-standing theme of the Women's Political Council that blacks should boycott the bus company. The cause had been there; the agony had been there; the leaders had been there. After a half century of pain and humiliation, why did December 5, 1955, become the day that the Montgomery Bus Boycott finally began? Why did the cries of "We have taken this long enough" soar through the black community with the power of a national anthem? It was as if every tear, every groan, every hurt had been stored up somewhere, and Rosa Parks's arrest was the last indignity. The dam burst. The flow of agony ran over with such force that it submerged fear, mistrust, doubt, and all the previous beliefs that social conditions existing for decades would continue unchecked. As a result, the desire to stand tall, to be confident in times of trouble, surfaced. It was as if souls were being liberated.

But the boycott could also be credited to something Martin used to call the "divine dimension." At the January 30, 1956, mass meeting, two months into the boycott, he said, "There comes a time when time itself is ready for a change," he offered. Often, he would point to the Zeitgeist as being responsible for the birth of the movement. The leaders do not ask for the task, but are tracked down by the spirit of the times until it consumes them; they reach a point where they become the symbol of both the disaffected and the movement swirling around them. It was the spirit of the times that tracked Martin, coupled with the Holy Spirit that motivated, inspired, and directed him. He became that lead symbol. From black barbershops and beauty shops to Negro schools and Alabama State University, the cry was the same.

On Friday, December 2, 1955, in response to Parks's arrest, E. D. Nixon, a fiery local civil rights leader, called Martin. By then, Nixon was echoing what many black people in Montgomery were feeling. "We have taken this type of thing too long," he said. "I feel the time has come to boycott the buses. It's the only way to make the white folks see that we will not take this sort of thing any longer."

Martin offered his church, Dexter, as a meeting place to discuss the idea of a boycott. To his delight, forty leaders showed up, representing every segment of African American life. There were doctors, lawyers, union leaders, federal government employees, and a great number of ministers. The ministers were important because of their influence on their congregations, of course, but their presence also showed a meeting of the minds with Martin and Ralph, who had been preaching the social gospel that religion had to deal not only with heaven, but with the hell playing out on earth.

The decision was unanimous. Yes, they would boycott. From that very first meeting, the Christian ministry provided the leadership of our struggle, and Christian ideals were its source.

THE SATURDAY BEFORE the boycott, Martin and other members of the committee hurried about, working out details with black-owned taxi companies and owners of private cars, who would help transport people to and from work. Although I could not leave Yoki to help outside our home, our house initially served as a command post for the new group, which came to be named the Montgomery Improvement Association (MIA), and it was my responsibility to answer the telephone, which rang incessantly. People needed directions and encouragement. I also cooked the meals for the continuous meetings.

During the boycott, some of the strategy was planned at my dinner table. Very often, I sat in on the meetings as part of the inner circle. Juanita Abernathy and the other ministers' wives and I often served as conduits between the press, the movement volunteers and staff, and our husbands, relieving some of the stress, which built constantly from all directions. Eventually people from across the country and from many foreign countries made their way to our home to become a part of the Montgomery movement.

Far too much of the valuable role that women played in the Montgomery movement and other such efforts has been lost to history. It should be remembered that it was Jo Ann Gibson Robinson, an English professor at Alabama State College and then-president of the Women's Political Council, who put in place a plan for a citywide bus boycott more than a year before Mrs. Parks's arrest. Robinson and Mary Fair Burks, who was equally fervid, helped create and sustain the climate that supported the 1955 boycott. Robinson and her team played multiple roles during the boycott. She drove six hours a day for the car pool, helped shape policy as a member of the Montgomery Improvement Association's executive board, and played a central role in the start of the protest by producing and distributing thousands of leaflets announcing the boycott. Myriad other women were involved as well, making phone calls, organizing, hosting bake sales to raise funds, and so on. Women as old as eighty went to jail.

One of our first challenges was determining how to reach the fifty thousand black people in Montgomery, a problem that, much to our delight, was solved by one of the biggest enemies of our efforts: the white press. A white woman found one of our leaflets, which her maid had left in the kitchen. The enraged woman telephoned the local press to expose what her servant was up to, and their coverage spread the word better than we ever could have.

As the countdown continued on Sunday morning, almost every African American pastor in town urged his parishioners to honor the boycott. Not surprisingly, the news media mounted a fervent case against us. One morning paper wrote an article accusing the NAACP of planting Mrs. Parks on the bus, and likened the boycott to the tactics of the White Citizens' Council, a white supremacist group that had formed in 1954. These accusations really upset Martin. Instead of slinging off the comparisons, he struggled with the ethical question of whether he was doing the right thing. Alone in his study, he paced back and forth, caught up in self-examination.

Finally, he wrote, "Our purposes are altogether different from those of the White Citizens' Council. We were using this method to give birth to justice and freedom and also to urge men to comply with the law of the land. Our concern would not be to put the bus company out of business, but to put justice in business. What we were really doing was withdrawing our cooperation from an evil system, rather than merely withdrawing our support from the bus company."

On the eve of the boycott, I pondered with Martin the pros and cons of the movement long into the night, wondering whether we would succeed. We hardly slept. The next morning, we rose early and were dressed by 5:30 sharp. We woke in anticipation, not knowing what to expect. After having coffee and toast, I planted myself in front of the window to check out the first bus, which was to stop just five feet from our house. At 6:00 a.m., the bus rolled up, right on time, headlights blazing through the December darkness.

"Martin, Martin, come quickly!" I called. He ran in and stood beside me, taking my hand, his face lighting up with excitement. Not one person was on the bus. Then came the next bus. It, too, was empty. This was the most traveled line in the city. We were so happy that we could hardly find words to express our joy.

Everywhere in the city that day, the scenario was the same: sidewalks crowded with men and women trudging to work; students at Alabama State College walking or hitchhiking; people clustered in taxis. Some even rode mules. Others were in horse-drawn buggies, and a few were on bikes. Some people had to make treks as long as twelve miles that day. Never before had I seen such courage and unity in so many, from butlers to schoolteachers, from the maids to the ministers. Truly, as Martin said, "a miracle had taken place." Instead of the 60 percent cooperation we had hoped for, we reached nearly 100 percent.

The next bombshell was the news Martin brought me that evening about the activities that had happened on day one. Martin and Ralph had attended the 9:30 a.m. trial of Rosa Parks. After the judge heard the arguments, she was found guilty of disobeying the city's segregation laws and fined fourteen dollars, including court costs. She appealed the case. This was one of the first clear-cut instances in which a black was convicted of disobeying segregation laws. Heretofore, such cases had either been dismissed or those involved had been charged with disorderly conduct. Had the D.A. known that the Parks case would evolve into a test of the validity of segregation laws, and that it would fuel the protest, I am sure they would have dismissed the case.

Later that afternoon, Martin went to a meeting with E. D. Nixon, Ralph Abernathy, and other organizers. Much to Martin's surprise, when he walked into the meeting, he was quickly named president of the Montgomery Improvement Association, with the understanding that the organization would continue the boycott until certain demands were met.

When I heard the news, I wondered aloud: Why Martin? Maybe because he was new in town, maybe because others already had important assignments. (Ralph had been made chairman of the committee and was asked to draw up its demands.) In any event, here was Martin, home at six o'clock, confronting a stack of messages because the phone had been ringing all day in support of our cause. He updated me, telling me very hesitantly about his new position. I didn't need to be told of the danger that loomed ahead for any black person who stood up for his or her rights. Nevertheless, I reassured him: "You know that whatever you do, I am with you."

Martin went off to his study to work on his address for the mass meeting that night at Holt Street Baptist Church. He had only twenty minutes to prepare for what he told me would be the most decisive speech of his life. Reporters and news cameras would be there to send his words around the world, and he confided to me that for a moment he almost panicked at the thought of what he was about to do. Beating back fear with prayer, Martin asked God to restore his balance and "to be with me in a time when I need your guidance more than ever."

Martin and Ralph had been debating whether the press would call their efforts a failure if only five hundred people showed up that night, only half-filling the thousand-seat church. But when they got within five blocks of the church, they encountered a traffic jam. Cars were everywhere: in yards, parked on sidewalks. It looked as though someone were having a party. As they pressed their way in, they found about a thousand people in the church and about four thousand more milling around outside, a response that was much more than Martin and I could ever have imagined.

When Martin and Ralph approached, someone saw them and

announced that they were in the house. The crowd started applauding politely, then wildly. The space was so jammed that people had to lift Ralph and Martin above the crowd and pass them from hand to hand over the heads of the crowd and to the platform.

Opening an hour and a half late, the program started with "Onward Christian Soldiers," which literally sounded like a five-thousand-voice battle cry. When Martin was introduced, a cry went up. The cameras clicked. Without manuscript or notes, Martin retold the story of Mrs. Parks and reviewed the long history of abuses and insults that Negro citizens had experienced on city buses. He told the audience that there comes a time "when people get tired of being trampled over by the iron feet of oppression." He pleaded for unity: "It is the great need of the hour." He cautioned against fear: "Don't let anyone frighten you. We are not afraid of what we are doing because we are doing it within the law." He refuted the press's inappropriate comparisons between the movement and the Klan: "There will be no crosses burned at any bus stops in Montgomery. There will be no white persons pulled out of their homes and taken out on some distant road and lynched for not cooperating." He reiterated that ours was a Christian movement: "In all of our doings, in all of our deliberations . . . whatever we do, we must keep God at the forefront"; "Love is one of the pivotal points of the Christian face, faith. There is another side called justice. And justice is really love in calculation. Justice is love correcting that which revolts against love." He closed the speech by saying, "As we prepare ourselves for what lies ahead, let us go with a grim and bold determination that we are going to stick together. We are going to work together. Right here in Montgomery, when the history books are written in the future, someone will say, 'There lived a people, a black people, fleecy locks and black complexion, a people who had the moral courage to stand up for their rights and thereby they injected a new meaning into the veins of history and of civilization.'"

As Martin finished speaking, the audience rose, cheering in exaltation. And in that speech, Martin laid the spiritual foundation, set the moral tone, and provided a model of courage for the movement that was born in Montgomery that very night. As Martin himself concluded that day, "the real victory was in the mass meeting, where thousands of black people stood revealed with a new sense of dignity and destiny."

Since I was under doctor's orders to remain at home following the birth of Yoki, I could not attend the meeting. However, Martin and I knew that the speech he would deliver would probably be one of the most important of his life, so I arranged ahead of time to have it taped. In retrospect, I believe that night in 1955, the seed for the Martin Luther King Jr. Center for Nonviolent Social Change was planted in my mind. What happened in Montgomery would eventually become a living model for future generations, through an institution that would preserve and grow Martin's vision.

I suppose I have always had a feel for history. It's a gift my mother had. Martin was too busy racing around, preaching, and being at the forefront to record his efforts. I remember telling myself that the life Martin and I were living was important and that, just maybe, people might someday want to know what was said and done. I knew I could not depend upon most of the mainstream press to record these events accurately; I often agonized over the ways they mangled the truth.

So, beginning with Martin's first mass address, which officially launched the Montgomery Bus Boycott, I started saving his speeches, his papers, and all other memorabilia. Of course, this makes sense in retrospect, but back then, I thought that if we who are living these events don't document our story, whom could we depend upon to be the truth tellers, to pass on accurate information to the next generation? Who would teach them, motivate them? Would the next generation understand what we were doing when we ourselves were young people if we didn't pass on our story?

Of course, that night, December 5, 1955, I envisioned passing our story to the next generation as something Martin and I would work on together. And of course, on that night, victory was far away. The struggle was just beginning. Yet, we could see that black people were being empowered. A change had come. We were willing to walk the streets in dignity rather than ride buses in shame. Despite mass jailings, bombing of homes and churches, firings, and slander in the press, we would not cooperate with injustice. We kept on walking, and walking, and walking—for 381 days.

On January 20, 1956, Montgomery city leaders announced a "get tough" policy in a desperate attempt to stop the boycott. "Get tough" amounted to a series of trumped-up charges for imaginary traffic violations, intended to put fear in the hearts of the protesters. Martin was among the first to go to jail that day.

The whole episode started when my husband and Robert "Bob" Williams, Martin's former schoolmate at Morehouse College, who was teaching music at Alabama State College, drove downtown to pick up Mrs. Lillie Thomas, the church secretary of Dexter Avenue Baptist Church. At the edge of the parking lot, a policeman stopped Martin and asked to see his license. As Martin was showing it, someone overheard another policeman say, "It's that damn King fellow." When Martin stopped to let his passengers out, a policeman pulled up and said, "Get out, King. You're under arrest for going thirty miles in a twenty-five-mile zone." Martin told Williams to drive on and notify me. Meanwhile, after two policemen searched him from top to bottom, they put Martin in the back of the car and drove off.

I was at church when one of the church sisters came running up to me. "Mrs. King, Mrs. King, they got him. They've arrested Dr. King. Please do something." My heart sank, and a sense of indescribable agony gripped me. I knew that Martin, who had to help others relinquish their fears, was struggling with his own personal fear of being alone in jail. This was the South, the cradle of the Confederacy, and the stomping grounds of the KKK. It was not unusual for a policeman also to be a Klansman. Martin and I knew that not every black person arrested made it home alive. Later, when Martin told me about this experience, he described the sense of panic he felt come over him when the police car appeared to be taking him in the opposite direction from the jail.

"I thought the jail was in the downtown section, yet we were going in a different direction," he told me. "The more we rode, the farther we were from the center of town. Pretty soon we turned into a dark and dingy street that I had never seen before and headed over a desolate old bridge. By this time, I was convinced that they were carrying me to some faraway spot to dump me off. I began to wonder whether they were driving me out to some waiting mob, planning to use the excuse later on that they had been overpowered. I found myself trembling within and without. I asked God to give me the strength to endure whatever came."

Yet the police drove on to the police station, and ushered Martin into a dingy, smelly cell. A big iron door shut behind him. He later told me that, as it dawned on him that, for the first time in his life, he was behind bars, gusts of emotion swept through him like cold winds on an open prairie.

For me, the hours that Martin was behind bars seemed like days. While he went to jail physically, I went to jail emotionally. Just as he in his imprisonment could not get out, I felt the same way: imprisoned *outside*, since I could not get in to be with him and share in his suffering. But there was no time for tears. Immediately, I helped get the word out. Later that afternoon, Martin was released on his own recognizance, apparently because as soon as word of his arrest spread, so many friends and well-wishers congregated at the jail that his jailers wanted to be rid of him. It seemed that virtually every black person in town had either come to the jail or was at one of five mass meetings being held around town, to pray for him.

When Martin was released, he spoke at each of those five meetings. It had been the aim of the authorities to discredit Martin. However, his followers saw his release as a direct answer to their prayers, a blessing that only made him more of a hero in their eyes.

Later that night, when Martin and I were alone, I did not tell him of my deep pain, my feeling of utter helplessness during those hours when I couldn't hear from him. I never let on how deeply it hurt me to see him in the hands of people who meant him harm, or how, for the first time, I had to reflect on the possibility that he could be taken from me and our infant daughter. I agonized over how unbearable life would be without him. I did not share these feelings. Instead, I listened to his story and encouraged him. Later, when he told his account of the jailing, he said, "As usual, Coretta gave me the reassurance that can come only from one who is as close to you as your own heartbeat." These are words that I never stopped cherishing.

Shortly after Martin was released from jail, however, the hate calls to our home increased, keeping me awake and turning me into an insomniac. The threats and the prevalent danger depressed us both. One night, at a mass meeting, Martin found himself saying, "If one day you find me sprawled and dead, I do not want you to retaliate with a single act of violence. I urge you to continue protesting with the same dignity and discipline you have shown so far."

On another day, Martin came home feeling very weary. He looked at me and the baby and worried aloud that we might be taken from each other at any time. In the middle of the night, an angry phone caller warned, "Nigger, we've taken all we want from you. Before next week you'll be sorry you ever came to Montgomery." One Saturday, I received forty abusive and threatening calls. I admit I did not always respond with a nonviolent demeanor. One of the early morning hecklers chided me for taking the telephone off the hook. "It's my phone, and I'll do what I like with it," I answered angrily. In the background, Martin prompted, "Oh, darling, don't talk like that. Be nice. Be kind."

The phone harassment became so heated that Martin told his congregation, "If you call and you cannot get through, it is because we take the phone off the hook at night. It's the only way we can get any rest." One night, after I had fallen asleep, Martin answered another angry call. Later he told me that, at that moment, it seemed he just couldn't take any more. He slipped out of bed to make himself some coffee, but something stopped him in his tracks. He sat down at the kitchen table, put his head in his hands, and bowed his head. He began to pray aloud. "Dear God, I am taking a stand for what I believe is right. The people are looking to me for leadership, and if I stand before them without strength and courage, they will falter. I am at the end of my powers. I have nothing left. I've come to the point where I can't face it alone."

At that moment, when he could go no further on his own power, Martin felt a sudden dramatic shift. He told me, "I experienced the presence of the Divine as I had never experienced it before. It seemed as though I could hear the quiet assurance of an inner voice saying, 'Stand up for righteousness, stand up for truth, and God will be at your side forever.'"

That voice was right, because eventually, of course, we won. On November 13, 1956, the Supreme Court declared Alabama's state and local laws requiring segregation on buses unconstitutional. This was a landmark verdict. While the Court's decision and its long-standing merits now take up volumes in law libraries, a more difficult story to tell is the effect on the human spirit, which will last even longer.

On December 20, the bus integration order finally reached Montgomery. After 381 days of determined protest, we could once again ride city buses. And for the first time since almost anyone could remember, we could sit where we wanted to and ride with dignity.

The next morning, Martin became one of the first passengers to ride the desegregated buses. Rosa Parks, Ralph Abernathy, E. D. Nixon, and the Rev. Glenn Smiley (who was white) of the Fellowship of Reconciliation all joined him, gathering in my living room beforehand in preparation to take their place in history.

Right on time, at 5:55 a.m., the bus flashed its lights as it rolled up to the bus stop. How normal that looks today! On that day, though, its appearance was fraught with the dangers one might expect from taking off to be the first to land on the moon. As the lights from TV cameras flooded the bus, a smiling bus driver said, "I believe you are Dr. King."

Martin said, "Yes, I am."

"We're glad to have you with us this morning," the driver said.

It's hard to describe the emotions—exhilaration, pride, hope—that washed over us all as we boarded that bus.

Before 1956 came to a close, I was able to move from a supportive to a major role as fund-raiser for the Montgomery Improvement Association. Activists Bayard Rustin, Stan Levison, and Ella Baker founded a group called In Friendship, which raised funds for victims of economic reprisals in the South. They put on a big benefit concert at the Manhattan Center in New York City on December 5, 1956, to mark the first anniversary of the start of the Montgomery Bus Boycott. Ruth Bunche, wife of Ralph Bunche, who was U.N. undersecretary general for special political affairs, and "Minnie" Wilkins, the wife of the NAACP's Roy Wilkins, were among the honorary chairs.

I was the featured performer among the great stars, such as Harry Belafonte and Duke Ellington, who performed that night at the jam-packed center. It was a frightening and humbling experience. First, I sang a program of classical music, and then I told the story of Montgomery. Weaving spirituals and freedom songs into the narration I had written, I spoke of the oppression suffered by many people throughout the ages and said that God had always sent deliverers to them, as He had sent Moses to the children of Israel. "Today God still speaks to the modern Pharaohs to 'Let My People Go,'" I said. "It was one year ago today, on December 5, 1955, that the cradle of political, economic and social injustice began rocking slowly but surely. For a year we have walked in dignity rather than ride in humiliation. As we walked to and from our jobs, we sang a song to give us moral support."

Then I sang the spiritual:

> *Walk together, chillun, don't you get weary,*
> *Walk together, chillun, don't you get weary,*
> *Dere's a great camp meetin' in the promise' land.*

I then told the story of Mother Pollard, an elderly lady we had met during the boycott who said, "It used to be my soul was tired while my feets rested; now my feets tired, while my soul is rested."

My next song was another spiritual, "Keep Your Hand on the Plow," of which I said, "We are going to keep our hands on the plow because we are determined that there shall be a new Montgomery, a new Southland, yes, a new America, where freedom, justice, and equality shall become a reality for every man, woman, and child. We have felt all along in our struggle that we have cosmic companionship—that God Himself is on our side and that truth and goodness ultimately will triumph. This is our faith, and by this faith we shall continue to live."

At the close of the program, I sang one of Martin's favorite songs, the beautiful spiritual "Honor, Honor":

> *O run along lil chillun to be baptize'*
> *Mighty pretty meetin' by de waterside.*

Thus we had our songs, we had the Spirit, and we had our unity—which only frustrated the racist extremists. But despite the fact that the violence continued—blacks were dragged off buses and beaten up, a pregnant woman was shot in the leg—a nonviolent Christian movement had begun. The paralysis resulting from hundreds of years of oppression had broken; we were learning to walk again as new human beings. The weapons of our movement—faith, love, prayer, action, and obedience to God—would prove mightier than bombs, dynamite, tradition, or the Ku Klux Klan.

The boycott had become personal for me very quickly. It burned into my mind the price I might have to pay for refusing to bow down to a system that insisted upon reducing us to less than human. The knowledge that I could be killed, along with all the people I loved, had to settle within me. In addition, Martin was unfairly jailed for the first time, which made me understand that if we continued with the movement, I would have to adjust to his being snatched away from me without really knowing if he would ever return.

Montgomery made me face the reality that I could lose my own life and leave my daughter without a mother. When you are in your twenties, even with danger all around, you have a sense of invincibility. But before the Montgomery experience ended, I knew what "commitment" was all about, and I knew just how far I would go with this new movement.

Martin and I felt extremely blessed when we saw what was happening around us. At the beginning of the Montgomery experience, we had no idea that a local boycott would spread like wildfire until it was news worldwide. It was like a great revelation, a truth unfolding and exploding within us. Somehow, we knew we had been divinely placed. It was God's will for us to be in Montgomery. I felt that we were part of a great drama unfolding on the stage of history. It was what I had been prepared for all my life, and a great sense of fulfillment came over me.

I had a feeling that told me: We're supposed to be here. I have been called to be a part of this, and now I'm prepared to go all the way. If something happens to me, then let it be.

———— ❋ ————

SIX

The Winds of Change

A N OFT-HEARD REFRAIN in black churches is "I got up one morning, my hands looked new; I looked at my feet, and they did, too." Everything was brand new. That was the way it felt in the wake of the successful Montgomery Bus Boycott. The new year, 1957, dawned as a metaphor for a future that sparkled and gleamed with promise, potential, and fresh purpose. The days reminded me of the touch of lime with which I liked to flavor my sweet tea, how you could enjoy sweetness with a hint of bitterness, a reminder that life often brings both.

On February 18, 1957, *Time* magazine featured Martin on its cover, with a story about how he was emerging as one of the nation's remarkable leaders. It was a great honor, but being thrust into the national spotlight brought with it a new set of uncertainties and challenges. I had many questions, and I was seeking direction about what awaited me around the corner. Could I continue my career as a concert singer? Should I be expected to become a public speaker? How could I balance being there for Martin *and* being home with the children *and* being deeply involved in the movement? How could I compartmentalize myself in so many ways and still hold on to the corner of my life that belonged strictly to Coretta?

I soon found that there was no map or guidebook to help me answer my questions. I had to live life and believe that God would define me and shape me for my purpose. I began to understand that each crisis, even each new heartache, was just preparation for the leadership role that I would have in the coming years.

Martin's recognition in the mainstream media had resulted in his being celebrated as the ex officio president of black America, with requests for him to speak pouring in from around the nation and the world. While I was overjoyed at the opportunities Martin had to be a messenger for such a great cause, for me, the notoriety also came with a price, like threats and harassment and the fact that Martin could be detained at any moment. Martin had been jailed for the first time, so I now knew how that felt, how anxiety is like rocks piling up in the pit of your stomach, and you wake every hour in anticipation of bad news. Strangely enough, I so identified with Martin's suffering that I vicariously felt the weight of prison doors slamming behind me, too. When he was locked in, I felt locked out of his life, not knowing if he would return to his family alive or with his body broken. I understood what it meant to feel helpless and hopeful at the same time.

Nevertheless, life had a hold of me, and I became swept up in the strong currents of the movement as it rushed forward. Encouraged by the success of the Montgomery experience, other churches and colleges began planning protests and sit-ins to end segregation. Martin and his team of ministers soon understood that the problems of segregation were so deeply ingrained in southern soil that full equality could come only through changes in the law or, more precisely, federal intervention, which would mean increasing our efforts to organize and mobilize.

On January 10, 1957, I found myself thrust in the midst of the formation of the Southern Christian Leadership Conference. I opened and presided over the first meeting of the body that would eventually become the SCLC. Martin had sent invitations to nearly a hundred leaders in states across the South, asking them to attend the two-day meeting at Ebenezer Baptist Church in Atlanta. Our aim was to coordinate all the fast-moving activities swirling around racial injustice and broaden the movement's base.

Martin and Ralph had planned to open the meetings, but in the wee hours of that morning they had to rush back to Montgomery because Ralph's home and church had been bombed, as had three other black churches and the home of pastor Robert Graetz, the white pastor of a black Lutheran church, the only white person to serve on the MIA board. So Martin delegated to me the historic task of calling the august group together. I took this as one more sign that eventually I would have to expand my role from being a concert singer to also becoming a public speaker, a role I eyed with trepidation.

About a month later, on Valentine's Day, 1957, the SCLC was officially founded in New Orleans. However, it was headquartered in Atlanta, because Atlanta was a hub of transportation in the South. Ella Baker was its first acting executive secretary; Ralph Abernathy was elected treasurer; Martin was elected president. Practically all the leaders who answered the call and attended our first meetings were ministers, underscoring our commission as a Christian-oriented, nonviolent movement. Although the members of the SCLC were often labeled "passive resisters," that was a serious misnomer. As I stressed at our first meeting, we organized as a militant organization that believed that the most potent weapon available was nonviolent social action.

From the moment of the SCLC's inception, I had high hopes for its success. I saw tremendously seasoned and courageous men stepping forward to work with the organization. These leaders included the Rev. C. K. Steele, eminent pastor of the Bethel Baptist Church in Tallahassee, who became the leader of the Tallahassee Bus Boycott and movement; the Rev. Joseph E. Lowery, who launched the Mobile movement; and the Rev. Fred Lee Shuttlesworth, a civil rights leader in Birmingham. It was Shuttlesworth who became a symbol of the southern struggle as he fought the tyranny of the infamous Bull Connor, the commissioner of public safety in Birmingham.

WITH MATTERS BEING organized, broadened, and placed in the hands of able leaders, Martin and I took some time off to rest and to travel internationally. When I reflect on the years immediately following Montgomery, I think on those things that took me away from it: it was as if some other part of my life had to be broadened through travel, meeting foreign dignitaries, and witnessing the experiences of other activists and oppressed people around the globe. Some thirty years later, I would serve a brief ambassadorship in the United Nations, and as a private citizen, I would serve as a goodwill ambassador to many nations of the world. Periodically, my conscience and sense of moral integrity would force me to take public stands against the official foreign policy of my government. These early years traveling with Martin to foreign shores were my prep school.

Many invitations poured in for me and Martin, to visit nations around the world, but the first we accepted was the opportunity to witness Ghana become one of the first African colonies to gain independence from the United Kingdom. Not only were the chains coming off in our country, but Africa was breaking free as well. You can imagine the excitement Martin and I felt after seeing a new movement being birthed in the South; now we could witness the winds of change stirring in Africa, too. The two struggles, against colonialism in Africa and racial oppression in America, were tributaries of the same river, so we felt honored that Kwame Nkrumah, head of the government-elect of Ghana, invited us to celebrate the birth of their new black nation.

After many years of black struggle, the British Empire finally concluded that it could no longer rule the Gold Coast. It agreed to free Ghana on March 6, 1957. All this was because of the persistent protests of those who no longer wanted to be bound. Nkrumah himself had been arrested for sedition and sentenced to several years, but just as the jailers in America were forced to let Martin out of jail because of the movement's protests, the British had to handle Nkrumah gently. He served only nine months, and came out of prison the new prime minister.

On March 3, 1957, Martin and I boarded a plane to Accra to be present at the birth of Ghana's independence. Nkrumah had invited a number of prominent black American leaders, including Ralph Bunche, Lester Granger of the Urban League, Congressman Adam Clayton Powell Jr., A. Philip Randolph, and NAACP chief Roy Wilkins. Chief Minister Norman Washington Manley, the "founding father" of Jamaica, was also there. People came from seventy nations to witness this African country's break from European colonial rule. At a reception on March 4, Martin met Richard Nixon, who was vice president at that time. He greeted Martin warmly: "You're Dr. King. I recognized you from your picture on the cover of *Time*. That was a mighty fine story about you. I'd like to meet with you when you are back in Washington."

On March 5, we watched the closing of the last meeting of the Parliament under the British rule. The British, most of whom were white, were dressed in business suits, and the Parliamentary officials wore traditional white curled wigs and black robes. Nkrumah and his ministers wore the prison caps that had been part of their uniforms during imprisonment. Those caps held special significance for me. They were a reminder of my deep pain the first time I saw Martin jailed, and they hinted at the many other heartbreaks over jailings I was sure would come.

At midnight, the bells of Accra began to toll, and we stepped out of Parliament and were greeted by the sight of a great crowd, more than fifty thousand people cheering wildly. We watched the Union Jack, with its triple crosses of red, blue, and white, ease down the flagpole. We saw the red, yellow, and green flag of Ghana, a new, free nation, rise up. Then Nkrumah, speaking in English, said, "At long last the battle has ended. Ghana, our beloved country, is free forever. Let us pause one minute to give thanks to our Almighty God." Breaking the silence, there was a mighty roar as thousands chanted in unison, "Ghana is free." I looked at Martin and saw that he was weeping with joy.

Like many African Americans who were not free to eat, live, or work where they wanted, I identified strongly with the Ghanaians. At so many places in the South, I still could not be served a hot dog unless I waited at the back door. I could not stay in a first-rate hotel; I could not try on a dress in a downtown department store; I could not check out a book from a public library. In Ghana, it was exhilarating to see black people in charge. For the first time, I was in a situation in which black people were the majority in a land they could call their own. What an impact! It gave me such a great sense of pride.

I thought about our own situation: How long would it be before we, too, could be freed from our oppression and become full-fledged Americans? The Ghanaian experience was a great boost to our dreams of one day seeing blacks control their own destiny in America.

It was also quite a thrill for me to see how Martin was recognized in Ghana and in the other places we traveled (Nigeria, Rome, Geneva, Paris, and London) as we made our way home. Two years later, Martin and I took our second trip off of American soil, journeying to India to study the teachings of Mohandas K. Gandhi, the man who had made such an impact on our movement, who was the guiding light for our ideology and our techniques of nonviolent social change.

I found it a wonderful twist of fate that the activist Bayard Rustin, head of the War Resisters League, who had spoken about India to my eighth-grade class in Marion, Alabama, and later at Antioch, had signed on as one of my husband's mentors for the trip. Rustin, a hard-core Gandhian, had spent six months in India and was active in its independent political movement. Rustin's speech on the tactics of Gandhi, coupled with independent study, had whetted my interest in the effectiveness of nonviolence. Meanwhile, ever since his studies at Crozer Seminary, Martin had been pursuing the Gandhian doctrine of strikes, marches, boycotts, and other nonviolent demonstrations to achieve justice. Martin was first exposed to Gandhi's works when he attended a lecture by Dr. Mordecai Johnson, the first black president of Howard University. After hearing Dr. Johnson speak, Martin bought every book he could find on Gandhi's success as a leader and a proponent of nonviolence. Gandhi's nonviolent strategies resonated with Martin's deeply ingrained Christian ethics.

Gandhi, of course, is widely celebrated as the father of Indian Independence. His hunger strikes, imprisonments, and nonviolent protests were so effective with the masses that Britain left India, one of its largest and most profitable colonies, in 1947. Tragically, Gandhi was assassinated just a year later, on January 30, 1948.

As I studied the life of Gandhi closely, I wondered if Martin, who patterned himself after Gandhi, would face a similar tragedy. I know my husband had similar thoughts. After our trip abroad, Martin wrote a piece about Gandhi that could have been a self-portrait. All one had to do was scratch out the name "Gandhi" and insert "Martin Luther King."

Martin wrote:

The world doesn't like people like Gandhi. . . . They don't like people like Christ; they don't like people like Abraham Lincoln. They kill them. And this man who had done all of that for India, who had given his life and who mobilized and galvanized four hundred million people for independence . . . Here was a man of nonviolence falling at the hands of a man of violence. Here was a man of love falling at the hands of a man of hate. This seems the way of history.

As we took off for India, a transportation tie-up temporarily diverted us from our main destination, New Delhi, to Bombay. To my shock, we saw thousands of people dressed in rags sleeping on the sidewalk or huddled in doorways, lying wherever they could find space. Some carried everything they owned wrapped up in rags or newspapers. The legions of emaciated human beings picking through garbage, some wearing only dirty loincloths, were, our guides explained to me, a by-product of colonialism. Not even in Africa had we seen such poverty. Yet, despite the degrading living conditions, the crime rate was surprisingly low in contrast to that in the poorer areas of the United States.

In marked contrast to the suffering we saw in Bombay, Prime Minister Jawaharlal Nehru's palatial residence in New Delhi was as lavish as it was gracious. Over dinner, we were able to learn firsthand the difference in policy and philosophy Nehru had had with Mahatma Gandhi. We knew from our studies and from friends about the policy battles between the two. Gandhi had been completely dedicated to nonviolence, while Nehru was inclined to accept it as a useful revolutionary technique. Gandhi, a practitioner of the simple life, had not wished to turn India into a modern technological society; Nehru, who was more Western-oriented, felt that India could not survive without becoming industrialized. It would be interesting if the two leaders could have had this conversation today, in the early twenty-first century, as India and its neighbor, Pakistan, continue to develop their nuclear armaments.

After dinner, Nehru took us up a broad flight of stairs and into a formal sitting room to meet his daughter, Indira Gandhi (who was no relation to Mohandas Gandhi). This was a high point of my pilgrimage. From that first meeting, Indira and I became friends, enjoying a friendship that endured up to her tragic assassination in 1984. Indira would later serve as prime minister of India, from 1966 to 1977, and from 1980 to 1984, becoming one of the first women in modern history, along with Israel's Golda Meir, to lead her nation. I was so impressed with Indira's charm, grace, and intellect, and by watching her close up, I came to understand some of the strengths and perils of women at the top, particularly the ways that women can be condemned for doing exactly the same things for which their male predecessors are praised. On the brighter side, however, as early as the 1950s (and partially because of Mahatma Gandhi's commitment to the advancement of women), I saw how some Indian women held much higher positions than women back home. There were women in Parliament; and in 1959 a woman was even a justice in India's High Courts. Imagine that! I know that someday women in the United States will lead the country, not only in one of the highest courts of the land but also at the top, as president. It would be wonderful if I could live to see that come to pass.

Lady Mountbatten, the wife of Lord Mountbatten, Viceroy of India, was also a guest of Nehru's that night. The Mountbattens and Nehru, who held opposing ideologies, could have been bitter enemies, yet they remained friends because of Gandhi's policy of love and nonviolence, in which the main objective and ideal aftermath of a nonviolent revolution is reconciliation and the creation of the Beloved Community. When the battles are over, the refusal of the activists to engage in hate or hostility can produce a new relationship of friendship between the oppressed and the oppressor.

During our trip, we also met with leaders advancing the cause of the so-called untouchables, a term drawn from the caste system that had existed in India for generations. The untouchable, or Dalit, status is traditionally associated with occupations regarded as ritually impure, such as butchering, removal of waste, or leatherwork. Dalits work as manual laborers, cleaning latrines and sewers and clearing away rubbish. Engaging in such activities was thought to pollute the individual, and this pollution was considered contagious. As a result, Dalits were segregated, and banned from full participation in Hindu social life. For example, they could not enter a temple or a school, and were required to stay outside the village.

To learn more about the untouchables, Martin and I journeyed to one of the southernmost parts of India, the city of Trivandrum, in the state of Kerala, where Martin spoke at a school attended by students who, with government help, were attempting to emerge from the caste system.

They had no running water. Many didn't have beds to sleep in. This was counter to what Gandhi would have wanted. He would not have given his life to free India from British political domination and economic exploitation only for his countrymen to trample more than a hundred million of their brothers and sisters underfoot. Through his many non-violent campaigns, such as fasting almost to the death, barriers that had existed for thousands of years had fallen, but the issue of the untouchables was still a struggle within India.

With that bit of history in mind, when Martin spoke at the school, he drew upon the parallels between the situation in India and with black Americans in the United States. "I am an untouchable, and every Negro in America is an untouchable."

Nehru had told Martin and me how, because of the climate set by Gandhi, federal laws banned discrimination against the untouchables, and the Indian Constitution had made violation of that law a crime punishable by imprisonment. The Indian government spent millions of rupees annually developing housing and job opportunities in villages heavily populated by untouchables. In addition, the prime minister said, if two applicants competed for entrance to a college or university, and one of the applicants was an untouchable while the other was of a higher caste, the school was obligated to take the untouchable.

In my understanding, Nehru's reformist policy sounded much like the policy at home, which was being called "affirmative action." How-ever, the prime minister saw it as a way of "atoning" for the centuries of injustice and suffering inflicted upon the untouchables. We found it dis-heartening that, in India, everyone from the prime minister down to the village councilmen had come to the conclusion, at least publicly, that declaring an ethnic group inferior was wrong, yet in America, segrega-tionists such as George Wallace won elections by declaring their opposi-tion to policies intended to foster equality for America's untouchables.

As Martin made speeches all across India stressing the debt America owed to Gandhian philosophy, I often sang on the same program; the Indians had a great love of Negro spirituals. As time went on, I sang as much as Martin lectured. Because the press in India had given our 381-day Montgomery Bus Boycott more comprehensive coverage than many publications in America, Martin had instant face recognition.

Wherever we went, we were besieged by autograph seekers. We held press conferences in all the larger cities, from Delhi to Calcutta, and Madras to Bombay.

Martin and I left India more convinced than ever that nonviolent resistance was the most potent weapon available to a minority group in its struggle for equality. What we had witnessed was the amazing climax of a nonviolent campaign. I had high hopes that our revolution would also reap a great harvest, and I fought my fears, trying to believe that Martin himself would live to see it.

After we returned home, I saw the effect of Martin's identification with the asceticism practiced by Gandhi. Like Gandhi, my husband had struggled with the issue of materialism. In his writings, Gandhi challenged the cultural condition that deemed his wife and children possessions. He often questioned how even a cupboard full of books might be excessive, because his spirituality compelled him to give up all that he had.

For me, that brand of asceticism was more than I had expected in our marriage, and it was more than I could accept. If Martin had had his way, he would have taken an oath of poverty, refusing even the most basic necessities, such as a house. He felt that much of the corruption in society came from the desire to acquire material things such as houses, land, and cars. He wanted none of these, he said, telling me once, "You know a man who dedicates himself to a cause doesn't need a family." That statement did not hurt me because I knew he was searching for a balance between asceticism and materialism. But I insisted that our family have a house—nothing fancy, but at least the basics. It took almost thirteen years of marriage before he agreed to buy a house, and when he did, he said he didn't need it; it was for me and the children. Finally, he decided that cars and a home were necessities, though he would strive to be more like Gandhi spiritually, adopting disciplines such as fasting in order to gain spiritual strength. Still, our house and car were in my name; he refused to own anything. And he never took to the pretentious habit of hiring chauffeured limousines or fancy cars; he would much rather drive a Ford than a Cadillac. Also, he wanted to have a house in a low-income neighborhood, and he wanted his children to grow up understanding the least of these. I didn't have a problem with that; I just wanted a house. Every woman wants a house.

Unlike Martin, I never sought out asceticism as a way of life, but like Martin, I never became a captive of materialism.

The travels Martin and I experienced together afforded us a chance to connect with world leaders, to get more than a textbook understanding of the developing nations of the world, and just as important, they helped us achieve balance in our lives. The travels, it seemed, served as a device to lift us up from the fire and to cool us down from the overload of movement demands, which sometimes pushed Martin to the point of exhaustion. The cooling-off period, however, never lasted long. While I tried not to feel apprehensive, it did seem as though each calm was followed by another storm. After every high point, evil lurked around the corner.

SEVEN

I Will Never Turn Back

O UR TRIP TO Ghana was life changing for Martin and me for a variety of reasons, one of which is that it was there that I realized I was pregnant with our second child. On the way from Accra to Kano, Nigeria, I began to experience morning sickness. The scents from the marketplaces left a heavy, putrid smell in my nostrils that exacerbated it. I felt nauseated, but said little, preferring to wait until a private moment to share with Martin the news he had been longing to hear. Once again, we would celebrate the birth of new life. We had lengthy debates over the naming of our first boy. I hesitated to name him after Martin; Martin was rising to prominence, and I sensed that the name of a famous father might be a crushing identity to carry. Nevertheless, on October 23, 1957, my son was born, and named Martin Luther King III.

At that time, I tried to curtail many of my activities to stay home with my two children. I always felt that if I failed at being a good mother, whatever else I did would not much matter. However, I soon learned that my resolve to function as a stay-at-home mother would constantly be interrupted by knocks at my door. At times, I yielded to the church mothers' constant requests to babysit my babies. I realize how nervous it made me feel the few times I had to be away, and how it made the mothers who babysat Yoki and Marty even more nervous when they answered the phone to "Hi, it's Mrs. King again!"

In addition to helping with civil rights efforts, I also still felt an inner stirring to return to the concert stage. Music was such a part of me; I could not let it go. Moreover, I could see its value for the movement. Music was an opportunity not only to drive home a message, but also to change minds. I returned to the stage on April 25, 1958, at Parker High School in Birmingham, at a program sponsored by Alpha Phi Alpha, my husband's fraternity. I continued the format I had developed, using dramatic storytelling mixed with songs to tell the story of the Montgomery Bus Boycott. I saw how these kinds of performances were excellent fundraisers for the movement, while giving me the personal satisfaction that came from using the arts to influence minds and hearts.

I had always preferred to sing and leave public speaking to Martin. Yet, sometimes he would push me forward to represent him when he was tied up with other business. I agonized over the shift in our roles at such times. Should I not stay where I was comfortable, as a singer, and further perfect that craft instead of doing something that seemed like trying to walk on eggshells? I settled the issue of whether I could make the shift from concert stage to public speaker's podium in March 9, 1958, when I was invited to deliver the annual Women's Day Address at the New Hope Baptist Church in Denver, Colorado. A dear friend of ours, the Rev. M. C. Williams, was the pastor. I spent hours preparing my message while traveling from Montgomery to Atlanta by train, and on to Denver by plane. I arrived in Denver on a Friday and spent that evening and a good part of Saturday polishing my speech. Realizing the importance and seriousness of what I was about to do, I also spent much time in prayer and meditation.

In the final version, I used the Book of Esther to present my theme: "I will never turn back. And if I perish, I perish." The Book of Esther is one of my favorites in the Bible. It is a study of how God used an orphaned Jewish girl in Persia to save His people after the evil Haman, the king's second in command, targeted the Jews for destruction. Esther was one of the unlikeliest people to be used in the grand scheme of shaping a nation, but through her courage, the Jews were saved. I love the line in which she comes to understand that she was brought to the kingdom "for a time such as this," even though taking a stand was against the law. "And if I perish, I perish," she vowed.

In delivering that message, the words of Horace Mann, the first president of Antioch College, were still alive within me. He encouraged his students by telling us that we should "Be ashamed to die until [we had] won some victory for humanity." That April, for the first time, I publicly gave voice to the vision and path I believed God had put me on. There were times in my life going forward when I had to brace myself with the mantra "If I perish, I perish," to find the strength to press on.

That night, I knew God was with me, because when I rose to speak, I felt the most powerful sense of His presence. I knew I had not been called to preach like Martin, but in many ways I felt I was preaching my trial sermon. After my presentation, three people came forward to give their lives to Christ. Their response settled the question of whether I should step forth as a public speaker as well as a singer. It was, for me, a truly unforgettable moment, infused with joy, resolve, and purpose.

In the wake of that pivotal moment, life continued on a high. Martin and I continued to travel and devote ourselves to organizing. Everywhere we went, people recognized Martin from the exposure he had received on the cover of *Time* magazine. As I feared, though, that notoriety attracted more harm to him, and not always from the hands of whites. As bad as the racial environment was in the South, I never felt that any one race had a monopoly on evil, and the specter of violence always hovered around us.

I worried about Martin incessantly when he was away from home, and always dreaded *that* call—like the one that came on September 20, 1958, from Dr. O. Clay Maxwell of the Mount Olivet Baptist Church in New York City, a family friend. After a short greeting, he said gently, "Mrs. King, I want you to prepare yourself. I have some bad news for you."

Instantly, my heart raced. Was this the news I had feared for so long?

"Is he dead?" I asked immediately.

"He's alive, but it's serious," Dr. Maxwell said. He went on to explain what had happened: a demented black woman had stabbed Martin as he was autographing his newly released book, *Stride Toward Freedom.* (Because of the way the weapon had been inserted, the surgeon had to remove it by making two incisions, leaving a cross-shaped scar on Martin's chest.) As soon as we could arrange a flight, Ralph, Christine, and I flew from Atlanta, arriving in New York at daybreak the next morning. Rev. Thomas Kilgore of the Friendship Baptist Church of New York City, Bayard Rustin, Stanley Levison, and Ella Baker met us at the airport. They shook with nerves as they shared the gory details.

Martin had been autographing books at a table in the shoe department of Blumstein's Department Store when a black woman came up to him and asked, "Are you Dr. King?"

He answered, "Yes, I am."

Mrs. Isola Ware Curry, a forty-two-year-old woman, then said in a voice dripping with anger, "Luther King, I have been after you for five years."

In the next second, my husband felt something sharp plunge forcefully into his chest. Someone grabbed the woman, another tried to take out the weapon, but Martin had the presence of mind to stop him. He told me later that he felt no great pain at first, but realized, because of the position of the weapon, that the wound could be fatal.

Martin was rushed by ambulance to Harlem Hospital, where he lay in bed for hours while preparations were made to remove the blade from his chest. At first, we were anxious about the delay, but then we learned the reason. Dr. Aubrey Maynard, the chief of surgery who performed the operation, told me that the razor tip of the blade had been touching Martin's aorta, and that his whole chest had to be opened to remove it.

"If you had sneezed during all those hours of waiting," Dr. Maynard told Martin. "Your aorta would have been punctured and you would have drowned in your own blood." Later, the *New York Times* summarized, "If Martin had sneezed, he would have died."

The doctors told us what a remarkable, fearless person Martin was. Think how many of us would have reacted if we had looked down and seen a blade sticking out of our chests: panic and fear, certainly; maybe we would even have tried to remove it. Any of those choices could have been fatal. The doctor said Martin's calmness helped save his life.

Later, my husband wrote for his column in *Ebony* magazine:

If I demonstrated unusual calm, it was not due to any extraordinary power that I possess. Rather, it was due to the power of God working through me. Throughout this struggle for racial justice, I have constantly asked God to remove all bitterness from my heart and to give me the strength and courage to face any disaster that came my way.

This constant prayer life and trust in God have given me the feeling
that I have divine companionship in the struggle.

Reflecting on why a nonviolent person became the victim of such violence, he commented, "To believe in nonviolence does not mean that violence will not be inflicted upon you. The believer in nonviolence is the person who will willingly allow himself to be the victim of violence but will never inflict violence upon another. He lives by the conviction that through his suffering and cross-bearing the social situation may be redeemed."

It was heartbreaking for me to see Martin plugged into so many tubes. One minute, he was perfectly healthy; the next, perfectly helpless. During the many nights I sat in Harlem Hospital, I tried to make sense of what had happened and to reflect on it with spiritual curiosity. Was this a trial, a test of some kind? I thought of the crowds that always followed Martin, of their love for him and what he stood for. On one hand, it was like Palm Sunday, when Christ went to Jerusalem and the people glorified him. On the other hand, the experience of the stabbing was somewhat like Gethsemane, a dark and arduous period during which maybe not only my husband was being tested, but his followers as well—including me.

I often heard Martin speak of being able to accept a blow without striking back. As I sat by his hospital bed, I began to understand that now was our chance to put our beliefs into action. As soon as Martin was able to speak, he issued a statement: "This person needs help. She is not responsible for the violence she has done me. Don't prosecute her; get her healed."

Eventually Mrs. Curry was committed to an institution for the criminally insane. I never held any bitterness against her; rather, I believe her act helped prepare us for a deeper appreciation of the struggle. During that time of wounding, we saw how blacks and whites around the world cared for Martin. Letters and cards poured in from everywhere. Worshippers in churches and synagogues prayed for his recovery. Even during this most painful moment, we saw how our movement was touching hearts and minds around the world—and that was more than enough to emblaze our desires, to show us that, somehow, we were on the right course.

As activists, we were also learning the true meaning of a phrase found in the biblical story of Joseph, which is a staple in Christian circles: "What the devil meant for evil, God changed it for good."

———— ✾ ————

EIGHT

Pushed to the Breaking Point

V IOLENCE AND OPPRESSION take many forms, and the form that took its toll on me was Martin's repeated, unwarranted arrests, which reached truly disruptive and dispiriting proportions in 1960, leaving me pushed to the breaking point. I felt so alone and vulnerable. I had tried to control my emotions and tie down my feelings, but I felt I could stomach no more. The feeling of losing my grip on life was not normal for me. As much as my ability to cope with tragedy had surprised me, this sudden sense of weakness startled me even more.

Overall, Martin's imprisonments—in which he would be joined by thousands of young people, seniors, colleagues, clergy, blacks and whites—became one of the most effective tools in nonviolent warfare. Martin saw jailing as the ultimate refusal to cooperate with evil and unjust laws; the unwillingness to comply, adjust, or compromise. It meant surrendering your body to be put in chains while allowing your spirit, your soul, and your sense of right to reign free. Gandhi, Kwame Nkrumah, Nelson Mandela, Fannie Lou Hamer, Rosa Parks, Apostle Paul, and Jesus Christ Himself all surrendered their bodies to their jailers and, in many ways, large and small, forever changed the face of history through their suffering and sacrifices.

From the lessons of history, I understood how, under the right circumstances, jail going as part of a struggle for freedom can be a positive force for change. I understood this from a historical and intellectual context, but also from a personal standpoint, given my own suffering at seeing Martin alone and in danger behind bars, to the extent that I wondered how much more I could bear.

Moreover, it was left to me to help our small children counter the teasing from other children who said their daddy was a "jailbird." I tried to make my children understand that Martin was not behind bars because he had done something wrong, but because he was trying to make things right for others. I said to Yoki, who was then five, and Marty, who was three, "Your daddy went to jail to help people. Some people don't have enough to eat, nor do they have comfortable homes to live in or enough clothing to wear. He goes to jail to make things better." I felt it was important for them to see his jail going as a badge of honor.

To return to the beginning of the story, in January 1960, Martin resigned from Dexter Baptist Church after a momentous ceremony, and we moved from Montgomery to a rented house in Atlanta. There, Martin became copastor with Daddy King at Ebenezer Baptist Church.

Before we could get settled, though, on February 17, 1960, Martin was charged with falsifying his state income taxes in Alabama. The implication was that he had taken money from the movement and not accounted for it. The auditors said that he had claimed a brand-new station wagon and an air-conditioner for our home, yet we had neither. Rather than detracting from Martin's character, as intended, the trumped-up charges were correctly viewed by the movement's supporters as harassment. This lesson was not lost on Martin's enemies, who understood that if character assassination did not work, other, more lethal weapons were available.

Although Martin was innocent, the weight of the unwarranted charge sent him into a depression. He confided in me his fear that he would be trying to prove his innocence for the rest of his life.

Martin and I had little hope of justice, but in a surprising development, on May 28, a southern jury of twelve white men acquitted him. Only then did Martin stop beating himself up about the charges. Shortly afterward, a cross was burned on our front lawn in Atlanta, but even that did not steal our joy or mar our victory.

We did not have long to celebrate. Five months later, Martin and 280 people were charged with staging a sit-in demonstration to integrate

Atlanta lunch counters. The charges were almost immediately dropped for most of the demonstrators, but Martin was detained and indicted for violating probation on an earlier traffic offense. The trouble had started back in May, when he was transporting Lillian Smith, a well-known southern writer, to Emory University Hospital in Atlanta, where she was undergoing cancer treatment. A policeman, no doubt noting that the woman was white, pulled Martin over and gave him a summons for driving with an out-of-state license. This happened in DeKalb County, a suburb of Atlanta, which was Klan country.

When Martin went to court the next day to face the traffic license citation, a judge named Oscar Mitchell fined him twenty-five dollars and, although Martin's lawyer didn't disclose this detail to Martin, placed him on probation for six months.

Later, in October, as Martin was being released from the sit-in charges in Atlanta, DeKalb County officials came and arrested him on the grounds that he had violated his probation from the earlier "traffic license" offense by participating in the sit-in. A hearing was set for three days later, during which time Martin remained behind bars. I attended the hearing at the DeKalb County courthouse, along with Martin's sister, Christine; his brother, A.D.; and Daddy King. Because the offense was minor, we were dumbfounded when Judge Oscar Mitchell denied bail and sentenced Martin to four months of hard labor on a state road gang at Georgia State Prison, a maximum-security prison in Reidsville.

It was such a shock that Christine burst into tears. When I saw her crying, I could not hold back my own tears. All through the movement, I had held myself together, but on that day, partially because of the shock of the sentence and the fact that Martin had been in jail for a week prior, I broke down. I was also five months pregnant with our third child, which I am certain aggravated my feelings.

Daddy King was upset himself, but he scolded me for crying. "You don't see Daddy crying," he told me. "I am not taking this lying down. I have to hold up for my wife, hold up for my daughter-in law and my daughter."

I felt helpless and alone. I was worried that our baby would be born while Martin was in jail, and I was worried about how Martin would fare without the usual companionship of Ralph Abernathy, who had become his regular cellmate. I was also told that if Martin were made to work on a state chain gang, he would be exposed to anyone who wanted to take a shot at him. In the climate we faced, Martin had to be freed or he would likely face death.

Try as I might, I could not erase my knowledge of the years of history, of what could happen to black people in the South at the hands of southern whites. It had only been five short years since the brutal murder of fourteen-year-old Emmett Till, who was beaten and killed while visiting relatives in Mississippi. The national news coverage of the funeral and the open casket showing Till's disfigured body added to the fear that no black person was safe in the South, especially one with the notoriety of my husband.

I watched in horror as Martin was immediately taken from the courtroom, his hands in metal cuffs behind his back. When Daddy King, Christine, A.D., and I were allowed to see him for a few moments, I couldn't stop the tears from streaming down my face. When Martin saw me crying, he said, "Corrie, I have never seen you like this before. You have to hold up for me." He asked me for newspapers, magazines, and some money. I tried to pull myself together, to return home and gather his things, and to take care of our children.

The lawyer filed a writ of habeas corpus, asking the judge to hold a hearing the next day, which would grant bail for Martin instead of sending him to jail. I was getting ready to go to court when I got a call with terrible news: in the middle of the night, several men came to Martin's cell, shone a flashlight in his face, and ordered him to get up. Martin later told me that the terrors of southern justice, wherein scores of black men were plucked from their cells and never seen again, ran through his mind as the men made him dress, handcuffed him very tightly, and chained him all the way down to his legs. They then placed him the back of a patrol car, along with a large German shepherd. During the 230-mile night ride through rural Georgia, the men didn't tell Martin where he was going. "That kind of mental anguish is worse than dying," Martin wrote about the experience. "Riding for mile after mile, hungry and thirsty, bound and helpless, waiting and not knowing what's going to happen to you. And all for a traffic ticket."

Exhausted and humiliated, Martin arrived at Reidsville where he was thrown into a narrow cell and made to don a prison uniform. Notes from other prisoners telling him how much they respected him took some of the edge off his confinement and the brutality he was suffering at the hands of the prison guards. In a letter to me about his ordeal, Martin wrote:

> I know this whole experience is very difficult for you to adjust to, especially in your condition of pregnancy, but as I said to you yesterday, this is the cross that we must bear for the freedom of our people. So I urge you to be strong in the faith and that in turn will strengthen me. I have the faith to believe that this excessive suffering that is now coming to our family will in some little way make Atlanta a better city, Georgia a better state and America a better country. Just how I do not yet know, but I have faith to believe it will happen. If I am correct, then our suffering will not be in vain.

Meanwhile, Daddy King sought legal help. He planned to retain attorney Morris Abram, a well-respected civil rights lawyer, to help Martin get out of jail. But to our delight, the decision was taken out of our hands by a phone call. On the other end of the telephone was Sargent Shriver, the brother-in-law of Sen. John F. Kennedy, who was in the final week of his presidential campaign. "May I speak to Mrs. King?" Sargent Shriver said. "Please hold for Senator Kennedy."

After a brief greeting, Senator Kennedy expressed his concern for me and Martin. "I know this must be very hard for you. I understand you are expecting your third child, and I just wanted you to know that I was thinking about you and Dr. King. If there is anything I can do to help, please let me know."

Of course I told him that I appreciated his concern and would welcome any assistance.

After the call, things happened fast. I began to hear encouraging news about Martin's release. Even A.D. said, "I'll bet you he'll be out by tomorrow night."

A.D. was right. Senator Kennedy's brother, Robert (aka Bobby), who was also his campaign manager, called Judge Mitchell to learn why Dr. King couldn't be released on bail pending appeal. That story leaked to the press, and evidently Judge Mitchell had a change of heart: he allowed Martin to be released on bail. I received the news about Martin's release around noon the next day, and was of course overjoyed. Minister Wyatt Tee Walker chartered a plane to bring me, Yoki, Marty, Mama, Daddy King, Christine, and her husband, Isaac, to meet Martin.

That night, a mass meeting was held at Ebenezer. A standing-room-only crowd heard Daddy King, a former Nixon man, make the famous statement "I had expected to vote against Senator Kennedy because of his religion. But now he can be my president, Catholic or whoever he is. . . . He has the moral courage to stand up for what he knows is right. I've got all my votes and I've got a suitcase and I'm going to take them up there and dump them in his lap."

The crowd roared its approval when Ralph Abernathy told them it was time to take off their Nixon buttons. The case was clear: Kennedy had responded to King; Nixon had not.

A few days later, John Fitzgerald Kennedy was elected president by about a hundred thousand votes. This was a significant election in the shift of black Americans from voting Republican to voting Democrat. Many historians say—and I agree—that black voters, grateful for Kennedy's intervention on behalf of my husband, made the difference in the 1960 presidential election.

Ironically, my husband was not allowed to vote because Georgia officials ruled that he hadn't lived in Atlanta long enough to establish residency, and he had waited too late to obtain an absentee ballot from Montgomery. Nevertheless, in prison stripes from a backwater jail, Martin, with his nonviolent spirit and his defiant yielding to suffering, helped launch, at least for a time, a new covenant of grace into the political world.

———— ❋ ————

NINE

I've Been Called by God, Too

I F THE CHILD I was carrying had been born a girl, her name would have been Mahalia. Martin made that promise to Mahalia Jackson after the great gospel diva cooked him a sumptuous chicken dinner smothered in brown mushroom gravy. After such a feast, he was helpless to do anything but promise to honor her request to make her our third child's namesake. But it was a baby boy who arrived on January 30, 1961, and we named him Dexter, after the first church Martin pastored.

Having another child, looking into the eyes of my innocent newborn, brought with it the familiar and agonizing questions: Would the change we all wanted and were willing to die for come soon enough so my children could grow up in a world that welcomed them as equals and beloved human beings? I was birthing children that my Bible told me were made in the image of God. Would they be treated as such?

Our movement was caught up in a whirlwind of change whipping across America. I wish I could say that we knew what the consequences of our actions would be. But all we knew for certain was that the winds of change were blowing, sometimes in our favor and sometimes not.

Throughout 1960, the year before Dexter was born, the student movement, which staged sit-ins at lunch counters and department stores, had continued to shake the South. Martin and the students were very close. At the sit-ins, many of the young people carried signs reading,

"Remember the Teachings of Gandhi and Martin Luther King." That April, as the protests spread, Martin and the SCLC leadership sent Ella Baker to set up a meeting with the students, to help organize them and set up a presentation on nonviolence. Martin and the SCLC appropriated money to finance the meeting. Martin and James Lawson, then a graduate student in theology, were the keynote speakers. At that meeting, the Student Nonviolent Coordinating Committee (SNCC) was formed. Under Martin's guidance, the members pledged themselves to nonviolence.

Later, in December 1960, a U.S. Supreme Court decision extended the prohibition of segregation to all interstate trains and buses and all train stations and bus terminals. Those of us who lived in the South knew that there was no meat on the bone of that new law. Despite the Court rulings, when I traveled from my home in Atlanta to different parts of the South, signs designating "Colored" and "White" were still attached to waiting rooms, restrooms, water fountains, and lunch counters. On trains, blacks were still seated at separate tables and hidden behind a curtain in the dining cars. The symbols as well as the practice of segregation remained. Seeing those signs was humiliating. I dreaded going any long distance except by automobile.

Then, in March 1961, protests to test the law began: the Freedom Rides. These protests were primarily a project of the Congress of Racial Equality (CORE), which had the backing of the SCLC and SNCC. Martin served as chairman of the Freedom Ride Coordinating Committee, through which CORE, the SCLC, and SNCC strategized a way to keep the rides happening until victory was achieved.

Nothing had changed, but now, with federal law behind us, with students sitting down at lunch counters, and with whites and blacks alike boarding Greyhound buses, the numbness and the acceptance of segregation were wearing off. We had hope.

While the sit-ins and protests were taking new forms, my life also was taking a new shape, much like the patterns my mother used to sew in her quilts. While I was happy to be Martin's wife and the mother of his children, I was more than a wife while he lived and more than a widow after he died. On the one hand, I was a copartner with him, married not only to him but to the movement. Yet, there was also a corner of life that belonged exclusively to me. More and more, I served as public speaker when Martin asked me to stand in for him at certain functions. I continued to perform, giving concerts to raise money for the movement, and I continued my role as a spokeswoman for the peace movement that I had begun through the Quaker groups at Antioch.

Granted, Martin was always ambivalent about my role out front, which sent me traveling across the country instead of staying at home. I suppose I experienced the personal dilemma that baffles every working woman. What happens when you are expected to be Superwoman, to perform a dozen conflicting tasks at the same time? I was trying to balance my concert career with motherhood and my responsibilities as Martin's wife and chief confidante. Most of the time, Martin was very supportive of my work. Once, however, I did have to set the record straight. During one exchange, he told me, "You see, I am called [by God], and you aren't."

I responded, "I have always felt that I have a call on my life, too. I've been called by God, too, to do something. You may not understand it, but I have a sense of a calling, too."

Still not convinced, Martin turned to me and said, "Well, somebody has to take care of the kids."

"No problem," I said. "I will do that."

Looking a bit crushed, he asked, "You aren't totally happy being my wife and the mother of my children, are you?"

"I love being your wife and the mother of your children," I said. "But if that's all I am to do, I'll go crazy."

Despite his ambivalence, when it was especially important for me to be with him or to advance issues for which I had a special passion, Martin was really encouraging. One such event came in March 1962, when I was invited by the Women Strike for Peace to go as a delegate to Switzerland, to support international efforts to ban atomic testing. When I brought the invitation to Martin, he said, "This is important. You need to do that."

With his blessing, I was able to turn my attention to global issues of diplomacy and international peace. Women Strike for Peace was founded in 1961 by Bella Abzug and Dagmar Wilson, and was initially part of the movement to ban nuclear testing and end the Vietnam War. On November 1, 1961, the organization mobilized about fifty thousand women to march and demonstrate against nuclear weapons in sixty U.S. cities. It was the largest national women's peace protest of the twentieth century. In Washington, DC, about fifteen hundred women, led by Dagmar Wilson, gathered at the foot of the Washington Monument. President John F. Kennedy watched from a window in the White House.

On April 6, 1962, the U.S. Women for Peace delegation departed for Switzerland. In Geneva, we were joined by women from Scandinavia and other countries such as Australia and the Soviet Union. Our goal was to join the international effort to influence the atomic test ban talks being held there by the United Nations Committee on Disarmament. We were there for the sake of our children. We knew that radioactive fallout from atmospheric tests was affecting our children's milk, bone structure, and overall health. Less than two years after our visit, we felt that our efforts, along with those of other peace advocates, had helped make history when the United States and the Soviet Union signed a nuclear test ban treaty.

I returned home to Atlanta from Geneva on a Friday. To my sorrow, I did not have time to properly rehearse for a concert I was scheduled to perform in Cincinnati, Ohio, on Sunday. I performed the concert, a standard repertoire with French, Italian, and German songs, but I wasn't happy with it. I thought, "I have three kids. I have to figure out how to do this in a way that isn't so stressful."

And so I developed the idea of the Freedom Concert. I patterned it after Paul Robeson's performances, which I'd had the good fortune of first seeing at Antioch; he would give a political commentary before he sang. Similarly, I would open my concerts by talking about the struggle, the movement. I would narrate and sing, alternating parts of the story with a song, mostly hymns or freedom songs. The Freedom Concerts, though less taxing on my voice than the standard classical music repertoire I had been performing, were highly rewarding: they raised thousands of dollars for the SCLC, which badly needed funds.

So Cincinnati became my last concert with a standard repertoire. Afterward, I took a two-year hiatus and did not sing again publicly until I performed my first Freedom Concert, on November 15, 1964, at New York City's Town Hall.

As I stepped away from the concert stage during that hiatus, I stepped back into the pace of the movement, which was racing along at a dazzling, tumultuous speed, with both victories and perils around every corner. And when Martin was facing danger, I was facing danger, too, whether I was out in the street with him or awaiting his return to our home. The term *other half* aptly fit Martin and me. In fact, we were more than that. I often felt as if we were one heartbeat, one soul. When he was in jail, I was in jail. When he was beaten up, I was beaten up. In some instances, his whole family was in pain, due to the emotions my children internalized through me when Martin was endangered. I often said I was stronger in a crisis, but that describes only my response, not my inner feelings. When he was away, I had to wait with my own anxieties—and with the eager eyes of our four children, only two of whom could actually speak well enough to ask, "When is Daddy coming home?"

On one night back in May 1961, Martin barely escaped grave injury from a mob gathered outside a rally for the Freedom Riders at Ralph Abernathy's First Baptist Church in Montgomery. After Martin's speech, carloads of angry whites surrounded the church, throwing rocks through the stained-glass windows, showering the worshippers with shards of glass. The men outside cursed and threatened to burn down the church. With rocks and curses filling the air, Martin and the congregation prayed and sang hymns, including "We Shall Overcome."

As Martin left, a gas bomb whizzed past his head. One of his aides, Rev. Fred C. Bennette, picked up the bomb and threw it over Martin's shoulder, away from him, and someone pulled Martin back into the church, where he stayed most of the night with the worshippers. Eventually someone reached the U.S. attorney general, Bobby Kennedy, who sent federal marshals to disperse the mob. As was our routine when Martin came home, our family filled the house with prayer and songs of praise. The climate we faced on a daily basis gave us much to pray about.

In the fall of 1961, some SNCC and NAACP leaders turned their focus to Albany, Georgia, a town of about fifty thousand residents (40 percent black) about 180 miles south of our home in Atlanta. Albany was the heart of hard-core "redneck country." Early that November, SNCC-trained high school students began a peaceful protest at an illegally segregated bus terminal in Albany, and although none of the students was arrested, their actions inspired a movement to desegregate all of Albany.

A series of sit-ins, boycotts, and other forms of nonviolent protest started up, so that by December, more than five hundred people had been jailed in Albany. Then Dr. William G. Anderson, a respected black osteopath and a friend of Martin's from their days as college students in Atlanta, called Martin for help. On December 15, Martin spoke at Shiloh Baptist Church in Albany; the next day, he and Ralph joined a protest there, and were arrested. Martin's arrival had attracted even more people to protest. In fact, I had never seen anything like Albany. Black maids were going to jail under assumed names to keep from being fired by their white employers. I saw children who had been arrested and released, enlisting to go back to jail again just to be with Dr. Martin Luther King Jr.

While other people's children wanted to be jailed with a hero, my own children just wanted Daddy home. Since our family lived within a five-hour drive of Albany, I often left baby Dexter with caregivers and drove with our two oldest children to see Martin. Yoki was seven and Marty was five during Martin's confinement in Albany. To avoid explaining why we had to go in the back door of a restaurant to avoid being called "nigger," I always packed our lunch. We also tried to avoid stopping at the segregated restrooms. Albany would be the first time the children saw their father in prison clothes, in a small, dingy cell. I wondered how they would feel. They were confused when the cell door did not open and Daddy did not come out, but moments later, they played happily up and down the darkened jail corridors. It was only as they grew older that the tougher questions came.

In Albany, Martin reached an agreement with city officials: if they released him, he would leave town (which was something they badly wanted), as long as they also agreed to desegregate the buses and also release all the other protesters on bail. Martin left town, the city officials failed to keep their end of the bargain, and on July 10, 1962, Martin and Ralph returned to Albany to face trial. They were convicted of leading the big December march. I attended the trial, and was surprised when Martin and Ralph were given suspended sentences. In fact, they were released from jail to stop the public attention that was being focused on segregation there. Rather than integrate public facilities, Albany officials closed the city parks and the public library. While we did not win a large victory at that time, our loss helped the SCLC learn valuable lessons. True, effective change was hampered by a lack of registered black voters.

AROUND THIS TIME, I began to agonize over what would become of our movement if something happened to Martin. The movement had many bright, committed people and great civil rights leaders, such as Whitney Young at the Urban League and Roy Wilkins at the NAACP, but the media had essentially anointed Martin president of black America.

I understood that leadership training was basic to the SCLC concept, but I did not know if it was possible for a charismatic leader to establish a permanent organization, since that type of leadership is built on the personality or appeal of that particular leader. For instance, the Marcus Garvey movement became a shell of itself when J. Edgar Hoover, the same man who tried to discredit my husband, succeeded in a campaign to imprison Garvey. Movements headed by other charismatic leaders, including Gandhi, collapsed without the leader or a structure to continue the leader's passion and programs.

When the heads of General Motors or AT&T move on, the established structure and rules provide a foundation for continuity under the next leader. But in our movement, we were making up the rules as we went from city to city. All too often, the media and the powers-that-be wanted to deal only with Martin, reinforcing the notion that the movement had only one spokesman. In addition to putting a lot of pressure on Martin, this created tension among some of the other movement leaders. But Martin did not think of himself as the chief; he preferred, and worked well with, a coalition.

It was a coalition that was growing by the day as scores of young people joined the movement. The involvement of dozens of America's best and brightest, who cast their lot with us, engaged their minds, and readied their bodies for a bloody battlefield, helped reduce some of the angst I had about our future direction. Most were college students or recent graduates. Some, like Andrew Young, had already received movement-related battle scars. A graduate of Hartford Theological Seminary, Young was a pastor at Bethany Congregational Church in Thomasville, Georgia. He knew what it felt like to watch the KKK parade around town in full regalia as a warning against the voting rights drive he was leading there. While the SCLC was well connected through the network of black Baptist and Methodist churches, Young's ability to plug us into white liberal circles was invaluable. He later moved up through the SCLC to become executive vice president, the rank he held at the time of Martin's death. He would become one of my closest friends and, after Martin's death, a surrogate father to our children.

The Rev. James Bevel, along with his future wife, Diane Nash, came from the Nashville movement. James Orange, one of the finest organizers in the country, came from Birmingham. Willie Bolden, Lester Hankerson, and Ben Clark came to us from the Savannah movement, led by that staunch agitator Hosea Williams. Like Williams, Bernard Lafayette specialized in conducting training in nonviolence. Septima Clark brought to the SCLC's Citizenship Education Program valuable insight from her experiences teaching adult education in her native Charleston, South Carolina. The Rev. Walter Fauntroy, whom I would later help get elected as the first, nonvoting delegate to Congress from the District of Columbia, also became a valuable aide, to the point at which Martin would say, "He is one of two persons who could run SCLC after I'm gone."

Still, though the future was always in our minds, we didn't have much time for long-term planning or soul searching or reflection, as there were too often more pressing matters to attend to. That was the case as the work of the civil rights movement moved on from Albany to one of the biggest and most demanding campaigns yet: Birmingham.

———— ❀ ————

TEN

So Evil Only God Could Change It

ARTIN ONCE SAID of Birmingham, "All the evils and injustices the Negro can be subjected to are right here in Birmingham." I soon found that truer words had never been spoken. Birmingham was notorious for ordinary day-to-day terrorism. The city had been hoisted to national infamy by black newspapers like the *Pittsburgh Courier*, which called it the "worst city in America." Between 1957 and 1963, eighteen unsolved bombings of black churches and homes occurred, earning the city the ignoble title of "Bombingham."

Bull Connor, the city's infamous commissioner of public safety, was notorious for his efforts to enforce segregation, deny black citizens their civil rights, and strong-arm any protests. I was told that when the NAACP tried to meet, he sent his police to bust up the meetings, and had thus succeeded in keeping that organization out of Birmingham. In 1962, Bull Connor closed sixty-eight parks, thirty-eight playgrounds, six swimming pools, and four golf courses rather than comply with a federal court order to desegregate public facilities.

Rev. Fred Shuttlesworth, who convinced Martin to make Birmingham the next major campaign, barely escaped death when his home was bombed to ruins in 1956. When he tried to enroll his children at a public school in 1957, he was chain-whipped on a public street by a white mob, and his wife was stabbed—with the cops present. In none of these incidents were any arrests made. Birmingham was the largest city in a police state presided over by Governor George Wallace, whose inauguration vow was "Segregation now, segregation tomorrow, segregation forever."

Once Martin and his SCLC team understood the viciousness of Birmingham, I knew what Martin's reaction would be. What better place to stage a nonviolent direct action than in one of the most violent enclaves in the nation? Before taking that action, however, in early 1963, Ralph Abernathy and Fred Shuttlesworth met with the Kennedy brothers to urge the federal government to initiate national civil rights legislation, but those efforts didn't work. Then, early in April, the Birmingham city government obtained a state circuit court injunction against protests, and Martin decided he would defy the injunction and go to jail. The timing of those protests, however, depended on the birth of our fourth child. I was eight months pregnant, and Martin was determined either to slow things down or to speed things up so he could be with me and see his child being born before going to jail.

During the month of March, Martin dashed back and forth between Birmingham and Atlanta, keeping a watch on me. My pregnancy was becoming difficult. I had extreme hip discomfort, as I'd had when I was pregnant with Marty, and could not walk down the stairs. My doctor confined me to bed rest, and Martin had to run up and down the stairs, preparing my meals and bringing me a bedpan. Unable to stand seeing me suffer, he tried to get our doctor to induce labor.

Moreover, Good Friday was approaching. Because of its major symbolic and religious significance, Martin wanted the demonstrations to take place so he could be in jail on that date. He didn't want events to overtake him and snatch him away from me when he was really needed. A friend recommended that I take a dose of castor oil to induce labor, and Martin and I agreed. Nothing happened. The next day, I took a larger dose, and on Thursday, March 28, as soon as I reached the hospital and was settled, my beautiful little darling daughter was born. We named her Bernice Albertine after her two grandmothers, and called her Bunny.

The very next day, however, Martin left for Birmingham. Five days later, the protests began. Did I feel abandoned or neglected because of my husband's quick departure after the birth of our daughter? The question has been raised before, but my answer is not complicated. For the most part, Martin and I shared values. I knew he loved his family, but we both had a higher calling and purpose that was much larger than the fulfillment of our own desires. As much as I loved Martin, I knew he belonged not just to me but to his calling. It had to be his first priority.

On April 3, lunch counter sit-ins began in Birmingham. Arrests followed. Over three days, about five hundred people had been jailed. There was a city injunction against protesting, but Martin took a leap of faith. He chose to break the injunction by organizing a march and provoking the police into arresting him on April 12, Good Friday. He announced his decision at Zion Hill Church, where the march was scheduled to begin. In his address, he made the link between the redemptive act of the suffering of Jesus on Good Friday and what lay ahead for those who faced sudden arrests or beatings. As he left the pulpit, women and men shouted out to him, "There he goes, just like Jesus." Then people poured out into the aisle, following him to the march.

It looked like every police officer on the force was waiting. All along the streets, blacks were encouraging themselves by singing freedom songs. When Martin passed, they applauded.

As the march neared downtown, Bull Connor ordered his men to move in. Two muscular policemen roughly clutched Martin and Ralph by the backs of their shirts and shoved them into a police car. Martin and Ralph were separated and held in solitary confinement. Even their lawyers could not see them.

And neither could I. Because of the complications from my pregnancy, I was confined to my house in Atlanta. I waited by the phone, but there was no call from Martin. Saturday came. Still no Martin. I woke up on Easter Sunday despondent. I knew how badly Martin had wanted to be in his pulpit.

In desperation, I called Rev. Wyatt Tee Walker in Birmingham.

"What have you heard, Wyatt?" I asked.

"Coretta, I haven't been able to get a phone message to him. Martin is being held incommunicado."

Wyatt suggested I put in a call to President Kennedy. For a moment, I thought: Me? Call the president?

Kennedy had been helpful to us before. Still, it seemed a bold move to reach out. I mulled it over. I had heard Martin was sleeping on a steel cot with no mattress. I thought about the evil ways of Birmingham, how somebody could kill him.

Resolved, I tried to get the number where the president was staying in West Palm Beach, but to no avail. I told the White House operator to find Vice President Lyndon Johnson, but that didn't work, either. After explaining my situation, the operator, a kind and sympathetic woman, suggested I call Pierre Salinger, the White House press secretary. I reached Salinger immediately, and he promised to make every effort to have the president call me.

While I was waiting for a call from the president, Harry Belafonte called. Harry and I had become close friends ever since performing at the same benefit concert in New York on the one-year anniversary of the start of the Montgomery Bus Boycott. From then on, whenever tragedy or a crisis hit, which was often, he showed up ready to help. I could lean on Harry. That day, I was very depressed and spilled out my troubles. I explained that I was not trying to get Martin out of jail, because I knew he wouldn't want that. I was just concerned about his safety. I told Harry about the phone ringing off the hook with inquiries about Martin, the demands of a two-week-old baby, and my desire to go immediately to Birmingham to be with Martin. Harry took charge, telling me that, if Martin wouldn't object, I should hire a nurse and a secretary at his, Harry's, expense. How well he knew my husband. Martin objected to anything that might suggest we were living pretentiously or "high on the hog."

While we were talking, a familiar voice called on the other line. "Mrs. King, this is Attorney General Robert Kennedy. The president wasn't able to talk to you because he's with our father, who is quite ill. He wanted me to call to find out how we can help."

I expressed my concern for his father's illness, but then I poured out our situation, trying to make it clear that I was only calling out of concern for Martin's safety and not trying to get him released from jail. Bobby told me how sorry he and the president were about what was happening with Martin, but said that they themselves had trouble dealing with Bull Connor. Bobby promised to do his best to help, however.

After hanging up, I felt encouraged. I remembered that it was Easter, and my spirit began to lift. This was the first Sunday in my adult life that I had not been to church. I turned on the radio and listened to a church service. As I thought about it, my understanding of Easter seemed to expand. I was lonely, worried, and depressed, and I thought that maybe Martin felt the same way. Yet what I was experiencing was nothing compared to the suffering of our Lord, Jesus Christ. Through His suffering, Christians were redeemed. Somehow, I knew that Martin's and my suffering would not be in vain—it was constructive suffering that would help bring down the walls of segregation. It was not happenstance, but meaningful suffering to help people, both black and white, reach a higher purpose. Jesus had been crucified, but in the end He triumphed. I encouraged myself to hold onto my faith that what I was going through was meaningful, too.

At about five o'clock the next evening, I heard two-year-old Dexter babbling away into the phone. I picked up the receiver and heard an exasperated operator say, "Will you please get that child off the phone?" The next voice I heard was President Kennedy's. He told me that he had sent the FBI into Birmingham to check on Martin's situation, and he assured me, "He's all right."

After hanging up, I felt such relief. About fifteen minutes later, Martin called. Martin always fasted for strength before going to jail, and his voice sounded tired and lifeless. I told him about my conversation with the president, and a smile returned to his voice. I learned that after my call, he had been allowed to take a shower, and been given a pillow and a mattress.

While in prison, Martin wrote his famed treatise, "Letter from a Birmingham Jail." He wrote it on the margins of newspapers and on scraps of toilet paper. For some reason, some of the world's most powerful writings have been penned by leaders imprisoned for political causes. There is something about the confinement, the isolation, and unjustness of those prisoners' situations that helps focus their minds on their principles. With little left to lose, their bodies already imprisoned, there is nothing left to do but state their principles unequivocally, what they will live and die for. Just as Apostle Paul wrote the prison epistles Ephesians, Philippians, Colossians, and Philemon, strengthening believers while being scourged and put in stocks in Roman jails, Martin found the strength while suffering to challenge white clergy to speak out against racial injustice.

Finally, I felt well enough to fly. Juanita Abernathy and I flew to Birmingham to visit our husbands, and on Saturday, April 20, they were released. Shortly thereafter, in response to the invitation of SCLC staffers James Bevel, Andy Young, Dorothy Cotton, and Bernard Lee, thousands of black high school and college students attended mass meetings and training sessions on the philosophy of nonviolence and then marched through Birmingham in what would come to be known as the Children's Crusade.

Naturally, the press, which had not criticized the segregated social system for abusing black children, accused the movement of exploiting the children. But neither the negative media attention nor the arrests dampened the marchers' enthusiasm. Somehow they understood that the movement was about them. Their numbers were being arrested, but they kept marching, wave after wave, until nearly a thousand children were locked up. For the first time in the civil rights movement, we were able to put into effect the Gandhian principle of filling the jails to obtain justice.

Heartfelt, heroic scenes like those of the marching children, however, only increased the venom coming our way from Bull Connor. On May 3, as a thousand children and teenagers marched toward the police, Connor ordered his troopers to open their water hoses. Jets of water, at hundreds of pounds of pressure, knocked down children, ripping off the clothes of some. Then Connor unleashed the police dogs. Some of the snarling beasts ran through the crowd, biting the legs and arms of children.

Two days later, on May 5, came an unforgettable and astonishing development. Rev. Charles Billups led a group of adults from the New Pilgrim Baptist Church to the police barricade. As they knelt in prayer, Connor ordered the dogs loosed and the hoses turned on. Connor shouted, "Turn on the hoses, dammit." But a miraculous thing happened. As the black people rose from their knees, Connor's men fell back to each side, their hoses sagging in their hands. A force stronger than their hoses was working. It was a soul force, what Gandhi called *satyagraha*, a moral power outweighing physical pressure. Under the eyes of a watching world, the spiritual force of that little band of blacks broke through the ranks of the armed police. Billups led his people past the police, singing. As they knelt in prayer, the police froze in their tracks, disarmed by our nonviolent army.

On Friday, May 10, an agreement was announced that accepted most of our demands word for word. The stores were to be desegregated, hiring of African Americans upgraded, charges against protesters dropped, and the Senior Citizens Committee of the Chamber of Commerce would meet regularly with black leaders to reconcile their differences.

Nonetheless, the terror of Birmingham didn't end there. The night after the agreement was signed, the home of Martin's brother, A.D., who was a pastor in Birmingham, was bombed twice. When the first bomb exploded, A.D. grabbed his wife, Naomi, and pulled her safely into a back room—just as a second bomb blew off the whole front of the house. Still another bomb blew up the office of the Gaston Motel, where Martin had been staying.

Hardly four months would pass before four little girls, Denise McNair, Carole Robertson, Cynthia Wesley, and Addie Mae Collins, were killed when a bomb hit the Sixteenth Street Baptist Church in Birmingham, the very church where Martin had preached to the children only months before. When they died, they had just finished listening to their Sunday school lessons and were in the ladies' lounge in the basement, freshening up. Like many parents, I thought of those children as my own.

What could be more evil than bombing children in church on a Sunday morning?

OVERALL, HOWEVER, BIRMINGHAM was a victory, a high point in our movement. We forged a rough and blood-drenched road, but Martin never looked for easy victories. I learned from him the value of searching for the worst cases, of allowing people to catch the spiritual dimension of their struggle and victory. The way I see it, Birmingham was so evil that only God could change it—and God did. Never before had black people taken such unified, direct action to change the conditions of their lives.

On the significance of those days, Martin wrote:

I like to believe that Birmingham will one day become a model in southern race relations . . . that the negative extremes of Birmingham's past will resolve into the positive and utopian extreme of her future; that the sins of a dark yesterday will be redeemed in the achievements of a bright tomorrow. I have this hope because once on a summer day, a dream came true. The city of Birmingham discovered a conscience.

At that time, it required a great leap of faith to believe in Martin's words, in his hope for Birmingham to radically change. Although Martin never saw what his prophetic words proclaim, I was fortunate enough to see his dream come true.

———— ✿ ————

ELEVEN

I Have a Dream

OUR VICTORY IN Birmingham helped give President Kennedy the courage to propose a Civil Rights Bill that would continue the dramatic movement under way to further integrate blacks into American society. All that was needed was to build congressional support, which would not be easy.

Nevertheless, in 1963, there was excitement and victory in the air. Blacks in city after city began to take the shackles off their minds, to believe what was once thought impossible: they did not have to tolerate being treated as less than human. They could see the possibility looming, that after more than three hundred years of existence in America, perhaps the day was coming when they would be granted the full rights of citizenship.

But as astonishing as the events of 1963 were, they were incomplete, like the thunder before the rain. We had experienced the thunder. Now leaders in the movement were ready for something more, for a downpour, for our communities to experience a flood of opportunity in all sectors where we had been deprived and discriminated against, from schools to labor unions, from hospitals to housing.

As bigger crowds all over America began to welcome Martin—35,000 in Los Angeles, and 125,000 in a Detroit parade Martin led with Walter Reuther, head of the United Auto Workers—an idea began to gel in the minds of those of us around him. The timing had come to put all our energies into one mammoth event. We needed to link the hidden and subtle obscenities of northern racism with the more blatant forms in the South, pile them at America's doorstep, and demand full redress. We could show that the Negro Revolution had come of age, as American in its desires and dreams as the American Revolution.

I remember saying to Martin, "People all over the nation have been so aroused by the impact of Birmingham. You should call a massive march on Washington to further dramatize the need for legislation to completely integrate black people into American society. I believe one hundred thousand people would come to the nation's capital at your invitation."

There were others sounding the same theme. James Bevel, who successfully advanced the idea of the Children's Crusade in Birmingham, proposed marching from Birmingham to Washington in imitation of Gandhi's spectacular Salt March to the sea. But given that Birmingham is twelve hundred miles from the nation's capital, the idea became too much of a hardship to actualize. A. Philip Randolph, founder of the Brotherhood of Sleeping Car Porters, had threatened to lead a massive march on Washington in 1941, but he canceled the march after President Franklin D. Roosevelt issued the historic Executive Order 8802, which called upon defense industries to hire workers without discrimination on account of "race, creed, color, or national origin." Twenty years later, in drumming up support for the 1963 march, the seventy-four-year-old Randolph reiterated how difficult finding work still was for blacks, with unemployment rates more than double that of whites. Moreover, the violence of Birmingham was still fresh on the national conscience.

To settle the matter, Martin, as president of the SCLC, and Roy Wilkins of the NAACP organized a conference, for July 2, gathering together the heads of other major civil rights groups, including Dorothy Height of the National Council of Negro Women, James Farmer of CORE, and Whitney Young of the Urban League. The SCLC's Fred Shuttlesworth, SNCC's James Forman, and Norman Hill of CORE also attended, but Wilkins insisted that, since these three were not major civil rights chiefs, they be ejected from the room. It was hard for me to understand how Wilkins could get away with such a demand, considering the battle scars of a man like Shuttlesworth. Moreover, Fred had come all the way from Birmingham to attend the meeting. Wilkins also evicted Bayard

Rustin, whom A. Philip Randolph wanted to help organize the march. Wilkins had warned Rustin by phone not to show up, feeling that recent attention to Rustin's arrest on a sodomy charge in California and his admission, in the aftermath of McCarthyism, that he belonged to the Young Communist League could prompt negative publicity. Randolph, however, got his way, and Rustin reappeared as coordinator.

Young and Wilkins spoke against the march, arguing that too many things could go wrong. Others in the group felt the victory of Birmingham spoke loudly enough, and worried that if inadequate numbers supported the march, the forward thrust of the movement would be seriously crippled. There were also concerns that this would be an all-black march, which could alienate southerners and work against the passage of the Civil Rights Bill.

Despite the wrangling back and forth, supporters of the march won out, and the March on Washington for Jobs and Freedom was set for August 28, giving us fewer than sixty days to organize, plan, and transport the one hundred thousand people we expected to attend. The mobilization was nothing short of a miracle.

The night before the march, Martin and I checked into the Willard Hotel in Washington, DC. It was about midnight when he finished the outline for his speech, but completing it was difficult, since he was trying to keep within the eight minutes he had been allotted. The speech began with Lincolnesque phrases: "Five score years ago, a great American, in whose symbolic shadow we stand today, signed the Emancipation Proclamation." Martin then inserted language pertaining to America issuing blacks a check that "has come back marked insufficient funds."

As I listened and watched him insert, delete, state, and restate his premises, I did not hear the famed "I have a dream" phrase that would so electrify the gathering. He had used that phrase so eloquently at Detroit's Cobo Hall the previous June. Since that had been a smaller audience, however, the press in Washington treated the "dream" flourishes as new.

At about 3:00 a.m., I took my last look at Martin cutting, paring, and shaping his speech. I felt guilty for being too sleepy to serve as a sounding board. Martin gave his handwritten draft to Wyatt Tee Walker at 4:00 a.m. for typing and reproduction, which meant it was too late to forward a summary or excerpt to the march committee's press office, as had been asked of him.

Near sunrise, I awakened. Martin was at the hotel window. He probably hadn't caught more than an hour's sleep. He was watching the street to get wind of the crowd size. We were anxious, hoping that the crowd would reach one hundred thousand. The initial news reports we heard were discouraging: commentators predicted a meager turnout. One news report said, "A very small number of people have assembled, only about 25,000."

As we reached the Mall, however, our spirits began to soar. The reporters were seriously underestimating the crowd. By 10:00 a.m., we estimated that there were about 90,000 people—and they were still coming. By bus, train, plane, and automobile, crowds flocked to the Mall, and would soon soar to more than 250,000 people, a number that exceeded our wildest dreams. Some were cycling, and a few arrived by foot. Forty percent of the marchers were white, and the crowd came from every state in the union. The crowd applauded their leaders, but it was the leaders who, in their hearts, were applauding the crowds for their dedication and commitment.

Martin and I had discussed at length whether I would march, and since I usually joined him for every march, I was not pleased that his answer was "Well, the wives are not going to march."

He explained that the planning committee had decided the march would be led by the top leadership, and no place was reserved for their wives. Although I understood, I was extremely disappointed. I would not bring up my grievance, however, because I knew Martin needed my support during the awesome task of delivering his speech.

On the Mall, I was separated from Martin, and found that no seat had been reserved for me on the platform. Thankfully, Ralph Abernathy helped me get a seat directly behind Martin. I looked around to see Lena Horne, Ralph Bunche, Marian Anderson, and about fifty members of Congress seated on the steps of the Lincoln Memorial. Sporadically the crowd would chant, "Pass the bill! Pass the bill!" in reference to the pending civil rights legislation.

Not many in that tremendous gathering had any idea of the battle royal going on behind the scenes. Different civil rights leaders were jockeying to be seen and heard. Martin, aware of some of the discord, strained to avoid distraction. There was much calamity over attempts to coerce John Lewis to soften his speech. Try as they might, march leaders could not stop Lewis from using anti-Kennedy rhetoric, which the leaders feared might sour JFK toward the civil rights bill. In addition, the debate was still raging over Shuttlesworth, who had been excluded from the list of speakers; the writer James Baldwin vigorously defended him. Finally, Shuttlesworth was given his proper respect and allowed to make brief remarks.

No woman was allowed to make a major speech, though Daisy Bates, substituting for Myrlie Evers, delivered 149 words. This was very upsetting to me, especially when there were so many battle-weary female veterans who deserved an opportunity to speak. Fannie Lou Hamer, Rosa Parks, Daisy Bates, Diane Nash Bevel, Ella Baker, Dorothy Cotton, Juanita Abernathy, and Dorothy Height—the list was endless. But that's how chauvinistic the leadership was at that time.

Although no woman was allowed a prominent speaking role, Mahalia sang. We listened to her soulful voice as it rang out: "I've been 'buked, and I've been scorned." Then the moment that so many had come so far to experience arrived. A. Philip Randolph rose to introduce Martin. The applause echoed like thunder. From one side of the Lincoln Memorial to another, people began chanting Martin's name.

He started slowly, a little husky at first, emerging into the strong and beautifully resonant tone that came when he was inspired to do his best. He orated the themes I had heard the night before, but when he got to the rhythmic part of "Now is the time," the crowd caught the timing and began shouting "now" in cadence. Their response lifted Martin to new heights of inspiration. In a moment of transformation, he turned aside from his manuscript and the "I Have a Dream" rhetoric, which was not on paper but was tucked inside him, began to roll off his tongue.

As he spoke, it seemed to me like heaven itself had opened up and poured out visions of hope. When Martin ended, there was an awed silence, then a tremendous crash of applause, shouts, and amens. Thousands cried out in ecstatic agreement with his oration. They kept on shouting and applauding, and for that brief moment, it felt to me like the kingdom of God had come to earth.

I sat, awed by the magnificence of the occasion. At the time, I could not know the waves the march would continue making. It provided a trail for many other groups to follow—from feminists to antiwar vets, from the physically challenged to the Million Man and Million Woman marches of the 1990s.

Ironically, some of the very leaders who had fought against Martin and the march, like Wilkins and Young, were now reaching for him. I reached for him, too, putting my arm in his so as not to be swept aside by the crowd. As I walked along, the federal marshals made room for me. "Step aside, that's Mrs. King," they urged the crowds.

Despite the magic of the hour, I was soon brought back to earth. Having talked several times to JFK by phone, I very much wanted to meet him face-to-face to thank him for the times he had intervened to help Martin when he was in prison. As the top leaders readied themselves to be driven by limousine to the White House to meet with Kennedy, I tried to convince Martin to allow me to sit in on the conference.

"Gosh, I would like to go," I remember saying. Martin said, "You can't go because you are not invited. It's against protocol."

I thought to myself: protocol, the devil! Why couldn't I go?

If the president had been LBJ, who wasn't a stickler for protocol, it wouldn't have mattered, I thought.

"Martin, if I don't meet him now, it may never happen," I said, not knowing how prescient those words would be.

In any event, Mrs. Wilkins and I rode with our husbands only to the White House gate. Then we got out of the limousine, hailed a cab, and returned to the Willard.

Isn't this awful? I thought as I rode back to the hotel. Later I joked about the new women's movement that was forming. "I need to join it," I quipped.

I fought not to allow these minor personal rejections to detract from the beautiful glow of the day's momentous events. But I must admit that I was hurt by the missed opportunity to meet President Kennedy, who had befriended me when I sorely needed him. The missed opportunity would become even more painful. Three months later, he was assassinated.

The tragedy of Kennedy's death affected me deeply. On that awful day, November 22, 1963, Martin saw the news bulletin flash across the TV screen at our home in Atlanta. "Corrie, I just heard that President Kennedy has been shot, possibly killed!" he called. I rushed up the stairs to Martin, and we held hands, praying and hoping together that the president would pull through. We felt that he had been a friend to the cause and a friend to us personally. When it was announced that the president had died, Martin was strangely silent. When he did speak, his words sent chills through me: "This is exactly what's going to happen to me. I keep telling you, this is a sick society."

For a moment, I couldn't find my voice. When I did, I had no words to comfort him, to assure him that it wouldn't happen. I felt he was right. I moved closer to him and grabbed his hand more tightly, holding on for dear life.

Yoki, who was eight at the time, had heard the news at school. She came running in the door and into my arms. "Mommy," she sobbed, "they killed the president and he didn't do a single thing to anybody. We'll never get our freedom now."

As best I could, I shared with her my belief that the president had had a divine purpose, that he was meant to help bring about a just and fair society. Like the Bible said, I truly believed that "All things work for the good of them that love the Lord." Kennedy's unearned sacrifice and undeserved suffering would be redemptive for the entire nation. And indeed, his death moved the nation in such a way that the Congress felt legislation advancing the cause of the least fortunate, legislation that included our Civil Rights Bill, should be passed as a tribute to his memory. Some eight months after President Kennedy's death, on July 2, 1964, Lyndon Johnson would invite Martin and other civil rights leaders to the White House to witness the signing of the historic bill, which would, among other things, once and for all outlaw racial segregation and discrimination in all publicly or privately owned facilities open to the general public.

But at President Kennedy's funeral, victory was far from my mind. I watched Jackie Kennedy and felt a great sense of pain for the loss of her husband and the father of her children. As I kept thinking about Martin, I identified with her ordeal. Many people considered Martin's work to be more dangerous than that of the president. If they could kill a president, what did that say about Martin's chances for survival in America? In a strange way, Kennedy's funeral further prepared me to accept what I knew in my heart would be our own fate.

TWELVE

Heartbreak Knocked, Faith Answered

A LTHOUGH I AM a woman of strong faith, I admit that my spirit sometimes struggled to overcome the heaviness of the trage- dies around me. When heartbreak knocked on my door, I learned to let faith answer. Things would get better. Evil would not pre- vail. It was something I had to train myself to believe in order to keep on going. I also learned that I had to hold on to the good and empowering moments, so that I could return to them and steady my grip when the inevitable next tragedy struck, such as when we got the horrible news of the infamous Klan murder of three Freedom Riders: black Mississippian James Chaney and two white New Yorkers, CORE staffer Michael Schwerner and volunteer Andrew Goodman.

Still, even in the wake of shock and sorrow, we took solace that these heroes had not died in vain and that the fruits of the movement's success were apparent. Breathtaking changes were rippling across America. Imagine the newness I could see, taste, and touch as I witnessed changes I had once thought would not happen in my lifetime. As a result of the Civil Rights Act, visible signs of forced racial separation were coming down. On trips through the South, I could enter through the front door of many restaurants and expect to be served. I could use the public rest- rooms and ride city buses as well as Greyhounds. There were hotels that would admit me. I could take my children to a movie and not be segregated in the balcony.

These experiences, which sound ordinary today, were so extraordinary in 1964 that they felt comparable to the first man landing on the moon. In a sense, that is what it was: a landing at a new frontier, a new step for humankind. There was still resistance, but we could now have a healthy anticipation that one day separate "White" and "Colored" water fountains would be mere relics of a shameful past. Then, on October 14, 1964, came an especially exciting achievement. It was a day that seemed to fall out of the clouds of heaven. After a staggering speaking schedule that took Martin from one end of the country to the other, as well as to Germany, I urged him to check into St. Joseph's Hospital in Atlanta for a much-needed rest. At about nine that morning, after he checked in, I was at home, busy screening his calls. Most were from supporters or admirers concerned about Martin's health. And then there was the steady flow of harassing and vulgar phone calls—the usual.

Then came one caller with a deep, official-sounding voice: "This is the Associated Press. I would like to speak to Dr. Martin Luther King."

When I told the reporter that I was Mrs. King, he said, "We have just received word from Norway that your husband has been named the recipient of the Nobel Peace Prize for 1964."

I gripped the phone, trying to remain calm. The press had announced that Martin was high on the list for the honor, but no one thought he had one iota of a chance of winning.

As soon as the reporter hung up, I called Martin: "How is the Nobel Peace Prize winner for 1964 feeling this morning?"

"What's that?" he asked sleepily.

"Martin, the Associated Press just called us. It's official: you are the winner of the Nobel Peace Prize."

He was stunned. He said, "Okay," and hung up. Moments later, he called back to check if the news was real or if he had been dreaming.

I was brimming over with joy. The Nobel Prize. He would be only the second African American to receive the prize after Ralph Bunche in 1950. It was exactly the lift Martin and the movement needed. It would push us to new heights, would show that our work was about not just civil rights but human rights, and it would place our efforts on a world stage. I sat by the phone and said a prayer of thanksgiving.

Then I got dressed so I could join Martin at the hospital. Together, we walked into the glare of flashbulbs and cameras as the media gathered for a statement.

The reporters hit Martin with a barrage of questions. The inevitable inquiry came up. "Where will the money go?" a reporter asked. The prize came with a $54,000 stipend, which Martin explained would be given to the movement. Later, the prize money was divided among different civil rights organizations, including the SCLC, SNCC, CORE, the National Council of Negro Women, the NAACP, and the American Foundation on Nonviolence. That, of course, was not a surprise to me. Martin generously gave away most of the money he earned.

When the reporters left, we went back up to Martin's room to share our thoughts. We were tremendously happy but recognized the burdens in store: the prize and all the publicity would detract from our time together, which, as it was, was quickly being winnowed away.

News of the prize came in October. We did not leave for Oslo until early December. In the meantime, while the Oslo events were the icing on the cake of a long and arduous struggle, a clandestine effort was under way to hack the cake itself to pieces.

With the announcement of the award, FBI director J. Edgar Hoover's heavy-handed smear campaign to ruin my husband's reputation and destroy our marriage swung into high gear. While the public saw Martin being feted internationally with the highest, most noble honors, out of sight, Hoover's knives were being sharpened, and traps were slowly and methodically being set to try to engineer Martin's demise.

On November 18 we began to understand just how deep-rooted the suspected FBI spying against Martin and our movement was, and to understand at least some of the lengths the Bureau would go to harass, intimidate, and ruin us. On that date, Hoover told a group of reporters that Martin was the "most notorious liar in the country." This statement reverberated in the press, among supporters and detractors alike. At the time, Martin was in Bimini, an island in the Caribbean, working on his Nobel address. His peaceful seclusion was shattered by an invasion of helicopters carrying members of the press. Martin had no idea what was happening until Dan Rather disembarked from his helicopter and began firing questions at him. Martin told me he was upset as he carefully denied Hoover's denunciation of him; he was also careful not to blast Hoover, for violent speech only begets violence.

Apparently what had ticked Hoover off was the Nobel Prize itself. We later learned that Hoover grew furious when he learned that Martin had received an honor that Hoover thought he himself deserved. For years, Hoover had urged his friends in Congress to nominate him, to no avail. Moreover, Hoover did not take kindly to Martin's criticism of the FBI for not aggressively pursuing the assailants who were killing, intimidating, or denying the constitutionally protected rights of civil rights workers.

Because of the furor in the press over Hoover's attack on Martin, when Martin returned from Bimini, we had a heartfelt talk, bringing up concerns we had not told each other before. Each of us had been discounting as "paranoid" our suspicions that our home phones as well as our office phones had been tapped. Now we put two and two together.

I recalled a suspicious incident from the Albany campaign when Juanita Abernathy; Andy Young's wife, Jean; Dr. Anderson's wife, Norma; Wyatt Walker's wife, Ann; and James Bevel's wife, Diane, had planned to lead a march to protest the jailing of demonstrators. Surprisingly, Martin, Ralph, and several others were then given suspended sentences and released, thus defusing our march. At the time, I felt as though someone had been eavesdropping on our strategy meetings.

For his part, Martin told me that in June 1963, JFK had taken him aside in the Rose Garden of the White House, where they were meeting to discuss civil rights legislation. President Kennedy warned Martin that Hoover thought Communists controlled the SCLC. Martin said it was clear from their conversation that the president did not buy Hoover's story, but the very fact that he passed on the warning *outside* the White House, where no monitoring devices could record their conversation, showed Kennedy's grave concern. Although the bugging of our homes and phones could not have gone on without the president's knowledge, he did not speak of his own role in the bugging operation, or that of Bobby, the attorney general.

Martin talked about how many of the movement staff had reported being followed by men with the military bearing of FBI agents. We talked about how Atlanta police chief Herbert Jenkins, a friend of Daddy King's, had told Daddy King that the FBI was planning to wage a campaign against Martin. Jenkins said that Hoover had even asked him to cooperate.

Jenkins advised Daddy King, "You tell your son to be careful, because if Hoover's men cannot catch him in some compromising position with women, they are going to frame him." Then he added, "If I hear this again, I am going to say it's a lie."

After he retired from the police force, however, Jenkins wrote his memoirs and cited this very conversation with Daddy King. It was amazing how many people, from presidents to police to members of the press to the ordinary man on the street, feared Hoover.

Martin and I were not naïve. We talked about the many ways in which the system tried to destroy leaders. It started by trying to convince people you were a thief. This had already been attempted with Martin, and had failed. The next step was always character assassination, usually with allegations of sexual wrongdoing. If that didn't work, physical destruction followed.

We did not go ballistic over Hoover's schemes, however, even though the writing was on the wall. We knew he had a vendetta against us, but we felt that we were the good guys, fighting to ensure democratic beliefs for all Americans. We took the regrettable position that we didn't care if the FBI followed us. Maybe one day it would even do its job and protect civil rights workers, instead of adding to our troubles.

It was so like Martin to think well of people, to appeal to their higher principles. He thought if he could just meet with Hoover, he could convince him that they were both working for the betterment of the nation. With the help of Archibald Carey, a black Chicago attorney who knew Hoover, a meeting was set for December 1, eight days before Martin would be honored in Norway. Martin, Ralph, Walter Fauntroy, and Andrew Young attended the meeting at the Justice Department offices on Constitution Avenue in Washington, DC. They went specifically to discuss Hoover's "notorious liar" statement, but instead, Hoover spent the hour-long meeting rambling on about the virtues of the FBI and how difficult it was to find "qualified" black agents. He even politely congratulated Martin on being awarded the Nobel Peace Prize. Martin said that no mention was made of the FBI surveillance, charges of Communist activity, or the sexual escapades that our friends in the media had warned us were being planted in the press.

In fact, Martin thought the meeting was cordial. "I can't understand the controversy around Hoover, because he treated us so warmly," Martin told me. "Hoover kept emphasizing that the agency had identified the assassins of the three civil rights workers and was close to making an arrest."

Yet, to our shock, as reported in the press and, later, revealed in the secret recordings of JFK, Hoover gave an entirely different version of events. He claimed that he confronted Martin about his Marxist philosophies and lectured him for an hour about his lack of morals. He implied that Martin had engaged in extramarital relations. He even reported that he told Martin he was not "going to take any lip" from him. Martin said that none of those things was ever discussed.

Hoover and his evil machinations were the last thing on my mind, however, on December 4, when our party of about thirty people left Atlanta for Norway. We took two separate flights; I led one delegation and Martin the other. We had stopped flying together as a means of protecting the children.

It was a remarkable trip. On the first leg, Martin preached a sermon in St. Paul's Cathedral in London. Except for the Nobel ceremony itself, this was the high point of the trip. Martin was the first non-Anglican to address this august body. His message, entitled "Three Dimensions of a Complete Life," was one of his favorite sermons, and it had sentimental significance for me. It was the first sermon I heard him preach after we met in Boston.

On December 8 we arrived in Oslo for the ceremony itself, which was two days later. The first evening, there were no official engagements. So, over dinner, family, friends, and SCLS staff and supporters took the time to rejoice and to recall our long struggles in making such an uphill climb. Present with us were Mama and Daddy King, A.D., Christine, Carol Hoover, Andy Young, Harry Wachtel, Ralph and Juanita, Bernard Lee, Wyatt T. Walker, and Freddye Henderson. It wasn't often that we could sit together and reflect. We were always in the vortex of a crisis: someone was going to jail, being beaten, or having their churches and/or homes bombed. After dinner, Martin, Andy, Ralph, Wyatt, and Bernard Lee formed a quintet and sang freedom songs. This was something we had often done in the midst of a storm, but that night, it was a moment of unblemished joy.

It was Daddy King, however, who brought us all to tears when he talked of his struggles to rise up from the depths of life as a sharecropper. He talked about how hard it was for him and Mama King to live with the knowledge that what Martin was doing was so dangerous. He talked about the threats the two of them had endured. "You don't know how it feels when a stranger calls you on the phone and tells you he wants to kill you, or kill your son."

Caught up in the emotion of his talk, we all cried, mostly from the realization that a people who had started so far back in life, as farmers, sharecroppers, and servants, could come so far—and not by ourselves. It was as though our whole race were running with us.

The next morning, December 10, we woke early to get ready for the ceremony. Martin had to wear formal dress, striped trousers and a gray tailcoat. We fussed a lot with his ascot. Despite his vow "never to dress up like that again," he looked very handsome, so young and eager, almost like a boy going to his first dress-up dance.

The formalities were held at Oslo University in a long, narrow auditorium decorated with hundreds of white flowers. The hall held about seven hundred people, with several thousand gathered outside, trying to catch a glimpse of Martin.

First in the hall was King Olav, with Crown Prince Harald. Everyone stood, and the Norwegian Radio Orchestra played the Norwegian national anthem. The ceremony was brief, shorter than some of my husband's regular Sunday Ebenezer services. We smiled graciously, but were amused when, in an effort to honor the African American community, the orchestra played selections from Gershwin's *Porgy and Bess*. The refrain of "Summertime and the livin' is easy" was much too bucolic to capture the scenes of fire hoses and police dogs in Birmingham.

Accepting the prize, Martin said he saw the award as "profound recognition that nonviolence is the answer to the crucial political and moral questions of our time." As usual, his message was full of optimism and hope: "I refuse to accept the view that mankind is so tragically bound to the starless midnight of racism and war that the bright daybreak of peace and brotherhood can never become a reality." He then went on in his Nobel Lecture to present one of his most definitive teachings on nonviolence, teachings that we can still study and be guided by today, including, "What the main sections of the Civil Rights movement in the United States are saying is that the demand for dignity, equality, jobs, and citizenship will not be abandoned or diluted or postponed. If that means resistance and conflict we shall not flinch. We shall not be cowed. We are no longer afraid." And, "In a real sense nonviolence seeks to redeem the spiritual and moral lag that I spoke of earlier as the chief dilemma of modern man. It seeks to secure moral ends through moral means.... Nonviolence is a powerful and just weapon. Indeed, it is a weapon unique in history, which cuts without wounding and ennobles the man who wields it.... [I]t is the only way to reestablish a broken community. It is the method which seeks to implement the just law by appealing to the conscience of the great decent majority who through blindness, fear, pride, and irrationality have allowed their consciences to sleep."

THAT NIGHT, THE SCLC family gathered for a private tribute. A case of champagne was brought in, and we all toasted to Martin. When it was my turn, I talked about what a privilege it was to be a coworker with a man whose life had made such a profound impact on the world. We were all straining to reach new heights with our rhetorical flourishes when Daddy King brought us back to reality, rising to say, "We couldn't have come this far by ourselves, no, not ever. Now I want us to toast the one who made it possible for us to be here tonight. I want to make a toast to God." It was a hilarious moment to see so many teetotalers trying to offer something so incongruous to God.

Most of us were so proud of him. As I watched Ralph Abernathy, though, I questioned whether he shared our joyous feelings. When the prize was first announced, Ralph talked late into the night with Martin about how he thought it should have been given jointly to both of them, and how he felt the money should have been divided equally.

Ralph's hurt feeling that he was not getting his just due and was operating in the shadow of Martin had been simmering for years. It was during the Nobel ceremonies that Abernathy's downcast mood became more noticeable in contrast with the abundant joy of others. For years, Ralph had been complaining about not getting enough attention. This was understandable: Martin's great intellectual gifts, his charisma, and his oratorical skills caused him to overshadow most of those around him. We were all in Martin's shadow.

Martin, however, greatly appreciated Ralph's ability to motivate the masses. He felt that Ralph understood him and his philosophy and would be a good successor if something happened to him. I saw Ralph as a valuable friend and confidant to Martin, as well as a leader in his own right, but as Martin used to say to me privately (usually after a long session during which Ralph complained to him about not getting press attention or about being treated like a second fiddle), "Ralph does not understand his role. He wants us to be coleaders. He does not understand that the people have made me a major symbol and do not respond to a coleadership arrangement. I wish he could understand and accept his role."

Martin did everything he could to push Ralph forward, but he had no control over how he was positioned in the media. In Norway, he sensed his friend's rather edgy feelings, but the beauty of the occasion kept his spirits high.

We returned home by way of Paris, where we checked into a hotel for a few days' rest. Martin's sister, Christine, his mother, and Dora McDonald, his secretary, all suggested we end the trip with a night out on the town. Martin resisted, reminding everyone that as a Baptist minister, he couldn't go to establishments where alcohol was served. Others countered that no one in our party would drink anything stronger than ginger ale.

I didn't join the fray; I simply retired to my room to get ready. When I reappeared, I was wearing one of my concert dresses, a stunning burgundy velvet with an off-the-shoulder neckline. Martin immediately insisted that I change into something more appropriate, by which I'm sure he meant more "matronly." I was startled, because the outfit was the same one I had worn on other occasions, without any complaints from him. Choosing not to argue, though, I offered to change clothes and stay at home with him. I realized later that it was a good thing I did. Martin was exhausted; he took a sedative and went to sleep.

As soon as he fell asleep, a UPI reporter called to inform us that the suspects in the murder of the three civil rights workers had been arrested in Mississippi. The reporter wanted to interview Martin. I called Harry Wachtel, a New York attorney who served as Martin's confidant and legal counsel and as the SCLC's liaison to the U.S. Justice Department. I told him about the UPI request and asked him to provide a statement for Martin to look at when he woke. Wachtel readily agreed. We felt a sense of relief and hope that justice was about to come to Mississippi.

We returned to the States via New York City, which gave Martin a hero's welcome: fireboats on the Hudson River and jetted streams. Mayor Robert Wagner presented Martin with the Bronze Medallion, the highest award the city could give. Martin and I, along with the members of our party, were also luncheon guests of New York governor Nelson Rockefeller and his wife, Happy.

In further recognition of the Nobel Peace Prize, President Johnson invited us to the White House to congratulate Martin. We were flown from New York City to Washington on the New York governor's private plane. During the meeting with President Johnson, Martin took the opportunity to discuss the importance of full voting rights in the South and beyond, laying the foundation for the movement's next major campaign.

After his being the darling of Europe, it was interesting to see the lukewarm welcome Martin received in Washington. There were no receptions or ceremonies to congratulate a man hailed for his greatness everywhere except a few corners of his homeland.

Finally, our weary band of travelers returned to Atlanta. As in DC, while there was a large turnout of blacks waiting to greet Martin, he received a virtual cold shoulder from Atlanta's white citizens. While some were proud that a hometown guy had won such an honor, others couldn't deal with its being a black man.

To complicate matters, Martin and the SCLC had been picketing the Scripto Company in a push for better working conditions for blacks. Scripto was one of the largest factories in Atlanta, and the SCLC picketing naturally did not produce much enthusiasm in the business community. In turn, tickets for a city-sponsored dinner to celebrate the Nobel were moving so slowly that Martin soured on the whole event, saying, "I don't care whether they honor me or not." (In his book *An Easy Burden*, Andy Young cites FBI records showing that Bureau officials discouraged many Atlanta businessmen from participating.) Things turned around only after Mayor Ivan Allen called the business leaders to a closed-door meeting at the Piedmont Driving Club, where J. Paul Austin, president of Coca-Cola, described the embarrassment of being in a city that didn't want to honor its own Nobel Peace Prize winner.

In the end, the dinner at Dinkler Plaza Hotel was a sold-out affair, the ballroom filled with about fifteen hundred people. It was the first integrated event of the kind that the city had ever experienced. The audience was about 65 percent white and 35 percent black. Judges sat next to cooks; porters were seated next to politicians. Five years before, an event such as that would have been unthinkable in a southern city.

It was a wonderful evening, but again, the glow couldn't last for long. In opening the mail that had been piling up in the months before our trip to Norway, I came across a package postmarked from Miami dated November 2. The package contained a reel of audiotape and a letter, which I opened. After Martin spoke, he was often sent an audiotape of the event, to keep for his records. But the poorly typed letter in this package read:

King, we've found you out. This is just a sample of the goods we have against you. Your end will come soon. You are done for, there is only one way out for you. You better take it. You have thirty-four days before you will be exposed and publicly defamed.

The letter had been sent some thirty-four days before Martin was set to receive the Nobel Peace Prize. There was no question in my mind that it was prodding Martin to commit suicide. Under stress, Martin often suffered from depression. In the sick minds of those who'd sent the letter, I'm sure they thought they were pushing my husband over the edge.

Through the grapevine, I had heard rumors that Hoover's FBI had prepared a suicide letter and a doctored tape to embarrass Martin. "This must be it," I said to myself. I set up our reel-to-reel recorder and sat down to listen. Although I have since read scores of reports talking about the supposed scurrilous activities of my husband, there was nothing at all incriminating on the tape. It was recorded at some social event and was of very poor quality. I recognized Bernard Lee's voice, but on the entire tape, I didn't hear Martin's. People were laughing, talking. Now and then I heard a dirty joke, some profanity. But there was nothing about Martin having sex or anything else that resembled the lies Hoover and his people were spreading. "Oh, this is nothing," I said to myself, cutting it off. I gave the tape to Martin. He and several staff members, including Ralph and Andy, secretly met and listened to it together.

Later, we learned what great lengths the FBI had taken to prepare the suicide package. Hoover had ordered that the doctored tape be mailed from a southern state; an FBI agent flew to Florida with the small package, mailed it, and returned to Washington. Hoover reasoned that I would confront Martin and then leave him, putting him in such a weakened state that he would become ineffectual to the movement. An impending divorce would also reduce his stature. Despite my refusal to fall for any of the bait, rumors spread through the media claiming that we'd had a screaming match and saying I was on the verge of walking out. Once again, nothing could have been further from the truth. Martin and I did not have the slightest argument over the tape.

There are so many stories about Martin and me and our life that were fabricated, pure and simple. For example, there was a rumor that Martin had a secret bank account stashed away in Switzerland—which was ridiculous, because we often did not have enough money to pay our bills. In Oslo, when the entire family was there, the FBI claimed they picked up a bug on Martin that proved he was cavorting with prostitutes and running buck naked down the hall with them. As ridiculous as that might sound, it's a typical example of what we were up against. Can you imagine that Martin, with his father and mother; his wife, sister, and brother; his staff and all his friends there, would pick this opportunity to do something so out of character?

But I understand, the question everyone wants to know is this: Do I believe my husband was unfaithful? All I can speak for is what I know. I don't have any evidence, and I never had a gut feeling that told me he had strayed. I never experienced any feelings of being rejected. I believe that women know if their husbands are unfaithful. They feel it. I understand that men can become very indifferent and cold, but I never sensed anything of that sort from Martin. I'm not saying that Martin was a saint. I never said he was perfect. Nobody is perfect. But as far as I am concerned, our marriage was a very good marriage, and it was like that all the way to the end.

Why is it so hard to believe that—in light of everything we know about the FBI and Hoover's counterintelligence operation (COINTELPRO), which was tasked to eliminate black groups such as the Black Panther Party, and of other vicious tactics—that the Bureau would not do something like spread false rumors about Martin Luther King, a man Hoover hated so much that he tried to push him to commit suicide? Why is it so hard to believe that Martin was not guilty and the FBI was? Why is it so hard to believe that he was not unfaithful to me when I am the one who would know?

There are people who like to feel that everybody is fallible, and that Martin was like everybody else. I don't think he was like everybody else. I think Martin was a much more moral person than most of the people around him. Again, I'm not saying he was a saint, but I really do believe that it's the sickness of our society that leads people to look so desperately for someone or something to bring down.

Those who really knew Martin knew he had a guilt complex. If he did anything wrong, he felt compelled to confess it and repent. I was often the one to whom he confessed his private wrongdoings. This is one of the main reasons I do not believe any affairs took place. All that exists about my husband is innuendo and hearsay. No one has ever been able to prove anything.

Were any of us perfect? No, we all fell short. But when speaking of historical significance, it is important to note that when the ultimate question is asked about who the real sinners or saviors of this century were, the answer clearly shows that Martin Luther King Jr. helped transform America. That is the end of that matter.

THIRTEEN

———— ✾ ————

Securing the Right to Vote
Was a Blood Covenant

YOU HAD BETTER enjoy yourselves, because when we go into
Selma, someone is going to get killed." Martin spoke these
words while we were in Oslo. Throughout that entire trip, he
had talked as if he'd had premonitions of more supporters from our
movement becoming martyrs. From the mountaintop of Norway, we
sensed that we were returning to a valley, where tragedy surely awaited.
The name of the particular valley was Selma.

A medium-size town between Montgomery and Birmingham, some
thirty miles from my hometown of Marion, Selma was originally a
cotton center and slave market. During the Civil War, it was second only
to Richmond, Virginia, as an arsenal and supply depot for the Confederate
Army. It had few equals, however, in its resolve to maintain the ideology
of white supremacy.

For blacks, Selma was rock bottom, a place where words such as
democracy, representative government, and *citizenship* had no meaning.
Most of the black population had never participated in governmental
business as citizens, even though their roots, like those of many other
African Americans, stretched back three hundred years.

Think what it means to have no vote in the major political, economic,
and social policies that govern your life. In Selma, victims of brutality
couldn't even say "ouch" too loudly; the town was nothing more than a

police state. Keeping blacks in line were the White Citizens' Council and Jim Clark, the Dallas County sheriff, whose counterpart was Birmingham's Bull Connor. Clark and his posse savagely used cattle prods on blacks "uppity" enough to try to exercise their constitutional right to protest or speak out against disenfranchisement.

While the majority of the folks in Dallas County (57 percent) were blacks, less than 1 percent of that majority was registered to vote. In comparison, two-thirds of whites were registered. Neighboring counties were even worse. For example, in nearby Lowndes County, not a single black in the entire county was registered to vote.

In 1965, all that would begin to change.

The next big movement campaign was a push for voter registration and voting rights—an attempt to secure for blacks the freedom white men and women earned by being born. Entrenched racism made the assignment seem as difficult as desegregation of public schools had been in the 1950s.

When, on our way home from Oslo, Martin met with President Johnson to discuss the importance of the right to vote in safeguarding all other rights, LBJ tried to convince Martin that the time wasn't suitable. It was similar to the way in which President Kennedy initially dismissed our efforts to secure equal public accommodation. "I can't get a voting bill through because I need the votes of the Southern bloc, and they won't give it," Johnson said. "It's just not wise and expedient."

But we were not to be deterred. In Selma, I would march with Martin as often as I could. I was also raising funds for the movement through my Freedom Concerts and continuing my work as a peace advocate. But my highest priority was back home in Atlanta, with my children. For their sake, I tried to shield them from the terror and the blood being spilled in Selma.

In a slight taste of what was to come, only a week after the Selma campaign began Martin was attacked. The first day he was there, a white man followed him. The stranger's behavior did not alarm Martin's staff because the man seemed rational. He followed Martin into the Hotel Albert; as Martin was checking in, he hit Martin on the head so hard that Martin staggered and would have fallen to the floor if a staff member had not grabbed him. The man was held until police arrived to arrest him.

Although Martin was not seriously injured, he suffered terrible head-aches from the blow. The incident worried me greatly, for I saw how easily someone who meant Martin harm could hurt him.

The first casualty of the voting rights campaign was not in Selma but in Marion. We had been holding mass meetings and demonstrations in my hometown. One night, in the middle of a march, the streetlights were suddenly turned off; in the darkness, the police and their white racist buddies charged the demonstrators, clubbing and beating them. Eighty-two-year-old Cager Lee was beaten bloody. His grandson, twenty-six-year-old Jimmie Lee Jackson, pushed his grandfather and his mother, Viola Jackson, into a café to escape further harm, but several troopers followed them. When a trooper hit Viola, Jimmie Lee struck back and was shot in the stomach. Eight days later, he died.

Jimmie Lee's aunt, Juanita, was a former teacher, and had been one of my best friends in high school. Jimmie Lee was his mother's sole supporter and had never been convicted of any crime. Ironically, the "crime" for which his life was taken was written in the Constitution as an inalien-able right to peaceably assemble, but for us, that promise was penned in invisible ink.

Martin preached Jimmie Lee's eulogy, hailing him as a martyr. Afterward, my father, who was then sixty-five years old, and my brother, Obie, joined the mourners as they walked through drenching rain to the cemetery. Obie, a minister in the AME Zion Church, had become a movement stalwart. In 1969 he integrated a post office in a small town near our parents' home, becoming the first African American postal carrier there. Until Obie took action, small rural areas in the South had seen no black mail carriers since Reconstruction.

The tragic news didn't stop with Jimmie Lee's death. Three days after he was killed, we learned that Malcolm X had been assassinated by mem-bers of the Nation of Islam in a ballroom near Harlem. When I heard the news, I felt a tense pain in my chest and a great sadness, especially that his death was so senseless. It was not a martyr's death, which is very often redemptive. Just a few weeks earlier, I had met and talked with Malcolm X in Selma, and I'd felt I was gaining a clearer understanding of his principles.

Malcolm had come down to Selma after Martin and Ralph were

arrested and jailed for leading a march of about 250 blacks and whites from Brown Chapel AME Church to the Selma Courthouse. Juanita Abernathy and I had gone to participate in the protests. When we arrived at Brown Chapel for a noonday march, Andy Young told me, "You have to come inside and meet with the people. Malcolm X is here, and he's really roused them up. They want to hear from you." In response, I gave a short inspirational speech, emphasizing the benefits of nonviolence and urging the protesters not to give up hope.

Afterward, Malcolm and I had a chance to talk. He apologized for not going to the jail to see Martin, explaining that he had a plane to catch for London, where he would address the African Students' Conference. Despite all the media reports of his inflammatory rhetoric, he was low-key and humble during our conversation. He told me, "I didn't come to Selma to make Dr. King's job difficult. I really did come thinking I could make it easier. If the white people realize what the alternative is, perhaps they will be more willing to listen to Dr. King."

I saw then that he wanted an opening by which he and my husband might work together. I knew that he had been to Mecca, that he had broken with Elijah Muhammad, that he was altering his violent rhetoric and was moving away from ideas of hatred toward racial unity. I believe the whole cause of social change would have been advanced if he and Martin had been able to combine their efforts going forward.

I could not reconcile my own beliefs with Malcolm's insistence on separation of the races; nor could Martin and I condone violence or racial hatred of any kind. Yet, we shared with Malcolm a strong desire for African Americans to reclaim their racial pride, to take joy in themselves and their race through a physical, cultural, and spiritual rebirth. We also believed that, in many respects, the black race reflected values that were wanting in the white cultures that had so long oppressed us. Both Martin and Malcolm were disappointed in the failure of white Christians to fight against the sin of racism, but Martin never would have stepped away from Christianity. Martin felt it was not Christianity itself that had to be rejected, but those who failed to practice the Christian ethic.

On February 3, the day I spoke with Malcolm, President Johnson held a press conference in which he expressed his support for equal voting rights. It was his first direct response to Selma. "I should like to say that all Americans should be indignant when one American is denied the right to vote," he said. "The loss of that right to a single citizen undermines the freedom of every citizen. . . . I intend to see that that right is secured for all citizens."

A few days before, a federal judge had issued an order requiring the registrar in Selma to process at least one hundred voting applications a day. Slowly but surely, we were making progress.

A month later, Martin flew to Washington to meet with President Johnson to urge him to expedite the new Voting Rights Bill, and to make sure it included provisions for federal registrars of voting applicants. To ensure that President Johnson got the message, two days later Martin signed off on an idea proposed by James Bevel for a fifty-mile march from Selma to the state capitol in Montgomery. The goal of the march was to focus the eyes of the nation on Selma and the issue of voting rights.

During the Albany campaign, Martin had learned that a movement whose leaders were all in jail at the beginning of the campaign was like a ship without a rudder, so at the last moment, he was persuaded not to lead the march. He chose the SCLC's Hosea Williams and SNCC's chairman, John Lewis, to take his place.

The March 7 march began on an upbeat note. The five hundred marchers, blacks and a sprinkling of whites, started out with a prayer and slowly moved up Highway 80 on a sunny afternoon. Not a policeman was in sight as Williams and Lewis led the group six blocks to Broad Street and began to cross the Edmund Pettus Bridge, which spans the Alabama River in East Selma. Martin's brother A.D. also joined the march. Suddenly, as the marchers reached the apex of the bridge, they saw a sea of blue-clad Alabama troopers awaiting them. Some were on horseback, with gas masks hanging from their belts and billy clubs in their hands. In what seemed like seconds, the troopers charged the demonstrators with wild rebel yells and began firing tear gas.

The evening news broadcast unforgettable images of the harrowing events: firing tear gas, slashing with bullwhips, and using electric cattle prods; chasing fleeing men, women, and children all the way back to Brown Chapel. The cameras also picked out the expressions of some whites on the sidelines, their faces distorted with hatred. A few called out, "Get those niggers! Kill them! Get the S.O.B.'s!" The tear gas was so bad that elderly people lay helplessly vomiting onto the road, while the troopers charged right over them.

Martin was horrified by the melee, which came to be known as Bloody Sunday, and he agonized over not being there. Immediately, he announced that he and Ralph would lead another march on Tuesday. Just as fast, the Alabama authorities got a temporary federal injunction to stop them.

When Bloody Sunday broke out, I was at Second Baptist Church in San Francisco, on the third leg of a five-city Freedom Concert tour to raise funds for the SCLC. As soon as I heard how badly the people had been beaten, I became very nervous. I hadn't heard from Martin and didn't know where he was. When I did talk to him later that night, he told me how one of the papers reported that a pretty credible threat on his life had been made.

"I had better come home to be with the kids, just in case they hear the rumor," I said.

"No, you're making a contribution right where you are," Martin told me.

"Fine, but if anything happens to my family, I am going to take the next plane out of here."

I finished my concerts in Portland and Denver, raising about twenty thousand dollars, which in those days was considered "good money," and returned to Atlanta. For a while I busied myself with the care and schooling of our children, trying to create a reality as free as possible of the death and bloodshed in Selma. There was always music in our home. Many people did not know that Martin had a deep baritone voice and enjoyed singing. Our children were musically inclined as well. Yolanda played the piano, the clarinet, and the bells. As a beginner in piano, Bunny showed promise. Marty had a good ear for music, and Dexter was working on learning the trumpet. The boys were also learning to sing bebop music with near-perfect pitch. We had recently purchased our very first home (after renting or living with friends and relatives for thirteen years), and I was determined that it be not just a roof over our heads, but also a refuge.

Martin's heavy responsibilities meant that the tasks of renovating and settling into our new home fell to me. Often this was the case—I bore much more of the domestic responsibilities and, with Martin away so much, was left to bring up the children virtually alone. Only on occasion did I feel sorry for myself, like when both Marty and Dexter had to have their tonsils out at the same time. Martin was so busy that I went ahead and made plans for their surgeries without telling him. When the boys woke up and needed his attention, Martin was not there. That evening, I had the television on and saw Martin at the White House, witnessing the signing of the Voting Rights Bill. I felt very supportive of his being there, but I also had this feeling of being alone, of being entirely by myself. More often than not, though, I accepted the fact that Martin could not do all he did and still be an active father. He sometimes berated himself for not being a "good parent." When he did that, I always came to his rescue, reminding him of the quality time he spent with the kids when he could. And when he was home, he was wonderful with the children. Occasionally, when I went to the hairdresser or went shopping, he would babysit; he and the kids would have a wild time together, roughhousing. And I tried to help our children see that what Daddy did helped change things for others for the better.

I remember how Yoki cried when we had to tell her she couldn't go to the Funtown amusement park in Atlanta because the park didn't allow "Negroes." Years later, when Funtown was desegregated as a result of the movement's efforts, Martin and I took Yoki, Marty, and Dexter there, and we used the experience to show them that people working together could change things.

On the Tuesday after Bloody Sunday, Martin decided that the march from Selma to Montgomery would go on despite the federal injunction against it. He had a distaste for defying federal injunctions, because he depended upon the judiciary in Alabama to prevent unlawful interference with the voting rights campaign. But the situation was urgent.

Martin made a nationwide appeal, asking clergy and laypeople to join him in Selma, and they came in droves. Nuns, priests, ministers, rabbis, and ordinary people flocked to that small southern town. In all, on that Tuesday, about fifteen hundred people, more than half of them white, marched out of Selma on the way to Montgomery. Once again, the troopers were lined up shoulder to shoulder on the Edmund Pettus Bridge. When the police gave the order to halt, the marchers knelt in prayer.

Then, in an effort to prevent a nonviolent confrontation from turning into another orgy of mob rule, Martin told the crowd to turn back.

Martin's attempt to strike a peaceful compromise, however, couldn't smother the hot fires of extremism. The night of the march, three clergy who had responded to Martin's call were viciously beaten as they left a black-owned café. Four Klansmen in sports jackets attacked them with wooden planks. The Rev. James Reeb, a white Unitarian minister from Boston and a father of four, was left unconscious. He died two days later.

On Monday, March 15, more than two thousand people attended a memorial service for Reeb. In Martin's eulogy, he noted that "Reeb's death may cause the white South to come to terms with its conscience." That night, President Johnson spoke to the nation about the ongoing violence. He compared Selma to the famous Lexington and Concord battles of the American Revolution, and to the Civil War's Battle of Appomattox. "In Selma," he said, "long-suffering men and women peacefully protested the denial of their rights as Americans. . . . What happened in Selma is part of a larger movement which reaches into every section and state of America. It is the effort of American Negroes to secure for themselves the full blessings of America." In a call for unity, he said, "Their cause must be our cause, too. Because it is not just Negroes but really all of us who must overcome the crippling legacy of bigotry and injustice."

With a flourish, President Johnson ended with our time-honored battle cry: "And we shall overcome." More important in his speech, he designated the Voting Rights Bill his highest priority.

Yet, even though we now had support at the highest levels, the Selma movement dragged on. After two murders and nearly thirty-eight hundred arrests, only about fifty African Americans were registered to vote. Then a miraculous turnaround occurred. The federal injunction against the march was lifted; the president federalized the Alabama National Guard, and committed four thousand regular army troops to Alabama. This meant that, despite Governor Wallace's protestations, the march could proceed. For the first time, our efforts fell under the protection of the federal government. On March 21, two weeks after Bloody Sunday, Martin led five thousand supporters of both races out of Selma and across the infamous Edmund Pettus Bridge.

I had to honor a commitment to speak at Bennett College in Greensboro, North Carolina, that day, but I said to Martin, "I would rather march in Selma." He encouraged me to go ahead and make my contribution in North Carolina and then join the group on Monday, which I did. When I arrived, I saw how tired he was. His feet were in poor condition. Fortunately, the march had advanced to the point where there was a medical unit, and even a commissary, to aid the marchers on their fifty-mile trek.

On March 24, some of the nation's most noted artists held a concert in Montgomery to celebrate the end of the march. Among them were Peter, Paul, and Mary; Sammy Davis Jr.; Odetta; Tony Bennett; and of course our friend Harry Belafonte. Despite the cover of harmony, there was an undertow of anxiety. Several more rumors of plots to assassinate Martin were swirling and circulating. That night, as we stood on the stage, I thought about what sitting ducks we were, out in the open night with the bright stage lights beaming down on us.

When I was asked to speak at the concert, I'd tried to beg off, but Martin and Harry Belafonte insisted. So I spoke about what it meant for me to return to Montgomery some ten years after leaving. I also spoke to the women about the future of their children, using the Langston Hughes poem "Mother to Son."

The next day, it was time for the last leg of our march, in which a crowd fifty thousand strong made its way to the capitol in Montgomery. Not so long ago we had to back off the sidewalk if a white person approached us head-on. Now we walked through the center of the town. Some boasted that we walked like we owned the town, but we were proud, not defiant. What we had always wanted was to create a climate of inclusion and shared responsibility, not to trade one form of oppression for another.

Some people on the sidewalks, white and black alike, seemed happy to see us. When Martin looked their way, they cheered. In another twist, we were no longer treated like enemies of the state. Finally our lives had some value, were deemed worthy of protection. We had maximum security all the way. Federal troops circled the highways. Sharpshooters were stationed on rooftops, and helicopters buzzed about overhead.

Marching past Dexter Avenue Baptist Church was thrilling for me. Shortly before we arrived, I saw my mother and father standing in the crowd. I sent for them to join us. Daddy King was also with us. Having our parents marching with us was a unique experience for Martin and me. Martin's sister and brother, Christine and A.D., also marched with us. You could say it was a family affair. Ralph Bunche, Mrs. Rosa Parks, and many others were there, too. I was greatly honored to have my parents join me on the platform for the ceremony, with the state capitol looming in the background.

During the speeches, I daydreamed, drifting back through a decade of events. In ten short years, we had seen miracles occur. Things thought impossible were now reality. Things that people like Jim Clark had said would happen only over their dead bodies were occurring, and those who had sworn to stop us, Jim Clark included, were alive to see civil rights legislation come to pass. Despite George Wallace's ringing declaration, "Segregation now, segregation tomorrow, segregation forever," we stood in an ever-changing, increasingly integrated society.

What a long way we had come! From thousands of people bravely challenging a bus system to hundreds of thousands of visible supporters marching across the South, we had desegregated buses, public transportation, and terminals. Our right to use public accommodation was guaranteed, and we were progressing toward school integration. And finally, by gaining the right to vote in the South, we were on the way to full citizenship. Cities known for their intransigence would go down in the history books as the birthplaces of national legislation: Montgomery led to the Civil Rights Acts of 1957 and 1960; Birmingham to the Civil Rights Act of 1964; and now Selma would produce the Voting Rights Act of 1965. It is a fact worth restating—especially for those who do not now use their franchise—securing the right to vote was a blood covenant, a right won and sealed by the deaths of men and women, whites and blacks, whose blood spilled onto Alabama soil.

When I looked out at the crowds, I saw many church people, both white and black. They were more involved now than at any time in our history. I told Martin later that it was perhaps the greatest witness by the church since the days of the early Christians. Perhaps my father summed up best how many of us felt: "This is the greatest day for Negroes in the history of America."

That night, the airport was jammed with thousands of people going home. They were a happy, fulfilled crowd: black and white together, eating and laughing in a spirit of brotherhood and sisterhood. It was a scene that captured what we had fought for, a chance to be free of race hatred, an opportunity for all people to live and laugh together as equals.

That image was soon shattered, however, by a telephone call we received when we reached Atlanta. Mrs. Viola Liuzzo, the white wife of a Detroit Teamsters Union official, had been shot to death on Highway 80 while driving some demonstrators back to Selma. Her murder sent a chill through me. If whites would kill a white woman for helping blacks register to vote, I thought, what would they do to blacks who attempted to vote? Mrs. Liuzzo's death was a reminder to watch and pray. The battle was not over, and there were many more rivers to cross.

Chicago would be that next river.

———— ❀ ————

FOURTEEN

Moral Concerns Know No
Geographic Boundary

S HORTLY AFTER OUR Selma campaign ended, Martin told me, "The doctor is always telling me how badly I need a vacation. So come on to the Bahamas with me."

We were still in the process of getting our new house in Atlanta renovated. We had scheduled the movers months ago; there was no way I could pick up and go as quickly as Martin wanted. "I'm leaving on Sunday," he told me, "and I want you to come at least by Wednesday." So the movers came on Tuesday. My friend Freddye Henderson and I stayed up all night putting up curtains, decorating, and trying to get things in order. We didn't want the house to be a mess when Martin and I returned from the Bahamas.

In my mind, I was thinking: How can I get all this done, put everything in place, and still be with Martin? I bet people might be saying, 'Oh, look at that woman running after that man.'" Yet, I lived with the terrible reality that our days together were numbered. I knew that sooner rather than later I would not have Martin, and I didn't ever want to feel that Martin had asked me to do something I did not do. I was willing to make whatever sacrifice I could.

It was hard, though. That Tuesday night, I received only one hour of sleep. At the end of the day, I felt as I did the first day I marched in Selma.

My legs felt disjointed, like they were coming apart from the hips. And I was so tired.

Still, the next morning, I dropped everything anyway and took off, leaving all the unfinished business behind. As an admitted perfectionist, that was difficult for me. Yet it was astonishingly easy for me as Martin's soul mate and wife.

We had a lovely (and rare) getaway to the Bahamas, and when we got home it was right back to business. In 1965, Martin made a dramatic shift in the movement, from South to North, from the battleground of the Bull Connors and Jim Clarks to the plantation of Chicago's mayor, Richard Daley. In keeping with Martin's style of leadership, which chose to challenge the worst examples and draw them into the public eye, Chicago became the SCLC's next target. Its towering housing projects loomed like upright concentration camps, placing abject black poverty within sight of white opulence. These visuals, combined with the deep despair of many of the impoverished blacks, made the city an ideal challenge.

Switching gears proved more difficult than we could have ever imagined. The black community was spread out over such a large area. It was not as tightly knit in the North as it was down home, which meant there were many more factions to pull together. Moreover, we had never gone up against a sophisticated political machine, one much more devious than that we had experienced at home.

Martin's primary goal was to prove to naysayers that nonviolence could work in a tough and gritty urban context. His mission was to dramatize the conditions of the black poor, to create an understanding of their plight among the powerful, to equip blacks to change their conditions, and to bring whites and blacks together in a spirit of cooperation.

In Chicago, Martin decided to live among the "least of them" and rent an apartment in the ghetto. I agreed to pack up the kids and move with him, since we did not know how long the campaign would take. Martin arrived in Chicago first, in January; I joined him once he'd found an apartment, and we planned to bring the children in at the beginning of the summer.

In all my life, I had rarely seen anything like the conditions we faced in Chicago. The level of poverty called to mind our travels through Bombay a few years before. Our apartment on the West Side, among the poorest of the poor, was in a dingy building that had no lights in the hall except for a single dim bulb at the head of the stairs. There were no locks on the front door; drunks came in and used the hallway as a public toilet, so it always smelled of urine. Our apartment was on the third floor, up three sets of rickety stairs. The old refrigerator didn't work; neither did the dilapidated gas stove. The heat didn't work, and sometimes it felt as cold inside as out, with temperatures that often dropped below zero in the winter. As we became friendlier with our neighbors and were invited into their apartments, we learned that, as bad as our accommodations were, others had it even worse. On the third floor of one building, we met a family of ten who were crowded together in a tiny apartment with no heat or running water.

I had never seen such depressing conditions, but no matter how miserable we were, we understood that our suffering could not be compared to that of those who lived permanently in the housing projects and had little chance of escaping or improving their lot. Our rent was eighty dollars monthly, which was more than the whites paid in nicer areas in the suburbs. What exploitation. Poor blacks were trapped in a vicious cycle: redlining by white real estate agents and selective covenants restricted them to concrete ghettos where education, medical services, and transportation were grossly limited. Few educational options led to unemployment, which in turn forced many blacks to opt for welfare to feed their families. Those on aid could not own property, not even an automobile. This policy ultimately confined the trapped ghetto dwellers to jobs near their homes, limited though they were. Prices for food and clothing around the ghetto were also hiked up, intensifying the financial exploitation and ensuring the confinement of project residents to the bottom rung.

Our children's arrival was delayed when James Meredith, who had been the first black student to integrate the University of Mississippi, was shot and wounded by a white man during a march in Mississippi. Martin flew to Memphis to see James in a hospital there; then Martin and Stokely Carmichael and a number of others restarted James's march from the spot where he had been shot. When they reached Tougaloo, Mississippi, fifteen thousand black people were gathered there, the largest such gathering in Mississippi history. Yoki and Marty and I joined Martin to march from Tougaloo to Jackson. James Meredith had recovered enough to join us as well.

After that march, we took all four children up to Chicago with us. We had some furniture by then, some bought secondhand and other pieces that had been donated. Although we lived as simply as we could back in Atlanta, our way of life in the South was totally different from life in the ghetto that summer. There was nothing for the children to do except go outside the apartment building and play in the black dirt. There was nothing green anywhere. Even the playground was black dirt. The moment they were dressed and went outdoors, their clothes were soiled. And when I tried to keep them inside, their tempers flared; there were shouting and pushing matches, which didn't happen often at home, where they had plenty of room to run off their pent-up energies.

The Chicago Freedom Movement's first big rally and demonstration, which had been in the works for more than a year, was planned for July 10, 1966, at Soldier Field. An unprecedented forty-five thousand people showed up. We took all four children to the platform, including Bunny, who was only three. Mahalia Jackson sang. There were speeches. And then Martin read his list of demands for social justice in Chicago. The demands were of real estate boards, banks, the mayor, the city council, the Chicago Housing Authority, politicians, businesses, unions, the governor, the federal government, and of the people. This was a Sunday, so of course City Hall was closed. Still, Martin led that enormous crowd to City Hall and nailed the demands to the closed City Hall door, just as his namesake Martin Luther had done with his Ninety-Five Theses centuries ago in Wittenberg. The march was a beautiful nonviolent demonstration.

We had planned to allow our three older children to march with us, but when Bunny heard her sister and brothers talking, she started asking "When are we going to march?" And when the speeches were over, she said, "But we haven't marched yet." I said to Martin, "What are we going to do about Bunny?," and he replied, "Let her march with us." He was particularly unable to resist her wishes in those days. So, even though she fell asleep and was carried more than half the distance by Bernard Lee and Andy Young, Bunny marched with us, and that was the only time our family ever marched together. I wish we had thought to get a picture of it.

The next evening, before a mass meeting, Martin and I went to dinner at Mahalia Jackson's house, and after dinner, on our way to the meeting, we ran into our first riot. The outbreak had started when police turned off fire hydrants that young people, who lacked access to swimming pools, were using to cool off. The youths started throwing rocks and breaking windows, and then the gangs got involved. Several black youths were beaten; others were arrested. Two gangs, the Cobras and the Vice Lords, threatened to tear the city up if the prisoners weren't released. Martin, Andy Young, Bernard Lee, Mahalia, and I all went to the police station, and Martin persuaded the authorities to let us post bail.

That night, angry crowds milled in the streets. SCLC staff were out all night trying to calm things down. Our children were safe on the other side of town, visiting some friends of ours, which enabled me to be out on the streets for most of the night with Martin.

The next day at noon, I addressed a women's meeting at the YWCA on the predominantly white North Side. I had been up nearly all night and was depressed, depleted, and completely exhausted. I proposed that one hundred women sign and send a telegram to Mayor Daley supporting Martin's proposals. Initially, some were reticent about signing because their husbands held jobs with the city. I pushed the point, saying, "What are you afraid of? The time has come when we have to make a decision and make a choice." After that, they signed the telegram. They also decided to form a permanent organization called Women Mobilized for Change. It was an integrated group, and eventually grew to one thousand members.

That night our whole family stayed with Mahalia, and the day after that, the children and I returned to our apartment. The next night, Wednesday, July 13, Martin was addressing a mass meeting on the West Side, and I was going to speak to a group on the North Side, taking the children with me because I didn't have a babysitter. While the children and I were getting ready to go, we heard glass shatter in the street. The children, who were looking out the window, saw some boys breaking a plate-glass shop window and shouting, "Black Power!" That was when it hit us: we were in the middle of a riot. People arrived to take us to the meeting on the North Side. I was addressing the group, with the children, including an overtired and restless Bunny, on the platform alongside me, when I was interrupted by someone saying there was an emergency call from Martin, who had heard about the rioting near our apartment and was worried about us.

He and I promised to stay in frequent communication by telephone, and I took the children back to the slum apartment that night. It was a nightmare. We traveled back through more glass breaking and through more shots being fired. The rioting went on for most of the night. Eventually we went to bed, listening to the shooting. Needless to say, it was a frightening experience.

Soon after the rioting ended, I took the children back to Atlanta. As a family, we had spent only a few weeks in Chicago. Meanwhile, the SCLC changed its focus in Chicago to concentrate solely on demonstrations for open housing and an end to economic exploitation. There was tremendous resistance to these efforts. Bricks and bottles were thrown at Martin and his aides as they marched through the lily-white suburb of Marquette Park in a push for open housing. Some of the same type of people who had confronted us in Selma and Birmingham confronted us as we marched in that Chicago suburb. Swastikas and Nazi flags waved. Someone hit Martin in the head with a rock, which brought him to his knees, although he was not seriously injured. He told me, "I've been in many demonstrations all across the South, but I can say that I have never seen, even in Mississippi, mobs as hostile and as hate-filled as in Chicago."

Finally, on August 26, 1966, the Chicago movement came to an end. The SCLC, Mayor Daley, the Real Estate Board, and the Chicago Housing Authority inked an agreement on open housing. It did not live up to its promise, however. As soon as we left, city officials continued to do business as usual.

That said, there were at least two lasting victories. In 1962, in Atlanta, the SCLC had established a program called Operation Breadbasket, which aimed to take the movement to the next level in its fight for equal economic rights. Now that we were able to get on the bus, we needed to be able to afford the cost of the ride—or even to own the bus company. In Chicago, starting in 1966, Operation Breadbasket, under the able leadership of the Rev. Jesse Jackson, pushed for job promotions, business opportunities, and an end to economic exploitation of the poor, such as the supermarket chains' practice of selling inferior products at exorbitant prices in the ghetto. In addition, some of the gang members we lived and worked with put down their guns and dependence on violence and marched with us, using nothing but their bodies and their faith to protect themselves against the evil of their enemies.

Despite the Daley Machine's unwillingness to honor its commitments, I believe the seeds of nonviolence and direct action we planted, along with our challenge to decades of entrenched economic exploitation, have produced a rich harvest that lingers to this day.

Personally, I saw Chicago as a first step in spreading our wings. We broke out of the box and moved beyond our southern borders. The northern drive was not without its critics, of course. There were those who believed we should not have stepped beyond the Mason-Dixon line. To the contrary, I say that moral concerns and matters that prick the conscience know no geographic boundaries. After receiving the Nobel Peace Prize, Martin also began to talk more about carrying the philosophy of nonviolence beyond American soil.

In 1965, at an SCLC retreat, Martin asked me to make a general statement about why we should take a public stand against the Vietnam War. I talked about how it would continue to drain resources from education, housing, health, and other badly needed social programs. I said, "Why do you think we got the Nobel Prize? It was not just for civil rights. . . . Peace and justice are indivisible."

Still, the Rev. Otis Moss of Cleveland was the only SCLC board member who encouraged Martin to support peace in Vietnam. All the other members argued that his position would dry up donations to the SCLC, because an antiwar stance would upset too many whites and make us appear unpatriotic.

For the next two years, Martin agonized over his silence, quietly working behind the scenes on antiwar public policy, raising his concerns about the war in private meetings with the president and in a meeting with UN ambassador Arthur Goldberg, where Martin called for a halt to the bombing of North Vietnam while more peaceful diplomatic efforts were pursued.

In the meantime, since the spotlight shone so brightly on Martin, the press overlooked my agenda and activities, which had been deeply pro-peace and antiwar since my days at Antioch. I was called upon to participate in a number of antiwar campaigns. For example, in 1965, Martin and I were invited to speak at a major rally in Madison Square Garden protesting the Vietnam War, and while Martin decided not to attend, I participated. In fact, I was the only woman and one of only two blacks invited to speak. I also continued my affiliation with Women Strike for Peace, the group I traveled to Geneva with in 1962 on a peace mission.

Until 1967, Martin had been content to leave it to me to march, protest, and mount public challenges to the war in Vietnam. With my history of antiwar activism, it was easier to assuage his conscience about not being more strongly involved himself. We were always a team, so he felt that "Well, at least one of us is involved."

In March 1967, Martin led his first antiwar march, in Chicago, and a few days after the march, he made it clear through the press that he had marched as "an individual, as a clergyman, as one who is greatly concerned about peace" and not as the leader of the SCLC.

Then, on April 4, 1967, he gave a speech at Riverside Church in New York City, to a large gathering of clergy and laymen. It was entitled "Beyond Vietnam" and was one of the most courageous and prophetic speeches he ever delivered. He pointed out that "if America's soul becomes totally poisoned, part of the autopsy must read: Vietnam." He noted that African Americans were "dying in disproportionate numbers in Vietnam" and called it a "reflection of the Negro's position in America. . . . We [are] taking the black young men who had been crippled by our society and sending them eight thousand miles away to guarantee liberties in Southeast Asia which they have not found in southwest Georgia and East Harlem."

Martin knew what would happen once he took this position. Virtually every major newspaper in America, including much of the black press, lambasted him. Members of Congress, his fellow civil rights leaders, and "brethren" of the cloth joined the parade of criticism, accusing Martin either of not sticking to the civil rights struggle or of aiding communism. SCLC funds did suffer. Friends such as Roy Wilkins blasted him publicly. But his answer was this: "Cowardice asks the question 'Is it safe?' Expediency asks the question 'Is it politic?' And Vanity comes along and asks the question 'Is it popular?' But Conscience asks the question 'Is it right?' And there comes a time when one must take a position that is neither safe, nor politic, nor popular, but he must do it because conscience tells him it is right."

In spite of the opposition, Martin took part in the Spring Mobilization for Peace in New York City on Saturday, April 15, 1967. When the march was announced, I told Martin, "Finally, I will be able to march with you. All these years I've been marching for peace alone, or as the only black and certainly the only woman." But Martin said, "I want you to go to the West Coast and lead that one. They need you out there. I will be on the East Coast." I told him how much I'd looked forward to being with him, but in the end, I went to San Francisco, where I was needed. About sixty thousand people participated in the San Francisco march, and about two hundred fifty thousand participated in the New York march led by Martin.

After the march, the criticism against Martin's pro-peace views grew even stronger. But he was merely practicing what he had often preached and what we both believed: "If you have never found something so dear and so precious to you that you will die for it, then you aren't fit to live," he wrote.

In 1942 white racists burned down the 1920 Heiberger, Alabama, house built by Coretta's father, Obadiah ("Obie") Scott. He built this second home in Marion, Alabama. Coretta lived here a year before leaving for Antioch College in Yellow Springs, Ohio.

Coretta Scott in the lap of her mother, Bernice McMurry Scott, with her sister, Edythe; Heiberger, Alabama, 1927.

Coretta Scott (above, at right) playing cards with her friend Fran Lucas (far left) and another student, during their Antioch College years.

Coretta Scott, graduate student at the New England Conservatory of Music, in the Boston apartment of Martin Luther King Jr., doctoral candidate at Boston University. The two were courting at the time.

Martin Luther King Jr. and Coretta Scott wedding portrait; Marion, Alabama, June 18, 1953. From left: Christine King, A. D. Williams King, Martin Luther King Jr., Naomi King, Coretta, Martin Luther King Sr., Edythe Scott Bagley, Bernice Scott, Alberta Williams King, with flower girl Alveda King and Obadiah Scott.

Coretta was preparing for a career as a classical singer when she met and married Martin in the early 1950s. Later, her "freedom concert" helped to fund the civil right movement.

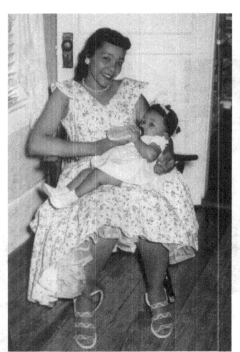

Coretta with Yolanda Denise King, the first of her and Martin's four children, in the parsonage of Dexter Avenue Baptist Church; Montgomery, Alabama, 1956.

Coretta with her sons, Martin III (age six) and Dexter (age two), in the home they rented in Atlanta, Georgia, December 1963.

The Ebenezer Baptist Church choir, including Coretta Scott King (second row, far right) and her sister-in-law Christine King Farris (second row; second from right), at a Sunday service.

Martin hugs Coretta during a news conference in Atlanta following the announcement that he had won the 1964 Nobel Peace Prize.

Martin with Coretta, his parents, Mrs. Alberta Williams King and Rev. Martin Luther King Sr., and his siblings, Christine King Farris and A. D. Williams King, after the Nobel Peace Prize ceremony, Oslo, Norway; December, 1964.

A King family portrait. From left: Dexter, Yolanda, Martin Jr., Bernice, Coretta, and Martin III in the study of Ebenezer Baptist Church, Atlanta, 1966.

Coretta comforts her youngest child, Bernice (age five), during the funeral services for Martin at Ebenezer Baptist Church, April 9, 1968. Dr. King had been assassinated five days before in Memphis, Tennessee.

Jacqueline Kennedy offers condolences to Coretta Scott King on the day of the funeral for Martin Luther King Jr. in Atlanta, April 9, 1968. (EBONY)

[above] *Coretta leads a prayer before a hospital workers' march to the Charleston Medical Center during a strike for fair wages in Charleston, South Carolina, August 8, 1969.* (AP)

[at left] *Coretta speaks at a press conference in Washington, DC, August 18, 1977, briefing reporters on worker demonstrations for jobs planned for fifty cities during Labor Day week that year.* (HENRY GRIFFIN/AP)

Coretta gestures at an architectural rendering of the King Center. Immediately after her husband's death in April 1968, she began securing his legacy of nonviolent social change; the King Center building complex, an important aspect of this legacy, was completed on January 15, 1982. (FLIP SCHULKE ARCHIVES/GETTY)

Scott family portrait, circa 1970. Left to right: Edythe Scott Bagley, Dexter King, Yolanda King, Martin III, Bernice McMurry Scott, Bernice King, Obie Scott, Obadiah Scott, and Coretta.

The King family, circa 1973. In front: Martin Luther King Sr. with great-grandson Jarrett Ellis, Angela Farris, and Bernice King. Standing, from left to right then up: Naomi King, Isaac Farris, Christine King Farris, Coretta, Alberta King, Isaac Farris Jr., Dexter King, Vernon King, Martin III, Darlene King, Yolanda King, Derek King, Alfred King, and Alveda King.

COUNT JACKSON

President Jimmy Carter and First Lady Rosalynn Carter sing with Martin Luther King Sr., Coretta Scott King, Andrew Young, and other civil rights leaders at Ebenezer Baptist Church in Atlanta, January 1979.

Coretta Scott King and her daughter Bernice (left) and son Martin III (right) are arrested for protesting apartheid at the South African Embassy in Washington, DC, June 26, 1985.

In the White House Rose Garden, November 2, 1983, President Ronald Reagan signs legislation establishing a U.S. federal holiday to commemorate Martin Luther King Jr.'s birthday. Representative John Conyers of Michigan first proposed the bill in April 1968.

Coretta with her son Dexter King as he becomes president of the King Center, 1989. Beside them is Rev. Barbara Williams-Skinner, chief operating officer of the King Center at the time. (BETTMANN/GETTY)

Nelson Mandela and Coretta Scott King dance at a victory celebration in Johannesburg, South Africa, on May 2, 1994, after Mandela and the ANC won the country's first integrated elections. (DAVID BRAUCHLI/AP)

Coretta Scott King and Dr. Barbara Reynolds working on Mrs. King's memoir at Hippocrates Spa in West Palm Beach, Florida, 1998.

Coretta Scott King with her close friends, Betty Shabazz, widow of Malcolm X, and Myrlie Evers-Williams, widow of Medgar Evers in January 1995.

Bernice King, Oprah Winfrey, Coretta Scott King, and Yolanda King in 2003 in the Atlanta condominium that Ms. Winfrey provided for Mrs. King.

In April 2002, Coretta Scott King celebrates her seventy-fifth birthday with her children, Martin III, Yolanda, Dexter, and Bernice at Stone Mountain Lake in Atlanta.
(GUERRY REDMOND ATLANTA)

Maya Angelou and Coretta Scott King during the launch of the Maya Angelou Life Mosaic collection by Hallmark at the Metropolitan Pavilion in New York City on January 29, 2002. Dr. Angelou and Mrs. King met early in the civil rights movement and became close friends.

———— ❀ ————

FIFTEEN

I Don't Want You to Grieve for Me

I N THE EARLY months of 1968, Martin was terribly distressed. I had not seen him like this before, and it was heartbreaking for me. When he became depressed, I could usually find the words to help comfort him, to lift him out of the depths of his discouragement. But now my words took root only for a moment.

Since 1964, riots had been breaking out in urban cities across America each summer. (Harlem and Rochester and Philadelphia in 1964; Watts in 1965; 7 major riots across the country in 1966, and then, in 1967, 159 race riots across the country.) Hundreds were injured; scores were killed. Each summer, as the temperatures started rising, so did tempers, anguish, and rage. Usually the root cause was police brutality, but sometimes it was a lack of jobs; sometimes the cause was not easily understood.

Martin and I felt that if the rioting continued, America would either fall into the throes of anarchy or become a right-wing police state. Of course, neither was acceptable, and Martin felt that something had to be done to steer the nation away from this deadly intersection. While he condemned the violence, he also understood that moral and economic issues lay at its root, issues that America might not have the resolve to fix.

During each of those harrowing hot summer days, Martin took the rioting to heart. It was so like him to be his own toughest critic. Here he was, a prophet of nonviolence, watching as values entirely opposite of his moved to the forefront. The movement had accomplished so much (civil rights bills had passed; schools, lunch counters, and housing were being desegregated), but maybe it wasn't happening fast enough. So little time, so much to be done. If the riots continued, there would be only more bloodshed, and Martin worried that people would give up on nonviolent protest and direct-action campaigns in response.

In those times of desperation, I prayed for him. I kept trying to find the right words, ones that would help him see past the cities in flames and connect with the millions of people who had faith in him and were convinced he was their best hope. When I could make him stop in his tracks and look at me, I would hold him and say, "I believe in you." I would see the spark coming back into his face, but, still, he agonized.

Not only did he agonize, he was haunted. Martin was haunted by the faces of poverty that he had seen in rural Mississippi, and in the ghettos of Chicago. He had left Chicago, but Chicago wouldn't leave him. Far too often, he had seen little children with clothes too skimpy to protect them from the city's harsh winds. A closer look revealed mucus in the corners of their eyes, a reminder that, although they were surrounded by some of the finest medical centers in the world, vitamins and flu shots were luxuries their families could ill afford. Martin had seen an apartment where rats attacked a baby in his crib, a scene that spoke to the flimsy, filthy housing conditions in a state we liked to call Up South. In Mississippi, too, Martin replayed searing images in his mind: ill-clad children sitting in one-room schoolhouses without books or lunches, malnourished in a state where corporate farmers were receiving billions not to plant food or cotton. The problems of the poor were invisible: out of sight, out of mind. Martin wanted to make the plight of those in the lower classes visible to the world. He wanted to dramatize the hidden face of American poverty. We believed that just as segregation was immoral in a democracy, poverty was immoral in a nation as wealthy as the United States.

Fortunately, as Martin and the SCLC were mulling over the issues of the poor, Marian Wright (later Edelman, founder and president of the Children's Defense Fund) helped Martin make a way out of no way, as the gospel lyrics promise. Wright, an attorney, was director of the

NAACP Legal Defense Fund in Mississippi. She visited Martin in his Atlanta office, bringing with her four black farmhands, men who had been jobless since the government farm programs began paying farmers not to grow crops. Wright proposed that Martin and other religious and labor leaders lead a protest in Washington, with a sit-in and fast at the office of the secretary of labor, W. Willard Wirtz. The plan was to protest until the problems of the chronically unemployed were addressed. As Martin and the SCLC mulled Wright's proposal, the fast and sit-in were thrown out, but the concept of dramatizing the extent of poverty in America seemed workable.

The effort would be called the Poor People's Campaign; it would not be solely about blacks, but would include Puerto Ricans, Native Americans, Mexicans, and poor whites. The prospect of establishing a rainbow coalition that could eventually see beyond racism and challenge the systems that demeaned all persons excited Martin. The overall objectives were "economic security, decent sanitary housing, and quality education for every American." The planning team decided to focus on ten cities and five rural areas.

Martin threw himself into these efforts. It was not unusual for me to awaken before daybreak and see him at his desk, deep in thought or scribbling notes on a yellow legal pad. I knew he was getting little sleep, but he seemed like a man with no time to rest. It was as if he were racing against a clock, one that was ticking off precious minutes all the while. The faster he ran, the faster the clock. Martin performed as if a great force were driving him onward, forcing him to find solutions to the problems that tormented him before time ran out.

He and I both felt tragedy moving swiftly toward us. It was a sensation I'd had for years, but it had recently become more intense. Ever since the Montgomery Bus Boycott, the heat of terrorism had been bearing down, stalking us. It felt like just yesterday that terrorists bombed my front porch with me and our baby Yoki in the house. I suffered through Martin being jailed, through his being taken, handcuffed and chained in the backseat of a police car, down dark Georgia roads—places where black men and women had no doubt been lynched. I had answered countless phone calls to hear someone threatening to kill Martin, me, and our family. We knew that FBI director J. Edgar Hoover had labeled my husband a public enemy, a threat to the United States of America. How could we *not* know we were living on borrowed moments?

Death was something that neither of us welcomed, but it did not paralyze us, either. Guided by the writings of the Apostle Paul and the life of Jesus, we knew that Christians are often called by God to participate not only in the victory of a risen Christ, but in His agony and His suffering. Martin sometimes even placed himself in the historical context of Jesus, especially when he said he would be "crucified for his beliefs." As he told me, "If I am crucified, remember to say, 'He died to make men free.'" He also told me, "I probably don't have a long life ahead of me, but if I die, I don't want you to spend your time grieving. You go on and live a normal life."

In an effort to build support for the Poor People's Campaign, Martin went on a series of what we called "people-to-people tours" to recruit poor persons from across the nation for a peaceful demonstration to be held that summer in Washington, DC. Everywhere he traveled, people came in large numbers to hear him and to pledge their support. Martin also came up with the novel idea of having a lowly mule train go from Marks, Mississippi (which was in Quitman, the poorest county in America), to the nation's capital.

I thought the campaign was actually the most difficult project the SCLC had ever attempted to organize: instead of mobilizing a city, we were mobilizing a nation. There was scarcely a power center that our campaign would not touch.

On March 10, 1968, I went to the press conference at Atlanta's Paschal's Motor Hotel at which the Poor People's Campaign officially launched. In January, I'd had surgery to remove fibroid tumors. I was supposed to recuperate and stay off my feet for about three months, but I felt an urgent need to press on and attend the news conference regardless, and to continue my efforts to personally record and document important events.

Leaders of about seventy nonblack groups representing Puerto Ricans, Mexicans, Native Americans from reservations, and poor Appalachian whites were at the press conference that day, countering the criticism that we were planning an all-black crusade against the economic power structures of America. Cesar Chavez, the cofounder of United Farm Workers, was ailing, and sent a representative. Wallace "Mad Bear" Anderson spoke for a poor Iroquois confederation from upstate New York; and Peggy Terry, reportedly raised by a Kentucky KKK family yet now a member of CORE and SNCC, was also there.

Despite this diverse group of fired-up people who had traveled across the nation to the heart of black Atlanta to address an American problem, the press coverage was negative—as I'd anticipated. Now that the movement was showing enough muscle to unify protesters across a broad spectrum of ethnic and economic groups, we had become the enemy. We were opposed not only by much of the media, but by members of Congress and some of the Johnson administration, although LBJ himself had been very supportive of our past efforts.

As I attempted to rest in the wake of my surgery, Martin decided that he, too, would take a short break. The doctors had been ordering it; he knew he needed a rest, and everyone around him agreed that he was pushing himself too hard. Sometimes he would keep his inner circle (Andy, Bernard Lee, and Ralph) up until 4:00 a.m. probing and pushing for the correct course of future actions. Andy once wondered aloud if Martin had declared a moratorium on sleep. At the suggestion of his doctor, he finally decided to take a short vacation. On March 12, right before he left, he phoned me from his office and asked, "Corrie, did you get the flowers?"

"Not so far," I told him. He explained that he'd gone to a florist and picked some out especially for me. I eagerly awaited their arrival, and indeed, as he returned home to pick up his bag to go to the airport, the flowers arrived. They were beautiful red carnations, but when I touched them, I was surprised to discover that they were artificial. Martin had never given me artificial flowers before. It seemed so unlike him.

That night, I complimented him on their beauty, but asked whether the florist had picked artificial flowers by mistake.

It was not a mistake at all. "I wanted to give you something that you could always keep," he said.

Those red carnations were the last flowers I ever received from Martin. Did he have a premonition of what was to come? I will never know for certain, but the flowers certainly suggested that he did. They were his prelude to good-bye.

When he returned from vacation and refocused his energies on the Poor People's Campaign, a garbage workers' strike in Memphis grabbed our attention. On February 23 a small, peaceful march by the sanitation workers union Local 1733 of the American Federation of State, County, and Municipal Employees (AFSCME) was broken up by police officers using clubs and mace, the squad cars charging in like a cavalry. This outraged not only blacks but some whites as well, including the predominantly white AFL-CIO labor union. At the invitation of Jim Lawson, who headed the SCLC's Memphis affiliate, Martin agreed to lead a protest march on March 28.

Before the protest, however, on March 23, Martin took advantage of an opportunity to take Marty and Dexter on a people-to-people trip through rural Georgia. Whenever he could, he tried to include the children in his work; we wanted them to have an understanding of his commitment and the cause he championed. As much as I wanted them to take the trip together, I do remember how worried I was when they were late returning. My concern was complicated by their flying in a small chartered Cessna. When they finally arrived, four hours behind schedule, the boys were exhausted, though flying with their father and hearing the crowds applaud him was hugely exciting for them. Martin was also exhausted, but after putting the boys to bed, he immediately went back to work. Increasingly, he seemed to be trying to fill every waking hour with something productive.

In retrospect, I think that trip was one of the greatest gifts Martin could have given the boys. I am sure it was Martin's hope that they would freeze the memory and carry that picture of their father's commitment with them for the rest of their lives. It was like a snapshot of his character. After all, Martin had no money to leave behind. All he could implant in their consciousness was an outline of his character.

On March 28, Martin went on to Memphis as planned. I was in Washington, participating in a press conference with the Women's International League for Peace and Freedom. In my statement, I discussed the ways in which the Vietnam War, which I had been very vocally against, was negatively contributing to the urban crisis. Social programs for food, housing, and health were being raided to foot the cost of an ever-expanding war. The situation appalled me.

Shortly before I boarded the plane for home, I called our Washington office to touch base. As soon as I said who I was, a staff member told me that violence had broken out in Memphis while my husband was leading the march.

I needed to know if Martin was all right, so I called Rev. Walter Fauntroy, who headed the Washington office. "Yes, he's fine, but he is terribly depressed," I was told. I felt relieved, but I also knew how badly Martin was hurting. He abhorred violence, and I knew that he would be blaming himself.

Later that evening, Martin told me what had happened. He and Ralph arrived late to the march, which had attracted about eight thousand demonstrators. The unrest had already started when they arrived, and almost immediately Martin sensed that something was wrong. His staff had not taken time to perform the nonviolence workshops that customarily preceded a march, and he saw Black Power signs scattered throughout the crowd. There was no proper lineup, and Martin told me he could sense a lack of discipline.

As it turned out, things were worse than he thought. Some of the younger black nationalists, from a group called the Invaders, had threatened to tear the place up if their agenda did not receive immediate attention. Martin said he soon heard the sound of breaking glass, followed by shouts and screams. In the distance came the sound of sirens. People were running in all directions. Martin said he yelled to Lawson to call off the march because it had turned violent. Ralph, Martin, and Bernard Lee were spirited away by a black woman driving a Pontiac. She took them to a Holiday Inn near the Mississippi River. When Martin turned on the nightly news, he saw that the scene was pandemonium, a mini-riot.

As I'd guessed, Martin was extremely despondent. "I feel responsible," he told me. "This is terrible. I can see the headlines now. Now we will never get people to believe in nonviolence."

The national press was unrelenting in its berating of Martin for the violence and in its declarations that the era of nonviolence had ended. An editorial in the Memphis *Commercial Appeal* stated flatly, "King's pose as the leader of a nonviolent movement has been shattered." Much later, however, we received confidential information that the youthful Invaders, who were at the root of the trouble, had been infiltrated by the

FBI, which used them to discredit my husband. It seemed that Hoover had vowed that King would never have another peaceful demonstration. Memphis offered an opportunity to prove it.

At that point, Martin felt he had no choice but to return to Memphis and lead another march to prove the efficacy of nonviolence. That march was scheduled for April 8.

Although he sounded so very low that night—a feeling that showed at the evening press conference—the next morning I learned that he'd had a miraculous turnaround. A different Martin appeared. The fire was back; the words and ideas flowed again. I understand he did a yeoman's job explaining to the press what he thought had gone wrong, in defining the frustrations of the black leadership and restating his commitment to nonviolence. Bernard Lee said, "I had seen him in a lot of press conferences, but rarely was he as profound and eloquent."

One perplexed reporter who had been to the earlier press conference noticed the change and asked, "Dr. King, what has happened to you since last night? Who have you talked to?"

Martin answered, "I have only talked to God."

On April 2, Martin met with the SCLC staff and reiterated his belief that a peaceful march in Memphis was key to a successful Poor People's Campaign. The meeting was very lively. It was a little like the Last Supper, at which Christ told Judas that he would betray Him and spoke to Peter and the rest of his disciples. Most of the staff were not supportive of Martin's going back to Memphis. They felt it was getting in the way of their bigger project, the Poor People's Campaign. When Jesse Jackson continued to press his objections, Martin barked at him, "If you're so interested in carving out your niche, go ahead, but for God's sake don't bother me." The meeting became heated, and Martin got upset, but it ended well, with a decision to go to Washington by way of Memphis.

On April 3, Martin prepared to return to Memphis on a 7:00 a.m. flight. Ralph came over to pick him up at our home. As was usual when Martin traveled, I rose early to prepare breakfast, but neither Ralph nor Martin ate. I followed Martin to the door, kissed him good-bye, and wished him well. The children were still asleep and didn't see him leave. It was an ordinary farewell, like thousands of others. As always, Martin promised to call me that evening.

We later learned that Hoover had leaked a story to the local media in Memphis deriding Martin for staying at the Holiday Inn, then considered too "fancy" for a black leader. Martin, ever sensitive to criticism, checked into the black-owned and -operated Lorraine Motel.

As promised, Martin called me that night. He explained that although Memphis mayor Henry Loeb had obtained a federal injunction against the march, he was going to lead it anyway. He told me that he was going to address a mass meeting that night at the Mason Temple.

Then Martin said, "I'll call you tomorrow."

In one of those inexplicable ironies of history, he wasn't feeling well that night, and decided to let Ralph speak in his stead. When Ralph arrived at the Mason Temple, the headquarters of the Church of God in Christ, about two thousand people had gathered, rather than the hundreds expected given there was a violent rainstorm raging. A tornado had also been sighted in the area, but even such inclement weather couldn't keep the people away. The congregation was cordial, but Ralph sensed they were hungry for Martin. He called him at the hotel and explained the situation, asking Martin to come and address the waiting crowd.

My husband's entrance in the giant hall at Mason Temple created tremendous excitement. Cheers and applause rang out as he walked in the door and down the aisle to the pulpit. Instead of the standard introduction, Ralph took the time to do a lengthy, rather unique summation of Martin's life from birth to his present involvement in Memphis.

Then all eyes focused on Martin, and he spoke for nearly two hours without notes. He gave his "I've Been to the Mountaintop" speech, which hit such high notes of oratory prowess that it can be compared to Lincoln's Gettysburg Address or the Farewell Address of George Washington. Martin spoke solemnly about the fate of prophets, which had not changed much from the Old Testament era. Most of the biblical prophets and disciples of Christ met tragic ends.

Even in his agony, though, Martin's concern was still for the masses. "I've seen the Promised Land," he told the gathered throng. "I may not get there with you. But I want you to know tonight that we as a people will get to the Promised Land. . . . Mine eyes have seen the glory of the coming of the Lord."

When he finished, there was hardly a dry eye in the church—including for Martin himself, who was overcome with emotion. Earlier, he'd had me copy out several stanzas of "The Battle Hymn of the Republic," which included "His truth is marching on," the line he'd planned to use as a conclusion. Caught up in the inspiration of the moment, he forgot to deliver the line.

In that speech, he also spoke about me, about how we had traveled the Jericho Road together in Israel. He connected our travel to that of the Good Samaritan, who picked up a wounded man who'd been beaten by robbers. Most of the others traveling by considered what would happen to them if they stopped. But the Good Samaritan asked, "What will happen *to him*, the wounded man, if I don't stop?" Martin said that this was the question we must ask when considering the plight of others, like the striking sanitation workers: "What will happen if we don't stop to help them?"

Better than anyone else, Martin knew what those who loved him could not bear to contemplate: that his time on earth was not long. Without being morbid, he tried to prepare his family, his friends, and his congregation. On February 4, 1968, at Ebenezer, he had preached "The Drum Major Instinct," a sermon that had always seemed to me the most fitting eulogy for him. In those days, the SCLC had a national radio station that broadcast the speech, and I had a staff member make me a copy. One evening, my sister, Edythe, and I settled back in my home to listen to it. When we reached the part in the tape at which Martin talked about his funeral, Edythe, who loved Martin dearly, shook her head.

"Corrie," she whispered, "Martin is definitely not going to be with us long."

Usually I was quick with an optimistic retort. This time, it seemed I had run out of words of hope. I did not answer my sister. I merely pretended not to hear.

On the afternoon of April 4, I took Yolanda shopping for an Easter dress, having bought the boys Easter suits the Friday before. I had not been home very long when the telephone in my bedroom rang. It was 7:08 p.m.

For most of our married lives, Martin and I knew that one day there would be a scene like this, a moment that would take one (or both) of us away from the other forever. But no matter how many times you rehearse it, it never feels real until it happens.

The caller was Jesse Jackson.

"Coretta, you had better take the next thing smokin'. Doc has been shot."

Again, I thought about how Martin had tried to prepare me for the inevitable. *You know I probably won't live a long life. When I die, I don't want you to grieve for me. You go on and live a normal life.*

Still, I held out hope that Martin was alive, and asked for details. Jesse tried to spare me. "He was shot in the shoulder."

"Where is he?"

"They've taken him to St. Joseph's Hospital, but maybe you should come to the Lorraine Motel, where we're staying, and we'll take you. . . . No, maybe you should go to the hospital; no, why don't you just come here?"

I turned on the television. I saw Martin's face, and the commentator in the background talking about how my husband had been shot on the balcony at the Lorraine Motel. By that time, all of the kids except Bunny had run into my bedroom. I tried to turn the news off, but I was too late. "Oh no, don't tell me!" Yolanda cried and ran back out of the room. In a few seconds, Andy Young called.

"Have you heard about Martin?" he asked.

"Jesse called me."

"Well, I tell you, it's pretty bad, and you need to come right away. He's not dead yet," he added. "He's still alive."

The fact that Andy had to say that made me feel like this was going to be fatal. Martin wouldn't live; I had that strong sense.

But I did what I always did in a crisis: I remained calm. I could have broken down and gone to pieces, but I didn't. I kept trying to think about how I had to hold up for my children.

"You need to bring somebody," Andy said to me.

"Juanita Abernathy. I've called her and she's coming."

"Yeah, bring her, and somebody else, too. Bring Dora McDonald."

Dora McDonald was Martin's secretary. She always seemed to have things under control, and everybody in the office admired her. She was always calm in her demeanor; you never saw her going to pieces.

The phone kept ringing. Atlanta mayor Ivan Allen called to say he was coming over and would provide me with a police escort to the airport.

He came with his wife; Christine and Isaac, Martin's sister and brother-in-law, also came, and we all went to the airport together.

As I was getting ready to leave, seven-year-old Dexter asked me, "Mommy, when is Daddy coming home?"

I took a deep breath. "Dexter, you know Daddy got shot in Memphis today, and I don't really know when he is coming home. When I get there, I'll let you know the answer."

I kissed the children good-bye and headed to the airport. As soon as we got there, I heard a page over the public address system. It was for me. This is probably it, I thought then. The mayor said, "Let's get the page at the gate."

In the meantime, I saw Dora McDonald coming, walking real fast, straight toward me. "Mrs. King, let's find someplace to sit down where I can talk to you."

And in that moment I knew Martin was dead.

The only place we could find was the ladies' restroom, in the outer part, near the counter. I saw Dora's pained expression. We embraced and held on to each other. I began weeping. Finally, the mayor just walked on in and said very formally, "Mrs. King, I have the sad responsibility as mayor of the city of Atlanta to inform you that your husband is dead. Would you like to go on to Memphis, or would you like to stay here for the night and go in the morning?"

"I need to stay here and go back and see about the kids. I'll go in the morning."

There was nothing I could do now. On the way home, I had an agonizing conversation with myself. What am I going to tell the kids? How would I tell them? I had to think about all the arrangements that had to be made. So much to be done.

I've got to prepare myself. I've got to be strong, I thought.

It was the Lenten season, leading up to Passion Week. Martin often made analogies in life to Good Friday and Easter. "We go through our Gethsemanes as Christ did, but then Easter comes and there is a rebirth and a resurrection," he would say. So I thought about how this was a good time for him to go, to be identified with Christ and His suffering: Like Christ, Martin will be resurrected in the faith and actions of his people. His spirit will live on. Just thinking about the parallels in his life with that of Jesus gave me some consolation, which I sorely needed. I had to go deep within to find the inspiration to go home and face my children.

When I returned home, my youngest child, five-year-old Bunny, was asleep. Yolanda was sitting, calmly waiting for me in the foyer. "Mommy, I'm not going to cry," she said. "I'm not going to cry because my daddy's really not dead. His spirit will never die, and I will see him in heaven."

Even as she insisted that she wasn't crying, tears were streaming down her soft little cheeks. "Mommy, should I hate the man who killed my daddy?" she asked.

"No, darling. Your daddy wouldn't want you to do that."

Marty seemed confused. He didn't want to talk at all.

Earlier, Dexter had asked me, "When is Daddy coming home?" and trying to answer the question that was breaking my heart, I'd said, "Do you know your daddy was shot?" But Dexter had no concept of death or the finality of what had happened, and I wasn't ready to attempt to explain further, so I told him to go to sleep and promised that I would talk to him in the morning.

That night, I received a call from Ralph. The authorities needed my permission to perform an autopsy. I was so tired and drained. I told him that I thought Martin would have wanted it, but said, "You make the decision, Ralph."

Calls were pouring in, offering help and condolences. President Johnson called. He proclaimed Sunday, April 7, a national day of mourning. Harry Belafonte called to say he would be at my side. But nothing anyone could have said or done would have eased the sorrow welling in my heart. I talked to Daddy King, who was understandably heartbroken. "I always felt I would go first," he said through his tears. A.D. had flown into Memphis to be with Martin on the day he died. Even as adults, they had kidded each other and wrestled much as they had as boys. In fact, hours before Martin died, he and A.D. were horsing around with each other, having a pillow fight. They even used to play tricks on Mama King by calling and disguising their voices, each one claiming to be the other. A.D. was terribly distraught. A year later he, too, would be dead, but I believe he began dying the same day his brother died.

The next morning, I rose early to get to Memphis and talk to the many callers expressing sympathy. Among them was Sen. Bobby Kennedy, who offered a private plane to bring back Martin's body. I accepted the offer gratefully as a gesture of friendship, though Ralph and Andy questioned my decision because of the political implication of Bobby being a political candidate. Senator Kennedy also arranged to put in three more phone lines in our home to handle the continuous flow of callers.

On Friday morning, I flew to Memphis. Martin's sister, Christine, her husband, Isaac, and Jean Young, Juanita Abernathy, Fred Bennette, Dora McDonald, and Bill Rutherford of SCLC waited with me inside the plane while Martin's body was brought aboard. When I saw the casket being lowered . . . the moment froze in my mind. My beloved Martin, the love of my life, was gone from me. The finality of that was overwhelming.

We landed back in Atlanta, where hundreds of people had gathered at the airport. Ralph, Andy, and Bernard Lee flew back to Atlanta with us. The children were brought to meet us and boarded the plane; Andy took Bunny in his arms. I remembered then that I'd left without preparing them to see their father in a casket. I hadn't really talked to any of them, except Yoki, or done enough to help them understand that their father was dead. But how do you explain such things to a five-year-old? I took Bunny from Andy and held her in my arms. She was innocently bouncing around. "Mommy, mommy, where is my daddy?" she asked.

I didn't say anything, couldn't find the words. "Mommy, where is my daddy?" she repeated.

I thought, my God, how can I tell her? I don't know what to say.

Finally, I spoke. "Bunny, you know your daddy is asleep in the back of the plane and he's lying there in his casket. When you see him, he won't be able to speak to you. His spirit has gone to live with God."

"Is he hungry?" she asked before becoming very quiet. As a family, we stood in the doorway of the plane; somebody wanted to photograph us standing together.

I have looked at that picture many times over the years. It is such a perfect image: everyone has the right expression, the one that reflects his or her feelings at that moment. We have forlorn looks on our faces, every last one of us.

We left the airport and went on to Hanley's Funeral Home. I was concerned about what Martin would look like, as the bullet had severely shattered his jaw. The undertakers had patched his face, however, and it looked pretty good.

When the kids saw their father's body at the funeral home, I thought it would help them understand. Bunny still didn't say anything when she saw him, nor did she ask any questions. I wanted to explain death to her, not its finality, but its continuation of life through the spirit. That's a difficult concept to explain to children, though. In retrospect, I regret that I didn't better prepare Bernice and Dexter, my younger children, but I did the best I could.

The family decided to have Martin lie in state in Sisters Chapel at Spelman College from Saturday afternoon until Monday afternoon. Then he was carried to Ebenezer Baptist Church to stay until the funeral on Tuesday.

Many thousands of people of all classes and colors waited for hours to pay their last respects to my husband. When I went with the children to Ebenezer on Monday, lines of people stretched around the block. For so long, Martin had been in the heart and soul of the masses. Now they wanted their time with him. I kept saying to myself, "Oh, I wish he knew how much people loved him." I remembered the times he had been depressed and needed a lift. If only he could have seen how much his sacrifices meant to people.

The news of Martin's death was televised to the world. His murder reverberated through the national psyche like the assassination of JFK or Abraham Lincoln, or the bombing of Pearl Harbor. Virtually everyone could remember what he or she was doing when they heard the terrible news. People expressed their grief in many different ways. They cried. They gathered in churches across America and told their stories about meeting Martin, about working with him. There were prayers for us, his family.

And some rioted.

The impact of my husband's assassination was felt deeply by millions around the world, but it resonated especially in black neighborhoods. Some people took their grief to the streets. Riots hit more than one hundred cities across the nation. Washington, DC, was hit the hardest. The violence, the fires, and the shootings were such ironic tributes to a prophet of nonviolence. Yet, I understood the language of despair, even though I could not condone it.

Atlanta, where we lived, was one of the few cities that did not go up in flames, and I believe that was because many of us, white and black leaders alike, went on the offensive. That Saturday, I made a statement saying that nothing could hurt Martin more than for those he left behind to solve their problems with violence. "He gave his life in search of a more excellent way," I said, "a more effective way, a creative rather than a destructive way. He never hated. He never despaired of well doing and he encouraged us to do likewise."

That was my first press conference without Martin. It gave me a strange, empty feeling.

On Monday, I took another out-of-character step. With coaching from Harry Belafonte, I decided to continue with the march in Memphis. Harry had told me, "People across the nation are so down. If you could find the strength to go to Memphis, if people could see your strength and determination, it would lift their spirits." Immediately, I thought, this is what Martin would want me to do. It felt right. I would finish what Martin and the movement had started. As I thought about the perpetrators of this evil act, I said to myself, they only killed his physical body. They can't kill his spirit.

For fourteen years, I had been with Martin in the thicket of controversy. My husband and I had been emotional twins. He thought of me as so close I was only a heartbeat away. I was his confidante. He was my best friend. I was his best student. He was the icing on my cake, the cream in my coffee. We could finish each other's sentences, feel each other's wounds, and share each other's jokes. Now I had to stand in for him, representing us both, without him.

That Monday, I flew to Memphis on a private plane provided by Harry. Along with Harry, I took Yoki, Marty, and Dexter, as well as Justine Smadbeck, who as director of the Jessie Smith Noyes Foundation had granted me a scholarship to the New England Conservatory of Music. We were rushed from the airport by limousine to the head of the march. Only about a month ago, there had been eight thousand people prepared to march. Now more than six times that many had gathered.

We marched for about a mile to City Hall, where many speeches applauding Martin's life were given. The children, still in somewhat of a daze, needed to hear others saying such good things about their father.

A speech had been prepared for me, too, but when I looked at it, it seemed so flat that I spoke without notes, from the heart. I challenged the crowds to "see that Martin's spirit never dies, and that we will go forward from this experience, which to me represents the Crucifixion, on toward the Resurrection and the redemption of the Spirit."

I ended with a question: "How many must die before we can really have a free and true and peaceful society? If we can catch the spirit and the true meaning of this experience, I believe this nation can be transformed into a society of love, justice, and brotherhood, where all men can really be brothers."

I learned later that when I stepped forward that day, some news reports said I was making my debut as a leader. That was not my objective. I had a commitment even larger than Martin's. I wanted to be useful and available to God, and I was praying to God for direction, a way to perfect my life after Martin and to continue our work and follow the calling we had both cherished. I was separated from Martin now, but never from the movement, never from the Cause.

As the day of Martin's homegoing grew closer, time seemed to stand still and hover over me like a heavy cloud. The preparation, however, made the process easier to bear. As long as I kept myself busy, I didn't have time to cry. The planning was therapy.

In planning the homegoing, I kept foremost in my mind what Martin would have wanted. I also wanted to ensure that people who came would have some opportunity to be part of a service. Eventually, we had to create two services. One was an outdoor memorial at Morehouse College, where Martin was an undergraduate and where Dr. Benjamin Mays, who was Martin's mentor, had been president.

The family also wanted to have a march. This would be Martin's last march.

But how would we transport Martin's body? We felt that he should have something fancy, like the kind of caisson that carries the bodies of presidents. Yet, we also wanted something simple.

"What about the mule train that Martin talked about taking to Washington during the Poor People's Campaign?" A.D. suggested.

Gosh, that's a great idea, I thought. Martin would like that.

This meant finding the mule and the wagon. Hosea Williams was very good at handling creative situations of this kind. He searched around and actually found a wagon outside an antique store. But this was the day before the funeral, and the store was closed; they couldn't ask the owner for it, so they borrowed it. (Of course they took it back!)

Next, Hosea and the others found some mules on a farm outside Atlanta. I was elated about the mule and wagon carrying Martin because he'd been so excited by the idea of taking mule trains from Mississippi through Jackson, on through Alabama and Georgia and into Washington. The mule, which was used in farming, symbolized poverty and the desperate plight of the poor in this country.

There was much debate about the eulogy. Christine, Edythe, and Martin's secretary, Dora McDonald, had joined me at our home to discuss it. We fought back tears and an overwhelming feeling of grief as we tried to decide who would preach it. Christine told me that no one could do it better than Martin himself had months before, at Ebenezer.

"Every now and then I think about my own death," he had told the congregation. "Tell them not to talk too long," he said, but added his hope that they would say that "Martin Luther King tried to give his life to serving others. Yes, if you want to say that I was a drum major, say that I was a drum major for justice. Say that I was a drum major for peace—I was a drum major for righteousness—and all the other shallow things will not matter."

I had a copy of the recording which I had listened to with my sister only a few months before. I listened to it again at two in the morning, before the homegoing service. The rightness of using it fell upon me.

Early on the morning of the funeral, I greeted a steady stream of mourners, from Hollywood celebrities to neighborhood residents, at our home. At one point, I looked up and saw that someone had escorted Jacqueline Kennedy back to my bedroom, where I was receiving a few guests. I had felt deeply for her when her husband was assassinated only five years earlier. Her visit inspired me; I had always admired the grace and dignity she exemplified in the aftermath of President Kennedy's death. Her strength and courage helped lift and hold a nation together. I will never forget that, on the day of JFK's funeral, she invited a group of children upstairs at the White House to celebrate John John's birthday with a party. That was her way of trying to create a normal life for her children.

Likewise, I didn't want my children to get caught up in the tragedy of their father's death or the aftermath of the riots that followed. I wanted them to go on living as normally as possible. The way Jackie conducted herself helped me understand that I could get through this, too. I saw her as a model of what could be done.

"Oh, how nice of you to come," I told her. "You have been a great inspiration for me. I know how difficult this must be for you."

I extended my hand. I have a tendency to hug people, and I wanted to embrace her, but I could see that was not what she wanted. In fact, I could feel the tension in our handshake. She was very formal. Maybe she did not feel she knew me well enough to be any different. She looked at me and said, in reference to the address I made after the march I had led in Memphis, "You speak so well." I thanked her.

At the funeral, my children each handled their grief differently. Yoki told me, "I was thinking about myself, and I don't know what I would do if I were in your shoes."

My goodness, how mature she is for her twelve years, I thought. She's lost her father, but she's empathizing with me as the mother and the widow because she knows I've had to take care of everything in the family. She showed so much grace, and I was so proud of her. She cried a little at the funeral, but she never broke down and cried for days, like some kids can. In fact, none of the children did.

I believe Marty was confused. He did not say much. It was like he didn't know *what* to say. Dexter tried to express himself. "My daddy has gone to the heaven in the sky, but his spirit is alive," he told me, but I could tell he was just repeating what he'd been told. The boys were too young to make sense of murder, death, and eternity.

Little Bunny sat next to me during the homegoing service. It was April and very warm. At one point, she lay in my lap. We were captured in a Pulitzer Prize–winning photograph by Moneta Sleet Jr., for *Ebony* magazine. Another photograph from the funeral, captured by photographer Flip Schulke, appeared on the cover of *Life* magazine. The expression on my face in that photograph, which a reporter called the "Mona Lisa smile," aptly captured my great sense of fulfillment: in the end, the service was so beautiful.

When it came time for Martin's taped voice to be played for his eulogy, the sound of her father's voice confused Bunny. I believe she thought he was speaking from his casket. Over the years, she had to struggle with the fear of funerals and of death, of people coming back to life. Lots of children make these types of associations as they personalize death. With time, and after other experiences with death, she became able to manage those feelings, although she has never fully overcome them.

When we came out of the church and into the sunlight, we saw tens of thousands of people standing in the streets, having listened to the service over loudspeakers. Together, we began our march from Ebenezer to Morehouse College for the memorial service. We marched because Martin had spent so much of his life marching for justice and freedom. We were awed and deeply grateful that more than 150,000 people marched with him. It was the most meaningful, inspiring march Martin ever led.

I couldn't march all the way from Ebenezer to Morehouse with the funeral procession, however; the effects of my fibroid tumor surgery lingered, and I didn't want to overexert myself. I marched part of the way to Morehouse with the kids, and rode the rest of the way.

We were almost at the college when Bunny asked me, "Mommy, how is Daddy going to eat?" I struggled with what to say; I thought about saying something like "Well, he'll eat angel food cake," but I couldn't. I didn't say anything, hoping that she would soon forget it and wouldn't keep asking me questions.

Finally, we made it to Morehouse. It was a long, hard way—the rush and press of so many people, the slow clop-clop of the mules. As our procession passed, the huge crowds fell silent. Some knelt in prayer.

After the prayers and Scripture readings, Mahalia Jackson sang "Precious Lord, Take My Hand," which Martin had asked tenor saxophonist Ben Branch to play for him at a rally that would have taken place only hours after his assassination. Dr. Benjamin E. Mays spoke. Then it was time for the interment. A.D. had been escorting me throughout the day. As we reached the grave site, he turned to me and said, "Coretta, I can't go any further with you."

I understood. The grave site was the hardest part. It's such a separation. "Okay," I said, but I knew I had to have someone with me. So I turned to Harry, who was by my side. "I would like you and my daddy to surround me as we go to the cemetery."

I had a terrible feeling about leaving Martin there. When we were readying ourselves to go home, Bunny asked, "What's a spirit?"

Helplessly, I asked my sister, Edythe, "How do you explain spirit to a five-year-old?" Then I said, "Bunny, you know people loved your daddy, and he loved them. He loved everybody." I put my arms around her and said, "Bunny, I love you." I thought that if I could just convey a feeling of warmth and security to her, maybe she would get the meaning of how your body can die but leave behind a loving spirit, which lives forever.

That was the best I could do.

In the deep sorrow of the day, I was comforted by the thought that, at the end, we had all done our best for Martin.

"They may have killed the dreamer," I thought, "but they will never kill his dream."

I vowed that I would carry that dream forward. I prayed that my children and all our supporters could see that my Martin's spirit, strong and determined, would carry forth and his work would live on.

———— ✹ ————

SIXTEEN

With a Prayer in My Heart,
I Could Greet the Morning

MARTIN IS GONE. He's just . . . *gone.*

How many times I must have repeated that to myself over and over and over. It was like the saying of it could somehow confirm this surreal new reality.

There were times when I would open my eyes with the joyous expectation of Martin being there. Then it would hit me like a cold chill: He was not there, and he was never going to be there again. Never. I had to let him go. There is nothing like finality, the presence of an absolute absence.

I never cried in public because I did not want to project an image of weakness or negativity. I wanted the public to know that the King family had the strength to love, to forgive, and to go on despite this great tragedy that had beset us. But when I was alone, the tears would roll down my cheeks in torrents. In our bedroom, the scent of his Old Spice cologne lingered in the lining of his best black pinstripe suit in the closet. In the bathroom, his toothbrush faced mine. There was the imprint on the sheets where he had lain, his shoes, some muddy and scuffed from marches, neatly lined up on racks. It all made Martin seem near—and yet so far away.

We had talked about it, joked about it, prayed about it. He had prepared me, but when death actually arrived, the feeling of separation was overwhelming. Our bedroom was filled with emptiness. My nights were lonely. In church, the preachers often said that suffering would endure for a night, and joy would come in the morning. But, I assure you, morning does not return without a long passage through the lonely nights of heartache. Sometimes I felt that my joy would never return.

For months, I tried to console myself with the knowledge that Martin was in a better place and was happy. I knew I was crying for myself, feeling sorry for myself. Martin wouldn't want me to weep over him.

I was no longer a wife, but I was still a parent—and a single parent at that. This was the motivating thought that kept me going. No matter what else I did, I had to be a mother first. I had to *say* to myself, "You are a mother first." It took that kind of self-talk to get me out of bed in the morning. Sometimes I just wanted to stay there under the covers. But I could not break down. I did not want my children to see me out of control, because then they might lose their way. So I had my cry before I came out of my room, and then I opened the door with a forceful determination I had never known before. I did not just open it; I thrust it open. But it required determination that came from beyond myself.

When I came out of my bedroom, I had to leave my feelings, my heartaches, and my anxieties behind. It almost felt like getting in character for one of my operatic performances. I had to step out of the fog of painful reality into a zone where I could perform as a mother and comfort others. Sometimes I paused at the door, my hand on the knob, making sure I had my emotions in check. Then, with a prayer in my heart and a smile on my face, I could greet the morning.

While my first love was my children, I also understood that I had to spread myself across a great span, keeping my husband's mission alive and institutionalizing his legacy. I had to keep it present, relevant. And I had to continue my own mission, working for world peace abroad and nonviolence here at home. In death as in life, we have to go on.

For my children, the way was not easy. They each had to wrestle with and endure major problems. The loss of their father to an assassin's bullet was catastrophic. The riots and the looting that followed were so at odds with our principles of nonviolence that they were deeply confused. All of them had questions. They could not understand why their father, the prophet of nonviolence, had met such a violent end. They wondered if that same fate would take me from them. For a time after the assassination,

Bunny would pore through family photo albums and ask me who would be the next to die. Fears about death plagued her.

I think my two oldest children, Yoki and Marty, handled the passing of their father a little better than Bunny because they had such strong, wonderful memories of Martin. Because she was only five years old when he was taken from her, Bunny was more deeply scarred and confused. I worried about what was going on deep down inside her because she was always the quietest of my children. After school, all the children would report on what they'd learned, but when it was Bunny's turn, she'd often say, "I don't have anything to share."

How do you get children to love and trust others when they have been confronted with such devastating loss? One thing that was very important to me as a parent was always to set a good example in front of my children. You cannot tell children to act one way and behave differently yourself.

I have always tried to conduct myself in an honest and moral way, a commitment I made long before marrying Martin. As a Scott, I had high moral standards instilled in me at a young age. And basic concepts of honesty, love of neighbor, and helping others were ethics I tried to teach my children by the way I carried myself, the way I loved others, no matter how they treated me and the issues I championed. There were causes that I championed and others that Martin gave priority, but after his death, our causes, our callings, became one.

In the months immediately following Martin's death, thousands of requests poured in from all over the world, asking me to speak on behalf of Martin, accept awards in his name, and discuss issues that were important to me. Of course, I could not accept them all. I often felt overwhelmed, pulled in too many different directions. I engaged in constant prayer, calling upon God to guide me on the right path. I was in perpetual motion, trying to accept the many awards and recognitions.

In January 1969, my friend and special assistant Bernita Bennette and I left for a trip to India. Before arriving in the country, we stopped over in Verona, Italy, where the government bestowed upon me the San Valentino ("Universal Love") Award. I was the first black person and first non-Italian to receive this honor. We also stopped in Rome, where I had an audience with Pope Paul VI at Vatican City.

In New Delhi, I accepted the Jawaharlal Nehru Award, which was being posthumously given to Martin in a ceremony at New Delhi University. While in India, I addressed university groups, rallies, and a group of so-called untouchables, thus building on the relationships Martin and I had established when we visited India in 1959.

In March 1969, Bernita and I, along with my sister, Edythe, and sister-in-law Christine, traveled to London, where I became the first woman to preach a statutory service at St. Paul's Cathedral. Standing there in my academic gown and hat, upon the spot where Martin had preached en route to his acceptance of the Nobel Peace Prize in 1964, I found myself deeply moved. The British Martin Luther King Jr. Foundation had invited me to London, and the insight I gained there into the ways other nations were institutionalizing my husband's vision inspired me.

During that time abroad, I could feel myself making progress in my inner healing. I talked not of sorrow but of the privilege of being able to follow that which was meaningful and fulfilling to me. I urged the British to address their own racial issues through the power of nonviolence. I also had an opportunity to speak and share my concerns with Mrs. Harold Wilson, wife of British prime minister Harold Wilson, at No. 10 Downing Street. And before leaving Europe, I rekindled my singing career, performing Freedom Concerts in England, Germany, and Holland.

This rush of international invitations shortly after Martin's death was a humbling reminder that our mission was respected on a global stage. I had long understood civil and human rights to be a global challenge. How could I look at the downtrodden (the untouchables in India, for example) and not connect them to the same forces that had attempted to develop a caste system at home? The principles of nonviolence and the creation of a Beloved Community, in which every individual would be respected and treated with dignity, resonated in every corner of the globe.

But while I welcomed the opportunity to share our message, I could not keep my suitcase packed and continue on this sort of global trek forever. I had to settle down and focus, to find the place at which I could make the greatest difference to the human condition. I had an idea of what I had to do as an institution builder, but with so much coming at me simultaneously, I had to reflect seriously on what course I would take as an activist working to shape public policy.

At times, I felt my road ahead would be a lonely one. Martin had always had me, but now I had to go on without him. These feelings of loneliness, however, didn't last long. All around me, I had a strong nexus of family and friends, including Edythe and her son, Arturo, who came to live with me for the two years after Martin's death. Edythe even took a leave of absence from work. Christine, a professor at Spelman College, her husband, Isaac, and Martin's brother, A.D., and his wife, Naomi, were also staunch sources of support. Of course, I had my own mother and father and Daddy and Mama King, all powerhouses of love. And there were my friends, like Cecil and Frances Thomas, from my Lincoln Normal days, and Fran Lucas from my Antioch days, and Robert and Lettie Green, friends since the early 1960s. Harry Belafonte had continuously been a financial help as well as an adviser, and Andrew Young also pitched in as a surrogate father.

So I never had to walk alone, despite those nagging feelings in the early years that this would be my path.

As I sorted out the five-year to-do list that would carry me through 1968 and into the mid-1970s, I realized that my priorities would shift from time to time. However, I believed my immediate concerns had to include continuing my campaign against the Vietnam War and fighting for livable wages and better conditions for workers, the cause Martin gave his life for in Memphis.

I had long been a vocal opponent of the Vietnam War, and Martin had made many enemies when he came forward in April 1967 at Riverside Church in New York City to oppose that war; much of the black clergy and, especially, many white Americans thought he had overstepped the bounds of his civil rights mandates that day. But in the aftermath of Martin's death, I gained another perspective that further fueled my opposition to the Vietnam War, and not just to that war, but to all future military conflicts. First of all, the war generated a climate of violence that too easily poisoned our national life and sickened our national character. Night after night, the horrors of war, such as the napalming of innocent civilians, were brought into our living rooms through the national news. Children saw other children horribly killed. The frequency of war, the grossness of its horrors, and the instant communication of them are among the elements that pepper our culture with violence, and create an insensitivity to it. If we as a culture become numb to the sight of bombers destroying the inhabitants of whole villages and towns, then surely it becomes psychologically easier for a small group or an individual to plan the assassination of one man.

With me, assassinations are not some vague, general topic of discussion. They are the reason I do not have a husband. I do not regard the murder of my husband, of John Kennedy, or of Robert Kennedy as aberrations or random acts by deranged individuals. They were political acts in both motivation and consequence. Is it a mere coincidence that, shortly before their deaths, these eminent public figures were seeking social progress and fighting particularly to end racial inequality and war? If we face the ugly truths that bigotry has not only been abrasive to the black man and dealt a false sense of superiority and entitlement to the white man, but has also generated a spirit of violence that has deformed the internal compass of our whole society, we will begin to understand how those significant forces of violence have shaped us all. To lose great men to assassination and young men and women to the unnecessary violence of war is intolerable. It is a terrible scar on our national character that will continue to haunt us in uncivil, corrupt ways for centuries to come—unless we dare to change.

These thoughts fueled my resolve to continue speaking out against the Vietnam War. On April 27, 1968, less than a month after Martin's death, I agreed to play a major role in a rally in New York City by the Spring Mobilization Committee to End the War in Vietnam, a national coalition of antiwar activists. I marched with protesters around Central Park, and then I addressed their gathering. This is what I shared:

My dear friends of peace and freedom, I come to New York today with a strong feeling that my dearly beloved husband, who was snatched suddenly from our midst slightly more than three weeks ago now, would have wanted me to be present today.

Though my heart is heavy with grief from having suffered an irreparable personal loss, my faith in the redemptive will of God is stronger today than ever before. . . .

I would like to share with you some notes taken from my husband's pockets upon his death. He carried these scraps of paper upon which he scribbled notes for his many speeches. . . .

Perhaps they were his early thoughts for the message he was to give to you today. I am sure he would have developed and delivered them in his usual eloquent and inspired fashion. I simply read them to you as he recorded them. And I quote, "Ten Commandments on Vietnam":

1. *Thou shalt not believe in a military victory.*
2. *Thou shall not believe in a political victory.*
3. *Thou shall not believe that they, the Vietnamese, love us.*
4. *Thou shall not believe that the Saigon government has the support of the people.*
5. *Thou shall not believe that the majority of the South Vietnamese look upon the Vietcong as terrorists.*
6. *Thou shalt not believe the figures of killed enemies or killed Americans.*
7. *Thou shall not believe that the generals know best.*
8. *Thou shalt not believe that the enemy's victory means communism.*
9. *Thou shall not believe that the world supports the United States.*
10. *Thou shall not kill.*

These are Martin Luther King's "Ten Commandments on Vietnam."

You who have worked with and loved my husband so much, you who have kept alive the burning issue of war in the American conscience, you who will not be deluded by talk of peace, but who press on in the knowledge that the work of peacemaking must continue until the last gun is silent.

In this speech, I went on to address the women in the audience directly:

The woman power of this nation can be the power which makes us whole and heals the rotten community, now so shattered by war and poverty and racism. I have great faith in the power of women who will dedicate themselves wholeheartedly to the task of remaking our society. . . .

With this determination, with this faith, we will be able to create new homes, new communities, new cities, and a new nation. Yes, a new world, which we desperately need!

After the Spring Mobilization Rally, I delivered a similar message in June 1968, when I became the first woman to deliver a Class Day address at Harvard University. In that address, I continued my opposition to the war and called for an end to our aerial bombing of North Vietnam. Those were the first speeches I gave after my husband's death, and on the subject of war, I would continue to seek many opportunities and work countless hours to help our nation and our communities choose peace, not violence.

One such effort took place in February 1969. I attended a conference held by the group Clergy and Laymen Concerned About Vietnam at the Metropolitan African Methodist Episcopal Church in Washington, DC, a church famous for its activism. Frederick Douglass had spoken there, and so had my husband. After the conference, I led a delegation to the White House for a meeting with Henry Kissinger, who was then serving as national security adviser to President Nixon. The Rev. William Sloan Coffin, chaplain of Yale University, accompanied me. We presented Kissinger with a proposal to grant amnesty to those who had been imprisoned for refusing to accept deployment to Vietnam, as well as those who had fled to Canada to escape the draft.

Not much came from that meeting. Eight years passed before President Carter offered unconditional amnesty to those who had refused to be conscripted into military service during Vietnam. So I was taken by surprise by an encounter I had with Henry Kissinger in the mid-1980s, during the Reagan-Bush administration. After a "get acquainted" visit to Vice President George H. W. Bush, I came out of the meeting to find former secretary of state Henry Kissinger waiting to see me. We chatted briefly, and he reminded me of our 1969 meeting. I was impressed that he remembered, especially since I had been in his company several times since and we had made only polite conversation.

He said, "Mrs. King, you know something? You all were right and we were wrong about Vietnam."

To hear him say that after all those years was quite remarkable.

* * *

BACK IN THE late 1960s, I not only spoke out against the war but also sent a clear signal that I would always continue to fight for the rights of the poor. In May 1968, I turned my attention to the Poor People's March, which Martin had envisioned as a nonviolent protest focusing on broad economic issues, as opposed to the racial issues we had campaigned against in the past.

On May 2, I advanced the cause for the Poor People's March from the balcony of the Lorraine Motel, the very site where my husband had been killed a month earlier. Standing there, I began to relive that awful moment, but I pushed these thoughts away, fighting to keep my focus off myself. After all, I was there doing what Martin would have done. I was furthering the Dream.

The more I thought about this, the stronger I felt. The more I encouraged the crowd, the more I came alive. As I stood there, I felt a strange sense of camaraderie flowing between the protesters and me. Our hopes and aspirations had spontaneously connected in some way.

Perhaps it was then that I truly understood: I could heal as I pressed on. I could not wait until I felt better to heal; I just had to run on and let the healing catch up with me.

A few weeks later, I led the Mother's Day Parade beside Ethel Kennedy, the wife of Sen. Bobby Kennedy, an event that brought together more than five thousand welfare mothers to march in Washington, DC. We highlighted the plight of poor women and children, showing how, from rural Appalachia to the urban ghettos, children were going to bed hungry, their mothers unable to afford decent medical care. Ethel and I immediately forged a relationship, one that was not just superficial but heartfelt. I could never have imagined that only a month after she and I marched together, we would find ourselves sharing another bond: the assassination of our husbands.

In the wee hours of the morning on June 5, 1968, I received word that presidential candidate Bobby Kennedy had been shot as he walked through the kitchen of the Ambassador Hotel in Los Angeles. As soon as I learned of the shooting, I got on the first available plane to California, where I joined Ethel at Good Samaritan Hospital. Bobby had a devastating head wound, and although we were all hoping for the best, it was almost certain he would not survive. I checked into a hotel with my friend Bernita Bennette and waited.

It was such a horrible feeling—waiting for someone to die. I'd never had that experience before. I passed the time praying and preparing a statement, and then, at about 4:00 a.m. on June 6, I received the call telling me that Bobby had died two hours earlier. I readied myself to fly back to New York with Ethel and some more of the Kennedy family.

In New York, I checked into the Waldorf, where I stayed to attend the funeral. After the services, we went by train to Arlington Cemetery for the interment. There, the press caught up with me to tell me that the man alleged to have killed Martin, James Earl Ray, had been caught. They asked me to comment, but I did not. I was at Arlington to pay my respects to the Kennedy family, not to become the center of attention.

It was such a tragic time. First JFK, then Martin, and now Bobby. The hate in America kept piling up and striking down our nation's best and brightest. It was so demoralizing. Black people had lost their great hero when Martin died. Now white people, the liberals and the idealists, had lost their great hero, too. In a profound way, all of us had lost.

Bobby, Ethel, Jackie, and other members of the Kennedy family had been by my side at Martin's funeral, and now, just a few months later, we were joined again in a ritual that seemed never ending.

After the service, to change the sad tone, Rose Kennedy and I talked about motherhood. Recalling that she had raised ten children, I asked her what her secret for good parenting was.

"You train the older ones well, and they will help you with the others," she said, smiling.

After Bobby's funeral, I was drenched in sadness, but it was a consolation to get right back to work fighting for the causes that were important to him and to Martin.

After the Mother's Day Parade, I started receiving calls from various women's organizations that, I believe, saw me as a symbol for women. They wanted me to convene and head a coalition of women's groups across various religions and ethnicities, whose collective membership topped one hundred thousand.

I was certainly in solidarity with their request. I felt deeply that women were the conscience of the family, and we could be the conscience of the nation, too. We were more attuned to protecting the life we had brought into the world; indeed, I felt we were coworkers with God in His creative activity. In the past, I had wanted Martin to organize a women's auxiliary in the SCLC. Although he was less chauvinistic than most men in the movement, he failed to do so.

Unfortunately, I didn't see myself playing such a leadership role with these groups.

I prayed about it, but I didn't feel I had the resources needed to bring this important element together as a whole. And I didn't feel women were really ready to unite and unify. I was still waiting for God to call me and guide me to what I was to do. There were only so many hours in the day, and I had four young children at home. I had to carefully determine where I would focus my efforts. So I turned down these requests from women's organizations, though I knew I would always be not only supportive but also proactive in helping women with good causes reach their goals.

One cause close to Martin's heart, one I chose to make my own, was fighting for workers. Martin was one of the best friends the labor movement had ever had. In fact, he gave his life in Memphis fighting for better wages and working conditions for striking sanitation workers. In 1962 he had also joined workers on the picket line in a Local 1199 drive to organize New York City's independent hospitals, and he called on New York governor Nelson Rockefeller and urged him to support collective bargaining.

In 1969, I went to Baltimore to help local health care workers, many of whom were African American women and single mothers like me. I felt that lending my influence and support, and encouraging them to join up with Local 1199 (the Service Employees International Union) would help them win a better life.

My help with Local 1199 went beyond making a speech. I walked the picket lines outside Johns Hopkins Hospital on Monument Street. Unfortunately, the news stories gave me much more credit than I deserved, claiming that the decisive moment in the drive came when I stood outside the hospital and met with the workers, who were unsure about the possibility of organizing against one of the city's largest and most powerful institutions. Even today, the union's official history states, "When the aides and orderlies of Hopkins showed up to work on that August day and saw Martin Luther King's widow standing strong outside the hospital, they took heart." The hospital officials quickly recognized the union and negotiated substantial pay and benefit improvements. While the fight was won, it was not the result of one person's actions. It was won by hundreds of emboldened nurses, aides, porters, and orderlies.

On the heels of their victory, I agreed to serve as honorary chairperson of 1199's National Organizing Committee. In that capacity, I spearheaded the invitation for other groups to join us in unionizing South Carolina hospitals, and went to South Carolina myself to help organize striking hospital workers. I led marches and rallies; I worked to inspire the strikers to continue fighting for their rights and the rights of their children to lead better lives. Our initiative established the first unionized hospital workers in Charleston.

For more than fifteen years, I worked with 1199 in major cities such as Philadelphia and New York, remaining a close friend and ally and speaking at its conventions and black history programs whenever I could. I also became a stalwart supporter of other unions, since unions and civil rights went hand in hand. They helped fund our causes; we helped them organize their workers. Over the years, I spoke for hundreds of labor groups, such as the Amalgamated Clothing and Textile Workers, the United Furniture Workers, the United Food and Commercial Workers, the Industrial Workers of the World, and the International Ladies' Garment Workers' Union. I worked with both the National Education Association and the American Federation of Teachers. I testified for them when they had important legislation before Congress, such as the Senate Labor Committee's deliberations on behalf of full employment.

Through my union activities, I began to understand the power and the ministry of presence. Sometimes we win just by showing up.

Harry Belafonte helped me understand this quality, too. One day, he and I were sitting in a conference room in Chicago, waiting to discuss the founding of the Congressional Black Caucus with Rep. John Conyers and author Lerone Bennett Jr. Harry gave me an intense look and said, "Coretta, I don't know what your public plans are, but you have more power just sitting in a room than most people. You don't even have to say much. It's your presence that carries so much weight."

When he told me this, I was embarrassed; it crossed my mind that maybe this was a nice way of warning me not to make too many waves around male leaders, so as not to deflate their egos. Still, I took to heart what Harry was saying. I thought about the many occasions when I had shown up in all kinds of places, representing so many causes. This was the Ministry of Presence.

Of course, I also understood that when I showed up, the news media would tag me as "Martin's widow." How well I understood the power of my husband's name and what he represented! But sometimes I wondered how and when people would look beyond the name and see me as a woman of substance and commitment, working for the Cause each day of her life. Regardless of this concern, I tried to bring whatever I could that added impact, life, and hope to great causes that were helpful to humanity.

Though Martin was gone physically, I became acutely aware of how much he remained a part of me spiritually. When we married, our hearts and minds were joined together. As he always said, I was only a heartbeat away from him. We did not have a his-and-hers mission. We were one soul, one goal, one love, one dream. The movement had become embedded in my DNA. It was not something I could choose—or refuse. I knew what I had to do. All that was in me had to focus on keeping the Dream alive. Something had a hold of me; something kept me believing. I could not let go. I came to believe that it was my calling, my purpose in life, to help institutionalize and internationalize the movement and Martin's work. I felt that serving as Martin's partner in the struggle had readied me to continue climbing up toward that mountain top, toward that ideal that Martin had seen but could not reach. Most of Martin's closest aides went on to other agendas and jobs, as would be expected. But I understood clearly that, other than raising my children, I had just one goal: the legacy had to continue. As Martin's other half and the architect of the King legacy, I could play a crucial role as an agent of change, following dutifully as God ordered my steps.

I would go on to champion hundreds of different ones, but my highest public priority had to be giving birth to my "fifth child": an institution to celebrate and advance Martin's cause, mission, and legacy.

———— ❀ ————

SEVENTEEN

My Fifth Child

THROUGHOUT MY LIFE, whenever I didn't pray, things went badly. I would become frustrated and feel out of sync with the will and purpose of God. But whenever my life was guided by prayer, I felt good about what I was doing, and I was able to reach out to other people with love and understanding. In the wake of Martin's death, I pondered and soul-searched, trying to determine my future plans and goals, and of course I prayed. It was during this time of prayer that the idea of creating an institution dedicated to Martin's legacy rose to the top of my life's to-do list.

As John Russwurm, who cofounded the first black American newspaper, *Freedom's Journal*, in 1827, put it, "Who can tell our story better than we ourselves can tell our story?" I knew that if I left our story for others to tell, it would be misinterpreted and maligned. Through twelve and a half short years of ministry, Martin changed the world we lived in. I wanted to ensure that his legacy to humanity lived on—and could be replicated.

So on June 26, 1968, I founded the Martin Luther King, Jr. Memorial Center, and in July, only three months after my husband's assassination, I held a press conference announcing it. Eventually, the name was changed to the Martin Luther King, Jr. Center for Nonviolent Social Change, or the King Center. In those hectic first days after Martin was gone, I worked on the Center right there in my bedroom. I sometimes slept with files of Martin's sermons and news clippings neatly stacked alongside me on the bed—on the side of the bed that only months before had belonged to the love of my life.

I had conceived of the Center as an extension of Martin's personality—not just a place, not just a building, but a spirit, one undergirded with his philosophy of nonviolence and love in action. It would be the official living memorial, a place where we would teach his philosophy, methodology, and strategies of nonviolence in the hope of bringing about social change and eliminating what he called the triple evils of society: poverty, racism, and war. The Center would advocate not just for civil rights but for human rights. It would encourage community and economic development in Atlanta as well as agitate for national political empowerment and promote social and economic justice around the world.

I knew that I did not want the Center to be a monument set only in bricks and mortar, yet I did want a physical memorial as well, and I envisioned a state-of-the-art archive of my husband's sermons, speeches, and other pertinent writings, and also films documenting the civil and human rights movements. I saw conference space for programs devoted to issues such as penal reform, voter registration, economic reform, and training in nonviolent conflict reconciliation. And I wanted a "freedom hall," with an auditorium and meeting rooms, an all-faiths international chapel, an administration building, a memorial park, a community center, a natatorium, and of course a permanent entombment for Martin. Just as, at its best, the White House is viewed in the United States as the People's House, the King Center and its offshoots would offer a snapshot of what a Beloved Community in the World House could become.

Again, by the Beloved Community, I am not talking about a utopian dream of a perfect society in which everyone lives together without conflict. Many artists have produced lovely, bucolic renditions of the "peaceable kingdom," with lions and lambs lying down together and everyone having his or her own vine and fig tree. That is more like heaven than the Beloved Community on earth, which is not a perfect society.

To me, the Beloved Community is a realistic vision of an achievable society, one in which problems and conflict exist, but are resolved peacefully and without bitterness. In the Beloved Community, caring and compassion drive political policies that support the worldwide elimination of poverty and hunger and all forms of bigotry and violence. The Beloved Community is a state of heart and mind, a spirit of hope and goodwill that transcends all boundaries and barriers and embraces all creation. At its core, the Beloved Community is an engine of reconciliation. This way of living seems a long way from the kind of world we have now, but I do believe it is a goal that can be accomplished through courage and determination, and through education and training, if enough people are willing to make the necessary commitment.

In the early years, my mission called for raising the funds to build the Center—to hire staff, implement programs, and build some physical structures. In consultation with my family and a few close friends, who would eventually be put in board positions, I estimated that we needed to raise about twenty million dollars to fulfill this vision. Little did I know that raising the necessary millions would be easy compared to fighting off the gremlins close at hand, who battled me at every stage.

The long road to see this initial project to fruition was filled with difficult moments and what I now know were unnecessary setbacks. These challenges were often very painful for me. Of course, a nice way to describe the opposition and obstacles I encountered would be "growing pains" or "labor pangs," but when I experienced the attacks on my attempts to build the Center, it felt like backstabbing, plain and simple. For years, I have not talked much about this, but now I feel I must speak about the process.

The story of the Center could be an example for anyone who wants to know the truth about institution building, to grasp the flaws and contradictions that lie within the construction of both a human and a concrete infrastructure. I am a process person. To me, the story of establishing the Center includes not just the beginning and the ending, but also what went on in the middle. Throughout the long years, I often wondered if there would someday be an attempt to tell this whole story. Too often, the Center was a one-liner in some news report that gave a brief and unfair assessment of its accomplishments without any attempt to understand its purpose or any acknowledgment that establishing its essential programs and physical facilities took fourteen years of hard work.

Early on, the carping and mean-spirited treatment I experienced from some in the SCLC, the organization my husband cofounded, was very difficult. Almost from the start, some of Martin's chief aides fought my building efforts, saying, "Oh, you know Coretta; she doesn't know what she's doing, and she's just talking." Or, "There goes Coretta; she's just talking big talk, and she can't do that."

In 1973, I was maligned publicly by Rev. Hosea Williams, one of my husband's top assistants, a man who was with Martin in Memphis when he was killed. Reverend Williams attacked me in the media, saying that my fund-raising efforts for the Center were taking money from the SCLC and that I should have divided the money I was raising for the Center with them. Instead of coming to me and asking for funds, he slammed me in the press. He said I wouldn't give the SCLC any money, which was not true. In 1969, for example, the Center had split the proceeds from a screening of the Abby Mann documentary *From Montgomery to Memphis* with the SCLC.

Then Ralph Abernathy joined the fray. He told the media that the SCLC was in poor financial shape, a state that would have been avoided if I had headed its fund-raising efforts or had split the money I'd raised for the Center with the SCLC. I remember Ralph saying, "Now, Mrs. King has a right to found any organization that she chooses, but Martin Luther King Jr. never founded but one organization, and that was the Southern Christian Leadership Conference." In essence, he was saying that there should be only one organization—certainly not mine.

It was clear that what the SCLC leadership really wanted was for me to continue raising funds for them, just as I did when Martin was alive. Sometimes Martin would brag about how the SCLC could make payroll only because of the money I'd brought in through the Freedom Concerts. But now I felt a calling to another role. I had to be about my husband's business and about working for the nation that I wished the United States could become.

After watching these painful attacks on television, I wanted to get up and call some of the reporters I knew and defend myself, but I have always felt that negative or harsh counterclaims only keep the pot boiling. And I certainly did not want to turn up the flame. I just wanted to be faithful to my commitment to the movement.

To this day, I have never understood why Ralph thought I was such a threat to the SCLC. I was simply trying to build an institution that would deal with research, education, and training around my husband's legacy. I never wanted to compete with the SCLC in an area where it had done such a great job. Nobody could have done direct action better. But I felt strongly that younger generations had to be educated and trained, and who better to do that than Martin Luther King Jr.? What better than his message?

At one point, I recommended that the SCLC and the Center conduct leadership training together. I didn't have people out there who had that expertise, but the SCLC leadership refused; they wouldn't cooperate at all. In those early days after Martin's death, the media seemed to focus a lot of their attention on me, and I had the feeling all that attention made some SCLC people uncomfortable. I was Martin's widow, and the media had a tendency to come to me. That's the way it was.

I was on the board of the SCLC for some time; after a while, I stopped attending meetings because I was treated with such disrespect. At the root of their problems with me, I think, was that I appeared to them to be a strong woman, not one to be pushed aside. Remember, this was the early 1970s, and these were primarily Baptist preachers with a strong sense of male superiority. Most thought that women should stay in the shadows; however, I felt that, as women, we had much to contribute. In fact, for the longest time, way before I married Martin, I had believed that women should allow our essence and presence to shine, rather than letting ourselves be buried or shunted to the sidelines.

I was brought up in the southern tradition, and was taught to have manners, to be ladylike and polite. That, however, did not mean allowing other people to walk all over me or treat me like a wallflower. It did not mean allowing some struggles men have with women to overwhelm me. I tried to operate in the strength and the grace of the Holy Spirit, and that kept me going. Once I'd prayed about it and felt I had God's blessing, I never really doubted that I could build a great institution. I knew I could not quit. The naysayers would not stop me. When I didn't know exactly how to begin the venture, I prayed. When I didn't know where to look for funds, I prayed. When critics condemned me without cause, I prayed. And when the physical buildings of the Center were completed, I still prayed, thanking God for how far He had brought us and asking Him to continue His watch, to protect and guide us as we made our way forward.

Also, I remembered that only after death was Martin so loved; while he lived, he was often condemned. Could I really have expected to be treated any differently?

I did so wish for Martin during these tough moments. When he was alive, he had me. But in my crises, I did not have him to lean on. In my darkest hours, I felt so alone. I never stayed fixated on that for long, though; there was too much to gain. The very fact that Martin was gone gave me a fighting spirit, encouraged me to keep building and developing.

With or without the top men in the SCLC, I had to keep building the Center. I just believed that I was going the right way, and when I was able to raise the millions in funds we needed, I saw that as affirmation that I'd done the right thing. When you can raise that kind of money against all odds—well, that in itself is encouraging.

And I believed that if I just kept treating the movement men, even my detractors, in a loving way and working for the higher cause, of service and of keeping Martin's agenda alive, eventually the barriers would come down. This is precisely what happened: Rev. Ben Hooks, formerly with the SCLC, who went on to head the NAACP, came to me and told me what an outstanding job I was doing. For quite a while, he sent checks for a thousand dollars. One of my husband's biographers, Lerone Bennett, complimented me on "doing a miraculous job."

What I found even more rewarding was the about-face from some of the women around me who had initially spoken against me. They had been taught that a woman was supposed to stay at home with the kids. I didn't fit the mold, and they didn't understand what I was doing. When they saw me standing up and speaking out, they seemed to think I was a threat to their way of life. But then, as they watched more closely and saw what I was doing, they began to support us.

Also, far outnumbering the naysayers was a wonderful, supportive network of people, including my family and Martin's family. For example, Christine King Farris, Martin's sister, was absolutely dedicated to helping me with the Center from its inception, working alongside me daily, as did her husband, Isaac Farris Sr. He managed the King Center bookstore and eventually served as the project manager for the construction of the King Center. Daddy King was a strong force who occasionally accompanied me to raise money. Our niece Alveda, one of A.D. and

Naomi's daughters, was one of my first secretaries at the Center. In the early 1980s, Alveda's mother, Naomi, worked at the Center's bookstore, and in the mid-1990s, she assisted me from my home. My sister, Edythe, provided a lot of administrative support and helped with our initial cultural events. I also had trusted help from people who weren't family in the beginning. Over the years, Pat Latimore, Dorothy Lockhart, Narissa Neal, Laura Brown, and Halton Horton all helped with the children. Mr. Horton had started working for us when Martin was still alive, mostly as a handyman; after Martin was gone, Mr. Horton also helped as a cook and as a surrogate for me at the children's extracurricular activities, and he often drove them to school and to their doctor appointments. Daisy Dial cleaned and cooked for us for years. Bob Fuse and Gordon Joyner tutored the children. So I had the trusted help of family and of other people who became like family. When you are building a great institution, someone also has to help you take care of your home and your kids. I never could have done what I did without all these people.

THE KING CENTER started in the basement of our house. After Martin died, I had the basement built out for the purpose of providing King Center offices, a kitchen, and a playroom for the children. Martin's sister, Christine, became my number two person—my right arm. She initially oversaw the finances. She came to my home every afternoon after her day of full-time teaching at Spelman College. She'd pick up her kids after school and bring them over to be with my kids. Her kids, Angela and Isaac Jr., did their homework while she worked on the King Center's books. Afterward, we would sit in my bedroom or in the kitchen to talk about the King Center, current affairs, and family matters. Through the years, we talked almost every day, many times late at night by phone. She worked with me this way, a silent giant behind the scenes, for a long time and didn't get the credit she deserves. She was the accountability factor, someone who could keep the books and whom I could trust. I really can't say enough about what a pillar she's been to me, or to my family outside the King Center. She's always been there, supporting me in every way. She also would keep Bunny sometimes on weekends, when I would go out of town, since Bunny and her daughter, Angela, were close in age. As a volunteer at the Center, she was vice president, treasurer, and chief fiscal officer, eventually becoming senior vice president and ultimately vice chair and treasurer. She used her skills as an educator at Spelman to help write Kingian nonviolence curriculums, such as the Martin Luther King, Jr. Infusion Model for Teaching Nonviolent Principles (grades K through 12). She wrote the first intermediate-level textbook on Martin for schools. She was also in charge of the King Center's Early Learning Center, housed at the Community Center, and the Right to Read Program, and she chaired the King Ecumenical Service for many years and worked on the committee for the King Center's annual fundraiser, the Salute to Greatness Awards Dinner.

In 1970, as plans for the Center continued in earnest, I embarked on a global tour to promote *My Life with Martin Luther King, Jr.*, a book I'd published the year before. My travels took me to Great Britain, Germany, Holland, France, Spain, Sweden, and Italy, where I carried forth the message of nonviolence and unconditional love and also hosted Freedom Concerts to raise funds for the Center.

While in Amsterdam, I was invited to have lunch with Queen Juliana of the Netherlands, one of the longest-reigning monarchs in the world at that time. A dozen years later, in 1982, after Juliana's daughter Beatrix succeeded her as queen, Queen Beatrix came to the Center and gave us a sizable financial contribution.

Spain was a country that had lived under a dictatorship for so many years. Yet the message of love and nonviolence I carried with me on that trip in 1970 quickly touched the hearts of those I met, and the people proved to be so loving and embracing. They were perpetually hugging and kissing me; it was just overwhelming.

In Italy, crowds lined up to see me. Such love I was finding in these white European countries! Love that made for a particularly sharp contrast when I got horrible news from home about more hate. While I was in Italy, someone shot up Martin's crypt in the predominantly black South-View Cemetery in Atlanta. Several bullet holes marred the crypt's surface, as if it had been used for target practice. South-View Cemetery was founded in 1886 by nine former slaves who had been barred from whites-only graveyards and had opened South-View to all races, but through this evil act, the ugly past came racing back. Can you imagine people hating Martin so badly that they would still shoot at him even after he was dead? Following this incident, we quietly moved his grave to the grounds of what would eventually become the Freedom Hall Complex at the King Center. In 1973 we broke ground for Martin's permanent entombment, the International Chapel of All Faiths and the Freedom Walkway. For a time after that 1970 trip to Europe, the image of two distinct and opposite human realities—of being loved where I had never been, but subjected to hate where I lived—lingered in my mind.

Still, in the face of such upsetting developments, I remained ever energized, seeing through the building of the King Center with the start of the King library and archives, the hiring of staff, the revitalization of Martin's birthplace, and the location of temporary administrative offices. Then, in 1978, all my dreams for the Center came much closer to reality when Henry Ford II took on the task of heading an $8.4 million building campaign for the Center's Freedom Hall Complex, which included an auditorium and meeting rooms; the administration, programs, and archive building; and an exhibit hall. Also in 1978, we received about $3.5 million through our friend President Jimmy Carter, who hosted one of the major fund-raisers for the Center. I never expressly asked President Carter for the money, but several times he publicly credited the King family with helping get him elected. In fact, he repeatedly said that if it were not for Dr. Martin Luther King Jr. and his movement, which changed the culture of the South, he would never have made it to the White House. His administration, working with Coca-Cola executives, paved the way for us to apply to several funding sources. (Yes, we had to apply for funds like everybody else, but I feel sure we were shown deference because of our relationship with President Carter.) Hundreds of major corporations and unions also contributed. Taken together, the funds we raised provided the money we needed to build the Center. And by the time we completed construction in the early 1980s, we had paid it off. That in itself was a miracle.

I pushed for all construction to have 50 percent minority participation, and in the end we exceeded that benchmark, with more than 60 percent participation. We were so proud of that accomplishment. To me, this set an example of how affirmative action and job creation can be a plus, rather than something to fight about. I always believed that we had a unique opportunity among other African American families to continue the democratization of America, so we had to press to get the most equitable results out of whatever we did.

BEYOND ESTABLISHING THE physical site, I had to build the right team to staff and run the Center, which also proved, especially initially, to be an experience fraught with growing pains.

In the early days of the Center, other ideologies were competing with our strategy of nonviolent social change. Hundreds of riots stemmed from Martin's death, and police brutality was rampant. We saw the rise of Black Power and black nationalism, which captured the attention of many young people. For example, Stokely Carmichael, as chairman of the SNCC, made a radical departure from the agenda of former SNCC director John Lewis, who had been by Martin's side during the movement and who had been severely beaten as they attempted to march peacefully across the Edmund Pettus Bridge in Selma. As Carmichael rose to prominence, he made it clear that white members, once actively recruited to the SNCC, were now no longer welcome.

Carmichael's slogan of Black Power and the SNCC's new hostility toward whites caught on as the rallying cry of a younger, more radical generation of black civil rights activists. A clash of values between integration and separatism ensued. Carmichael vocalized his intention to build "a movement that would smash everything Western civilization had created."

Despite our commitment to nonviolence, overtones of black nationalism and separatism attempted to make their way through the doors of the King Center via our first executive director, Dr. Vincent Harding. A beautiful human being and history professor on loan to the Center from Spelman College, Vincent was the noted author of *There Is a River* and *Hope and History*. In the sixties, he had worked with Martin as a mediator between white and black communities. By the early 1970s, however, Vincent had started pushing Malcolm X's thinking over that of Martin's, denouncing whites and pushing for separatism. Of course, it was an apprehensive time. We saw more cities exploding in flames. Angry people were lashing out violently. Many blamed the government, the establishment, for Martin's death. There was so much confusion in this period.

Even as I was trying to launch a nonviolent training institute within the

Center, Vincent was propagating the view that "Nobody is interested in nonviolence these days," and he went about hiring several young staff members who supported his separatist views. In fact, he went so far as to set up the Institute of the Black World inside the Center as an effort to attract more militant proponents to his side. Seeing what was happening, I told him in no uncertain terms, "There will never be any element in the Center where people, no matter who they are or what color they are, cannot participate. Martin wouldn't have stood for this, and I will not stand for this."

In addition to our ideological differences, Vincent did not know much about money management; we found that he was spending funds that should have gone to pay taxes to the IRS. In light of how Martin had been harassed and accused of tax fraud, we were shocked. At a board meeting, Vincent finally told us, "Look, the IRS is going to come and close the doors if we don't pay the money we owe." Daddy King, then a board member, fired back, "Vincent, you had no right to spend the government's money." That mismanagement pushed the Center into financial crisis. In an effort to fix the problem and raise the money needed to pay those taxes, we had to take a severe step backward, which meant cutting staff. We were forced to give many of our employees only two weeks' notice. You can imagine the fallout.

Determined to pick ourselves up and move forward, we called a press conference to introduce our next executive director, Dr. Julius Scott, also a distinguished scholar. He would go on to become president of Paine College in Augusta, Georgia.

When I arrived at the press conference to announce the Scott appointment, the furloughed staff members were there with picket signs, passing out a very derogatory statement about me to members of the media. Naturally, I was caught off guard, but I announced the appointment as best I could. The press was not interested in reporting our efforts to move forward, though. They focused on the negative, and it took a while to live down that series of incidents.

Vincent Harding went on to establish the Institute of the Black World independently of the Center, and for the two years that Julius Scott served as executive director (on loan to us from and paid for by Spelman), we successfully developed the Institute on Nonviolence at the King Center, where, under the sponsorship of the National Education Association, we trained educators, labor leaders, community organizers, faith leaders, and students. This institute has been an especially rewarding program for me over the years, because I continue to meet people we trained in those workshops and hear about the wonderful things they are doing. But back then when Julius's time was up, we didn't have the money to pay a new executive director. That was a tough time.

Our search to run the Center ran into other snafus in the early seventies. Probably the most bizarre incident involved Thomas Porter, a graduate from the Antioch School of Education in Seattle, Washington. He had convinced us he was a pro at organizational structure. He also convinced me he was a convert to nonviolence, although I had heard otherwise. I believe in redemption, so I did not hold that hearsay against him. No one believed in him but me; and we soon found that I had made a mistake. Right away Tom started making demands and publicly saying things that embarrassed us. I took him with me to the Democratic National Convention in California, when I endorsed George McGovern. Junius Griffin, who at that time was the publicist for Motown, picked us up in a Rolls-Royce limousine; after that, Tom started giving people the impression that I was running around in big limousines, which the King Center couldn't afford. Then I took him to a black leadership meeting, where he embarrassed me by using foul language. He made a big fuss because I didn't get him a room in the main hotel, where McGovern was staying. I told him I wanted to meet with him when we returned to the Center, but he had the nerve to present me with a negative evaluation of me and the Center. I advised him against putting those things in writing, "because you can't take it back." Instead of apologizing for his behavior, at the next board meeting he said, "I have to have absolute control of the budget." Andy Young countered, "Tom, you must be planning to resign and go back home." So we gave him three months' severance, and he left. Our next mistake was that we did not fire Tom's assistant and staff hires, and they sent negative information about the Center to the board and others from whom we were seeking help. When we discovered all this, we had to fire Tom's assistant and staff, leaving only two people staffing the Center. We kept the whole thing quiet, but we had to close the Center for six weeks until we could regroup. And regroup we did. We kept regrouping.

We then brought in Calvin Morris, whom Andy had recommended. Calvin was a good speaker, but he did not have the best administrative skills, and all he wanted to do was to speak and preach. And then, he left to work on his doctorate.

As the Center developed, hundreds of staff members with favorable opinions of our work made themselves known. We eventually found excellent directors who helped us stay on course, and in 1979, *People* magazine's opinion poll named me "the most effective among women leaders." Still, early on, press about the Center sometimes blamed me for the challenges we encountered finding the right director. "Hard to work with," they said.

Looking back, those hard early years building a staff were just a few backward steps in what was overall a great march forward. In the decade between 1976 and 1995, we were blessed with several wonderful leaders, such as Maxi Jackson, who came in 1976 but had to leave to resettle his family back in Michigan; Lloyd Davis, on loan from the U.S. Department of Housing and Urban Development (HUD), who became the Center's first executive vice president; followed by Harold Sims; Dr. William (Chip) Wheeler; Dr. Ronald Quincy; and William Sonny Walker. These men put the icing on the cake, implementing programs essential to our commitment to nonviolence and social justice, activities that kept the Center bustling with commitment, excitement, and purpose.

I AM ALSO quite proud of the part the Center has played in revitalizing the Sweet Auburn neighborhood around our complex, an area that has become one of the nation's leading tourist sites, adding millions of dollars to the economy of Atlanta. Even more important, that revitalization made attractive housing surrounding the Center available to low-income residents.

During the early 1900s, Auburn Avenue, which is east of downtown Atlanta, was the center of life for upwardly mobile blacks. Famous names and black establishments were trademarks; patriarchs such as Alonzo Herndon, John Wesley Dobbs, and Rev. A. D. Williams, Martin's maternal grandfather, set a tone of pride and dignity. Businesses thrived, such as the *Atlanta Daily World*, the nation's first black daily newspaper; the

Mutual Federal Savings and Loan; and the Atlanta Life Insurance Company, one of the largest black-owned institutions in the nation. The Top Hat nightclub, later named the Royal Peacock, hosted top performers, including Bessie Smith, Louis Armstrong, and Gladys Knight and the Pips. A church aristocracy, which included Bethel AME, Wheat Street Baptist Church, and Ebenezer Baptist Church, provided a spiritual foundation. By 1960 the Prince Hall Masonic building on Auburn Avenue housed the SCLC offices as well as a historic radio station. And, of course, in 1970, Martin was interred on Auburn Avenue on what today are the grounds of the Freedom Hall Complex at the King Center.

It was around 1960, however, shortly after Martin and I moved to Atlanta, when I saw the handwriting on the wall. Urban blight and the migration of wealthier blacks to the suburbs (in light of desegregation plans) left behind lower-income families without recreation or access to health care and other services. By the 1970s, scores of residential buildings had become eyesores and were being razed. Once-prosperous businesses had become shells of their former selves.

I hoped to promote the preservation and restoration of this neighborhood, this valuable motherlode of black culture and history, partly by locating the Freedom Hall Complex of the King Center in the Auburn area. But the very first beacon in this neighborhood preservation would be the house where Martin was born.

One year before Martin's assassination, I met with Atlanta's mayor, Ivan Allen, to retain his help in restoring Martin's birth home; I had learned that this historic block was slated for demolition, and I wanted to give the community where Martin grew up a facelift, to help change its destiny from deterioration to revitalization. I began to lobby for the home to become a National Historic Site, and the birth home became the first completed portion of my vision for the Martin Luther King, Jr. Historic District; at first, we offered tours of the home; eventually, we invited the National Park Service (NPS) to partner with us to give regular tours to visitors. The birth home, a two-story Queen Anne frame structure, was built in 1895 and purchased in the early 1900s by Reverend Williams. Mama King (Mrs. Alberta Williams King) grew up in that house. When she gave birth to Martin on January 15, 1929, Daddy King jumped up and touched the ceiling, leaving a handprint, which we embossed so it would remain. The house was and still is just a stone's throw from Fire Station No. 6, where Martin had chased fire trucks as a boy and just a few feet from the King Center Freedom Hall Complex.

The designation of Martin's home as a historic site made him the first black American whose birth home earned recognition from the National Register of Historic Places. Because of our efforts, Ebenezer Church subsequently received a similar designation, and these efforts opened the way for additional funds for the Auburn Avenue restorations from state and private preservation organizations. We also received funds for the restoration of the birth home from sororities: Alpha Kappa Alpha, the grand chapter of Sigma Gamma Rho, and the Atlanta Alumnae chapter of Delta Sigma Theta. Work on the restoration of the home was completed in 1974.

Mama King worked diligently with me and Christine on the restoration, and took special pride in supervising the painting, wallpapering, and selection of most of the furniture. She played an indispensable role in helping us complete the birth home. Unfortunately, a tragic turn of events made it so that she wasn't with us when the home was dedicated in 1975. On June 30, 1974, she was shot and killed at Ebenezer while she sat at the organ playing "The Lord's Prayer."

MAMA KING, WHOM Daddy King called Bunch, was not a public figure, but she was deeply loved within the family and at her church. Indeed, Mama King had much more influence than one might guess. Martin used to say, "You know who the real pastor of this church is? Mother." Sometimes she would call Martin at 6:00 a.m. and tell him in her heavy voice what she thought he should be doing at the church. It seemed she never slept! She also did a lot of grandmothering, and would take care of the children from time to time while I traveled. Sometimes she watched after my kids, Naomi's kids, and Christine's kids at the same time. They would all play together, and Mama and Daddy King would get so much joy out of having all their grandkids together.

On that awful Sunday morning, the church pews were full as Mama King began to play the organ, the melody flowing through the sanctuary. She had a natural talent for music, and she served as the minister of music, directing some of the choirs at Ebenezer. Some of the deacons remembered that a young man, definitely a first-time visitor, came to the sanctuary just before service began and asked, "Is Reverend King preaching today?" The deacon responded "No." An usher seated the man near the front, to the left of the pulpit, on a pew right next to the Hammond B-3 organ where Mama King was seated. Daddy King and Christine were sitting in the first pew, to the right of the pulpit.

As Mama King was playing "The Lord's Prayer" the young man shouted, "I'm taking over this morning!" There was a popping sound, and Daddy King saw Bunch's hand fly to her face. Blood ran through her fingers; she fell forward, holding her side. The bullets were still flying. The young man had two guns, one in either hand, and he started shooting wildly across the church. He shot and killed one of the deacons, Edward Boykin. Another member of the congregation was also shot, but later recovered. Other deacons restrained Daddy King, who was frantically trying to reach his wife of forty-eight years.

The man pointed his weapons at the choir members and even at Daddy King's grandson Rev. Derek King, who was in the pulpit that day. The man kept trying to fire, but he had emptied his guns' chambers. He became frightened and tried to run out of the church. Derek tackled him and started beating him. If the police had not rushed in, the young man, later identified as twenty-three-year-old Marcus Wayne Chenault, might have died on the spot.

All these intricate and heartrending details were relayed to me the moment my plane landed. I had been in Chicago, giving a speech for the National Educational Association; Dexter had already gone to church earlier with his cousins. He was at the store across the street from the church when the shooting started. When I called the house to wake up the other children for Sunday school, I called too late; I had forgotten that Chicago is an hour behind Atlanta. As soon as Dexter heard about the shooting, he ran back across the street to the church, and before Mama King was moved to the ambulance, he saw her in a pool of blood. Still, in retrospect, I was comforted that all of my children, at least, were spared the horror of seeing their grandmother, whom they adored, shot down in front of their eyes in church, of all places.

A few weeks after the murder, Daddy King insisted that he meet with Chenault in prison. When he asked, "Why did you do it, son?" Chenault rambled on about Christians being his enemies. He was completely incoherent, making no sense at all. Eventually, he was found guilty of the attack and sentenced to die in the electric chair.

Ironically, Andrea Young, Andrew Young's daughter, happened to be a lawyer with the firm that aided indigent prisoners and was representing Chenault; she was working to get his sentence commuted to life in prison. She came to me for advice, and I told her that while I didn't believe in the death penalty, she had to talk through the case with Daddy King and Christine, who were suffering tremendously. He had lost both his sons and she, her two brothers. First Martin and then A.D., who was found dead in his own pool under suspicious circumstances a year after Martin's death. Now, tragically, he had lost his wife and Christine had lost her mother.

Watching the way Daddy King handled himself was a great inspiration to me. It was wonderful to see forgiveness and the love of Christ flow so freely. I remember him saying, "There are two men I am supposed to hate. One is white, and the other is black. James Earl Ray is a prisoner in Tennessee, charged with killing my son. Marcus Chenault is in a Georgia penitentiary after killing my wife. Nothing that a man does takes him lower than when he allows himself to stoop so low as to hate someone. I love the lesson of love triumphing over evil too much to make room in my heart for hate."

Our family had suffered so many tragedies in six short years. They kept us on our knees, praying for strength, and we found the strength to push past our pain and continue on our mission, which we had been uniquely challenged to carry out. Sooner or later, our Comforter would come. We had to keep growing, keep building, and keep moving on.

Shortly after revitalizing Martin's birth home, we bought the adjacent house at 503 Auburn Avenue and used it as temporary administrative offices for the King Center. Next, as part of revitalizing the Auburn neighborhood, I went to work on building a community center, which would include a gymnasium, a game room, a library, an early learning center, community services, and a fountain, as well as a separate natatorium. The community around the proposed Center badly needed social, cultural, and recreational resources for children and young adults. To provide for these necessities, I had to do some serious lobbying with officials in the city and with the Nixon administration.

Cutting a path through the Nixon labyrinth was no easy task. For years, I've known that the FBI was smearing me as an anti-American subversive. The media also reported that Patrick Buchanan, Nixon's speechwriter, had warned the president against meeting with me on the first anniversary of Martin's birthday, claiming that such a visit would "outrage many, many people who believe Dr. King was a fraud and a demagogue and perhaps worse. Dr. King is one of the most divisive men in contemporary history—some believe him to be a Messiah, others consider him the devil incarnate."

Still, I appealed to President Nixon for funds. After all, he was elected to be the president of all the people, and we were trying to build upon what was good and proper about our country, an effort we hoped even Nixon would want to be part of. I called his office and told him that we were building a memorial for my husband and needed his help for the community center. Through one of his deputies, we were promised help, and told that he would get his best people working on it.

That never happened. Later, we were told there was no money. And later still, we learned the real reason: beyond Nixon's personal dislike for the King family, Herman Talmadge and Richard B. Russell Jr., two U.S. senators from Georgia, had scotched the funding. Subsequently, Nixon passed word to all his Cabinet directors and heads of various agencies that there would be no money for the community center or the memorial. There was a rumor of a bizarre idea: the Nixon administration would offer us a recording of the 1970 birthday White House concert for Duke Ellington, which we could sell to raise money. This was an insult. Of course we appreciated Duke Ellington, but we were against the administration trying to pass off his birthday concert as monetarily significant.

Yet, as the Scripture teaches, just when Abraham was about to sacrifice Isaac, a ram in the bush appeared as a substitute. There is always a ram in the bush. In this case, the ram that saved the day was George Romney, secretary of HUD. As the former governor of Michigan, Romney had made high-level appointments of African Americans. Through that pipeline, he tapped Lloyd Davis, a former member of the Kennedy administration (and, it turned out, a future executive director of the King Center), and assigned him to review our application for funding; Romney wanted to ensure that all equal opportunity and fair housing requirements had been met, and since they were, he made sure discretionary funds were directed to us. With those funds, along with matching funds raised by me and other grants, we amassed the estimated three million dollars needed to build our community center and provide much-needed social and recreational services. We held the ribbon-cutting ceremonies during King Birthday Week in January 1976.

At the community center, we had an early-learning center, a reading academy (thanks to additional Right to Read funding from the Department of Health, Education and Welfare), and neighborhood services to train young people in nonviolence. We were also able to provide direct housing and food assistance to Sweet Auburn residents in need, and if there were problems our staff could not handle directly (whether with utility bills, child care, transportation, or employment), we referred those in need to the proper agencies. In addition, we maintained a presence on corporate and nonprofit boards, which allowed us to channel aid to needy communities through personal networking.

Seeing how the community center made a difference was thrilling to me. And the natatorium, the Olympic-size swimming pool, connected by a walkway to the community center, was used by many local swim teams and also attracted national swim meets. It was one of the nicest pools in Atlanta, which also made me happy. One reason I wanted that pool was because in Marion, Alabama, where I grew up, we were not allowed to swim in the public pools, which were for whites only. And as a child, I almost drowned trying to learn to swim in a pond, which looked like a big, dark hole to me. I was afraid to get in that pond in the first place, and after I did, I never learned to swim. I wanted the next generation to have a different experience. Similarly, I'd never learned to play tennis, because we didn't have tennis courts in Marion, so we constructed two courts near the natatorium. All the things I didn't have as a child, I tried to provide through the community center. I put in early-learning programs because I remembered how my lack of early training made it difficult for me to keep up in college. To see the children coming to the early-learning center was really gratifying.

204 Coretta Scott King

Of course, over the years, a great many extraordinary entertainers, from Flip Wilson to Stevie Wonder to Michael Jackson to Bono, visited the Center and contributed to its work. But another Atlanta cultural issue I was blessed to be able to address during the 1970s was opera. Blacks in Atlanta, as in other southern cities, had not been allowed to attend opera performances during the days of segregation. As a concert singer and someone who loved opera and the arts in general, I wanted this barrier to come down. I worked with Rudolf Bing, the general manager for the Metropolitan Opera, to make tickets available to blacks—and to members of all races. And because the Fox Theatre, where operas in Atlanta were performed, was teetering on the edge of financial collapse, I worked with local residents to save it, restore it to its original grandeur.

By 1980, AFTER our major campaign of lobbying the White House and Congress, the King Center board of directors and I succeeded in getting legislation passed to establish the Martin Luther King, Jr. National Historic Site. And in 1981, after years spent collecting the largest inventory of civil rights documents in the world related to the modern civil rights movement, including an oral history project, the Center formally opened the administration building, which houses the King Library and Archives. And in 1981, after years spent collecting the largest inventory of civil rights documents in the world related to the modern civil rights movement, including an oral history project, the Center formally opened the administration building, which houses the King Library and Archives. The building was opened for staff, the library and archives were opened to scholars and researchers from around the world, and, initially, the Center was also able to offer exhibitions to the public in the building. In addition, that same year, we worked with the City of Atlanta and the U.S. Department of Labor to train youth to provide services to senior citizens, such as minor home repairs and escort assistance, which helped two underserved populations and provided a service model for the nation.

On January 15, 1982, as part of the weeklong observance of Martin's fifty-third birthday, we celebrated the final construction of the Freedom Hall Complex. This completed the entire building phase of the Center.

Until 1982, when we used the term *Center*, we were referring to our organization, a work-in-progress housed in temporary offices. But in 1982, all our staff and programs were finally in their own administration building. We had come home at last. The completed complex also consisted of the International Chapel of All Faiths, the Freedom Walkway, Freedom Hall (a conference center with meeting rooms and a 250-seat auditorium), the screening room, the reflecting pool, Martin's crypt, which sits on a circular island in the center of the pool, and the eternal flame, symbolizing Martin's lifelong commitment to justice and peace.

The idea of a reflecting pool had come to me during my visit to the Taj Mahal in Agra, India, during my book tour in 1970. I saw this beautiful reflecting pool leading up to the mausoleum of white marble built by Emperor Shah Jahan in 1653 in memory of his third wife. It is a symbol of love. Martin's crypt was also a labor of love. At one end of the pool are several tiers, with five fountains on the top tier representing the five races in humanity and water cascades down from them, reminding me of that Scripture in the Book of Amos: "Let justice rain down like water and righteousness like a mighty stream." Inscribed on the white marble crypt are Martin's famous words "Free at last. Free at last. Thank God Almighty, I'm free at last."

I believe it is only right that the caring community that helped produce a Martin Luther King Jr. not deteriorate but remain creative, vibrant, and illustrious. Sweet Auburn is part of a legacy that keeps producing something better. Today, the neighborhood offers us all a unique opportunity to experience the environment that produced the man who sacrificed his life to save us. And within it stands the King Center—both a social and a sacred space, a pilgrimage destination with an estimated one million visitors from around the world every year, and most of all, through its educational and training programs, an epicenter for nonviolent change, both societally and interpersonally.

FROM THE VERY moment the Center began, with meager resources and a dispersed and inadequate administrative home, it still managed to do what mattered most: continue Martin's unfinished work through education,

research, advocacy, and nonviolence training. We did not allow the naysayers or our own missteps to bog us down or distract us from our mission.

Martin believed that each person could make a difference, and I
believed that the King Center could help each person obtain the tools to
make that difference without violence. Even before we opened our doors,
we offered education and training for every age group. At the preschool
level, the children sang songs and learned poems in the spirit of nonviolence; our emphasis was on love and concern for the kids. And our programs
for college students soon included a scholars' internship program, through
which students learned Kingian nonviolence and got on-the-job training
from internships in government offices or in social service organizations,
where they had a chance to apply the principles they had learned at the
Center; they also received credit for their learning and work from their
colleges or universities. By 1980, eighty students had gone through that
program. Also, even before we had a building, we had an Institute on
Nonviolence, which brought adults from as far away as California and
Maine for weeklong and summer workshops.

In its first twenty years the Center led more than twenty educational
programs and more than a dozen community and public affairs programs,
such as the new Coalition of Conscience and the American Indian Forum.

At the core of the Center—its heart and soul—has been nonviolence
education and training, which we have provided to tens of thousands of
people through the years. In one 1984 program alone, we partnered with
the FBI to train twenty-five thousand young people in nonviolence. Also,
every year we bring in about 300 young people to our Summer Institute on
Nonviolence. We also host the top executives of law enforcement groups,
judges, and prison personnel. Our goal is to use my husband's philosophy
and strategies to demonstrate alternatives to violence. The Center's police
training started in the early 1990s because of Charles Alphin Sr., a St. Louis
police captain, who began visiting the Center on his own time in the 1980s
to learn the techniques of nonviolence; he then applied them in the communities where he worked. Eventually, with his help, our Summer Institute for Youth expanded and included family members Martin III,
Bernice, Derek, Vernon, and Angela Farris as trainers.

In an effort to test the value of our nonviolence program, Charles
began bringing busloads of youth from St. Louis to the Center for nonvi-

olence workshops. One particular youth was a gang member who had been involved in a drive-by shooting. A kind judge let him out of juvenile detention to attend our workshops, along with 20 other youths. When he returned home he vowed not to fight anymore, despite being harassed for his decision. When he was released from detention he returned to the Center to delight us with his turnaround; he became active in our training programs and completely changed his life.

After Charles retired from the police force in 1992, I encouraged him to come to work for the Center as a trainer, and later, after I promoted him to director of education and training, our police training programs expanding nationally. A youth and law enforcement training at the Holocaust Museum in Los Angeles was one of many such programs. One of the success stories I am most proud of is our work with the police department in Miami that credited us with helping it prevent the kinds of riots that occurred in Los Angeles in 1992 after acquittal of the white police officer involved in the beating of unarmed black motorist Rodney King.

After those riots, the Los Angeles PD called upon us for assistance in keeping the peace. We attended a summit with gang leaders—the Crips and the Bloods—at the Martin Luther King Jr. Community Hospital in Watts. I listened and spoke and later invited gang members to the Center, facing strenuous objections for doing so. XXXOG is the highest level of gang memberships, yet Charles Rachal, a XXXOG Crip leader, and Bobby Lavender, a XXXOG Blood member, were among the nine gang leaders who accepted my invitation. On the heels of the training, I became fond of both men. We exposed any number of gang members to Kingian nonviolence as a lifestyle. It was gratifying to see how these young people, coming to the Center from various urban communities with no understanding of nonviolence at all, could choose Martin's teaching as a viable antidote to violence.

By 1984 the King Center had expanded its role as an international institution. We incorporated and pulled from what we had learned on the battlefields of America to build training materials that were in tune with diverse cultures and could be translated into various languages. We embraced the vision of the Center as a "world house," where people of disparate ideologies could embrace a common ideology of peace. We trained some of our staff members to become globetrotters, to literally stand between warring factions without being labeled spies or intruders. In 1985, the Center used Martin's birthday week to focus attention on world hunger and poverty, which were at unprecedented levels and which represented violence in one of its ugliest and most basic forms. I spoke about the conditions in some developing nations where the annual average income is less than three hundred dollars. Our brothers and sisters in those countries lack even a survivable diet; they take in a daily deficit of calories and nutrients that hinders the growth of their bodies and minds and permanently handicaps their countries. We issued a charge for all nations to wage an unconditional war not on any nation or people, but on poverty, racism, and violence. In 1989, we continued our efforts to get the U.S. corporate community to further its divestment in South Africa, as a nonviolent way of fighting apartheid; we also used the Center's offices and facilities as a nonviolent forum in which the opposing South African parties might mediate their differences and work for national reconciliation.

From the beginning, our trainings drew on Martin's scores of books, speeches, and sermons, but we turned to three sources in particular to teach his worldview and his concept of Kingian nonviolence: "The Pilgrimage to Nonviolence," a chapter from his book *Stride Toward Freedom*; the "Letter from a Birmingham Jail," which is in the book *Why We Can't Wait*; and "The World House," the last chapter from his 1967 book, *Where Do We Go From Here: Chaos or Community?*—as well as excerpts from his Nobel Lecture, and his close identification with the teachings of Mahatma Gandhi.

We gleaned from Martin's writings the clearest statements on nonviolence, and abbreviated them to become the Center's Six Principles of Nonviolence, which, along with Martin's Six Steps of Nonviolence, are the basis of everything we teach.

The Center's Six Principles of Nonviolence are:

1. Nonviolence is a way of life for courageous people. It is an active, not a passive, form of resistance to evil.
2. Those who practice nonviolence must seek to win friendship and understanding from their adversaries, and not try to vanquish, humiliate, or defeat them.
3. Those who practice nonviolence recognize that evildoers are not

evil people, and that they are often victims of systemic injustice themselves. Therefore, we seek to defeat injustice and not people.

4. Unearned suffering for a just cause is redemptive because it can educate and win the hearts of adversaries and the public. This understanding empowers the nonviolence practitioner to accept suffering without retaliation, so as to advance the victory of a just cause.

5. Nonviolence is rooted in unconditional love instead of hate. By recognizing that all life is interrelated, nonviolence resists violence of the spirit as well as of the body.

6. Faith in the ultimate triumph of justice empowers the nonviolence practitioner to endure suffering and defeat as temporary phenomena, knowing that justice will prevail because God is just and the universe is on the side of justice.

We have always coupled these Six Principles of Nonviolence with the Kingian Six Steps of Nonviolence:

1. Information gathering. Gather as much data as possible about the problem and the conflict from all sides.

2. Educate the community about the information we have gathered.

3. Make a personal commitment to solving the problem and resolving the conflict nonviolently, checking motives along the way.

4. Negotiate. Meet with the opposition, discuss differences, and try to come to a win-win resolution. If negotiations fail, only then do we go to step five.

5. Direct action. Direct action can take the form of economic withdrawal, such as boycotts or picketing, or marches, protests, or other types of demonstrations.

6. Reconciliation. The goal is to reestablish community and, ultimately, to create the Beloved Community, about which people have heard me talk so often.

I AM SO proud of the ongoing education and training in nonviolence that is the heart of the King Center's work.

Will there ever be a true reconciliation out of conflict and violence through nonviolent means?

Will the disparities between rich and poor no longer exist and will each person have, as Martin wanted, "Three meals a day for their bodies, education and culture for their minds, and dignity, equality and freedom for their spirits?"

Will the human family lead to the realization of the Beloved Community?

Will people achieve peace within themselves, each other, their families, their communities, their nations?

I still believe, as I said once to an interviewer at *Ebony* magazine, that "because of so many ongoing social ills and injustices, another movement is inevitable. It is interesting how a movement is triggered at a certain moment in history. I can't help but believe that at some time in the not-too-distant future, there is going to be another movement to change these systemic conditions of poverty, injustice, and violence in people's lives. That is where we've got to go, and it is going to be a struggle."

When that struggle comes, those who have been trained in Kingian nonviolence will be ready.

ALL THOSE YEARS we were building the King Center and revitalizing Sweet Auburn, I challenged myself and the Center board and staff to extend our ideals and be Martin's voice in action. I never stopped speaking out for justice outside Atlanta's city limits as well as within them, making hundreds of speeches, engaging with blacks, women, the physically challenged, gays, and poor and deprived children. I used my nationally syndicated newspaper column and my thrice-weekly show on CNN to help give voice to my husband's vision.

In 1979, the Center's board of directors drew up its first legislative agenda, which included calling for implementation of the Humphrey-Hawkins Full Employment Act, for full voting rights for the District of Columbia, for the Martin Luther King Jr. birthday bill, for the Equal Rights Amendment, and for ratification of the UN human rights covenants.

By 1984, the year French president François Mitterrand visited, the King Center had already become an international institution, a World

House where people of disparate ideologies could embrace a common ideology of peace. Distinguished international visitors included Nicaraguan president Daniel Ortega, Prime Minister Robert Mugabe of Zimbabwe, the King and Queen of Nepal, and prime ministers, Cabinet-level ministers, and official delegations from Canada, England, India, Japan, Kenya, Liberia, Romania, Saudi Arabia, South Africa, the Soviet Union, West Africa, and West Germany, to name a few.

And in 1986 during the first national holiday, the King Center, in conjunction with Ebenezer Baptist Church, where I worship, hosted the National Conference Against Apartheid, which was attended by a powerful list of religious leaders (from Rev. Joseph Lowery, then head of the SCLC, to Bishop Desmond Tutu of South Africa), ambassadors from several nations, U.S. State Department officials, presidents of trade unions and colleges, and heads of prominent South African and international organizations, among others. The national march and parade following the conference were attended by thousands, including former president Jimmy Carter, who was honorary grand marshal. Mrs. Rosa Parks and Peter V. Ueberroth, the commissioner of Major League Baseball, were grand marshals. The U.S. Air Force provided a "Fly Over Tribute" to Martin.

Also, from the beginning, the Center was a site for important commemorations and celebrations that helped keep Martin's message alive.

Every year, starting in 1973, the King Center presented the Martin Luther King, Jr. Nonviolent Peace Prize to a world citizen who embodied and emulated Martin's spirit and mission. Andrew Young, Cesar Chavez, Rep. John Lewis, Rep. Joseph Lowery, Randolph Blackwell, Benjamin Mays, Stanley Levison, Zambian president Kenneth Kaunda, President Jimmy Carter, Rosa Parks, former Atlanta mayor Ivan Allen, Harry Belafonte, Martin Luther King Sr., Sir Richard Attenborough, President Corazon Aquino of the Philippines, and the Rev. Jesse Jackson all received the prize, and in 1990 we presented the award to Mikhail Gorbachev, the last general secretary of the Soviet Union, who brought about massive economic, social, and political changes and helped bring an end to both the Soviet Union and the Cold War.

One of the Center's commemorations of which I am most proud occurred in 1988. I had long been concerned about the lack of proper recognition given to the women who participated in the civil rights movement. The King Center organized a conference to address the issue, and was able to get the Division of Continuing Education of Georgia State University to sponsor it with us. This conference, entitled Women in the Civil Rights Movement: Trailblazers and Torchbearers, was one of the most historic events held on the issue. Some two hundred women from diverse racial, cultural, economic, and professional backgrounds came together to discuss new directions and a future agenda for women. We honored Rosa Parks at the conference on the occasion of her seventy-fifth birthday, acknowledging her contributions with a special exhibit at the Center and hailing her as the "Mother of the U.S. Civil Rights Movement." A conference room in Freedom Hall was dedicated in her honor. In conjunction with the conference, I established a Trailblazers and Torchbearers advisory board, which included Juanita Abernathy, Joan Baez, Daisy Bates, Mary Frances Berry, Unita Blackwell, Xernona Clayton-Brady, Marian Wright Edelman, Christine Farris, Eleanor Holmes Norton, Rosa Parks, Bernice Johnson Reagon, Modjeska Simkins, Maxine Waters, and Jean Young.

Even though I acknowledge and celebrate all these and many more King Center milestones and other successes, I was humbled and surprised when a reporter looking for a comparison asked me to name another African American woman who had built an institution from the ground up that was hailed internationally as a tourist destination. I hadn't thought of my accomplishment in those terms, and the truth is that contributions of all kinds came to the King Center, from labor, civil, and human rights groups; from arts communities, fraternities, and sororities; from prayer warriors and people of faith from around the globe; from corporations large and small; from legislative leaders across the nation, both Democrats and Republicans; and from international diplomatic corps, U.S. presidents, and heads of state from around the world.

The King Center is a mecca for spiritual growth and activism, safeguarding and championing Martin's legacy to all nations. It has spurred redevelopment in Atlanta, creating a citadel of diversity that helped attract the 1996 Summer Olympics and that continues to draw visitors from around the globe. I never expected to see so many people close to me who wanted this child of mine stillborn. Nevertheless, out of much pain and with much prayer, the King Center came forth. As with my flesh-and-blood children, I am a proud parent.

In the decade after Martin's death, it was of utmost importance to me to put my children first, to make sure they knew how special and loved they were. I could see the difference that this was making almost daily. I remember Martin III telling me, "Mama, a kid can live without a father, but no kid can make it without a mother," yet all my children knew they had to share me with my fifth child.

There were times of agony and times of joy, but there are no regrets, especially when I see what the Center means to the world.

This miraculous Center was conceived in me, and birthed by thousands of midwives—and my other children will finish raising up this sibling of theirs to independent adulthood when I'm gone.

———— ❋ ————

EIGHTEEN

We Must Learn to Disagree
Without Being Disagreeable

I N A TRULY democratic society, we would not still need the Voting
Rights Act to protect people of color. But we do. Subtle and sophisticated forms of discrimination persist today, including gerrymander-
ing, manipulation of polling hours and locations, and burdensome rules
designed to depress minority voting strength. Perhaps the largest group
of disenfranchised citizens is the six hundred thousand residents of
the District of Columbia, the majority of whom are people of color.
Our struggle for voting rights will not be complete as long as the people
of the District, who pay taxes and serve our country in the military, do
not have voting representation in the House and the Senate.

So, when all is said and done, am I satisfied with the progress made
since the passage of the 1965 Voting Rights Act?

No. Not yet.

But by the early 1970s, the 1965 Voting Rights Act, which so many
blacks and whites in the civil rights movement marched, bled, and died for,
was opening the gates of political empowerment for a historically disenfranchised people. Many of our ancestors, including my parents and grand-
parents, were disqualified from voting either by poll taxes and grandfather
clauses or by the terrifying specter of armed vigilantes. Here was a new day.
Millions of blacks in the South were finally citizens of the land their ancestors had helped build through the inhumane institution of slavery.

Voters still had to be educated and registered, suits had to be filed to break down intractable obstacles and unethical backroom practices, and worthy candidates had to be found, along with the large sums necessary to back them. For us, voting, a short walk to the ballot box for most Americans, still often seemed as complex as buying a house and being expected to bring our own basement and roof. Step by bloody step, we had to build a system that connected us to the democratic order, an order designed at the birth of the nation to keep black Americans locked out. And my goal at the King Center was to continue the nonviolent flow of the movement so that more and more of those whose race, class, or gender had left them voiceless and invisible would become heard and seen, and would have full access to the American Dream.

When the Voting Rights Act passed in 1965, fewer than 300 blacks held major elected office in the United States. By 1972, according to the Joint Center for Political and Economic Studies, there were 88 black mayors, 140 judges and magistrates, 13 congressmen, 246 state legislators, 740 city councilmen, and about 675 school board members. Although those estimated 2,000 black elected officials constituted 0.4 percent of the 521,760 elected officials in the United States overall, these numbers were a real step forward for Black Power, which had started from so far behind.

In 1972, Black Power politics was riding a wave of passion and energy, calling for a crusade to organize around the self-interests of race and for breaking ties with white backroom party bosses, such as Chicago's mayor Richard Daley, who counted on the black vote to win, but who refused to share resources. Emotionalism, that drumbeat of the masses, was at a peak. "The hands that picked cotton in 1964 will pick a president in 1972," vowed Jesse Jackson.

So I waded deep into these waters, and became involved, for the first time ever, in presidential politics. While Martin never endorsed candidates, because he felt that would leave him most free to be critical of both parties when necessary, I had, for years, endorsed candidates in Atlanta and in other local elections, and it had proved to be equal parts empowering and complicated. I had won some political skirmishes, lost some, and was even publicly humiliated several times. But in light of the high stakes in play in 1972, I felt I had no choice but to exert my influence at the highest levels.

My quandary centered on whom to endorse. For decades, I had been fighting for the right to vote, to *elect* decent politicians. However, I soon learned that *selection*, not just *election*, was the key. Fortunately, we were not bereft of decent choices for the Democratic presidential ticket. Among them were Congressman Eugene McCarthy of Minnesota; Senators Edmund Muskie of Maine and George McGovern of South Dakota, Hubert Humphrey, who had been vice president in the Johnson administration; and Shirley Chisholm, the first African American woman in Congress, who made history by entering the race.

My main focus was ridding our nation of Richard Nixon and his reactionary policies on race, war, and poverty. During his presidency, I had made several trips to the White House to talk to him about civil rights. We weren't exactly strangers. I first met Nixon in 1957, when Martin and I had traveled to Ghana. Nixon was there as vice president, representing President Eisenhower, and Martin had just been featured on the cover of *Time* magazine. Nixon had read the cover article, and he complimented Martin. On that occasion, he was funny, witty, and approachable, but Martin never really trusted him, because of the smear campaign Nixon had waged against Rep. Helen Gahagan Douglas of California, whom Nixon had falsely targeted as a Communist sympathizer.

It still stung, too, that Nixon had refused, and then blocked, funds for the King Center. At one point, frustrated by his recalcitrance, I essentially called him out. Everyone who knows me would agree that, in the nonviolent spirit, I go out of my way not to be offensive; nor do I use intemperate language. But I was at a press conference, and the media were asking me questions about what the Nixon administration had done for my husband's memorial. I answered that Nixon had not done anything, because he was too busy playing to a southern strategy that denounced black people via coded language and negative stereotyping.

While I didn't use the exact word *racist*, by the time I was finished describing Nixon's uncharitable and discriminatory actions, it was obvious what term best described him. One of my Republican advisers soon got word from the Nixon camp asking that I "please soften" my statements concerning the president.

In 1972, then, while still trying to figure out whom to endorse, I considered Hubert Humphrey. He was a friend to labor and to the civil rights movement, though he had proven to be wishy-washy on the Vietnam War, which incensed peace activists and did not endear him to me as a candidate. Also, I thought Nixon would easily defeat him.

Then there was Shirley Chisholm. In 1971 she and I had both appeared at Jesse Jackson's Operation PUSH (People United to Serve Humanity) program in Chicago, on a panel dealing with the criminal justice system, and there, during a lull in the proceedings, she leaned over and filled me in on her planned history-making run for the White House.

"Oh, that's wonderful," I said, trying to be careful to encourage her without promising my endorsement. She certainly was a bold, uncompromising person, and a strong advocate for the people in her congressional district in New York, but I was still assessing the field.

Much of 1971 had been devoted to male candidates talking about who among *them* would be the broker for black America. There were several strategies. One involved organizing the estimated twelve hundred black delegates going to the convention in Miami into a single bloc and brokering that bloc for platform concessions for black America. There were several black agendas to which candidates had to pledge themselves to earn the black vote. Most included commitments to appoint black Cabinet members, to consider a black person as running mate, and to put forward plans for national health insurance and full employment.

The other, rather dramatic strategy for amassing political power was to create a black political party that would put forth its own presidential candidate. This strategy evolved from the call for unity at the National Black Political Convention, held in Gary, Indiana, in March 1972. It was the first time black Americans had held such a gathering in forty-four years. Gary was a majority black city with a newly elected black mayor, Richard Hatcher. More than eight thousand people showed up for the convention, all looking for a way to flex their new political muscle.

This was where I first met Betty Shabazz, the widow of Malcolm X, who, years later, would become one of my very best friends. We were on a panel together, and as two women, both of whom had lost their husbands tragically, we instantly identified with each other and greeted one another warmly.

For many, the call for a separate black political party was the perfect pitch. Many felt that the Democrats were taking blacks for granted, while the Republicans were ignoring them. The idea of a third party, or a third political force, was championed by Rep. John Conyers, Rev. Jesse Jackson, and Imamu Amiri Baraka (né LeRoi Jones). At that time, hardly anyone believed that a black third-party candidate could win a national presidential race, but the thinking centered on what man—they were not thinking about women—could become a spoiler by denying either of the two parties a majority in key states that had a significant number of black voters. The men were strategizing among themselves, strutting around like peacocks as they argued over which of them would emerge as the top power broker.

Then, in a surprising move, New York Democratic congresswoman Shirley Chisholm stole the black kingmakers' thunder by using the convention to announce her own bid for the presidency. Privately, a few of the men condemned her as a pawn of New York mayor John Lindsay, but publicly, they were at a loss for words. They could not afford to openly or publicly attack her; nor could they jump in the race themselves and run against her.

There was no shortage of private jabs aimed at Chisholm. Once she caught wind of these putdowns, she roared into a meeting room where some of her detractors were gathered and let them have it. "Brothers, please get off my back. I am not here to compete with you or fight you. Use me as an instrument. If I were to tell the whole truth, I would say that not everyone here is fighting to liberate us. Some have been exploiting us."

I respected her courage, but I didn't see how she could win, insulting men like that.

One night shortly thereafter, Jesse called me. "Shirley's going to call you; she's trying to get all her ducks in a row. I advised her that she needs to call on you and Maynard Jackson." Maynard was then vice mayor of Atlanta, and he would be elected Atlanta's first black mayor the following year.

Sure enough, Shirley called. We talked for quite a while. Much of the conversation focused on how smart she was. She said her husband had told her that so many of the men were against her because of her brains. After going on and on, she asked me for my support.

"At this point," I told her, "I am not endorsing anyone. I certainly encourage you to run; it's wonderful. We need more women in politics. I wish you all the best. If I decide to support you, I will get back to you."

Not long afterward, and after consulting Andy Young and other advisers, I called Shirley back and explained to her that I would probably go with McGovern because he looked like the strongest candidate and the one who could accomplish my purpose: defeating Nixon. She was calm and understanding.

My decision not to support Chisholm rankled some of those around me. Many of them did not like her, but were too intimidated by the possible negative fallout to support anyone else as long as she was in the race. Even my good friend Harry Belafonte asked me if I anticipated Shirley's wrath. I assured him, "I don't have a problem with Shirley. Men have a problem with Shirley, or maybe Shirley has a problem with men, but we get along fine."

Before I formally endorsed McGovern, I pulled together several advisers. Together, we mapped out a document that made certain demands on him in exchange for our support. Chief among my concerns were that there be monetary policies to cut the unemployment rate, an increase in the dismal number of black federal judges, and strategies for including blacks in the mix of federal contracting. I also asked that Walter Fauntroy, a movement friend who was the nonvoting congressional delegate from the District of Columbia, give one of McGovern's nominating speeches.

Through Yancey Martin, a black aide to McGovern who was handling the candidate's outreach to African Americans, I sent a message to the campaign saying that I was ready to make my endorsement if McGovern supported and signed the document we had prepared. When McGovern and I had spoken earlier in the year about the potential for my support, he told me, "Coretta, I can't tell you how important your endorsement is to me. In fact, it will be the most important singular endorsement in this election."

"I will be in touch with you when I make my final decision," I'd said.

And he replied, "You just have someone call me and let me know."

"No, I'll do it myself."

And now, a few weeks later, I was making that call and officially endorsing him.

Then I received a frantic call from Walter Fauntroy, who had gone to work for McGovern. "Coretta, they're trying to take the nominating speech from me and give it to Newark mayor Ken Gibson." (Gibson was the first black mayor of Newark.)

"No, they won't, Walter. McGovern made this promise to me, and he will keep it."

I immediately called Yancey Martin. "Put me through to Senator McGovern, please." It took a while to track him down, but while I was holding, I told Yancey, "I know all of you think I'm nice and sweet, but if you renege on your promise to Walter, I am going to show up in Miami and set things straight."

In that phone conversation, I exposed an unusual side of myself. Rarely do I get so angry that I resort to threats. However, once I get riled up enough to go that far, I do not make *empty* threats.

Very quickly, McGovern called back and explained that he had made the change I wanted. "I just want you to know that Walter will indeed be making a nominating address, and Ken Gibson will do something else with the vice president." He went on to tell me the whole story, and I noticed that he kept talking and talking, not allowing me to get a word in. When I turned on the television that night, I saw a news clip about McGovern and his courtship of black leaders. The news clip included the conversation he had been having with me. So that explained why he'd kept talking: the conversation was being filmed. Wouldn't it have been nice if he had told me it was being recorded and would be aired?

McGovern did secure the nomination, but he lost in November. After that defeat, to my great dismay, we were once again stuck with Richard Nixon. But with the Watergate scandal, which ended with Gerald Ford taking the White House and infamously pardoning Nixon, the Democrats looked like they were in peak shape to retake the White House in 1976. This time, I would be better prepared to fight for the inclusion and representation of African Americans, women, and the poor.

In the lead-up to the 1976 election, I met with Daddy King; Andy Young, who was then serving in Congress; Jesse Hill, the vice president of Atlanta Life Insurance Company; John Lewis; Rev. Joseph Lowery; and Herman Russell of Russell Construction, probably the wealthiest black businessman in Atlanta, to brainstorm about how we would work to influence the 1976 election. I was surprised to note that as our little group gained ground, the press began referring to us as the Atlanta Mafia.

We decided to put our weight behind Georgia governor Jimmy Carter. As governor, Carter had appointed many African Americans to statewide boards and offices. His predecessor in the governor's office was arch-segregationist Lester Maddox. In comparison, Carter was a striking example of "the New South."

Rev. Fred Bennette, a top SCLC aide, knew Carter and called him to Andy's attention. Andy felt that if George Wallace were stopped, Carter would have a good chance of winning. He decided to endorse him. In addition, Carter had asked Daddy King for his support early on. He came to the King home, sat on the front porch, and asked Daddy King if he would support him if he decided to run.

"Run for what?" Daddy King asked.

"The presidency," Carter answered.

"Of what?" Daddy King asked.

In any event, Daddy King signed on with Carter. I also liked Carter and was grateful for his generous fund-raising help with the King Center. I had talked with him privately on several occasions, and I was excited that a man who I knew possessed strong moral convictions actually had a chance to become the leader of our country. To me, Carter was a symbol of not only how much the South had changed, but how great walls and barriers of all kinds could come crashing down when the right spirit was released into the universe.

Unlike LBJ, who as a Texan was considered more western than southern, Carter was Deep South. To some across the Mason-Dixon line, there was little difference between a George Wallace and a Jimmy Carter. Yet, the two were miles apart. Carter understood and had internalized the political changes brought about by the movement and knew he was a direct beneficiary of the emerging black vote. In his campaign stumps, he emphasized the ways in which Martin was a major factor in the changing South. He also discussed the ways in which his views on foreign policy, which had a strong human rights focus, were deeply influenced by my husband.

Vernon Jordan, an Atlantan whose mother ran a successful catering business in the city, was also early into Carter's camp. However, Vernon was well aware of the dangers of stepping over the line of nonpartisanship, and he advised me not to endorse Carter. "I don't think you can continue to get away with endorsing candidates. I've been warning you about that ever since you endorsed Ed Brooke," he said. In 1967, Brooke, a Republican, became the first black elected to the U.S. Senate since Reconstruction.

"Well, you know, as long as I can get away with this, I will do it," I told Vernon.

As Jimmy Carter's campaign progressed, the "Atlanta Mafia" moniker hung heavily around our necks. Although I did not relish the term, it did telegraph our weighty role in Carter's campaign, a role we expected to carry over into his administration. We gave Carter credibility with black Americans, liberals, and progressives, and we would be ready to recommend people to high-level positions and influence policy once he was elected.

I decided to wait until after the primaries to do most of my campaigning for Carter. When Carter first announced his candidacy, Andy told me, "Daddy King and I can take care of this one; you don't need to get involved yet." Andy always had this sense that somebody in our group was going to mess up. If all of us were in the same basket, then there'd be no one to pull the others out if things went wrong. In a way, he was counting on me to come to their rescue if things fell apart.

Things didn't exactly fall apart, but they did take a potentially devastating turn when Carter admitted to having "lusted in his heart" in a *Playboy* magazine interview; on another occasion, he angered blacks with a peculiar term: *ethnic purity.*

In today's context, with all that has gone on in the White House and with the personal affairs in which candidates have engaged, "lusting in one's heart" would not be even a blip on the scandal meter. But in the 1970s, "lust" of any kind was fairly scandalous. Daddy King defended Carter, while others seized on his stalled momentum for their own advantage. After Carter's success in the Iowa caucus, the New Hampshire primary, and the Florida primary, some liberal Democrats feared his success and began an "ABC" ("Anyone But Carter") movement to try to head off his nomination. Daddy King pointed to Carter's leadership in ending the era of segregation in Georgia and helping repeal restrictive voting laws that had especially disenfranchised African Americans. Daddy King silenced Carter's critics by confronting them in his incomparable "stern preacher" style: "Listen, the man has told you he is sorry and asked for forgiveness. Haven't you ever done anything you needed forgiveness for? So you go ahead and forgive him and leave him alone."

The cloud soon lifted.

At Carter's request, in 1976 I ended up giving my first address at a Democratic National Convention. I spoke on civil rights in New York City's cavernous Madison Square Garden. Daddy King gave the Benediction. The crowd's response was heartening.

To me, though, these gestures were only symbolic. What mattered to me was what came later. Carter received about 90 percent of the black vote, which made a difference in thirteen states, carrying significant weight in the Electoral College. Carter won the presidency, and the votes of black Americans made his win possible. True to his word and his ideals, he was a good president for America, and especially for African Americans. As a result of Carter's administration, Andy became the first African American to be named Ambassador to the United Nations; Patricia Roberts Harris, who was black, became the first woman to hold two Cabinet posts, at Housing and Urban Development and at Health and Human Services; Ernie Greene, one of the Little Rock Nine (whose integration of an Arkansas high school changed history), took the reins of the Comprehensive Employment and Training Act (CETA), the administration's job training program; John Lewis was named associate director of ACTION, the federal agency for volunteer service; and Louis Martin became special assistant to the president, advising Carter on issues crucial to black America. President Carter appointed me to be a public delegate to the United Nations.

Because of our campaign-year activism and our postelection inclusion in the Carter administration, blacks influenced a good portion of the federal budget, and President Carter fought hard to save the nation's ailing cities by approving a multibillion-dollar urban policy package designed to increase investment, jobs, and housing opportunities in the inner cities.

I worked with the president on an area that I considered profoundly important to the direction of this country: the appointment of black judges to the federal bench, especially in nine of the Deep South states, where there was a shocking lack of black representation. In 1949, after Judge William Hastie was appointed to the U.S. Court of Appeals for the Third Circuit, he remained the sole African American federal appeals court judge until 1961, when President Kennedy appointed Thurgood

224 • Coretta Scott King

Marshall to the Second Circuit in the District of Columbia. Kennedy also made Wade McCree and James Parsons district judges in Michigan and Illinois.

A delegation of state representatives (some of whom, such as the Texans Eddie Bernice Johnson and Sheila Jackson Lee, went on to serve in Congress) asked me to be the leader in taking up with the president this issue of black judges. I remember a particular meeting at the White House in which President Carter turned to Griffin Bell, his attorney general, and said, "I don't know about you, but I really think that people who have lived under conditions of oppression and are not being treated as equals should not be penalized now. We should lift those barriers. And I do intend to appoint some black federal judges."

Indeed, the most significant breakthrough in history for black judges was made during the four-year Carter administration, when 37 of Carter's 258 appointed judges were African American. (In the three Reagan-Bush terms after Carter left office, only 19 African American judges were appointed, out of a total of 579 appointments.) Thanks to our lobbying efforts, Carter appointed three black judges in the Deep South, two in Alabama and one in Georgia. In Alabama, we wanted Fred Gray, a young attorney who'd handled cases for my husband and Rosa Parks, to be one of the judges. But white politicians apparently decided to punish Gray for his commitment to civil rights and blocked him. U.S. senator Howell Heflin of Alabama, who had initially supported Fred, did an about-face, saying, "We might be able to help you if you give us another name." We tried to force the issue, but found ourselves up against a brick wall, so we came up with another name and were able to get him appointed. We considered that a great victory, although he was not our first choice.

I was pleased with the strides Carter made and felt he was well positioned to be reelected in 1980. However, just as black involvement helped make him in 1976, lack of support from our community proved to be his downfall.

One of the groups I helped found was the Black Leadership Forum, which harnesses the advocacy and brain power of seventeen member organizations, including the Congressional Black Caucus, the King Center, the National Council of Negro Women, the National Urban Coalition for Unity and Peace, the National Coalition of Black Elected Officials, the

National Newspaper Publisher Association, the NAACP, the NAACP Legal Defense Fund, the SCLC, Operation PUSH, the Urban League, and so on. The forum's first leader was Vernon Jordan. During a meeting we were holding with the Congressional Black Caucus a few months before the 1980 presidential election, I began to experience a sinking feeling. Carl Holman, director of the Urban Coalition; Rev. Jesse Jackson; Joe Lowery; and others were sitting around saying that they hadn't yet made up their minds whom they were going to support. The whole scene was so appalling that I spoke up. "Well, who else is there for you to support? The choice is Carter or Reagan."

Ironically, one factor that had some black leaders up in arms against Carter was something I'd helped create: the Humphrey–Hawkins Full Employment and Balanced Growth Act. That law was very dear to my heart. It was my first attempt to shape the writing of legislation that would affect the destiny of millions. For a while, it looked as if the measure would die in the Senate, which was especially frustrating because, at the time, unemployment for black and brown people was 12.6 percent, more than double that of the national average (5.9 percent). Many black Americans blamed the president—unfairly, I believe—for the snail's pace this bill took toward passage, and this caused major disruptions between the White House and black political leaders.

In any case, not many black leaders were working hard to get out the vote for Carter; nor were they supporting the other blacks in the administration. One day, Andy and I were talking about the large number of blacks Carter had appointed. I told Andy, "You know, it's tough being the first black in an office or corporation. I understand some of them are having a rough time. They are outnumbered, and they can't fight that well from the inside. We need to form a coalition on the outside so we can help them. I'm sure they need some support."

As usual, Andy turned the tables back on me, saying, "You would be the ideal person to call this kind of group together. I tell you what, why don't you get the Black Leadership Forum to do it? Bring it up and let this group head the effort."

The opportunity to follow up on Andy's suggestion soon came, at a leadership meeting in Chicago. I arrived with what I thought was a strong proposal: to support and defend our people in government who might encounter problems balancing the interests of the underserved with those of their supervisors. I talked about how these men and women needed our help because they were struggling to fight from the inside, but the forum was unmoved by this proposal.

I could only surmise that some black leaders sat on their hands because they were envious of some of the other blacks—specifically those Atlanta power brokers, "the Atlanta Mafia"—who were close to Jimmy Carter. Others, such as Hosea Williams and Ralph Abernathy, went to extremes by campaigning for Ronald Reagan, who beat Carter by a landslide.

Carter carried only six states and the District of Columbia, earning 49 Electoral College votes to Reagan's 489. Sure, the spectacle of Americans being held hostage in Iran and a faltering economy worked against him, but I still think Carter could have won if black leaders had closed ranks behind him. I think he felt, although he never said it aloud, that the very people he'd stood up for hadn't stood up for him. I agree, we didn't stand up for him. That lack of black support for Carter hurt us, and it hurt for a long time. President Carter had worked so hard for us. And if he had stayed in office another four years, we would not have experienced Reagan's damaging supply-side economics or his anti–affirmative action budget cuts to the Equal Employment Opportunity Commission and to the Civil Rights Division of the Justice Department. Sometimes we are our own worst enemy. People may not like to hear that from me, but it is the truth.

Reagan had signaled his divisive, mean-spirited politics during the campaign. On August 3, 1980, soon after receiving the GOP nomination, he gave his first major postconvention speech—in Philadelphia, Mississippi, the town where, in 1964, the three civil rights workers James Chaney, Andrew Goodman, and Mickey Schwerner were murdered by the KKK. And on that hallowed ground of civil rights martyrs, Reagan's speech centered on states' rights, and was a direct appeal to white conservative southern voters, harkening back to the days when the federal government aided and abetted state-organized segregation and looked the other way when the rights of African Americans were being violated.

With Carter out of the White House, it did not take long for those who cared about blacks, the poor, and the working class to begin agonizing over the nation's quick retreat from the progressive gains made during the Carter years: The first four years of Reagan's presidency were disastrous for black Americans. The Reagan administration's public relations campaigns scapegoated poor blacks and labeled them undeserving of federal education dollars, of housing or employment training programs, of food stamps or dependent children benefits. Reagan's administration painted a false and tainted image of poor black women as "welfare queens," who were living large on public assistance. The goal of this dishonesty was to make voters believe that federal spending on social programs was mostly wasted on pointless handouts to black recipients, which was far from the truth. For starters, welfare benefited vastly more whites than African Americans. Beyond that, in the 1980s, more than 85 percent of the federal budget was allocated to defense spending, Social Security, Medicare, and payments on the national debt—all utterly colorblind expenditures. Yet Reagan carefully cultivated the impression that "government spending" meant "free money for black people," which caused a decrease in support and compassion for those in need, including job training, not only for blacks, but for depressed communities regardless of their race.

With so much at stake, I trained my efforts, laser-like, on the 1984 presidential election, looking for a Democratic candidate who could replace Reagan.

Black leaders were all over the political map about how to accomplish this goal. One of the hottest issues among African American leaders was Jesse Jackson's announced bid for the presidency. Jesse's run earned on many strong positives and sharp negatives that it split black leadership, which, because of its divergent interests, cannot always act as one monolithic voice. The so-called Atlanta Mafia, along with then speaker of the California State Assembly Willie Brown, and mayors Coleman Young of Detroit, Wilson Goode of Philadelphia, and Tom Bradley of Los Angeles, all supported Walter Mondale, while many other influential blacks supported Jesse. The key issue, however, is that although we took separate routes, our goal was the same: improving the lot of black America.

On the one hand, Jesse's run perfected the politics of inclusion, a vision Martin and I had always cherished. In his Rainbow Coalition were farmers, Appalachian poor, Asians, peace activists, Native Americans, Third World activists, unionists, the elderly, and gay rights activists, as well as African Americans. Jesse's run would give more blacks experience in running campaigns, and would motivate others to run. On the other hand, there was resentment among some elected black officials that, while they had stood for election in their respective districts and waited their turn to have political influence, here was a man who had never run for anything being perceived as the singular voice of black America. In other words, in this election year there would be only one political broker for black America. Martin had often warned against hoisting one person onto a pedestal as a single spokesman for blacks. The press had done exactly this to him, and he paid for it with his life.

My own reason for not supporting Jesse had nothing to do with the reports of conflicts that have been published in the press and many books. These reports of Jesse projecting himself as the "new King" and as the claimant to my husband's mantle of leadership did not concern me. There was never any question in my mind as to where my husband's mantle rested. It rested with all his followers, who could represent what Martin stood for with honor, dignity, and integrity. Also, as Martin often said, I "was only a heartbeat away" from his work in the movement; I would not abdicate to anyone else my responsibility to aid in the shaping and maintaining of his legacy.

Jesse was no stranger to me. I had known him for years. When he started Operation Breadbasket in Chicago for the SCLC in 1967, I shared with Martin how effective I thought he was. After Martin died, I began hearing criticism from others in the movement about Jesse. I was told he was obsessed with recognition; when you work with him, people told me, he has to be the star; everything is all about Jesse at all times. Over the years, I treated the reports of Jesse's self-promotion strategies as hearsay, but I started watching him and eventually came to see that what others were saying had some basis. Each time I attempted to go deep enough to reflect on Jesse's reputed exploitation of my husband before he was even in the grave, I grew so pained that I could not put my true feelings into words.

I tried to encourage Jesse. "You are so talented, highly intelligent, and handsome," I told him. "You have everything going for you. You just need to get yourself out of the way and allow God to use you."

Jesse didn't seem upset by what I was telling him, but it didn't seem to get through to him, either. I felt troubled about him; I felt that he needed to stop being so self-centered and to stop using people. Leadership is not about that. Leadership requires serving others without regard to public recognition. And I was concerned because I knew the movement needed strong male moral leaders to help fill the vacuum created by Martin's death.

Finally, I said to myself, "Maybe God will work with him and through him, and there could be a conversion, a miraculous conversion, and things will work out."

Jesse went on to develop quite a following. He knows how to use the media like few people I have ever met. At a major meeting of nationally acclaimed black leaders in 1983, he laid out his case for running for the presidency, and Andy and I were the only ones in the room who did not raise our voices in support. I did not try to hide my decision; I stood up and spoke forthrightly. I told the group that while Jesse was creative, articulate, and intelligent, I believed his run would be divisive. There would be a number of Democratic candidates, and this would make it more difficult for the front-runner to attain a clear majority. Again, I had one goal in mind: I wanted to see the defeat of Ronald Reagan, who had done so much damage already to the gains we had made through the activism of the 1960s. "I see a shift backward," I told the room. "We don't need four more years of Reagan. I understand that blacks have to get used to running, and white people have to get used to seeing them run, but the greater good right now is the defeat of Reagan. Besides, we all know that the country at this time is not going to vote for a black president, so why, with so much damage already done, why not keep our eyes on the prize of unseating Reagan?"

Needless to say, Andy and I took an unpopular position—with painful results. At the Democratic National Convention, Andy, who was then the mayor of Atlanta, was on the floor addressing a caucus of African American delegates, attempting to explain a technical point in one of the convention planks, but before he could finish, someone booed. Slowly the booing grew louder. As I viewed on television the heavy-handed treatment Andy was receiving, it really pained me. It was not necessarily the volume of the booing as the meaning of it that hurt so much. I hate to admit it, but the hostile sounds reverberating through the convention hall brought me to tears. While I sat there I thought, "Now that is a crying shame. We can't let Andy be booed like that."

As I continued to watch Andy's ordeal, I fleshed out what my response should be. I paced back and forth, thinking aloud, "We can't let this picture stand. Andy is loved by black people all over the world. This is not the way he should be coming into America's living rooms."

When I saw that other leaders were not rushing to Andy's defense, I decided I could not remain silent. I asked for an invitation to address the black delegates, a group comprising mostly Jesse Jackson supporters. They were the same ones who had unceremoniously booed Andy.

I knew what lay ahead for me during my speech. Throughout my adult life, I had put myself in harm's way for my people. I had never shied away from danger, seen or unseen. But the thought of facing down my own race unnerved me momentarily. Those you love the most can always hurt you the most. I was disturbed by the thought processes of those I would be facing, because I understood that the hostile speech that had rained down on Andy was a kind of violence. It can pierce the heart and the soul. I also thought about those who were priming the delegates to pour out their hateful speech, the kind of people who throw rocks and hide their hands. They might have marched with Martin, but they did not practice what he preached. Somehow they did not internalize what Martin always said: "We must learn to disagree without being disagreeable."

The next morning, I walked to the podium to face the convention's caucus of black delegates, and began to give a detailed chronology of Andy's career and sacrifices—not just for blacks, but for all people. "Here is a man who paid his dues, not only for us, but for future generations. He has never betrayed our trust."

Unfortunately, I didn't make it very far into my remarks before the booing started. I tried to continue. I thought about Andy, about all he stood for, and I couldn't fight back the tears. I did something then that I had never done: I broke down in public, in front of the delegates and before the TV cameras that were beaming my remarks to thousands of viewers. Somehow, I was not ashamed of my tears. They purged my hurt and my pain, and in one of my weakest moments, I felt renewed strength.

Seeing my condition, NAACP leader Hazel Dukes called to me, "Mrs. King, Mrs. King, come on, sit down." She thought I was overcome and wanted to spare me any future pain. But I wiped my eyes, braced my shoulders, and started again. I did not stop until I had finished talking about how Andy had fought the good fight for all of us, and deserved respect. I finished saying what I had to say and left the podium. As I returned to my seat, I heard applause following me.

I understand from people who were backstage at the hall that Jesse could have primed his people not to be rude, or he could have stopped the booing once it started. But his strategy, I was told, was to let the anger build and then to step out and clean things up, making himself look good on camera.

I soon healed from the ordeal, and felt stronger because I had fought for Andy, rather than hide so as to protect myself. Once again, I saw a premise working that I didn't like but had learned to accept: often you can go out on a limb, and when you are attacked, few people will come to your rescue if it means crawling out on the limb with you. But that's all a part of what's involved in leadership.

As expected, Ronald Reagan and George H. W. Bush won handily over Walter Mondale and Geraldine Ferraro. One of the casualties of the election year was the idea of a woman on the ticket of one of the two major parties. Ferraro was the first woman in the United States to be nominated on one of the tickets by a major party. How long, I wondered, would it be before a woman on the ticket was seen as an asset rather than a liability?

As hard as we had worked to unseat Reagan, the ending was like walking in a daze.

Even worse news came in the immediate wake of the election. Daddy King died on November 11, 1984.

THE DEATH OF Daddy King quickly overshadowed whatever meaning politics had for our family that year. He had lived for ten years after the murder of Mama King, but I still believe Daddy King died of loneliness. He was also weak after being operated on for prostate cancer, which drained his energy. In his later years, Daddy King wanted his grandchildren to be with him as much as possible and take turns staying with him. He had a housekeeper during the daytime, but at night, he'd be by himself. While his grandchildren adored him, it was hard for them because they were young and thought that staying with him was too confining. I kept telling them, "You know Daddy King isn't going to be with us forever, so can't you just for this time give him as much attention as possible?" They scheduled the time, but periodically somebody wouldn't show up, and then Daddy King would feel rejected. We could have gotten someone to stay with him, but he didn't want that; he wanted his family. And I suppose he felt that no one had time for him and he didn't want to be in the way.

He had started having more attacks in which his heart would start beating fast, and he had to be rushed to the emergency room. In October 1984 a cardiologist at Crawford W. Long Memorial Hospital confided to Christine, Daddy King's only surviving child, that he did not have long to live.

So, early on a Sunday morning that October, Christine called me about Daddy King's condition. I readied myself to go to the hospital and called all my kids to meet me there, except Yolanda, who was in New York. When I arrived, I could tell the doctors were very nervous about his prognosis. Dr. Bernard J. Bridges, a friend of the family, was there. He was a King Center board member and had also treated Martin. When I entered Daddy King's room, I felt his hand. It was cold.

He said, "Coretta, I think I'm dying. I hate to leave you all, but I think I'm going to have to go."

I squeezed his hand. "Well, you know you always told us that everything would be all right, so everything is going to be all right."

I and many members of the family gathered in the waiting room, forming a circle and holding hands. Isaac Sr. said, "In times like these, this family always prays." He then asked Daddy King's grandson Derek, a preacher, to pray. I had Yolanda on the phone. I told her we were getting ready to pray for Daddy King and I asked if she would like to join us. As he prayed, Derek kept breaking down. After he finished, we sat, immobilized, awaiting the worst news. Suddenly a smiling Dr. Bridges dashed in and made a startling announcement: "I don't understand what happened, but his heartbeat has returned to normal."

Isaac Sr. said, "You know, a miracle has taken place. We just finished praying."

We were overjoyed and stunned at the same time. We weren't ready for good news. Of course we were happy, but our emotions were all geared up with preparing ourselves for the inevitable, and the surprising news pushed us into a state of shock.

As people of faith, however, perhaps we shouldn't have been so surprised. We had just prayed for Daddy King's health to be returned, and before our eyes, we were seeing the power of prayer in action.

All of a sudden, we heard somebody down the hall bawling loudly. We rushed to see who it was, and found it was Dr. Bridges, who had broken down crying. I guess the tension had built up in him so much that he couldn't hold it. Here he was, the doctor, trying to save his friend, and it had happened. We hugged him, united in a moment of gratitude and spiritual understanding. Then I rushed back in to see Daddy King—and what a turnaround! He was sitting up, smiling. "I think I'm going to be around for a little while," he told me. "But not much longer."

"Dad," I said, "You don't know how long God has for you to be here." But he smiled and repeated himself. "I won't be here long."

We stayed around the hospital for the rest of the day, talking about how wonderful it was that God had given us another chance to be with Daddy King, especially his ten living grandchildren (one of A.D. and Naomi's daughters, Darlene, had died suddenly, at age twenty, while jogging). To his grandchildren, Daddy King was immovable; he was so strong, and he would always fix everything. To some of them, he was the only father they had known in the wake of Martin's and A.D.'s deaths.

Daddy King lived another month, giving everybody a chance to visit him and hold him one last time. The Sunday that he passed, I was in New York. I had gone to the theater that afternoon. When I checked my phone messages, I saw that I'd had a barrage of calls from Yolanda and Bernice informing me that he had passed.

The first thing I thought about was how earlier that morning I'd had strong thoughts about him. I'd wondered how he was doing. I guess that was an omen, though I didn't know it at the time. I called the airport, thinking the last plane to Atlanta had gone, but I found that my friend and date to the theater, Dr. Lonnie MacDonald, had called Eastern Airlines and explained to them what had happened. They held a plane for me so that I could return home that night.

When I arrived in Atlanta, Andy met me at the airport. Andy was always there when anything happened. When Mama King was murdered, he was there right away. Two years later, when A.D. and Naomi's daughter Darlene passed, he was there. I was so glad to see him. I was so glad that I could be there for Christine, too, because both her mother and father were gone now.

On the morning of November 11, 1984, Daddy King had attended church services at Atlanta's Salem Baptist Church to hear his favorite preacher, Reverend Jasper Williams. That afternoon, he suffered a heart attack and was rushed to Crawford W. Long Memorial Hospital where he died that evening at 5:41 p.m., with his surviving child, Christine, at his side. He was eighty-four. Daddy King's death marked the first time any senior member of the King family had died a natural death.

AS TIME TRUDGED on after Daddy King's death, not only did I miss his voice, but I sure could have used his shoulder to lean on. Once again I continued to try to push open the system for the powerless. I still had to take my lumps. I had my share of embarrassments, and I certainly had a good measure of egg on my face.

For the next election, 1988, which pitted Republican incumbent vice president George H. W. Bush against Michael Dukakis, I began to assess my role in national politics. I had devoted the Center to the hard work of voter education and registration. I had lobbied for causes ranging from gun control to gay rights to full employment. Not many liberals or progressive politicians in the last decade had run for office without asking for and obtaining my assistance. Yet I was not entirely pleased. I just couldn't see how, in keeping with my focus on nonviolence, I could continue to support one candidate over another. When it came to the point at which there were black candidates running against other blacks, it just didn't feel right to me.

I thought to myself, It looks like I'm *against* somebody if I'm *for* somebody else. My best bet is probably to be independent or nonpartisan.

I had addressed every Democratic National Convention since 1976, but never a Republican one. I decided that it would be a good time to continue rising above partisan politics, so a few months before the 1988 Republican National Convention, I went to see Bush. I wanted to determine if there was a way I could impart a message of goodwill to the delegation. In explaining my intentions, I told him, "My husband's dream of equality was not a Democratic dream or a Republican dream. It was for all America. I want to appeal to the convention delegates as an ambassador of goodwill, to continue this quest for political and economic inclusion for all Americans, from the very poor to the rich, for farmers, city dwellers, and suburbanites, Ivy League colleges, major corporations, and even minimum wage workers."

Instead of supporting my mission, the vice president looked at me rather blankly. "Coretta, I guess that can't do any harm. Let me check with my people and get back to you."

His people got back to me, telling me that I could make a presentation to the platform committee, which was like sentencing me to Siberia. I decided that, instead, I would put together a five-minute statement and have my deputy read it into the record at the convention, something that scores of organizations were doing. But even that token gesture was not honored. No time was allotted for my statement.

Bush sent word back to me, however. "Although I can't grant your request, I would be pleased if I could welcome you and be your host to the convention. You'd be our special guest."

I dreaded every minute of it, but I felt I had to go. I worried because I knew that I would have a lot of explaining to do, and I wasn't sure that people would understand my gesture as an attempt to move above party politics for the good of the country.

In the meantime, Bush let his staff know that he wanted me to sit in a special place at the convention, which I did. An aide gestured for me to move to a phone where Bush could talk to me. When I got up, I saw that the phone was right next to Barbara Bush, who had been gracious to me in our few encounters. She reached out to me and said, "Coretta, I really appreciate your coming, and I hope you're not embarrassed by being here."

Trying to put her at ease, I said, "Oh, no, no."

When I finished talking to her husband and got ready to move back to my seat, she urged, "Don't move. Just sit here."

There I was stuck. The cameras were right on me and Barbara Bush. The national television audience saw all of it. When I got back to

Atlanta, I found there'd been a barrage of calls into my office, most of them angry. Some people were even in tears. Others felt betrayed, afraid that I was going to jump ship and work for the Republicans, as some of Martin's cohorts had already done.

It took a lot of explaining, and I am still not sure that many people understood my gesture. Personally, I listened to the speeches at the Republican National Convention, and it was very hard for me to keep a straight face. I didn't agree with much that was being said. It was a very hard experience for me.

I decided then and there that although I would continue attending both Democratic and Republican conventions, I would not make any more endorsements. I had more understanding now of why Martin never publicly endorsed candidates. In August 1988, I sent a statement to the press that began:

> On many occasions over the past twenty years, I have been asked by friends seeking high political office in the United States for my endorsement. As a matter of conscience, I have endorsed a few candidates because of the consistency of their lives, values, and philosophy with the dream of Martin Luther King, Jr. However, I have always believed that it is my mission in life to perpetuate his dream. His dream pictures a world free from racism, poverty, and free from war and violence.
>
> This dream is non-partisan. This dream transcends politics and political parties. I believe it is my job to keep the dream before this nation and its leaders. The leaders of our nation are both Democrat and Republican, liberal and conservative. It is for this reason that I am not endorsing candidates for public office. I am not endorsing one party over another. A non-partisan position is more consistent with the spirit of nonviolence, which can help build bridges of hope and trust. A non-partisan position can more effectively bring the diverse peoples of this nation together to end racism, poverty, and war.

For forty years, I had been working in the political system, attempting to make things better for those without a vote or a voice. I may have decided to work differently, but I was not going to stop working.

NINETEEN

------ ❀ ------

Injustice Anywhere Is a Threat
to Justice Everywhere

I NOW KNOW that all my life there has been a trajectory, a jagged path connecting me from Nowhere USA to the front door of the World House. When I was a teenager sitting on my porch bench in Marion, Alabama, in the still of the night, with no sound but the crackling of pine cones, I would sometimes look at the moon and wonder what was on the other side. I would also wonder about our big world itself and all the other kinds of people out there somewhere. I knew that one day I would be part of something larger.

My early yearning was for the better and the greater, for the kinder and the more graceful; it was for the opposite of what I saw in the white people I grew up around, those men and women who looked at me with hate and spite, as if I had committed a crime just by being born black. I had experienced meanness, but I yearned for kindness. I wanted to be part of whatever would bring peace, love, and fairness to wherever I would find myself.

Working with Martin brought me nearer to becoming a citizen of the Beloved Community of which I dreamed, and the King Center allowed me to advance those efforts, even on an international stage. I had always seen the work we were doing in the movement as part of a global human rights struggle, and I identified with all suffering people around the world, no matter what color they were. In the end, I really consider myself a human rights activist.

One particularly meaningful and exciting human rights opportunity came in 1977, when President Jimmy Carter appointed me a public delegate to the Thirty-Second General Assembly of the United Nations. I would wager most people have never heard of a UN public delegate. Each year, a few Americans are appointed to these posts by the president. I served with actors Robert Redford and Paul Newman, and with W. Averell Harriman, the former governor of New York. From my vantage point, as a black person born into second-class citizenship and as a woman born into third-class citizenship, the chance to occupy a first-class seat with a window to the world left me both awed and humbled. And my UN role allowed me to expand the message of nonviolence and human rights, to form relationships with world leaders, and to deepen my calling to the World House.

On March 17, 1977, I was intensely proud to be seated directly behind my dear friend Andy Young, who was then the U.S. ambassador to the United Nations, when President Carter, one of the first U.S. presidents to make human rights the center of his foreign policy, addressed the UN General Assembly. As expected, President Carter spoke about the major challenge of reducing the staggering arms race. "The Soviet Union and the United States have accumulated thousands of nuclear weapons," he told the assembly. "Our two nations now have five times more missile warheads than we had just eight years ago. But we are not five times more secure. On the contrary, the arms race has only increased the risk of conflict." Somewhat less expected, however, was Carter's emphasis on human rights; he called on the body to commit itself to the peace and the well-being of "every individual, no matter how weak, no matter how poor."

He refused to continue overlooking the human rights abuses of our allies, which had been the custom. He was also credited with ending more than thirty years of U.S. political and military support for one of Latin America's most abusive leaders, President Anastasio Somoza of Nicaragua. After too many years of Richard Nixon, it seemed to me that our country was finally preparing to practice at home some of the democratic values we professed to others around the world—as well as moving human rights from the sidelines of foreign policy to the front row. It was amazing to be at the United Nations at that time.

I suppose this meant so much to me personally because many of those around me were criticizing me for not focusing solely on racism and civil rights at a time when I saw the opportunity, the moral imperative even, to advocate for a variety of issues: global warming, famine, nuclear proliferation, peace in the Middle East, terrorism, drug cartels, gun trafficking, apartheid, gender equality, ending violence against women and girls, and the invasion or occupation of other countries.

At the United Nations, Andy and I seized every chance to insert nonviolent alternatives into the unfeeling talk of militarism. We put human faces on collateral damage and maintained our stance that poverty was one of the dire consequences of budgets heavily larded with weaponry. We called attention to the ways in which ethnicity and race contributed to disparities in the dispensation of funds for refugees. It seemed that the darker the populace, the fewer the resources made available and the slower the distribution of those resources.

I was a nonvoting delegate in the United Nations; however, it was my job to build healthy, positive relationships wherever I could. How well I understood that so much is accomplished through informal relationships! Wherever and whenever there was an opportunity, I listened, and I spoke out about the value of treating every life with human dignity and respect. I found that I could carry the message of human rights to the Russians, the Israelis, the Greeks, the Iranians, the Cambodians, and whomever else I met in the hallways or spoke to at luncheons and over dinner. If you get to know people and they come to like you, you can influence them. Even with the ongoing tensions between the United States and the Soviet Union, Andy and I made friends. I remember going to a dinner with the Soviet delegation at which Andy teased them that they looked like Harvard grads: they spoke very good English and looked very American. We would all joke back and forth in this manner, despite the wider political pressures. Our delegation, like all the other delegations, had only one vote. But we had moral persuasion, and I know that counted for so much.

While I felt good about the idea of the United Nations as a deliberative body with at least the stated goals of peacekeeping, many of our government officials and bureaucrats, especially the Republicans, did not share my view and did not want to fund the UN or its mission. I always disagreed with their assessment. Our involvement in the UN places the United States within the only international forum that currently exists for the consistent promotion of ideals guided by our embrace of liberty, democracy, equality, individual rights, and free market economics. It also allows us to listen to the views of others. In the view of its critics, though, "the U.N. is too messy, too loud, too ineffective; it contains too much of the wrong kinds of colors, religions, and non-religions." Yet, when I met with the delegates from other countries, I saw their belief that the United Nations was the best hope for peace, and for closing the gap between rich and poor nations.

Although my UN posting was only three months long, I never really departed. I maintained the relationships I built during my time there, and continued to work for the issues I'd taken on. I also carried with me the lasting impact of getting to share sacred space with Eleanor Roosevelt merely by walking the same halls that she walked and by stepping into the human rights environment she helped create. Eleanor Roosevelt and Mary McLeod Bethune (the daughter of slaves and the founder of Bethune College, a private school for African Americans in Daytona Beach, Florida) are the two female pioneers I consider to be my greatest role models.

As a human rights activist, I deeply admired Eleanor's life. She was called the First Lady of the World, and I identified with the globetrotting humanitarian work she carried out after her husband's death. Even though she died sixteen years before I walked in the doors of the United Nations, I felt her spirit there. The language we were using, the goals and ideals, the policies that President Carter, Andy, and I employed to champion for human rights—Eleanor laid the framework for all this. She helped create the UN Commission on Human Rights, and as its first chair, she helped draft the Universal Declaration of Human Rights, the most widely recognized statement of those rights to which every person on our planet is entitled. Its preamble states that "All human beings are born free and equal in dignity and rights."

While those words sound basic, it is difficult for many nations to accept them. To do so means making monumental changes in their forms of government. Acceptance of that basic preamble requires agreements that allow freedom of speech and religion, pledges to prohibit discrimination and torture, promises to facilitate the right to work, and accordance with the scores of legally binding human rights treaties currently in existence. The Declaration is used as a yardstick to measure governmental performance (or lack thereof) both by UN bodies and nongovernmental organizations. Whether we are talking about oppression, genocide, or sex trafficking, the Declaration guides our path. The hand of Eleanor is forever upon us.

I also admire Eleanor as a great civil rights leader. When the Daughters of the American Revolution denied Marian Anderson the right to perform at Washington's Constitution Hall in 1939, Eleanor resigned from the group in protest and helped arrange another concert, on the steps of the Lincoln Memorial. She also had Anderson perform at a White House dinner. In addition, she arranged the appointment of Mary McLeod Bethune (my two role models were friends) as director of the Division of Negro Affairs of the National Youth Administration. To ensure Bethune would be received properly when she visited the White House, the First Lady greeted her at the gate and embraced her. They would walk in arm in arm, smiling.

I wish I had been there to see those two great women together. When I was working so hard to build the King Center, I thought of how Mary helped raise money for her college by selling pies on the side of the road. Together and apart, Eleanor and Mary left lasting legacies. Their stories inspired me and brought light to my darkest moments.

Serving in the United Nations was one of the most fulfilling experiences of my life, and a role of which I am deeply proud. I had a sense that by being on this world stage, I could grow in my understanding of life-changing issues. Simply being in that environment was inspiring and empowering. Similarly, I was honored when President Carter also appointed me to serve as commissioner of the International Women's Year Conference. The appointment gave me the opportunity to be a key organizer and participant in the National Women's Conference, which was empowered by Congress to assess the status of women in the United

States and make recommendations to the president and Congress. The event took place from November 18 to 21, 1977, in Houston; it was the first meeting of its type in the United States since the 1848 Women's Rights Convention in Seneca Falls, New York. Approximately two thousand delegates from fifty states and six territories participated in the meeting, which was attended by an additional fifteen to twenty thousand observers.

Gay rights were without a doubt one of the most contentious issues at the women's conference that year. Several women's groups went so far as to advocate for a constitutional ban on same-sex marriage, and to define marriage as the union of a man and a woman as husband and wife. While I did not issue a formal statement at that time, in private conversations I spoke in defense of gay rights. I could tell from those same private conversations that there was quite a buzz at the conference over my support for gay rights and my conviction that gay and lesbian people and their families deserved to have legal protections, whether by marriage or civil union. But I would not budge.

I believe unequivocally that discrimination against people because of their sexual orientation is wrong. It is unacceptable in a democracy that protects the human rights of all its citizens. Racism, sexism, anti-Semitism, and bigotry based on sexual orientation are all forms of intolerance that are unworthy of America as a democracy. If the basic right of one group can be denied, all groups become vulnerable. Those who oppose discrimination and support equal opportunity should stand firm in support of universal human rights. As my husband once said, "Injustice anywhere is a threat to justice everywhere." Furthermore, in the civil rights movement, gays and lesbians could be found on the front line of every campaign led by my husband, from Montgomery to Memphis, and they made many courageous contributions during those long, hard years. At the National Women's Conference, I refused to turn my back on them, and I will continue to appeal to state legislatures and the federal government, to ensure civil rights protections against discrimination based on sexual orientation.

In 1993, I made a strong stand for gay rights, speaking out firmly against discrimination in the armed services by writing a letter to the U.S. Congress on this matter. I compared the arguments for banning gay people from military service to similar arguments made against black people. When military leaders said that they themselves were not prejudiced, but were concerned about what "others" might think, I pointed out that this was not very different from businesses that cited "customer" preference as justification for their refusal to hire African Americans to work in their stores.

Another issue for which I was an enthusiastic champion was ending apartheid in South Africa.

FOLLOWING THE SUCCESS of the Montgomery Bus Boycott back in 1955, other boycotts had spread to southern cities in the United States, such as Birmingham and Tallahassee. Much to our surprise, however, in 1957, blacks also launched a bus boycott in Johannesburg, South Africa, in an effort to call attention to their plight and show solidarity with our movement. That protest shook us up. It made us focus our attention on how brutally the white Afrikaners in South Africa were treating those they classified as black and colored. We recoiled at the news of the 1960 Sharpeville Massacre, in which Afrikaner police shot at two hundred blacks, killing sixty-nine of them, during a peaceful protest against unfair "pass laws," which were designed to keep the black and colored populations segregated.

The greatest apartheid-era catastrophe, however, and the one that galvanized the world's attention and fueled the movement to boycott companies supporting apartheid, was the one that happened on June 16, 1976, the year before Carter sent me to the United Nations. That June, students were protesting the government closure of many of their schools, and resisting an official policy that required them to be taught only in Afrikaans, the language of the Afrikaners, which most blacks did not speak. As part of this protest, the students organized a march in Soweto. More than 20,000 students turned up to the march, followed closely by the police. Tensions mounted between the blacks and the police. Angered by their plight, the children taunted the police, who responded with tear gas and then with live ammunition. They shot round after round. Children of all ages were gunned down, 360 children in all. Reports showed haunting images of small children, little children like Hector Pieterson, swatted down and killed without thought, like they had no more worth than pesky mosquitoes.

I made ending apartheid a priority of the King Center, and a personal one as well. In the mid-1980s, the resistance to apartheid was moving so slowly in the United States that it had to be embraced by the African American community to gain momentum. In 1982, when I addressed the World Council of Churches in Vancouver, I had met with Desmond Tutu, who was then secretary-general of the South African Council of Churches, and with Rev. Allan Boesak, a well-respected antiapartheid activist and president of the World Alliance of Reformed Churches. The two men had wanted to work with me, and I'd wanted to visit South Africa, and I understood that their churches could provide the right kind of sponsorship for my trip. Having a host for a visit was very important, because visiting South Africa was a delicate undertaking, laden with political complexities. Tensions between the apartheid regime and the majority black populace were high.

In 1983, when Reverend Boesak spoke at the King Center to commemorate the twentieth anniversary of the March on Washington, I renewed the subject of a trip to Soweto and to Cape Town. "I will be attending the United Nations International Women's Conference in Nairobi, Kenya, in 1985," I told him. "I really would like to come to South Africa on my way. Could either you or Bishop Tutu host the visit?" But, strangely enough, neither Reverend Boesak nor Bishop Tutu responded to that request. In 1985, while I was attending that conference in Nairobi, some of the other attendees there, insiders in the Free South Africa Movement, briefed me on the reasons for the cold shoulder concerning my proposed trip to South Africa. They told me that Randall Robinson, a very talented man and the head of TransAfrica and one of the leaders of the Free South Africa Movement, and Jesse Jackson had been working to turn some of the black South Africans against me, because they were working in the region and considered me to be infringing on their turf.

At the time, I didn't think much about what I'd been told. But the next time I saw Rev. Boesak in Atlanta, he did not seem eager for me to come to South Africa. In fact, it seemed that he was deliberately delaying me. In a conversation with Andy Young, Reverend Boesak intimated that it might take six months or more to plan my trip.

"Baloney." That was the response from Stoney Cooks, Andy's top aide, when I told him what Reverend Boesak had said. "You need to go right now," Stoney added. "It's not like you don't know anything about South Africa. You have held conferences on it, given speeches, and written numerous columns on sanctions and apartheid. You need to go now." He was right, of course, but one cannot just up and go to South Africa without some of the main leaders in Soweto, such as Boesak or Desmond Tutu, hosting you. So since they did not honor my request, I did not go at that time.

Still, I could not drop the issue. I was troubled in my spirit by the unrest in South Africa. The very instability that was complicating my plans was drawing me to travel there, because I understood the power of strategic nonviolent opposition. One of my board members, who was agonizing over the same situation, asked, "Of all the things we're doing with nonviolence and teaching nonviolence, why can't we help South Africa?" And I said, "I think we can."

I appointed a committee to come up with a plan, a program, and a way by which we could address the problem of apartheid. Perhaps a visit to South Africa would be helpful. Therefore, we proceeded to plan a trip, and I selected a group of people who I thought represented different segments of the community: Rev. Barbara Skinner, a member of the board of advisers, who could help us on our fact-finding mission with women; Christine King Farris, for education; Carol Hoover and Bob Brown, both King Center board members and business persons; Bernard Lafayette, to help advise on nonviolence training; and my son Martin III for youth outreach. In the end, we had about thirteen people ready for the trip. One of them was Ronald Quincy, a State Department representative who had been a White House Fellow and who later became executive director of the King Center.

As we prepared, we consulted Andy Young on the culture and the correct protocol. "What you're trying to do is very difficult," he told us. "It's almost impossible. If you go, you have to talk to everybody. You have to talk to the enemy, President Botha, and when you talk to one set of people, other groups will get angry with you. They won't speak to you. But I think if anybody can be successful in doing it, you can."

We also followed protocol and sought information and a briefing from the U.S. State Department. I let President Reagan know my plans, so that when I returned, I could tell him what I'd done and try to get his support; we hoped to get him to come around and support a strong antiapartheid act. I also called on Vice President Bush and Secretary of State George Shultz, telling them about our plans and asking for their advice and support.

Secretary Shultz encouraged the trip, as well as my plans to try to see Nelson Mandela. If I went over there and didn't try to see Mandela, he told me, people would ask why I hadn't at least made an attempt. He also said that the only way I could arrange that meeting was through then-president P. W. Botha. He added, "You and Dr. King stood for the philosophy of nonviolence and forgiveness. It would be a powerful thing if you could get permission to see Nelson and Winnie, and the three of you could be together. Can you imagine what that photograph would look like, going around the world? It would send a powerful message of unity and support for the Mandelas."

"Well," I told him, "we will try."

So, through the King Center, we made an appointment with President Botha. At our meeting, I planned to bring up the question of visiting Mandela. The State Department assigned a person to go with us, which was very helpful. In those days, many South Africans were deeply suspicious of visitors, and my people were very upset about my not taking security.

I also obtained a briefing from some of the U.S. lobbyists for the African National Congress (ANC), the lead party against apartheid, as well as from some ANC activists in South Africa, such as Oliver Tambo. When I spoke to them about nonviolence, I put it this way: "You know that economic sanctions are a form of nonviolence. You do not have to pick up a gun. Withdrawing your patronage is a weapon Martin used all the time. We didn't cooperate with people who discriminated against us, and who were doing evil and unjust things to us. If we can get sanctions against South Africa going in the United States, this would be a nonviolent tool." I think such explanations were helpful in showing an alternate vision; many people at that time did not see sanctions in this light.

If the goal is ending a violent and unjust regime, do you treat your enemies as persons beyond human understanding, as unworthy of any interaction? Do you designate them hopeless cases and slam the door? I see it as a crucial article of faith in nonviolence that even the most violent of adversaries can be approached in a true spirit of reconciliation. When he first organized his nonviolent resistance campaigns, Mahatma Gandhi held frequent meetings with Boer general Jan Christiaan Smuts, his principal adversary in South Africa. Gandhi once said, "In a nonviolent conflict, there is no rancor left behind, and in the end, the enemies are converted into friends. That was my experience in South Africa with General Smuts."

In 1985, at a time of national and international boycotts and protests against companies that invested in South Africa and calls for government sanctions against South Africa, I was arrested along with Martin III and Bernice in a protest against apartheid at the South African embassy in Washington, DC. At last, in 1986, it was time to go to South Africa. I had accepted an invitation to the enthronement of Bishop Tutu, who was about to become Archbishop of Cape Town, South Africa's legislative capital, located in the southernmost part of the country. Accompanied by my board members, I flew into Harare, Zimbabwe, on September 2, 1986, to attend the Conference on Non-Aligned Nations. While there, I met with President Kenneth Kaunda of Zambia; President Quett K. J. Masire of Botswana; President Samora Machel of Mozambique; Prime Minister Robert Mugabe of Zimbabwe; Oliver Tambo, past president of the Non-Aligned Nations conference; and my good friend Indira Gandhi, all of whom were members of the nonaligned nations. All agreed that whatever sanctions were imposed against South Africa, the United States must help provide economic aid to keep the country and the region from collapsing. From there, I went on to Johannesburg, South Africa, where I attended a dinner for Leon Sullivan, a Baptist preacher from Philadelphia who was a major player in helping businesses in South Africa work out fair labor practices. I also met with several South African businesspeople and civil and community leaders across racial lines. We also held international prayer breakfasts in Johannesburg and Cape Town.

When we arrived in Cape Town, however, we found that there was trouble brewing with regard to our arrival. Carl Ware, a top executive for Coca-Cola who had worked extensively in South Africa, called me; he said the word on the street was that Winnie Mandela and Rev. Allan Boesak were not going to meet with me because I had an appointment to see President Botha. I was also told that some black activists thought my meeting with Botha was aiding and abetting his murder and repression of black South Africans, a very serious and dangerous misconception.

Several sources also told me that Randall Robinson had called ahead and told people that I had been ill-advised, didn't know what I was doing, and was in South Africa "to stir up stuff." Bishop John Walker, the dean of the Washington National Cathedral, also in Cape Town for Tutu's enthronement, was so worried about what he had heard that he knocked on my door at my hotel one night to share his concern for me. "I am so upset, because we don't want your image tarnished by the negative things being said," he told me. He went on to say that the statements in question seemed to be coming from Randall Robinson and Jesse Jackson.

Randall had been working with TransAfrica on the problem of apartheid for a long time, but I had also been working on this problem for a long time. I'd even tried to work with Randall. Whenever he called a coalition together, I was there. I was at all the press conferences. I was at all the marches. I made statements. I was very actively involved. I'd even asked him for a briefing before I left for South Africa, but his strategy appeared to be to try to turn the fellows against me—and to question the potential of nonviolent protest in South Africa.

In any event, at a ceremony following his enthronement, Bishop Tutu graciously introduced me, the only person he introduced at that service. He also gave our delegation front-row seats across from his family. I had eight or nine people with me: Martin III, Christine, Carol Hoover, Ebenezer Church pastor Joseph Roberts, and several others. We have beautiful memories of that service.

When I finally had a chance to talk to Desmond, I said, "I want to understand what the problem is. I was trying to meet with President Botha because I wanted to see Nelson Mandela, and I was told that meeting with you and the president was the only way I could do it."

Desmond told me, "You see, there's nothing wrong with your meeting with our national president. I have met with him, but the problem is, because of killings that have taken place this year, some groups will take your meeting and use it against us. The enthronement is an act of reconciliation, and that's enough for them to focus on right now."

What Desmond was telling me fit in with what I'd been told Randall and Jesse were saying. Finally, I called off my meeting with Botha. I also called off a meeting with Zulu chief Mangosuthu Buthelezi, because I knew he was having problems with the ANC. The ANC had even said that if someone met with Buthelezi, he or she could not meet with the ANC. I took my board's advice and chose not to go ahead with the meetings.

In the aftermath of my visit to South Africa, I had a meeting with Randall and some of my board members. It was one of the most insulting meetings I ever attended. "Why did you go over then when you did not know what you were doing?" Randall demanded. He accused me of setting the Free South Africa Movement back ten years. He took aim at Bob Brown, a businessman on my board, who he claimed was dictating my actions in South Africa. Randall's accusations did not sit well with me. I remember defending myself firmly. Adding to my agitation was the fact that my board members did not defend me. Not even Walter Fauntroy, who was the first chair of the King Center board and whom I helped get elected to Congress. They all just sat there and listened.

I prayed about all these events. I realize now that I didn't do enough planning, but I also believe I was undermined. It was helpful to remember what Martin sometimes said when he preached a sermon entitled "Going Forward by Going Backwards." In that sermon, he related the parable of Christ being left in the temple as a child. His parents journeyed a whole day before they realized that He had been left; to recover this precious treasure, they had to go back. Now, I told myself, I have to go back before I can go forward. I have to build more direct ties with all the leaders of all the groups involved in South Africa.

We took quite a beating in the press for the on-again, off-again meetings with Botha, but I was optimistic about the good news we'd spread as we traveled the length and breadth of that tormented but mesmerizingly beautiful land. We built support there for economic sanctions, work stoppages, and an expanded Christmas boycott of downtown stores by blacks—all of which we presented as alternatives to guns. We also had a series of encouraging discussions with other white and black leaders, who expressed a desire for greater international cooperation.

And I was privileged enough to have met Nelson's wife, Winnie, who embraced me as a friend. Her words were a virtual torrent of pain as she shared with me how the apartheid system had stolen her life, how it felt to be denied the loving touch of her husband for twenty-three years, how she grieved over his forced labor in the Robben Island prison's rock quarry, which was damaging his lungs and his vision.

Most of the time, Winnie spoke about her husband, but she also talked about herself and her children. She described the brutality and the isolation she felt after being beaten in prison and then banished and dumped in a house some 230 miles away from her home in Soweto. The ramshackle structure had no running water or heat, and only dirt floors.

"I had to live that way for eight years," she told me. "I am a trained social worker, but I was not allowed to be employed. The plan was to break me emotionally and financially. My husband was taken; my livelihood was taken. But through the help of friends, my two girls, Zenani and Zindzi, were sent off to private school in Swaziland, where they could get a good education."

When Winnie talked about her children, her face relaxed. With pride, she told me of the marriage of her oldest daughter, Zenani, to Prince Thumbumuzi Dlamini of Swaziland, who was the son of the Swazi king Sobhuza II. But she also expressed her sadness over her inability to spend more time with her first grandchild, whom Nelson had named Zaziwe, which translates to "Hope."

Winnie even shared with me some of the letters Nelson had written her. One read, "Had it not been for your visits, wonderful letters and your love, I would have fallen apart many years ago."

After that first meeting in Soweto, Winnie and I developed a very sisterly relationship. In 1992 we brought her to the Center for King Week to participate in a panel following the Center's annual Salute to Greatness Awards Dinner, and she served as grand marshal for our King Week parade and march. Later in our private conversations during her visit, Winnie was very forthright, telling me directly that she came to the King Center to learn "the language of peace."

Still, though I have tremendous admiration for her, Winnie struggled with the central tenets of nonviolence. When her history is considered, I can understand this. Not only did she have to spend twenty-seven years of her thirty-eight-year marriage without Nelson, but the apartheid government regularly detained her. As she worked to keep her husband's name and movement alive, she was tortured, subjected to house arrest, kept under surveillance, held in solitary confinement at Pretoria Central Prison for a year and a half, and then banished to a remote town. Unfortunately, her reputation was damaged by charges of criminal behavior; it was also reported that, in 1986, she endorsed a local practice of "necklacing," during which suspected traitors were burned alive inside automobile tires soaked in gasoline.

I don't know whether those charges are true, and naturally I could never condone such acts of violence. I can, however, identify with her as a woman who is the wife of a man who led a revolution. In terms of what we have to do to keep things going when our husbands are no longer on the scene, when they are in jail or murdered, such women have so much in common. Winnie kept Nelson's memory and movement alive in the public eye. She held things together, and throughout her personal suffering (her jailing, banning, and torture), she reacted with so much strength and dignity. It is an awful thing to be banished and kept from your children. Who wouldn't be emotionally scarred by that ordeal?

Of course, I am also sympathetic to what Nelson went through. He is my hero. He led his nation into a democratic state and showed them that the ways you must behave once you become a nation versus being in a movement are very different. For him to go through all he did, come out of prison without being bitter and being able to show love to his enemies, I think he deserved whatever happiness he could get. And Winnie does, too. So when the news came, in 1996, that they were divorcing, I was sad but not necessarily surprised. To me, they were both good people who just could not make it. I think that in the years of separation, they grew apart. Winnie was so young when they married, and during Nelson's imprisonment, they didn't get to spend enough time together for their relationship to really bond them to one another.

Nevertheless, when Nelson Mandela was finally released from prison on February 11, 1990, Winnie was by his side to rejoice. The whole world rejoiced.

Shortly after Nelson was released, I received a call from Harry Belafonte. He told me that the ANC had asked him to ask me if I could coordinate and help raise funds for Nelson and Winnie Mandela's visit to America. Of course I readily agreed. In fact, I had already invited Nelson and Winnie to the King Center. I turned to Atlanta mayor Maynard Jackson first and asked him to head the committee. He told me he was busy with his crime program, but would support whatever I did.

"Maynard," I countered, "you are the number one citizen of this city and it would be appropriate for you to do this." He still couldn't take the lead, so I turned to Jesse Hill, my board chairman, and asked him to start raising the funds needed to bring in Nelson and his wife.

In the meantime, I went off to South Africa and Zambia, where I worked to convince the ANC and others how important it was for the Mandelas to come to Atlanta. We also needed to raise a few hundred thousand dollars, which was difficult; white people in Atlanta were not eager to raise funds for the ANC, which many associated with communism. So I went to Coca-Cola. I had a very good relationship with Donald Keough, the president and chief operating officer. He told me that he found the cause appropriate and was happy to support us in any way he could, but he feared a backlash. He didn't think it was wise to be publicly identified with the ANC, but he was happy to support us anonymously.

Then, suddenly, the positive flow was interrupted.

Randall Robinson apparently got wind of our plans. If Coca-Cola was involved, he said, his group was going to boycott the company. In other words, he was going to encourage the ANC not to allow the Mandelas to come to Atlanta.

Soon, we began to hear rumors that the Nelson Mandela event had been canceled. I first heard this from Harry Belafonte. He told me it was Randall's doing. And he said he'd told Randall, "You have to be out of your mind. We can't let this happen." Harry and I pushed back, and managed to get the Mandela trip rescheduled. However, the back-and-forth had tired Nelson out, and some of his activities had to be curtailed. He was just overwhelmed. And our staff was unnecessarily overwhelmed.

What was so disconcerting was that Randall Robinson had apparently urged this boycott; I heard that over and over, from many trusted sources.

In any event, a few months later, the Mandelas visited us at the King Center as part of their tour of Canada, the United States, and Europe. I, along with Mayor Jackson, Georgia governor Joe Frank Harris, and the Rev. Joseph E. Lowery, then president of the SCLC, met the Mandelas' chartered jet when it landed at Atlanta's Hartsfield International Airport. We greeted them as they deplaned and walked down a red carpet to their waiting armored limousine.

On the evening of June 27, 1990, about fifty thousand people crammed into Georgia Tech's Bobby Dodd Stadium at historic Grant Field to hear Nelson speak. It was my pleasure to introduce him. In his speech, he linked the struggles of the poor and powerless around the world to the great freedom expressions of the American civil rights era under Dr. King, and he thanked the Center's board and staff for their support "in their just cause for freedom and opportunity in a one-person, one-vote democracy South Africa."

Before his address, he pulled up to our Center, which he called the home of the civil rights movement, through a huge cadre of police cars blocking the street to allow the arrival of his entourage. He met privately with my family and staff and took part in ceremonies, during which we presented him with the King Center's International Freedom Award for 1990. He also laid a wreath at my husband's crypt.

The reaction to the visit by Steve Klein, the King Center's public relations person, summed up the event for many. "When he came through the door, everyone's jaw dropped," Klein said. "The Center has been visited by heads of states, prime ministers, presidents, kings and queens. But those visits didn't measure up to Mandela's. He was bigger than royalty. Mandela is somebody who actually earned the tremendous respect of people all over the world. He didn't inherit it."

My daughter Bernice put it this way: "Outside of Jesus Christ and my parents, he is the one. He had such a very calm spirit, very dignified . . . a forgiving spirit. It was so comforting for me to see him."

As I witnessed the enthusiastic outpouring of support from Americans of all races, creeds, and national origins who flocked to greet this world citizen everywhere he traveled, it felt like further proof that my husband was correct when he reminded his supporters that "the moral arc of the universe is long, but it bends toward justice."

In 1992, two years after Nelson's visit, the King Center became directly involved in South Africa in advance of that nation's first truly democratic national elections. The U.S. State Department gave the Center a grant to create a curriculum and to train South African activists in the principles of Martin's nonviolence philosophy. We were told that our help was needed to counter what State Department officials feared would be riots and murders when those first free elections were held.

It was widely assumed that the climate was ripe for violent confrontation on many fronts. In South Africa, 35 million black Africans had suffered excruciating violence under white rule, represented by 4.3 million white Afrikaners. We understood the possibility of violence both from people who were being forced to give up their power and from people who had been birthed in the crucible of violence and oppression. We were notified of horrific acts erupting between the various tribes, all of them arguing over the contents of the new Constitution being drafted and the outcome of the first national election.

When the call came for the Center to participate in the training, we were ready. I had been to the region several times; we knew the terrain would be different, but we also knew that we had shared experiences. As civil rights activists, we had all been on the firing lines of terrorism in America. From personal experience, many King Center staff knew what it felt like to be shot at or wrongly imprisoned, to have their homes firebombed or to be denied the right to vote. We also had a few staff members who had worked in South Africa.

Our three senior trainers, Harold Sims, Dr. Bernard Lafayette, and Charles Alphin Sr., incorporated bits of language that reflected the South African principle of *ubuntu* (which conveys a fervent belief in respect for human life) into the King Center teaching materials, including into the Center's six principles of nonviolence.

In South Africa, one great advantage in teaching the principles and the steps was, by good fortune, already having a supportive institution in place there. In the mid-1980s, Rev. Joseph Tshwane, a South African student at the Union Theological Seminary in Richmond, Virginia, had come to the Center to study Martin's principles of nonviolence, as scholars and students from all over the world continue to do. He was a charismatic figure and a recording artist, affiliated with a Presbyterian church. He had asked us for permission to establish the King-Luthuli Transformation Centre in Johannesburg. After consulting with local leaders in South Africa, including Bishop Desmond Tutu, the King Center helped Tshwane found the King-Luthuli Transformation Centre in 1987. Tshwane understood how to integrate Kingian principles with the *ubuntu* respect for life. In 1992, when the peace-training preparations for the 1994 election began, the preexistence of the Transformation Centre helped us avoid the appearance of imposing a Western concept on South Africa's people.

The combined ideologies of the King Center and the Transformation Centre and our shared emphasis on nonpartisanship also helped us avoid trouble from the heated divisions that had flared up between Mandela's party, the ANC, which was primarily Xhosa, and the primarily Zulu Inkatha Freedom Party, headed by the powerful chief Mangosuthu Buthelezi. So, as the unprecedented election, the first in which all South African citizens could vote, neared, seeds of nonviolence were planted, but we were aware that seeds of violence were plenteous as well. Alarming news headlines in papers such as the *London Daily Mail* predicted a race war, fueled by right-wing whites. Reports of potential all-out violence between the ANC and the Zulus also increased. Chief Buthelezi warned his followers to brace for violence and even death. Townships around the country were rife with violence. The ANC's headquarters in the Shell House in Johannesburg were bombed in April 1994, two days before the election. Nine people died, and the Zulus were blamed for this attack. Meanwhile, ANC guards had reportedly shot eight demonstrators.

Our staff, working alongside South African activists, were armed with little more than their Bibles and their faith that a peaceful transition was not only necessary but achievable. All around us, emergency plans were being made. There was a scheme in place to airlift up to 350,000 Britons out of South Africa should the country slide into chaos. Shortly before the election, our State Department recommended that all American workers leave South Africa, because of the virtual certainty that violence would overwhelm the country. Nevertheless, our small staff persevered.

In an effort to maintain our nonpartisan image with the different groups, our trainers wore aprons with the King Center emblem embossed on the front and the King-Luthuli emblem on the back. These men and women might have been killed if they had appeared to be siding with the wrong faction.

As our aides traveled through the countryside, South African police often searched their automobiles for materials that could be construed as propaganda to benefit one side or the other—materials we did not carry. Despite the potential for violence, our methods were so successful that the U.S. State Department rescinded its prior order for all groups to leave South Africa a week before the election.

Charles Alphin Sr. told us that we ended up being the only American group allowed to stay. We had helped train more than three hundred thousand people to do something they had never done before: participate in a truly democratic election.

A great example of how far South Africa had come in terms of race relations was the awarding of the 1993 Nobel Peace Prize to F. W. de Klerk, the white former president of South Africa, and Mandela. They shared the honor for their work in ending apartheid. De Klerk was the seventh and last president of the apartheid era. When he took office in 1989, he released Mandela from prison the next year and lifted a ban on the ANC that had been in place since shortly after the Soweto riots in 1976.

In 1994, not a lot of activists in or out of South Africa had put as much faith in a peaceful outcome as I had. But shortly after Mandela's release from prison in 1990, I heard white Afrikaners say that they expected blacks to start shooting whites, and they were shocked when this did not happen. And in another chapter of the same story, after the Emancipation Proclamation freed the slaves in the United States, these men, women, and children did not respond to the brutalities of their imprisonment with violence toward their former masters. That, too, is amazing. It is God's work, and it's important for me to say that.

That, overall, peace was maintained in South Africa in April 1994 is also a credit to Nelson Mandela. He set the tone of calm and stability by the sheer force of his personality and the power of his negotiating skills.

Rather than calling for anger or revenge, Nelson's philosophy, which so closely paralleled Martin's, emphasized reconciliation between all people. If he could emerge from twenty-seven years of imprisonment and forgive his captors, it seemed possible for his supporters to do likewise.

On April 27, 1994, Nelson and the African National Congress won the election with 62 percent of the vote; Buthelezi's Inkatha Freedom Party earned about 10 percent.

On May 9, 1994, news photographers captured my jubilation as I danced the *toi-toi* with Nelson at the Carlton Hotel in Johannesburg, celebrating his victory. As I glanced over my shoulder, I saw even uniformed police officers dancing. On that remarkable evening, I listened joyfully as Nelson praised Martin for helping provide the climate, and the King Center for helping train thousands of participants in the tactics of nonviolence. Nelson made the transition from twenty-seven years of imprisonment to his role as leader of his nation—all without massive bloodshed.

As I stood beside Nelson, I thought of how Martin had once said he was prepared to die to see his dream of a society in which blacks and whites were equal become a reality. And there we were, Nelson and I, joined in an embrace of victory. This great freedom fighter lifted my hand as we danced alongside the thousands of jubilant celebrants. We were two symbols of the rich harvest of the long-suffering, yet fruitful, revolution on the part of the dispossessed, an uprising that miraculously changed the oppressors as well as their oppressed. Nelson's election was one of the largest nonviolent democratic transitions of the twentieth century. Few thought they would ever witness the patient and peaceful assembly of millions of South Africans, who queued in lines that extended for miles to vote, braving the threat of bombs planted by those still living out the emotional scars of apartheid.

I personally felt a sense of unapologetic joy on that night. I saw God's timing in this miraculous historical breakthrough. I had prophesied that divine intervention could not only save but also redeem South Africa. The Holy Spirit works through people. You do all you can, and then God takes over. He creates the breakthroughs in our lives that make these kinds of miraculous historical events eminently possible. When God decides a change is coming, He uses people who will be obedient to His purpose and will. Then miraculous things begin to happen. That election was a powerful vindication of nonviolent resistance and its message, so often stated by Martin: "We must either learn to live together as brothers or we perish together as fools."

SADLY, DURING THE years we were working on peacekeeping in South Africa, Jesse Jackson and several of the men who had been my husband's top aides were, once again, involved in opposing the Center's efforts in the United States. In past years, I had been wounded by Jesse's self-serving moves; then in 1990, the year Nelson was freed from prison, I felt that Randall Robinson, leader of TransAfrica, and others were putting their interests in the way of our doing our best work in support of those we were called to serve. These critics, sometimes publicly, sometimes secretly, stated that it was wrong for the King Center to be involved at all in South Africa; they argued that we should stick to civil rights. I felt these criticisms were a painful burden, especially as some of these critics had worked closely with my husband. Although I was carrying out the same mission as Martin, they now seemed to be working just as hard against me as they had worked with him. But as the biblical story of Joseph demonstrates, what some mean for evil, God will turn around for our good.

Why am I talking about the sordid side of leadership now? Because future leaders need to know how to work together as a team, and how to avoid infighting, which hurts many and helps no one. Overall, our efforts on civil rights would be more effective if personalities, inflated egos, turf issues, and jealousies could be set aside for the bigger picture. How much more could be accomplished if we could work together rather than against each other?

Yet, despite the problems I've had, I have no hard feelings toward Randall or Jesse. In fact, in 1993, I presented the Reverend Jackson with the Martin Luther King, Jr. Nonviolent Peace Prize, the Center's highest award. Jesse has made many valuable contributions to our country. No matter what has happened to me personally, the cause is greater than any individual. All people have human frailties. Certainly, I am no exception. In all honesty, I hurt like any human being, but I have fought very hard not to allow my private wounds to blot out the good I see in others.

I took the same approach with Ralph Abernathy, who died of a heart attack shortly before Nelson Mandela's historic visit to the United States and to the King Center. People often ask me how I felt about the negative accusations he made in his autobiography, *And the Walls Came Tumbling Down*, where he claimed that my husband slapped around a spurned lover and then left his room to stay with another woman until the wee hours of the morning the night before he was killed.

If Ralph were to be believed, on the evening of April 2, 1968, after Martin, a deeply religious man, made one of the most prophetic and anointed sermons of his lifetime, "I've Been to the Mountain Top," he descended from the pulpit and engaged in this sordid behavior. First of all, I know my husband, and this would have been totally out of character for him. I also had a conversation with Martin earlier that evening. And although I do not need to rely on any of Martin's aides to substantiate or vouch for his whereabouts, not one of them said they saw or heard anything like what Ralph alleges occurred.

These kinds of revelations were mind-boggling, especially coming from Ralph, my husband's closest confidant, counselor, and cell mate. They ate and drank together. They marched side by side during the protests that brought down Jim Crow segregation in the South. When my husband was shot down, it was Ralph who cradled him in his arms as the blood seethed from his wounds. All this makes Ralph's incredible falsehood about his best friend especially disturbing.

Many people have asked me to react to Ralph's claim. Before now, I could not divulge my deeper feelings. I issued a very guarded statement to the news media, but what I really felt was this: I knew Ralph had run into financial difficulty. Scandal sells books; fidelity does not. Bad news about the unsavory behavior of a good man is a better page-turner than anything I have to say about my husband, a man who felt so guilty about the smallest infraction or sin that he could not carry the weight of it without telling me. As his wife, I know my husband. If Martin had an affair, I would have known it. I don't have one instance of proof of Martin's infidelity. Not one. The fact that Ralph said those things about Martin does not make them true.

I was in Harare, Zimbabwe, in 1990, celebrating that country's tenth anniversary of independence, when I learned that Ralph had died on

April 17 in Atlanta. I issued a statement, which in part read, "When our home was bombed and our lives were threatened, he was there. His strength as a tactician and a counselor to Martin during our struggle has been eloquently recorded in Martin's own writings and in the annals of the American civil rights movement." I hurried back for the homegoing, which was held at West Hunter Street Baptist Church in Atlanta, where Ralph had served for many years as pastor.

As we laid Ralph to rest, there were absolutely no hard feelings on my part or on the part of my family. We still had unconditional love for Ralph. Speaking at the funeral, Martin's sister, Christine King Farris, described "the Ralph I remember is, like a member of our family . . . Uncle Ralph." And in the years afterward, I never lost touch with the Abernathy family.

As the King Center developed, I was able to both dialogue with powerful leaders, including prime ministers and presidents, and participate in protests alongside rank-and-file working people of all races. I met with many great spiritual leaders, too, including Pope John Paul II, the Dalai Lama, Dorothy Day, and my friend Pastor Robert Schuller, of the Crystal Cathedral. By the mid-eighties, I could more richly appreciate the influence that God had given me to make a difference in the lives of others. It allowed me to pick up a phone and have my calls put through to presidents, queens, princes, mayors, governors, heads of state, and CEOs of Fortune 500 companies. These calls enabled me to help somebody, to promote good people, to intervene in situations that were going wrong. I even witnessed the historic handshake between Prime Minister Yitzhak Rabin and Chairman Yasser Arafat at the signing of the Middle East Peace Accords in 1993.

In 1984, in Washington, DC, I met with the ambassadors to the United States from forty African nations; we discussed ways to strengthen economic and diplomatic relations and focus more attention on resolving the issues of poverty and hunger. The meeting was arranged by Raouf Ghoneim, from the Embassy of the Arab Republic of Egypt, and hosted by G. Toe Washington, ambassador to Washington from the Republic of Liberia.

In 1988, in preparation for the Reagan-Gorbachev talks, I served as head of the U.S. delegation of Women for a Meaningful Summit in Athens, Greece, and in 1990, as the USSR was redefining itself, I was a convener of the Soviet-American Women's Summit in Washington, DC.

Some of my most unforgettable and remarkable experiences came through meeting various world leaders. Some, such as Indira Gandhi and Corazon Aquino, became my dearest friends. Some of my international interactions, however, are memorable because of the unexpected incidents that occurred. On June 10, 1994, Emperor Akihito of Japan and his wife, Empress Michiko, visited the King Center after lunching with President Jimmy Carter. I think I will always remember that day because of what went awry. For fourteen centuries, Japanese citizens were taught that the emperor was a direct descendant of the sun goddess. Although Akihito's father, Hirohito, renounced the notion of godhood, even the slightest hint of disrespect is viewed as shockingly unacceptable by the emperor's countrymen. We knew this, and we knew that, for whatever reason, it was not customary for the emperor to shake hands with people.

Yet when the emperor arrived, Rev. Hosea Williams, one of my husband's former aides, grabbed his hand and lectured him, saying that he found "Japanese people to be very disrespectful of black Americans." He loudly challenged the emperor, telling him, "We spend thirteen billion dollars a year on Japanese products. And not a single black American has a Japanese franchise." The emperor just smiled and nodded. I know he doesn't speak English very well, so I wasn't certain he understood. The *New York Times*, on the other hand, understood very clearly what was happening, and ran an article on it.

On a sadder note, I also responded to the call from my friend Corazon Aquino when her husband was assassinated on August 23, 1983. Corazon and I had met at the United Nations, and we became fast friends. When her husband, Benigno, was killed, I broke away from my trip in Africa to be by her side. Her subsequent rise to the presidency of the Philippines was quite spectacular. She considered herself to be an ordinary housewife, but when her husband was killed, Corazon, usually attired in her signature yellow dresses, led a people's revolution that in 1986 toppled the twenty-one-year authoritarian rule of President Ferdinand Marcos and restored democracy to the Philippines. She became the first female

president in Asia. Over the years, we enjoyed teasing each other about
our shared nickname. Her formal name is Maria Corazon Sumulong
Cojuangco Aquino, but she was called Cory. My husband and a few close
friends always called me Corrie.

Another one of my closest friends was Indira Gandhi, the first female
prime minister of India and one of the first women elected to lead her
country in the modern era. She remained in office close to twelve years,
which set a record. I first met her when Martin and I toured India in 1957
and visited with her father, then the prime minister. Indira was serving
as her father's chief of staff. Later, when she became prime minister, I
returned to India to accept the Nehru Award for Outstanding International Leadership from her.

Indira was elected in January 1966. At that time, as the world's
second-most-populous nation, India had 1.2 billion people. In 1982, following the world premiere of Sir Richard Attenborough's film *Gandhi*,
CBS (which had produced the televised version) paid my expenses so that
I might attend a reception at Indira's home. As usual, she was dressed in
an elegant handwoven sari. Unlike the palatial estate of her father, Jawaharlal Nehru, Indira's home was very modest, a place where even the very
poor would feel comfortable visiting. In fact, she had become a champion
of the poor, and had found acclaim as the leader of India's Green Revolution. Her administration took on the problem of serious food shortages,
which affected mainly the extremely poor Sikh farmers of the Punjab
region, increasing crop diversification and food exports as a way out of
the problem. Indira's strategy opened up new job opportunities as well.
During my visit, we talked about our hopes for ending the arms race, and
she confided in me her worries about a growing extremist, separatist Sikh
movement in India, which was threatening to divide the nation. In our
public addresses, Indira and I both called vigorously for an end to the
Vietnam War. Through the United Nations, in her capacity as a leader of
the nonaligned nations, and through my syndicated columns, press conferences, and talks with the Nixon administration, we pressed our antiwar
message. We also garnered criticism at the highest levels for doing so.

By watching her close-up, I came to understand some of the strengths
and perils of women at the top, particularly the ways that women can
be condemned for doing exactly the same things for which their male

predecessors are praised. On the brighter side, as early as the 1950s (and partially because of Mahatma Gandhi's commitment to the advancement of women), I saw how some Indian women held much higher positions than women at home. There were women in Parliament; in 1959, even the chief justice of India's Supreme Court was a woman. Imagine that! I know that, someday, women in the United States will lead our country, not only in the highest court of the land but at the top, as president.

On October 31, 1984, I received the heartbreaking call that I think she had been trying to warn me about. Indira had been assassinated. It was so agonizing, so shocking. According to reports, her trusted bodyguard, who was a Sikh, pulled out a .38 revolver and shot her at point-blank range. Another bodyguard, also a Sikh, then took out an automatic weapon and fired thirty rounds into her body. She died on the way to the hospital.

Immediately, I thought about how crazy these assassinations were. I believe firmly that people at the highest levels must plot and plan such things. I just can't believe that someone's own bodyguard would do such a thing unless he or she had been paid to do it. To make matters even more horrible, years later, on May 21, 1991, Indira's son Rajiv, who'd followed in her footsteps as India's prime minister and was such a beautiful person, was also assassinated.

Before Indira's death, however, she helped us establish a permanent memorial to Mahatma Gandhi, whose birthday we celebrated annually at the King Center on October 2. We have a Gandhi Room in our Freedom Hall, which contained his sandals, his eyeglasses, his walking cane, one of his prayer rugs, and a very nice picture of him. Indira personally ensured our receipt of many of his original possessions.

I miss my friend. She was such a brave soul.

The American civil rights movement and the King Center helped provide the leadership and inspiration as well as the training in strategy, tactics, and the moral capacities of nonviolence that captivated nations from Europe to Asia, from Africa to Central America. As early as 1989, we saw free elections in Hungary, Czechoslovakia, Poland, Brazil, and Namibia, Africa's last colony. We witnessed hundreds of thousands of people marching through the streets of Berlin and Beijing, Budapest and Pretoria, Moscow, Warsaw, and Prague, singing "We Shall Overcome" in a host of languages. They sang in Bantu and German, Tagalog and Polish, sang the same song of freedom we once sang in the streets of Birmingham, Montgomery, and Little Rock. The U.S. Information Agency published and distributed materials on the King Center in the Russian language throughout the Soviet Union.

When Daddy King, Mama King, and my sister-in-law Christine King Farris visited Hungary in 1978, they found no fewer than five churches named after Martin. The Solidarity movement in Poland also used the documentary *Montgomery to Memphis*, which we use as a nonviolence training film at the Center.

Students in the Chinese Freedom Movement were photographed in news magazines carrying signs and wearing T-shirts that displayed the words "We Shall Overcome." Martin often challenged world leaders to create a new foreign policy, one that would replace the evils of racism, poverty, and militarism with a new set of values dependent on moral power rather than military might.

Shortly before his assassination, Martin had strongly urged the institutionalizing and internationalizing of our nonviolent strategies. He felt they were vitally needed to continue the flow of democratic movements around the world. And without a doubt, institutionalizing and internationalizing nonviolence is our goal at the Martin Luther King, Jr. Center for Nonviolent Social Change.

We walk and work where Martin would have walked and worked if he had been allowed to live. As we continue expanding the cause from civil to human rights, we are committed to keeping alive Martin's dream of nonviolent global policies that, whenever possible, choose diplomacy over war and always show respect for human lives over hate, revenge, and bitterness.

TWENTY

Happy Birthday, Martin

A S YOU MIGHT have noticed by now, I can be a very determined woman. When I have put my mind to something, with hard work and God's grace, it has usually come to pass. Perhaps nowhere has this process been more obvious and more useful than in my efforts to establish Martin's birthday as a national holiday, observed now in all fifty states and also in more than one hundred nations. Only a few close friends and religious leaders believed this holiday would ever happen, but I never really doubted. I understand that sometimes a hard task simply requires that one person is particularly chosen to hear the charge, the divine calling, and to step out on faith. The people, the resources, the strategy will follow. That's what happened with me and the King holiday.

At the heart of things, we who believed in the King holiday had to have a vision. We also had to attract the best minds and map out a blue-print. The vision and the planning took time, and training. Many of the skills I used were ones I'd never even thought of developing until I had to use them. I learned how to lobby members of Congress. I organized a coalition of 750 political, religious, labor, and civil rights groups. I also had to experience failure—or results that were less than my expectations—and this failure taught me more about winning than many of the ventures I had previously labeled a success.

Often when writers or commentators speak about the holiday, it is said in a short sentence or a fleeting breath. There's no depth to it; no recognition of the hard work and the miracles it took for the holiday to come into being; no attempt to fully convey and do justice to the process or to the thousands of people around the world who directly involved themselves, providing their time, talent, and funds to help. Nor does any mention of the holiday properly demonstrate how God can use anybody to accomplish the most impossible feats.

God certainly used me.

John Conyers, a Democratic congressman from Michigan, first introduced a bill to establish Martin's January 15 birthday as a federal holiday in April 1968, just four days after Martin was assassinated, but the road to achieving passage of that bill was fifteen long and winding years, and there were a lot of twists and turns in the road.

I HAVE ALWAYS had a burning desire to alleviate poverty through good jobs, and by the mid-1970s, the double-digit unemployment rates among blacks, Hispanics, and the residents of Appalachia were worrying me deeply. In 1974, I helped develop and cochaired the National Committee for Full Employment with Murray Finley, president of the Amalgamated Clothing and Textile Workers Union (ACTWU). Our goal was to pass comprehensive legislation to address employment opportunity that, if enacted, we hoped would be as far reaching as the Civil Rights Act of 1964 and the Voting Rights Act of 1965.

Even though, in the end, our committee won fewer battles than we expected, the fight for full employment moved me inside the complex system of legislating. I saw how laws are made and, even more important, how good laws are broken and ignored. I was able to operate in a different way from Martin, who achieved victories as an outsider applying pressure on the inside power brokers. Times had changed; the movement had opened the doors to us. We had more legislators on the inside who were sympathetic to our causes. Still, I had to learn which doors to go through and how to properly use the influence I possessed. The drive for full employment was the bridge that brought me to an understanding of the art of lobbying. To be successful, we had to build strong coalitions. And I began to see that one of my strengths was as a coalition builder.

My work fighting for full employment deeply convinced me that jobs that pay fair wages are an answer to many of the social and economic problems that afflict so many nations. Unemployment is often blamed solely on individuals, who are depicted as too lazy to work. In reality, the bulk of the problem is global, and involves the tax breaks and low wages that entice nations such as ours to move corporations offshore or overseas, and to exploit cheap labor, in Asia, for example. On the line are the lives of decent, hardworking people who want to cross over into the dignity of work but who remain caught in the barbed-wire trap of historic global exploitation.

Whenever I could bring the issue of unemployment into a debate or a panel discussion, I was not timid about addressing it. Following on my work with the National Committee for Full Employment, I was also cochair of the Full Employment Action Council, and in 1977 that council organized Full Employment Week, a national demonstration for jobs involving more than a million people in more than three hundred cities and towns.

As it happened, a bill addressing the necessity for full employment was making its way through Congress in 1977. Rep. Augustus Hawkins (a Democratic congressman from California) had offered what became known as the Humphrey-Hawkins Bill, after Sen. Hubert Humphrey cosponsored it. Once I understood that this bill was already in the works, our mission became to support it. Murray Finley and I brought a lot of labor on board. We spoke to labor unions and at rallies, meetings, and conventions, trying to educate people about the need for full employment. We traveled all across the country.

On these travels, whenever I talked to the average person, especially students, I never felt that there was a lot of excitement surrounding the employment bill. Yet, when I added that we should have a holiday in honor of Martin's birthday, I would always get loud applause. My first mission was to make people understand that unemployment was a pressing issue that needed national attention. But I sort of tucked away that response about the birthday holiday for a later time. I began to feel that there were very strong national feelings in favor of the holiday.

As I tried to promote the full employment bill, I kept saying to my speechwriters, "Look, we've got to use the kind of language that's going to reach people and get them excited—get them disturbed." We tried to paint a vivid picture of what unemployment was doing to families and so on, but it felt too much like an intellectual argument. That worried me; still, I stayed with my assignment. I wanted so deeply to help bring down poverty rates, and I didn't want to drop the ball. The Full Employment Action Council determined that the correct measurement for full employment would be around 3 percent, which was considered negligible. This was the guiding formula we used in making our argument.

From the start, critics claimed that we were coming up with another welfare plan, so we immediately had to disprove a negative and demonstrate that our plan was not welfare. We were also hampered by the fact that we did not have the financial resources of the Business Roundtable, a group that was lobbying against the bill.

In the end, the Humphrey-Hawkins Full Employment Act did pass, and Jimmy Carter signed it into law on October 27, 1978, though by the time it passed, it was too watered down to make much of an impact. First, there was language in the bill which called for the impeachment of the president if certain measures were not achieved. Well, nobody was going to do that! Maybe that's why Congress passed it: they knew it would not be taken seriously. Second, while our good friend President Carter supported the bill, he was lukewarm about it; he could see businesses did not want it, and he needed their support. In addition, the president had the responsibility of implementing the bill, yet most of the jobs it affected were in the private sector. This was something no president could directly implement or enforce.

The act set specific numerical goals for the president to achieve. It stated that "By 1983, unemployment rates should be no more than three percent for persons aged 20 or over and no more than four percent for persons aged 16 or over, and inflation rates should not be over four percent. By 1988, inflation rates should be zero percent." The act allowed Congress to revise these goals over time. If private enterprise appeared to be falling short of the goals, the act expressly allowed the government to create a "reservoir of public employment. These jobs are required to be in the lower ranges of skill and pay to minimize competition with the private sector."

With unemployment continuing to run in the steady double digits for communities of color, it is sad that the major provisions of the Humphrey-Hawkins Act were not amended. Instead, they were put on a shelf and ignored. I can only imagine how many lives would have been changed or saved if the bill had been taken seriously. Joblessness contributes significantly to the "cradle to prison" pipeline, to inadequate access to health care, to mental illnesses, and to hopelessness, which is a major factor in violent crime.

U.S. service sector jobs are steadily disappearing. Customer service jobs, for example, have been exported to the Philippines, India, and Jamaica. Or, in the case of supermarket checkout workers, for example, these jobs have been displaced by scanners or other forms of technology. Yet, while the working- and middle-class workers suffer, the wealthiest Americans have gotten much richer. The Humphrey-Hawkins Act, which expired in 2000, might have created a twenty-first-century New Deal, gainfully employing unemployed Americans to rebuild our crumbling infrastructure and strengthen our communities.

In the end, I had to make peace with the bill being less than satisfying, but I found comfort in remembering how Martin dealt with such things. When you achieve a minor victory, you have to take it and make it more of a major victory.

He showed me this during the Democratic National Convention in 1964. When Fannie Lou Hamer led the Mississippi Freedom Democratic Party challenge at that convention, her small but mighty group asked that the old Democratic Party be unseated and the Mississippi Freedom Democratic Party be seated in its place, as it was more representative of the people. Martin was the negotiator for the Freedom Party, but that year, they could get only about two or three people seated. The SNCC then attacked Martin as an Uncle Tom, blaming him for the slow progress. I remember how Martin agonized over this situation and how the press was asking him all these questions, and in response, he said, "You know, we didn't get all that we wanted, but I consider it a victory, and we will continue to work at it. In the next four years, perhaps we will get all those seats." He felt that if we went back home and told our people that we'd lost, they wouldn't follow us anymore. I learned from watching Martin's work, and I tried to help our people see that while we didn't get all that we wanted in our efforts toward full employment, all was not lost. We did gain *something*, and that was the way we had to look at it. People need some sense of hope so that they keep on struggling, Martin would tell me. So after the Humphrey-Hawkins Act turned out to be less than I had hoped for, I said to myself, "Maybe we didn't get all that we wanted, but we need to keep mobilizing and maybe someday we can get a stronger bill."

When you are doing something significant and you are even moderately successful, you need to promote it in such a way that people understand what you're doing and what you've accomplished. If you don't, people will think you haven't done anything. When you promote what you've done, you can then try to understand how to improve upon what you did get: When the Humphrey-Hawkins Bill passed, we should have created an apparatus to monitor its application. But we didn't have the resources, so nobody really understood what had happened or how to provide proper follow-up or constant vigilance.

Despite these challenges with Humphrey-Hawkins, I did not come out of that four-year experience bitter, and the experience of learning how to pass a bill was vital for me. I had made many friends in Congress, and I had heard (could still hear) the roar of the masses calling for a Martin Luther King Jr. holiday. So I turned to our good friend Rep. John Conyers, still a Democratic congressman from Michigan in the 1970s just as he has been since the 1960s.

John Conyers is a real hero in the effort to honor Martin's life and legacy with a national holiday. Year after year after year, ever since Martin died, John, who is also one of the thirteen founding members of the Congressional Black Caucus, persisted in introducing the same King birthday bill over and over. In all, Congress rejected the bill more than seventy times.

Then, in 1979, following on my decade of speeches about the birthday, in every state of the union, I said to John, "It is time to bring the King Holiday bill to vote on the House floor again." It was obvious to me that the masses were calling for the King holiday. Some around me hesitated, though, afraid we still did not have enough congressional support. My response was, "You know better than that. If we hadn't had a small but effective coalition on the inside, we never would have passed Humphrey-Hawkins. There, the cards were stacked against us. Here, I believe there is enough sentiment among the people to help us get this bill passed."

John also felt the passion building. He was ready to bring the bill to the floor again. He asked me to come to Washington to meet with Tip O'Neill, the Democratic speaker of the House, and with Sen. Robert Byrd, the Democratic Senate majority leader from West Virginia.

Only a few short years before, I would have been anxious about meeting with Byrd. It was common knowledge that he'd been an active member of the KKK and that he'd filibustered the 1964 Civil Rights Bill. But while I was campaigning for Humphrey-Hawkins, I'd had a chance to meet with him, and he had assured me that his views had changed.

During that 1979 visit to Washington, I testified before the Senate Judiciary Committee and spoke with passion about the bill's importance and about how I wanted the holiday to be on the actual date of Martin's birthday. O'Neill and Byrd agreed to go forward with this plan. I went back to Atlanta, but several weeks later, John called me back to Washington to do more lobbying, to call on more congresspersons, and to testify before a joint hearing of Congress. The leadership agreed to use a rule that required a two-thirds vote on the bill for it to pass, instead of a simple majority. Because of that rule change and because some of our strongest supporters were absent when the bill came to the floor, we lost by about five votes in the House.

Nevertheless, I vowed to keep pushing with the same resolve and faith that I was putting into building the King Center.

In order for a national holiday to have meaning, it had to be embraced by all fifty states. Just the thought of how officials in some southern and western states regarded my husband was enough to rock the confidence of even my closest friends. As a matter of fact, even Andy Young said, "Do you really believe we're going to get a holiday?"

"Yes, we will," I said firmly.

Every year since 1969, the King Center had celebrated Martin's life and legacy with weeklong festivities and awards that began on his birthday, January 15. As the years passed, the Center became the de facto hub of a national holiday celebration. Each year, increasing numbers of Americans, and even visitors from foreign countries, made a pilgrimage to the Center for the birthday week. Across the nation, thousands of governmental agencies (federal, state, and city), businesses, communities, and church groups had also begun celebrating King Week. Although many honored Martin with sincerity and dignity, others failed to capture his spirit or ideology, or they dishonored him with crass commercialization. To achieve some type of decorum and uniformity, the King Center board had to issue a Standards of Conduct for honoring Martin, calling on groups "not to exploit Dr. King's name or good work for financial, political, or other selfish gain; to commit to nonviolence; and to agree that any fundraising activities designed to continue the work of Dr. King must first address the needs of the only living memorial, namely the Martin Luther King Jr. Center for Nonviolent Social Change."

Meanwhile, year after year, I undertook a letter-writing campaign, reaching out to mayors, state legislators, and governors across the nation, asking them to observe my husband's birthday as an annual holiday. In 1971 the SCLC had gathered three million pro-holiday signatures, though those weren't enough to sway Congress. In 1973 the state of Illinois became the first state to sign the King holiday into state law; this bill was sponsored by Assemblyman Harold Washington, who later became Chicago's first African American mayor. In 1979 we launched a new petition drive, which ultimately resulted in six million signatures. In 1980, I testified again before the House and the Senate; also that year, Stevie Wonder released "Happy Birthday," a song celebrating Martin and advocating for the holiday. In 1982, I testified again before Senate and House committees, and Stevie Wonder and I presented the petitions, carrying those six million signatures to House speaker Tip O'Neill and bill floor manager Rep. Robert Garcia of New York in special ceremonies at the U.S. Capitol. While all this work was going on, a miracle was coming in the form of the twentieth anniversary of the March on Washington and Martin's "I Have a Dream" speech, on August 27, 1983. In December 1982, on the White House Lawn, I announced the creation of a New Coalition of Conscience, a group of organizations to help sponsor the twentieth anniversary of the March. By that summer, there were 750 organizations in that group, and at the top of the group's legislative agenda was the

King holiday bill. Washington felt a groundswell coming. In June 1983, I testified once again before Congress on behalf of the King holiday bill, and in July, first-term congresswoman Katie Hall (D-IN) reintroduced the holiday bill, co-sponsored by Jack Kemp (R-NY).

On August 2, 1983, the House voted 338 to 90 in favor of designating the third Monday in January as a day to honor Martin. Sensing the mounting support for the bill, Senate majority leader Howard Baker (R-TN) sent the House version to the Senate floor without committee review. A few weeks later, the twentieth anniversary of the March on Washington firmly demonstrated just how much people cared about a holiday for Martin; Stevie Wonder again sang "Happy Birthday," which had become a rallying cry across America and was on the lips of the marchers who showed up, five hundred thousand strong, at the Lincoln Memorial. The efforts we had begun in 1969 had finally reached the tipping point.

Yet, even as the bill was gaining traction, Republican senator Jesse Helms of North Carolina staged a filibuster against it. On October 3, 1983, Helms read a paper on the Senate floor entitled, "Martin Luther King, Jr.: Political Activities and Associations," and gave a three-hundred-page document to members of the Senate detailing my husband's so-called Communist connections. Some senators were dismayed by Helms's actions, including Massachussets's Edward M. Kennedy and New York's Daniel Patrick Moynihan. Moynihan threw the document to the ground, stomped on it, and called it a "packet of filth."

Helms argued that anyone who objected to a King holiday would automatically be dubbed a racist, and urged the Senate not to be bullied into elevating my husband to "the same level as the father of our country and above the many other Americans whose achievements approach that of George Washington's by making him one of the few individuals honored by a federal holiday." He mounted a campaign to amend the birthday bill so that the holiday would be named "National Civil Rights Day," would include no mention of Martin, and would fall on a Sunday, when most Americans were already off from work.

Fortunately, Helms's efforts were unsuccessful, and the bill went to the Senate for a vote.

On October 19, 1983, with all members present, the Senate voted 78 to 22 to make my husband's birthday a national holiday. The Senate bill was co-sponsored by Senator Ted Kennedy. After fifteen years of lobbying, nine million petition signatures, hundreds of thousands of marching feet, telegrams from around the world, outreach from President Jimmy Carter and Pope John Paul II, the Martin Luther King Jr. birthday holiday was finally a federal law. The bill represented the first time a national holiday was established for someone other than a U.S. president or Christopher Columbus, who is credited as well as discredited as the first European to discover America. The bill, known as H.R. 3706, was the tenth federal holiday established by Congress.

On November 3, 1983, I, along with my children, Edythe, Christine, other members of my family, and leaders of the civil rights movement my husband led crowded into the Rose Garden. Vice President George H. W. Bush was there, along with representatives Katie Hall and Jack Kemp, Senators Howard Baker and Ted Kennedy, Senator Bob Dole (R-KS), and Samuel Pierce, Secretary of Housing and Urban Development. There, we witnessed the signing of the King holiday bill into law by President Ronald Reagan. Martin's holiday would be celebrated on the third Monday of January, beginning in 1986.

President Reagan was cordial during the ceremonies and displayed no angst to those of us gathered there, though he had opposed the bill until it was passed by Congress.

With the stroke of his pen, the holiday was finally law.

However, national holidays are legal holidays only for federal employees and the District of Columbia. To make it a truly national holiday, our work was still cut out for us. In preparation for the holiday's inauguration, we had to visit fifty states and forty-two cities, ensuring that each local government was correctly informed about the launch. Having learned from the Humphrey-Hawkins aftermath, we called for Congress to establish a federal commission to oversee how the holiday was institutionalized and to create some uniformity in how it was celebrated across the country. Congress passed that legislation, which President Reagan signed into law on August 27, 1984. I became a life member of the commission and its first and only chairperson. Lloyd Davis, a former HUD official and executive director of the King Center, was the commission's first and only executive director. Initially, the commission was slated to last for five years, but Congress twice extended its life, and it formally ended its mission in 1996.

With the federal holiday now in effect for more than a decade, it's easy to forget how difficult a task it was to accomplish. Just imagine someone locked in a tiny prison for fifteen years, handcuffed and shackled to the floor, able to peep out of only a small crack in the wall. His cries are unheard by the people walking by—except for one woman. She makes faithful daily trips to the prison. With each visit, she beats on the crack in the wall. One day, the wall breaks into splinters, and she sees that there was not just one prisoner, but many who broke free.

You might say I was the woman who kept beating on the wall. It was a labor of love, a long, hard labor. When the commission began its work in 1984, only twenty-seven states and Washington, DC, observed Martin's birthday in some manner. Arizona was infamously resistant. All three House Republicans voted against the bill in 1983. Arizona did not vote in favor of recognizing the holiday until 1992, after the NFL moved Super Bowl XXVII from Tempe's Sun Devil Stadium to San Diego, California, in protest over Arizona's resistance to the holiday.

While one of the most recalcitrant, Arizona was not the only state acting out of concert with federal law. In 2000, seventeen years after the law's official passage, South Carolina became the last state to sign a bill recognizing Martin Luther King Jr. Day as a paid holiday. By then, in all U.S. territories and at all U.S. installations around the world, Martin's birthday was observed as a national holiday, and more than a hundred other nations celebrated it as well. With the bill signed and with support for the holiday encircling the globe, I searched for proper words to express the joy I felt. The statement I released at the time captures it: "As a nation chooses its heroes and heroines, a nation interprets its history and shapes its destiny."

IF THE ACHIEVEMENTS of the King Center's local, national, and international programs and the global influence of the King birthday holiday ever gave the impression that racism had somehow disappeared since my husband's death, some events in January 1987 were a chilling reminder that Atlanta was still in Georgia, and that Georgia was still in the South, and that the South, as well as the United States, had much further to go toward freedom.

That January, as we prepared to observe the second annual federal holiday as well as National King Week in Atlanta, Rev. Hosea Williams, then an Atlanta City councilman, was invited by Dean Carter, a white karate instructor from Forsyth County, to commemorate the King holiday by participating in a "Brotherhood March" into Forsyth, an all-white county in Georgia. On January 17 a busload of about eighty African Americans, led by Reverend Williams, arrived in Cumming, Georgia, the county seat of Forsyth, to join Carter. Almost immediately, the marchers were attacked and beaten by a group of white segregation proponents. Reverend Williams was hit by a rock, and this was shown on the news. The incident drew national attention, and Reverend Williams and Dean Carter vowed to return on January 24 to continue the march.

I immediately offered my support, and with the King Center as a base of action, I got on the phone and mobilized a team. One of my first calls was to James Orange, who had been an important "ground crew" organizer for my husband and a staffer of the SCLC; he, along with other civil rights grassroots leaders, helped me organize a massive turnout to support Hosea Williams's and Dean Carter's return to Forsyth County. Andrew Young and Rev. Joseph Lowery also helped. This was a National Mobilization Against Fear and Intimidation.

As the day neared, it became clear that the number of people joining us for the march would exceed our expectations. Therefore, we had to quickly add seventy-five more buses to the hundred we'd already reserved. People arrived from all across the country, including civil rights leaders, college presidents, U.S. senators, and other elected officials. On January 24, I, along with several family members, King Center board members, staff, elected officials, and community activists, gathered at the Center to board the 175 buses and other vehicles to transport us to Cumming. As the number of arriving people continued to swell, we realized that even the buses we had reserved would not be enough to accommodate the overflow. Several thousand marchers were left behind to find their own way to Forsyth. On top of that, there were four to six inches of snow on the ground. The Georgia FBI unit, along with seventeen hundred National Guard troops, provided security. William Bradford Reynolds, assistant U.S. attorney general, flew from Washington to join the march. Members of the Guardian Angels also took part.

But right-wing activists also showed up in force. J. B. Stoner, the infamous white supremacist, was on hand, signing autographs. Former Georgia governor Lester Maddox mingled with about five hundred white counterprotesters, who waved Confederate flags and shouted insults at the marchers. Klan members showed up wearing Klan robes. My daughter Bernice recalls that our bus passed a spot where the counterprotesters had written "Go home 'Niger'" in the snow. We were pleased that with just seven days to mobilize, more than twenty thousand of us were able to converge on Forsyth County to stand up for justice and equality.

In the wake of our march, Oprah Winfrey arranged to broadcast her daily TV show from Cummings, the first time she aired a show away from her home base of Chicago.

Despite the violence that had greeted the marchers on the seventeenth, this incident was also a reminder of how much things had changed, and of the vital roles the civil rights movement, the King Center, and the King holiday had played in advancing race relations in the South: An abundance of whites joined us for the January 24 march, and the law was on our side.

THE KING HOLIDAY had been established and the King Center had evolved from a few filing cabinets in my bedroom to a staff of more than 60 welcoming about 2.5 million visitors every year, but I felt the urgent need to keep adding thunder to the left, to keep the voice, vision, and values of a humane, peace-seeking society at the top of the national agenda. The movement had to hold on to the social, economic, and political gains we had won while continuing to break through closed doors and glass ceilings.

As Martin had used sermons and books to challenge our political leaders and institutions, I used speeches, forums at the King Center, and hundreds of syndicated columns and television commentaries on CNN to continue presenting an alternative vision of what an equitable and just society should look like. I saw the media as a valuable tool, one that allowed the voiceless to have a role in participatory democracy. Without the media coverage of the marches and bloodshed of the movement, we would not have touched the hearts of good people across the nation.

The Reagan administration, however, thought otherwise. It was so bothered by my critique of national and international affairs that I was banned from appearing on Voice of America, the official external broadcast organization of the United States, and from traveling on any government-sponsored trips as a representative of the United States. I was thought of more as an enemy of the state than a public servant.

I had worked my entire life to make the dispossessed full participants in the American Dream. The Reagan cold shoulder was just a replay of how I ended up on President Richard Nixon's unofficial list of enemies. Of course, I am not naïve. If the Reagan administration had loved me, that would have meant I was not doing my job, that I had failed in my task of, as the great journalist Finley Peter Dunne wrote, "Comforting the afflicted and afflicting the comfortable."

During the Reagan years, I had much to say about the administration's painfully regressive policies, which cut survival funding for the working poor and their families. In America in 1989, one child out of every four was living in poverty—and fully *half* of all African American children were living in poverty. Yet, instead of increasing funds to fight hunger and homelessness or increasing access to health care, Reagan imposed draconian cuts on subsidies for the poor. In fact, he was excoriated for going so far as to advocate cutting school lunch budgets and allowing ketchup and other condiments to count as vegetables. And while subsidies for survival necessities such as school lunches were on the chopping block, the Pentagon was awash in hefty increases. One report in the *Detroit Free Press* showed that military spending had increased by $164 billion while programs for the poor were cut by $50 billion.

In 1990, President George H. W. Bush chose to react to Iraq's invasion of Kuwait with bombs, rather than with sanctions and diplomacy. That mission, called Operation Desert Storm, set the stage for a full-blown oil war disaster in Iraq a decade later, during the presidency of Bush's son George W. Bush. Under the false premise that Iraq held weapons of mass destruction, the younger Bush led the United States into a war that resulted in thousands of lives lost unnecessarily, and billions drained from our domestic economy.

During the Reagan and Bush years, I used my voice to push for a new war on poverty instead of a continued war on the poor. I was not just pleading the case for welfare; I was still arguing for a no-nonsense national commitment to full employment: a job at a decent wage for everyone who was able and capable of working. Such a policy would also include a higher minimum wage, a national health care system, and an expansion of public works. In the private sector, governmental incentives could encourage corporations and unions to create job training and child care opportunities in depressed communities, so that mothers would not have to put their children at risk in order to work and support their families.

Later, during the Clinton administration, I did not quiet my call for a more targeted war on poverty. Nor did I stop advocating for an end to supply-side trickle-down economic policies, which had resulted in double-digit joblessness and left one out of five black workers unemployed. While President Bill Clinton did not support our agenda to the letter, he did bring about major improvements over the Reagan and Bush years. Studies show that 7.7 million people were lifted out of poverty during Clinton's term, compared with only 77,000 during the Reagan years. President Clinton's economic legacy included a balanced budget and the creation of 22.7 million jobs, which dramatically decreased joblessness among people of color. According to the Department of Commerce, from 1992 to 2000, unemployment fell to 7.6 percent from 14.2 percent for African Americans, and to 5.7 percent from 11.6 percent for Hispanics. I appreciated the job growth under Clinton's administration, although I was very disappointed about the "three strikes, you're out" 1994 crime bill, which Clinton signed into law and which sent so many African American men to spend most of their lives in jail.

I battled the government on many other fronts. Just as Martin and I had pushed to end the Vietnam War, so I tried to bring that same passion to my outcry against the rush to war in the Gulf and challenged the warmongering maneuvers of President George H. W. Bush, which unfortunately escalated into disaster under his son. As early as August 1990, I was pleading with the administration of George H. W. Bush to choose diplomatic options to resolve conflicts in the Gulf. A war would benefit only the oil companies and arms dealers, I warned, leaving in its wake many thousands of widows and heartbroken children, financial disaster for U.S. taxpayers, and increasing terrorist retaliation against the United States.

Unfortunately, just as Martin was demonized for speaking out against the Vietnam War, I was harshly criticized (sometimes by other civil rights leaders!) for advocating caution, compromise, and diplomacy instead of rushing full steam ahead into war. In my heart, I have always been patriotic. I love my country, the land for which so many of my fellow citizens sacrificed their blood on battlefields both here and abroad. I do not mean to say that the United States should not have a strong defense; I advocate driving down a different road to get there. True homeland security ought to be more about providing health care for every citizen, more about protecting civil liberties, more about protection of pension assets for retired people, more about gun control and about protecting Americans against domestic hate crimes; more about feeding the hungry, housing the homeless, and making sure there is quality education for every child and a job at a decent wage for everyone who wants and needs one. This is how we make our country safe and secure for all citizens.

I will never stop sounding off about justice for all, regardless of the steps backward our country might be making. I will fight on and await the Zeitgeist. There is something about the Zeitgeist, the spirit of the time. Martin used to preach about this. The Zeitgeist pushes people from the dullness of yesterday into the bright sunlight of tomorrow; it is a time when all the alarms on the human clock ring. Someday, once again, those alarm bells will ring.

———— ❀ ————

TWENTY-ONE

Our Children

F OR ALL THAT I shared with Martin and all the uplifting work I
have done and continue to do, in my life my greatest joy has been
my children, Yolanda, Martin, Dexter, and Bernice. I've always felt
that nothing I did would mean anything if my children did not know I
loved them, if they were not strengthened by what they saw in me every
day. I strove always to be a role model, with consistent character and values. In front of them and in private, I sought to live an ethical life. Integration for me is not merely a civil rights issue, it is a soul issue, and this
means integrating your personal beliefs into your public life. There
should be no difference between public morality and private morality. What I preached publicly I tried to live out privately in front of my
children.

Over the decades, my children have achieved so much, but they've
also endured their own private struggles, many of which came with
the weight of bearing the King name. As a young mother, I remembered
the words Rose Kennedy once shared with me, about training the oldest
child to help with the youngest, and passed this style onto my firstborn,
Yolanda, whom we called Yoki.

Yoki was twelve years old when her father died. While he was alive,
she'd already been forced to deal with the King name, which can bring a
blessing or a burden, depending on where you are, in Atlanta or the

world. As early as the mid-1970s, Martin was the most famous man most Atlantans had ever known, and it was difficult for our children not to understand the specialness of our name when it was being emblazoned on street signs, schools, T-shirts, and, later, the King Center. Yoki was the only one of our children educated from elementary to high school entirely in the public system, as Martin and I had wanted. In the years following Martin's death, I took the other children out of public schools for security reasons.

As a child in elementary school, Yoki demonstrated an innate ability to handle her own problems. One day, she came home and told me that that she was tired of people asking her, "Is your daddy Martin Luther King?" So when the teacher stepped out of the classroom, she turned to the other students and said, "Look, all I want is to be treated like a normal child."

I was pleased with her response. To live a normal life as their best selves is all Martin and I ever wanted for our children.

Yoki always had strong opinions about what she wanted to do with her life. As a younger child, she, along with our older son, Martin, and the Abernathys' three children, Juandalynn, Donzaleigh, and Ralph III, were the first to integrate Atlanta's Spring Street Elementary School, and Yoki insisted upon attending Grady High School, the integrated public high school her friends went to. In 1972 she graduated with honors from Grady as the best all-around student and went on to the all-women Smith College, where she studied drama and graduated with honors in 1976, with a B.A. in theater and African American studies.

Yolanda started showing her theatrical talent when she was only seven. At nine, she wrote her first play, *Riches and Royalty*. I was amazed that she even knew how to properly format it. Not only did she write it, but she cast her siblings in it and produced it with costumes, all in a day and a half. The plot concerned children of the world bringing gifts to a queen, and she dressed Marty as Chinese, Dexter as African, and Bunny as East Indian. When it was over, my sister, Edythe, who was the drama teacher at Cheyney University of Pennsylvania, quipped, "Next time, give yourself two weeks instead of a day and a half." But in a child's world, a day is like an eternity. The fun of Yoki's theatrical pursuits continued:

When she was eleven, her backyard production of *Sleeping Beauty* came to an early end when the script required six-and-a-half-year-old Dexter to awaken the princess, his sister Bunny, with a kiss on the lips.

Understanding her precocious talent, I steered Yoki to a children's drama workshop in Atlanta that had been launched by Walter Roberts and Betty Lou Bredemus, the parents of the famous actress Julia Roberts and the actor Eric Roberts. Ironically, while Yolanda was receiving spectacular coaching and I enthusiastically supported the theater, the association drew our family into quite a controversy. Walter cast Yolanda, who was only sixteen, as a prostitute in the play *The Owl and the Pussycat*, in which she kissed a white boy. This caused an uproar around Atlanta.

Yolanda defended the role, telling me, "Mommy, I want to do this because there is nothing in the character with which I can identify. If I can do it well, then I can prove to myself that I can be a better actress."

Word got out about the forthcoming production, and soon the church people began calling Daddy King, telling him that if Martin were alive, he would never have allowed such a thing, etc. My mother also got wind of the controversy, and was concerned. And my sister, Edythe, told me that if I did not stop Yoki, I'd live to regret it. However, Andy Young advised that, although it was a rough play, we shouldn't stop her.

Despite this conflicting chorus, I had already made up my mind. I knew my girl, and I knew that she had a right to make a mistake, even though she was Martin Luther King Jr.'s daughter. If she made a mistake, she would learn from it.

Sure enough, the media attacked me and the play. Some criticized Yolanda's diction. She was playing the role as a southern black woman who had not been tutored in proper English, while, in contrast, the white lead had a polished British accent. Somehow people seemed not to understand that this was just theater.

I took on her critics, telling them, "She is Martin Luther King, Jr. and Coretta Scott King's daughter, and she certainly knows how to talk."

After the run of the play, I was getting ready to go on a vacation with my friends Dr. Robert and Lettie Green when Yolanda gave me a little note and asked me to open it after I got on the plane. My heart started beating faster; I thought that maybe something disastrous had happened.

Was she going to tell me she was pregnant? I was nervous to read it. But when I finally did open the envelope, I read a sweet note thanking me for allowing her to express herself and for "taking the blows for her."

Interestingly, when Yoki was a child and said she was going to be an actress, Martin asked me to tell her not to say that. "What's wrong with being an actress?" I asked him. Always acutely aware of how critically people judged preachers, he simply said, "It's the image." So I think if Martin had lived, she would have had a harder time becoming an actress.

After graduating from Smith, Yoki went on to New York University, where she received a master's in fine arts in 1979. She and Betty Shabazz's daughter Attallah Shabazz went on to found a theater company called Nucleus, which created an original play aimed at teenage children called *Stepping into Tomorrow*.

Yolanda always demonstrated a strong sense of social justice in the projects she took on, even playing Rosa Parks in the NBC TV movie *King*. She played Dr. Betty Shabazz in the film *Death of a Prophet*, with Morgan Freeman; and Medgar Evers's daughter, Reena, in *Ghosts of Mississippi*. She also played Judge Esther Green in the hit CBS series *JAG*.

I was proud of her confidence and poise. Seeing her in these roles called to mind a day when she came home from middle school and asked me, "Mama, why are Negroes ugly?" She told me she had heard this stark, brutal conclusion at school.

I reached under the living room table and produced a couple of issues of *Ebony* magazine. I flipped through the smartly colored pages and pointed out to her the many beautiful women of color. They were fashionably dressed and intelligent. After our conversation, I was happy the case was closed. But was it? The very next day, Yoki came to the conclusion: "Well, I think white people are ugly." I simply picked up a copy of *Ladies' Home Journal* and showed her images of beautiful white women, also fashionably dressed and intelligent. It took a while for her to understand that there is beauty in all races. Later, I taught her that beauty is more than skin deep, and beauty is as beauty does.

One night, when Yoki was at Smith, I got a very strange call from her about her appearance. "Mother, I want you to tell me the truth about something that's been bothering me," she said. "Did you and Daddy find me in a garbage can while you were traveling in Korea?"

"What are you talking about?" I asked her, baffled.

"Some kids at school were saying that I look Oriental and that I'm a Korean and you found me. Now tell me the truth."

Yolanda was so serious that I had to convince her that I'd carried her for nine months, and that she was a whopping nine-pound, ten-ounce baby. I think many kids must go through this stage of discovery, because Bernice also went through a period of thinking she was adopted because she didn't look like anybody else in the family. Finally, I found a picture of me when I was about nine, and showed it to her. It looked just like Bernice. The older Bernice gets, the more she favors me.

As an adult, Yolanda was very instrumental in setting up the arts component of the King Center. She started cultural affairs programming for the Center while she was still in graduate school, and after she graduated from NYU, in 1982, she felt she needed to come work at the Center as a way of "paying her dues," as she used to say. She then established the King Center's Cultural Affairs Department, with the help of her aunt Edythe. I had long felt that the King Center was not complete without drama, dance, music, and visual arts as ways of promoting nonviolent social change, and Yoki knew this. On the advice of Edythe, she formed an advisory committee with Ossie Davis, Ruby Dee, James Baldwin, Harry Belafonte, Sidney Poitier, Maya Angelou, and others. She showcased so much talent; she produced; she acted. She directed a production of James Baldwin's play *Amen Corner*, and Mr. Baldwin visited the Center to see that production.

In addition to overseeing the annual entertainment salute to Martin as part of the King Holiday Week, starting in 1982, Yoki's department put on Kingfest, a summer-long performance and visual arts festival that brought in national artists, featuring gospel, jazz, country, bluegrass, rock, and many other kinds of music. It was one of the few popular music festivals in Atlanta during those years. On certain Saturdays and Sundays, June through August, thousands of people would come and enjoy the artists she brought into the Center, including War, the Ohio Players, George Howard, Ramsey Clark, Tony Terry, Boyz II Men, and Vickie Winans. For each Kingfest, the Dream Team, which consisted of friends and associates of Yolanda's in the acting industry, would put on performances, humorous vignettes that dramatized issues of local, national, and international concern. These performances were created using Martin's philosophy and methodology of nonviolence. She also showcased a lot of local talent. Kingfest included a Kids' Day, when all the performances and visual art were provided by local children, and a Nonviolent Film Festival, which taught visual literacy. Through Kingfest, Yoki sought not simply to entertain, but also to utilize the universality of the arts to help bring together diverse segments of the community and to offer local artists' wares and a health fair, with free health screenings. And she inaugurated Kingfest International, where acts from all over the world showcased their culture, music, and food. You know, Martin loved the arts, music in particular.

THE TRAGEDY OF losing their father touched each of my children differently, but sooner or later they all cut their way through their personal thickets. I tried for years to discover how deeply Bernice had been affected by her father's death. Bernice, whom we called Bunny, was only five when he was taken from us. At that age, she could not put most of the horrible pieces together, but she did finally come to understand that her daddy was not coming home. Shortly after the funeral, I had to go to the bank to transact some business. It was the first time I left home without Bunny. As I walked past the door, she called out to me, "Mommy, don't go, don't go, you may get shot." Her cries jarred me. I said, "Look, I promise. Nothing is going to happen to Mommy." I hoped to God my words would hold true—at least until my children were adults. Had I been thinking, I would have taken her with me. Once, months later, I asked her if she was still worried about me when I traveled, and she said, "No, because I see you always coming back." I thought, "Well, maybe she is telling the truth to the best of her ability." But I always worried about what was going on deep down inside, because Bunny was always the quietest one of my children. After school, the other three would share what they had learned that day, but when it was Bunny's turn, she would usually say that she had nothing to share. It was a long time before she attempted to emerge from her personal exile.

Bunny was very attached to her daddy in the last year of his life. Before that, she hadn't warmed up to him because he was in and out of the house so much. Yet, near the end, Martin invested a lot of quality time in her because he was determined that she would remember him. When he came home, he would stand in the front hall and let her run and jump into his arms. He played little personal games with her. He had a kissing game that he played with the whole family, where he identified on his face what he called sugar spots. My sugar was right in the center of Martin's mouth, Yoki's sugar was on the side of his mouth, Marty's and Dexter's were each on one of his cheeks. In his last year, he played this game a lot with Bunny; he would say, "Now, where is Bunny's sugar?" and she would smack him on the spot he had pointed to, which was the forehead. He'd go around and call out each of our names, and she'd identify all the sugar spots. He would do that several times, so she would remember them. And then he would take her and put her on top of the refrigerator and let her jump into his arms, and they would laugh. He would do that with all the children, but I think that Bunny's getting to know him at that developmental stage and then having him snatched away was terribly devastating to her. Sometimes, in her frustration, she would refer to her father as "that man." Pointing to the sky, she'd say, "That man up there, I don't know him." She really wanted a daddy figure. Once, when she was six or so, a white male photographer was shadowing us for a news article. "Mama," she asked me, "is he going to my ballet recital tonight?" After I told her that he was, she asked me, "What would be wrong with him being our daddy so he could live with us in our house?"

In reality, it was very difficult for Bunny to trust people. Standoffish, distant, shy, angry—that's how strangers described her. But I understood why she was so reserved. For years, everyone she loved and was close to died. First, she lost her father. The next year, in 1969, her beloved uncle A.D. was found dead in his swimming pool under suspicious circumstances. This was shortly after the Fourth of July. Edythe, Pat Latimore, Narissa Neal, A.D. and Naomi and two of their children (Darlene and Vernon), and my children and I had just gone on a two-week vacation in Jamaica. A.D. taught Bunny how to swim on that vacation. But he had to leave after one week, while the rest of us stayed on. As we were packing up to return to Atlanta, I received a call informing me that A.D. had died. Bunny overheard me talking, and blurted out, "I'm not going to any more funerals." And then her grandmother was murdered in church in 1974. Occasionally, Mama King would take care of Bunny when I was traveling; then, suddenly, Mama King was gone, too. Bunny's two cousins around her age, Darlene and Alfred, also died suddenly (both while jogging) at the young ages of twenty and thirty-four, respectively. Then Daddy King died. So, even as she grew into adulthood, Bernice resisted getting close to anyone, sometimes consciously, sometimes subconsciously, because she was afraid that she was going to lose them. She was protecting herself from pain, fearful of developing relationships because they might lead to her being left again.

When it came time for college, Bernice, like many teenagers, vacillated between wanting to be independent (maybe even from me) and wanting to be with family. She sampled several different colleges before finding the school that she thought fit. Initially, she accepted a scholarship to the predominantly white Grinnell College, which is about an hour outside Des Moines, Iowa. That opportunity came about through Andy Young, who'd given a speech there and learned from the African American students of their desire to have more black students on campus. I advised Bernice to visit the school before applying, but she jumped at the chance to attend, primarily because her beloved uncle Andy had suggested it and because it offered a change of scenery from Atlanta. It wasn't long before she admitted that she wished she had taken my advice to visit the college instead of plunging headlong into the new experience. She'd wanted something different, but Grinnell was too much change coming too fast for an eighteen-year-old. Atlanta was a warm climate; Grinnell was often an iceberg. Atlanta offered a lively urban setting; Grinnell was a town of about seventeen thousand, with blacks numbering about sixty-five, all of whom were either faculty or students at the college. At Grinnell, there was not a single black church. The weather, the size of the town, and the lack of groups vying for social justice—all amounted to culture shock for her.

Once there, Bernice quickly confided, "Mommy, even the black people aren't black." By that I think she meant that the blacks she met there did not share the same kind of passion for black culture and the civil rights struggle that she was accustomed to. And I suspect the more staid and somber worship services in Grinnell had her longing for the upbeat gospel songs at Ebenezer Baptist Church.

Feelings of loneliness, and isolation from her family, drove eighteen-year-old Bernice to tears. For the first few weeks, she cried off and on. She wanted to return home immediately, but upon my advice she completed one semester at Grinnell and came home to attend Spelman College in January 1982. Spelman is one of the top colleges in America for African American women. After Martin's death, it had offered scholarships to both my daughters. Of course, Yolanda didn't use hers, but Bernice's was still available. So this worked out well. Before understanding that often the grass only looks greener on the other side, Bernice tried one more out-of-town experience. It lasted only a matter of days.

In August 1982 she enrolled at American University and was assigned to a coed dorm, where she would have to share a bathroom with a male and a dorm room with a white female. That kind of closeness in her private space, plus the rigors of the academic load, were too overwhelming at the time. Once again, the more Bernice experienced "different," the more she seemed to really want "familiar." She quickly returned to Atlanta to continue her education that fall at Spelman, from which she graduated with a degree in psychology, with a concentration in prelaw, in 1985.

Bernice was still trying to carve out a path for herself as the daughter of one of the greatest heroes of the century while finding a way to maintain her identity as a private person. I also knew she was still grief-stricken over the loss of her father at such a young age and was struggling not to be angry at whites in general for her father's suffering and eventual assassination.

Once home in Atlanta, she became engrossed in advancing her education. After graduating from Spelman, she enrolled in a dual divinity/law program at Emory University. Both ministering and lawyering require strong communication skills, and Bernice certainly has those. Early in her teenage years, she showed promise as an excellent speaker. She volunteered to step in for me on one occasion—she must have been just seventeen—and made her first major speech. I had to address the United Nations on the issue of apartheid, but I could not attend because of illness. I was trying to get Yolanda or Martin III to stand in for me when Bernice volunteered. Though it surprised me that she would volunteer, she took my speech and made it her own—and made the front page of the *New York Times* with it! They treated the address as if it were her speech, but of course I didn't mind. I was happy she'd done such a good job, even though I hadn't wanted her to step out into the public arena so soon. Once you do that, you have to be prepared to take the bitter with the sweet.

Although Bernice was headed down the right career path, she still suffered, I think, from the lingering pain of unresolved inner conflict. Her emotional path was not a straight line; it was jagged, sometimes two steps forward and one step backward. In law school, much to my surprise, Bernice apparently contemplated suicide, although it is hard for me to accept that she really meant to carry it out.

One evening, I received a startling phone call. It was from Bernice's roommate and good friend, Alice Eason. Alice told me that she had come down the stairs in the town house where they lived and seen my daughter with a knife in her hand. She thought Bernice was going to cut herself. I knew that the law school had placed Bernice on probation because of below-average grades. I later found out the school had extended that probation and that Bernice was facing the prospect of being released permanently if she did not improve her grades the following semester. At that time, she was already dealing with a heavy baggage of pain. Her father's death lingered over her like a dark cloud before a storm. But would she have actually committed suicide? She has said since then that she had the knife in her hand trying to figure out how bad the pain would be if she went on with her plan to take her own life, but after a miraculous encounter with the Holy Spirit that night, she felt comforted and changed her mind. When I received the call, I got on the phone with her aunt Christine and we rushed over to see Bernice. We told her how much we loved her and that we would do anything for her. I talked to her siblings and encouraged them to call her more often, and Yolanda absolutely drew closer to her.

Bernice, like her father, suffered from depression. Is that surprising? Who wouldn't, considering what Martin and Bernice had to deal with? Martin had the weight of the world on his shoulders, and often went for days without sleeping; Bernice grieved for him for a long time. Thankfully, in time, ministry became Bernice's salvation. I am very clear about that. She was compelled to follow that call. It was God's way of saving her life.

She often talked about how badly she missed Martin and longed to have a conversation with him. Finally, those conversations began happening. Martin came to her in several dreams. In one particular dream, she said he looked just like he did right before he left us. She said that he was sitting in a chair. Yolanda was standing next to him on his right, and Bernice was facing both of them. She told me, "I started pointing my finger at him like I was fussing at him. 'Why haven't you been in touch?' Yolanda answered, 'He has been in touch with me.'" After looking at Yolanda, Martin looked back at Bernice and said, "You will understand it's my ministry."

Bernice told me that Martin had appeared to her at a very strategic time. "It was an affirmation of my call into ministry because there was still some negative talk about women not preaching. That dream opened up my understanding of why my daddy was no longer with us. His suffering was part of his ministry, and he was telling me, as I continue on in ministry, that I will understand the sacrifice and the price that one will have to make for others." After that dream, Bernice said she finally found enough peace, understanding, and encouragement to enthusiastically continue on with her life.

Bernice went on to graduate in May 1990 from the dual-degree program at Emory University, with a master of divinity degree and a juris doctor degree. The same day she received both degrees, she was also ordained as a minister. I never heard any more about depression or suicide attempts. And after experiencing another dream about her father, she was making great progress, I felt, toward inner healing.

Bernice told me that she began believing that God was calling on her to preach when she was about seventeen years old. I had often wondered if a child of mine would get the Call, although I did not like to bring it up, for fear that it would seem like I was pushing them. Daddy King had expected the call to come for Martin III.

My heart swelled with pride when Bernice told me that an inner voice had encouraged her to follow in her father's preaching footsteps.

But I understood the difficulties. Because Bernice is the daughter of Martin Luther King Jr., her road in ministry would be easier, but not exactly simple. I must be clear: This is the South. Sexism in many black Baptist churches is as normal as passing the collection plate on a Sunday morning. Somehow, recalcitrant pastors and preachers remain; these men ignore Scripture references to Jesus's resurrection on Easter Sunday, when he came first to Mary Magdalene and empowered her to preach one of the greatest sermons ever given, "He Is Risen." Moreover, Jesus, who is called the Word in the Gospel of John, came into this world through the seed of a woman, not through the sperm of a man. If a woman can give birth to the Word, certainly she can preach His Word, too. Yet many black Baptist pastors, as well as white pastors in the Southern Baptist denomination, will simply refuse to ordain a woman. At some Baptist churches, if a woman is invited to preach, she is referred to as a speaker and is not allowed to preach from the pulpit; she must preach from the floor.

My daughter preached her trial sermon from the pulpit, not from the floor, on March 27, 1988, at Ebenezer. Of course, I, along with Yolanda, Martin III, and Dexter, and other immediate family from both Martin's and my side of the family were there in the congregation for her first sermon. Although Bernice didn't have the benefit of having Daddy King and Mama King's presence that day, she was honored that my parents, whom the kids called "Grandaddy" and "Nina," were there. Her sermon was entitled "Getting Above the Crowd" and was based on the story of Zacchaeus, a short man who had to climb a sycamore tree to get above the crowd to see Jesus.

Her trial sermon was so good; it was amazing. She fasted for seven days before she spoke, and I felt she had certainly heard from heaven. "Uncle Andy" was there, and he cried like a baby. Afterward, he asked me, "Did she ever listen to Martin's tapes?" Bernice told me that she had not, yet Andy and I both had heard speech patterns like Martin's. And she held her fingers like Martin used to, gestured with her hands like Martin. It was there in the way she tilted her head, in her flashes of humor. She was so much like Martin, it was incredible. The sermon, the style, and the substance actually caused Andy to wonder if certain facets of spirituality, not only the preaching, but also the understanding and revelations, are somehow inherited, passed through the bloodline.

Bernice is always fine when she is in the pulpit. When you see her standing there, you never know how she struggles to get her sermon together. With Bernice, things are black or white, right or wrong. There are no in-betweens. It can be hard to find friends to talk to when you are moralistic. She is not a saint, but she is very definite about her views of good and evil. I stay close to her.

I encouraged Bernice to pull closer to her two brothers. For the longest time, she felt that they picked on her when she was growing up. Still, she tried to play with the boys. She grew up with more boys than girls; her sister was eight years older than she. Now she is making strong female friends, especially in the ministry.

I have heard from many sources that Bernice is a mesmerizing, anointed preacher with many ministry gifts. But preaching is one gift, and pastoring is quite another, and she needed pastoring experience. So she went to her pastor, the Rev. Joseph Roberts, and asked if she could assist him at Ebenezer. She hoped to help troubled youth. Bernice is very good at counseling and resolving conflicts, and has a talent for mediation. Sometimes, when Dexter and I were at an impasse, she could come in, cut right to the chase, and help us reach a resolution. She thought Reverend Roberts could make use of these gifts and help her gain the necessary experience. But he instructed her to look for apprenticeship elsewhere. This was exactly the same thing he'd done with A.D. and Naomi's sons, Rev. Vernon C. King and Rev. Derek King, who preceded Bernice into ministry; he instructed them to look for apprenticeship elsewhere. It was quite a historic break. not to have an ordained member of the immediate King family in the Ebenezer pulpit. Fortunately, Bernice found another pastor, Byron Broussard, who was ready to use her gifts and help her gain pastoral experience, at Greater Rising Star Baptist Church, affectionately known as the "Love Center," located in an inner-city community in Atlanta. And later, Reverend Roberts did have her preach at Ebenezer. If she still feels called to pastor in the future, I think she could certainly start her own church.

THEN THERE IS Martin III, commonly known by his family as Marty. A very sensitive and obedient child, at times he seemed the most melancholy and confused about losing his father, but I am happy that he did not grow up to be angry or hostile. Even in talking about James Earl Ray, the man who was convicted of killing his father, Marty says, "I never hated him. I can't hate or hold bitterness against anybody. Maybe it's my religion or my family background, but it is just not in me to hate."

As the oldest boy, Marty was the one who had bonded most with Martin. He traveled with him, occasionally marched with him, and played basketball and biked with him. In fact, I purchased similar bikes for both of them the Christmas before Martin was taken from us. I remember on the day of the funeral how little Marty, who was ten, sat on the edge of my bed and said, "It just makes me so mad that I don't have a daddy."

Sometimes I wonder which is worse: never to know one's father, or to know and love him only to have him tragically snatched away. Even ten years after his father's death, Marty would on occasion take visitors down to the basement to share with them his most treasured possessions, tucked away in the bottom of a closet, objects that had belonged to Martin: a pair of denim jeans, a ministerial robe, a straw hat, a busted tan briefcase, and that purple bike, which still looked brand-new. Marty longed for the experience of riding off on those bikes with his father. Even into adulthood, Marty has said that he has never understood why anybody would dislike his father enough to kill him. From a moral as well as a human view, I have never understood it, either.

Marty was named Martin III despite my objections. In the back of my mind, I could foresee the problems a son might encounter trying to match the exploits of a famous and anointed father. I worried that Marty would grow up suffering from depression over the loss of his father or be crushed by the burden of his name. Even as a small child, the name posed a problem.

Marty and Yoki were among the first black children to integrate Spring Street Elementary, a public school in Atlanta. The day after enrolling, Marty told me that a little boy had walked up to him and said, "What's your name?"

"Martin Luther King the Third," Marty replied.

"Oh, your daddy's the nigger preacher."

Marty answered, "The word is *Negro.*"

Despite his strength, I understood how the word hurt Marty. He knew it was an insult, and I am sure it was the kind of thing he became sensitized to. When he was about eight years old, he started playing football and baseball, and one Saturday morning I took him to football practice, and he said, "Mommy, you see those big boys over there?" I said, "Yeah, what about them?" He told me, "They came up to me and asked me what was my name, and I told them I didn't know." I asked him why he'd done that, although I knew why: because he believed they would be hostile to him and beat him up if he revealed his name. That just tore my heart out, understanding that Marty had a great name but that it could also bring him pain.

Even before Martin died, the teasing was too much for Marty, so after Martin's assassination, I felt the need to transfer Marty to a private school called Galloway, which was predominantly white and turned out to be a good experience for him. I transferred Dexter and Bernice there as well. At Galloway, Martin became captain of the basketball team and was very popular. The principal said that Marty would often lecture other students about the evils of smoking, drinking, and the use of drugs.

At sixteen, Marty served as a page to Sen. Edward Kennedy. This was the same time that Caroline Kennedy served as a summer intern for her uncle, and the job turned into a lasting friendship between him and Caroline and John Kennedy Jr. In 1975, he graduated from Galloway. And one year later, while a student at Morehouse College, at the age of nineteen, Marty served as a consultant to President Jimmy Carter's election campaign. A few years later, he was a staff aide to Atlanta mayor Andy Young. In 1979, Martin graduated from Morehouse like his father and grandfather before him. He received his B.A. in Political Science.

Over time, he developed a passion for extending the social justice movement that his father and I had championed. He marched. He led protests. He went to jail. But he also left little doubt that he was intent on following his own passions and being his own man. Much to the surprise of some close to him, who had concluded that it was only natural for him to choose the ministry as a career, like his father and his grandfathers, he went another way.

He was the first of our children elected to political office.

On June 9, 1986, he announced his candidacy to become a commissioner on the Fulton County Commission, in Georgia. In explaining his decision, he said, "I've been blessed to be able to travel all over the world and meet all types of people." The privilege of those kinds of experiences had helped him to see how important it is to give back to the community that helped develop him. He understood that in the 1960s most of us could not be in the political arena. It would take years to accomplish things then that today can be done with the stroke of a pen. He saw the political process as the most direct way to help massive numbers of people, whether with jobs, with health care, or with housing. That is why he opted to run.

His association with Sen. Ted Kennedy also fueled his desire to launch into politics, and in 1986 both Caroline Kennedy and John Kennedy Jr. campaigned for Martin III, who was elected a member of the Board of County Commissioners in a landslide, beating a Democrat who has served there for thirty years by an 8 to 1 margin. He served until 1993.

The Fulton County Commission had about thirty-five department heads, almost all of them white males, but once elected a commissioner, Marty proved that in this virtually all-white arena, he was not going to be the Invisible Man. He worked hard to create the Department of Contract Compliance and Equal Employment; to ensure that the commission had a diverse workforce in terms of leadership; and also to ensure that people of color and women were able to gain government contracts through a system that had previously locked them out. When he came into office, probably fewer than 5 percent of the county's contracts went to women, small developers, or African American businesses. It was the same problem I had confronted when building the Center. I found that the best way to change low numbers of minority contracts was to tackle the numbers head-on and to demonstrate to both employers and workers that diversity, if given a chance, could be a win-win position for everyone. Martin did much the same thing, except from the inside. In 1987 he was named vice chairman of the National Labor Relations Committee of the National Association of County Officials.

Another program he launched inside the commission was A Call to Manhood, which was designed to provide "fathering" and mentoring to young children who were displaced and at risk for becoming school dropouts and being thrust into the prison pipeline. So many young boys are without fathers to give them attention, so they get attention in other ways, from gangs or drug dealers. Martin initiated "rite-of-passage seminars" for the youth and found them successful role models and tutors. When he left office as commissioner in 1993, both the contracting programs and A Call to Manhood stayed in place. A nice legacy.

As time went on, I could see that Martin III had several deeply planted, inbred "movement" values. If you engage in a serious conversation with him, you will see these values shining through. World peace, antipoverty, nonviolence—these are his concerns, and they are the three branches of the same tree. Like all my children, he has been involved in the King Center over the years, and at the Center, his passion was organizing youth workshops on nonviolence, which attracted young people, including gang members and other activists, from around the world.

Keeping the spotlight on the poor is vital to Martin. He is steadfast in his belief that the plight of the poor—of children who go to bed hungry, of homeless families sleeping in parks and under bridges, of the sick who can't afford to buy their medication—must become central to our nation's political discourse and to our media.

Martin III has a novel idea that I think would go a long way toward addressing poverty. He is looking at creative ways to revitalize the Martin Luther King Jr. thoroughfares. All over America, he says, there are close to a thousand of those thoroughfares, and unfortunately many of these streets bearing the King name are blighted. He applauds those politicians who led the way to name these avenues after his dad, but he is bothered that they did not follow through with funding for them. What a difference it would make if the government and business communities got behind a revitalization of these streets. With the right funding in these areas, people could have decent schools and housing so they could sustain themselves. This alone would help create a notable number of jobs and make a dent in unemployment. Unfortunately, so far, other political priorities have overshadowed this idea.

Marty's beliefs have also led him to become an outspoken opponent of the death penalty. He is fond of saying, "If we believed in an eye for an eye and a tooth for a tooth, most of us would be without eyes and without teeth." I am also proud of his campaign to thwart the continuing tragic cases of police shootings of unarmed black men.

In 1997, I was proud that he was unanimously elected the fourth president of the SCLC, during the fortieth anniversary of the civil rights organization Martin cofounded in 1957. As president, Martin III helped establish new SCLC chapters, led protests to change the design of the Georgia state flag, which still featured a large Confederate image, and to remove the Confederate flag from the statehouse grounds in South Carolina.

He also held hearings and focused national attention on police brutality. At the thirty-seventh "I Have a Dream" anniversary, on August 27, 2000, Martin III and New York activist Al Sharpton led a gathering of thousands at the Lincoln Memorial, where they demanded an end to police brutality and racial profiling. I introduced both Martin and Al Sharpton at that gathering. The crowd grew enthusiastic as it became obvious that neither of those two were going to sugarcoat anything. Martin is somewhat quiet and soft-spoken, but his words flame with passion and power. He told the crowd that America has not fulfilled his father's vision for racial justice, and he took the police to task for too many cases of police brutality and too many fatal shootings of unarmed men. On the minds of many there was the police shooting of Amadou Diallo. He was an unarmed immigrant killed in a hail of forty-one bullets the year before in New York City. At the rally, organizers focused attention on how unarmed black men were more likely to be shot by police than unarmed white men, how black men were too often randomly searched without cause, and how too often a routine traffic stop could turn fatal for blacks. Martin told the crowd that he was still awaiting the day "when we can raise our children to respect police first, and fear them last."

He also seized the occasion of the "I Have a Dream" anniversary rally to hold public officials accountable, just as Martin and I always tried to do. The day before the gathering at the Lincoln Memorial, Martin III and Rev. Al Sharpton met with Attorney General Janet Reno and with top aides to President Clinton to demand that the federal government withhold funds from any police department that practiced racial profiling or showed a pattern of brutality. The tragedy of the 9/11 attacks scuttled that approach, because fears of terrorism resulted in demands for more funding for, not more oversight of, police. Holding police accountable is not something Martin has given up on; it is a necessary change that is still a work in progress.

In 2003, Martin cosponsored the fortieth anniversary of the historic March on Washington with human rights organizations from across the country. Before the media, he clarified his role. "I know I can't be my father," he told them, "but what I can do is to take the message that was the blueprint that he left for us and I can share it with others and hopefully take the legacy to the next level. I was raised in a family dedicated to public service. It is only natural that I would feel compelled to continue the work. Why reinvent the wheel when it is clear that there is much work to be done? If we can come anywhere close to what my father envisioned, I know we'll have a better nation and world. So if I had a dream, it would be to see that the vision that my father gave his life to achieve is manifested. I firmly believe everyone in America deserves a decent job with decent pay."

Keeping the dream alive is not a mere slogan or headline with Martin. It has captivated him. He conceptualizes it and in ways large or small continues to reshape and repackage its tenets of peace, justice, and fairness for the next generation. Sometimes he steps back into politics to achieve the goal.

He is clear about his own style of leadership. He describes it this way: "My leadership style is to try to build a coalition and not be confrontational unless I have to be. I try to build support among, first of all, my staff. If the staff doesn't agree, I try to hear out everyone before I make a decision. Although some leaders lead dictatorially, I believe you can lead in a coalescing way. When you disagree, you don't humiliate someone because you disagree. You want to hear their point and then you want to bring them around, so I try to use persuasion as a leadership tool and try to see the best in everyone. I want to bring the best out of everyone."

I know that he thinks that today, when there are so many terrific and seemingly irresolvable problems, it is a time for new forms of leadership to emerge. For example, he challenges the business community to try putting people before profits by paying livable wages and providing health care, all of which should be in the business's self-interest. To Martin III, worker rights, such as a livable wage and health care, should be the headlights of a business's mission, not the taillights.

On the whole, I believe that while carrying Martin's name has been difficult for Marty, he has not crumbled. He has worn it well. He often told me that he knows better than to try to do what his father did. Martin Luther King Jr. was a national leader at twenty-seven; on the cover of *Time* at twenty-eight. If Martin had to compare himself to his father, he often says, he would have "flunked." Actually, "failed miserably" is how he puts it. Instead, he wants God to help him enhance what his father did.

April 4, the anniversary day of his father's assassination, usually saddens Marty, and though he has come to terms with it, he admitted to me, "On that day for many years, I would shed tears. Our father is gone, but because of the holiday and the many observances, it's like he's enshrined in time. He will be forever young. That is the one wonderful way of thinking that helped me get through it." He also told me, "The sad thing for me and my siblings, as adults, is not having had the opportunity to have a conversation with him, and that's what we've probably missed. Those are the things that there's nothing you can do about, but the ten years that we were together were incredible. We all will have fond memories forever."

What a feeling of comfort for me to know that Martin III is making a difference and paving his own way as his own man.

Perhaps because he was the older son, he wants to protect people. He even felt he was my protector. I take comfort in that, too. He has spent long evenings with me, patiently waiting in my bedroom until I finished my phone calls. He sought my advice on politics, love and marriage, business relationships, inner healing—whatever was in his heart. Even when he had his own house, he would come over most every evening to check on me, or just stay with me. It often seemed like he had never left home. For that, people whispered about him being a "mama's boy." It surprised me to hear that people did not know that my house, the one I raised all my children in, was now in a drug-infested part of the city, an area none of my critics would dare walk in, let alone live in. In fact, my house in Vine City was broken into twice. Once, when I was at home, Martin happened not to be at the house, I fell asleep sitting up in my bed after reading some papers. I was briefly awoken by a noise and thought a picture had fallen, and I just went back to sleep. I discovered that a burglar had been there only when I woke up the next morning and Pat, my beloved personal assistant, arrived and told me that a brick had been thrown through the living room window, which faced the front of the house. A walkie-talkie that had been in its charging station in the kitchen was missing. Only by the grace of God did I avoid being beaten, raped, or murdered.

The police eventually caught the man who broke in. He was a drug addict, and had sold the walkie-talkie to someone, who ended up using it, which allowed the police to trace it back to the burglar. During the interrogation, the burglar apparently told the police that he had actually stood over me for a spell, considering what to do with me. They discovered that he was responsible for the rapes and murders of three elderly women in the neighborhood. Why did he leave me unharmed? Maybe he recognized me from the pictures in the living room. Or maybe he saw a picture of Martin and me in the bedroom. I know for sure that it was just not my time to die—which is to say, I was grateful that Marty would come to watch over me and put my safety before his own comfort or pleasure.

Deep inside Martin III are the will and the strength to love unconditionally. We talk about this sometimes. He sincerely believes—much as both Martin and I, and of course much like his "Granddaddy" Daddy King, believed—that love is the antidote to racism and self-hatred. "His source of love that springs forth outward begins within," Martin likes to say. People really have to develop a true love for themselves. It helps to take account of one's self by writing down all the bad and good qualities you have and strive to eliminate the bad. Then say, "Even though I have those problems, I love me." He feels that you really have to love yourself before you can even begin to love other people. In 1990 he showed his ability to correct a wrong when he made a disparaging remark about homosexuals. After meeting with gay rights leaders, he apologized and referred to his words as "uninformed and insensitive."

Just imagine a hot sunny day, Martin and me sitting in lawn chairs in our backyard, sipping lemonade and chatting about our children, as proud parents do. I could see Martin and me scrambling to conclude what qualities our eldest son received from each of us. I think we would conclude that in some ways he resembles both of us: tender-hearted, passionate, determined, patient. And even with the weight of carrying the King name, he has found a way to achieve inner peace and outer strength as he faces the ups and down of trying to advance the causes he was born and bred on, but doing things his own way. He has taken the advice I offered to all my children: not to become a prisoner of the King name, but rather to "Always be your own best self."

DEXTER, NAMED AFTER the first church Martin pastored, was only seven years old when his father was murdered. He was always a deep thinker, prone to analyzing instead of accepting. Over and over in the aftermath of his father's murder, he would ask, "Why did my daddy die? How did he die? What is going to happen to the bad people who shot him?" Sometimes I felt as though he were asking the same questions repeatedly to get attention. Being the second son and the third child can make it hard to find one's place in a family. But it turns out he has, and always had, such an analytical mind. His sense of logic and administration, which he used to head the King Center, was demonstrated at an early age. At the Galloway School, he did very well in math. In fact, his elementary school math teacher said he had never worked with a child like Dexter, who would give up his lunch just to come in and work on math problems.

At around age twelve, he started his own photography business. He went to the Southern Rural Action Project, which was designed to help rural poor people, but Dexter attended the program one summer, and they offered him a photography course. He became a very good photographer. He took pictures for weddings and graduations and for different groups, such as the Institute on Nonviolence at the King Center. But being so young, he wasn't yet mature enough to understand how success can turn into a nightmare. Daddy King began announcing Dexter's picture-taking business from the pulpit. Very soon, he had far more orders than he could handle and often couldn't deliver the pictures quickly enough to satisfy the demand. It taught him a lesson, though, about the peril of moving too far too fast.

Dexter and his cousin Isaac Farris used to work together; they'd sit around and throw around big terms like *diversification*, but they didn't know what they were doing. They made a little sign that read, "K and F Sound Productions," which later became a rather sophisticated music production company. As a student at Morehouse College, Dexter would hire himself out as a disc jockey. He purchased some of the best equipment money could buy for his enterprises.

At a certain point, though, he was spending too much time on his business ventures and not enough on his schoolwork. I tried to convince him to close down his extracurricular activities. I thought they might be the reason he wasn't performing well in his studies at Morehouse, a prestigious, historically black private school for men in Atlanta. Four generations of Kings had graduated from Morehouse: Dexter's maternal great-granddaddy, Rev. A.D. Williams, in the class of 1898; his grandfather Martin Luther King Sr., class of 1930; Martin, who enrolled at fifteen and graduated in 1948; Dexter's uncle, A.D., who graduated in 1959; and Martin III, who graduated with the class of 1979.

Dexter, however, eventually dropped out. He had problems concentrating and focusing on his studies. He could read something over and over and still not understand it. He was soon diagnosed as having attention deficit disorder, or ADD, a condition that often makes it impossible to function in a controlled environment, one that does not leave room for wandering around. Doctors then were prescribing Ritalin to control ADD, which I wouldn't allow. I didn't want my son drugged. I had also read that some medications could produce symptoms worse than the diagnosis. In any event, Dexter felt the shame and the burden of being the son of Martin Luther King Jr. and not excelling. He left Morehouse and went back to deejaying. Music gave him meaning and a sense of well-being. But the exit from Morehouse also represented a break with a proud tradition of Morehouse graduates in the family, and this resulted in Dexter feeling like the black sheep—at least for a while.

One summer, he took a job working in a funeral home. He and his cousin started talking big. They said they were going to buy up a run-down funeral home right off Auburn Avenue and refurbish it. When he came home from work, he would tell us all about his experiences with dead people in the funeral home. He would try to sneak up behind me and put his hands on me, and I would tell him, "Don't you put your hands on me after coming home from a funeral home." It was all in fun, though, and another way that Dexter coped with his grief and overcame his fear of death.

In 1982, he went to work for the Atlanta Police Department, and I, a staunch advocate of nonviolence, faced a dilemma: having a policeman with a gun in my house. This was something I did not allow, so Dexter ended up keeping the gun in his car. He had always wanted to be a police officer; when he was in high school, he actually told the kids that he was a cop. He bought himself a cap that looked like a policeman's cap and some badges, and the kids believed him.

In the mid-1980s, he began to pour his passion for musical production and organization into the King Center. He also spent hours wrestling with the thorny issues of how to protect his father's legacy, to ensure that it was not exploited, and to endow resources for future generations. In addition, he hoped to produce more resources, eventually allowing us to contribute to other grassroots organizations. He had innovative ideas about using new technology to tell our story and promote the Kingian nonviolence philosophy.

In the late 1980s, I began to contemplate successorship. Too many leaders do not train anyone to succeed them, and this is why there's often so much confusion when a leader is incapacitated or dies. I felt that it would take time to train whomever I put in place to head the Center. Besides, I always felt that young people ought to be trained for leadership.

Yet, even as I wanted to let go, it was difficult to actually do it. Here again was the inner tug-of-war between Mrs. King, the institutional parent, and Coretta, the mother of flesh-and-blood children, whom I innately and unconditionally loved and supported. In a real sense, I gave birth to both: the institution, with the help of many midwives; and my natural children, through the love Martin and I shared. Couldn't I hang on to both? To all? To everything?

Of course, the answer was no. As founder, president, and CEO of the Center, I knew it had come time for me to decrease my role and allow my children to increase theirs. Subliminally, I knew they could not assert themselves as long as I remained a strong presence, but it was quite a challenge to begin letting go. Even understanding that this task would go to one of my four children did not make the decision easier.

I am the kind of person who likes to know exactly what's going to happen, especially in a matter as serious as heading the Center. I have to have a clear picture of the outcome; if I can't see my way clearly, I often hesitate—some would say procrastinate. After much prayer, I felt the urgency to step out and proceed on faith.

I let my children know how serious I was about the Center having an orderly line of succession. In the summer of 1988, I arranged for all of us to meet in a cabin in the northeast Georgia mountains. I picked the location for its isolation. We did not need interruptions. We all sat in a circle, and I asked each sibling about his or her interest in taking this role. Yolanda, who was well on her way to a successful acting career, said, "I'll do it if I have to, but I sure hope I won't." Martin, who was contemplating a political future, said, "I guess if I had to, but I really don't know." Bernice, who was pursuing her doctorate of law and master of divinity, said, "I'll handle a part of it if I have to." Then everyone looked at Dexter, who we all agreed had the best business sense of the siblings. He had a vision and a plan for the Center, which at that time employed sixty people and managed a few million in finances.

Dexter, at twenty-eight years old, accepted the responsibility. On April 4, 1989, twenty-one years to the date after Martin's assassination, the King Center board and I held a five-hour installation service. Appropriately, the installation was carried out at Ebenezer, a church filled with our family's history, both joyous and painful. People came from everywhere to celebrate. Motown founder Berry Gordy attended and donated tapes of Martin's best-known speeches. Jennifer Holiday sang. Adam Clayton Powell IV came, along with many other daughters and sons of the movement. In his installation speech, Dexter announced ambitious plans that included training one hundred thousand activists around the world in Martin Luther King Jr.'s philosophy and methodology of nonviolence, and to build a forty-million-dollar endowment within the next decade.

But six months later, Dexter resigned.

Some blamed me for not getting out of the way. Others blamed Dexter for getting *in* the way. Many other factors, including consistently negative press, especially in the *Atlanta Journal-Constitution*, contributed to this disappointing equation. But the major problem was a flawed structure. The board made Dexter the president, I was the CEO, and the Rev. Barbara Skinner was the chief operating officer. Then there was the board chairman, and an oversight committee. Dexter soon felt he was sandwiched between competing personalities. He asked for complete authority from the board, but never received it.

There were also deep, entrenched factions on the board. Many of the members were veterans of the civil rights movement. They would not embrace Dexter, who counted hip-hop artists among his good friends and wanted to cater to a younger generation. Undercurrents of talk suggested that he did not have the proper educational credentials to command respect as president. Some thought he needed to be more diplomatic; others wanted him to be a figurehead. In the end, he felt betrayed and disillusioned.

The press reported that we were at war, which was not exactly true. After Dexter left, we went back to my being president and CEO, and appointed Dr. Cleveland Dennard the chief operating officer. Dennard, a civil rights veteran, had served as president of Atlanta University for seven years and had earned respect as a management consultant. He was a member of our church, a good friend and supporter, and he agreed to be with us through our reorganization. But five years after the reorganization, I ended up with the same dilemma: Who would lead the Center into the next generation?

It was now 1994. Once again, we looked to Dexter. If he agreed to come back, we thought, then this time things would be different. I didn't know how much he had changed, but I knew *I* had. Dexter still burned with the same vision, and he had a holistic understanding of how the King entities (the Center, the Foundation, and the Estate) could work together and not against one another.

There were some actions I had to take to make this work. I agreed to take the title of founder; I would stay on the board, but not be an officer. As long as I was in a prominent position, I realized, people would not deal with Dexter; they would go around him to talk to me. This time around, when people came to me, I would tell them I was not in charge and would send them to Dexter.

When I went to the board to propose Dexter's return, there was resistance. I was sympathetic to their concerns that we have the right leadership—we had quite a reputation at the King Center for not getting the right people—but I reiterated the importance of institutionalizing Martin's legacy, and restated my support for Dexter.

Finally, the board agreed that there should never be a time when a King family member did not lead the Center. I had to get the young people prepared. I made it clear that, my personal feelings notwithstanding, I needed to step aside before I became too advanced in years, unable to focus, to be alert or get around. This time the board seemed to sense that we had reached the point at which change had to come.

During a very emotional meeting in October 1994, Dexter was voted in as CEO. The board made very positive statements about him and the future-looking leadership he represented. They thanked me for my dedication while embracing him. It was virtually a complete turnaround. The experience was so meaningful and humbling for Dexter that he broke down and cried. Later, he confided in me that the tears were an embarrassment. Reassuring him, I said, "Dexter, the tears helped people see you as a human being. You have feelings just like everybody else. Maybe people see you as being indifferent or cold and unfeeling, but now they see you in a different light."

ALMOST IMMEDIATELY UPON assuming his role as CEO, Dexter was pitched into a bruising conflict with the National Park Service as Atlanta prepared for the 1996 Summer Olympics. Years earlier, when the International Olympic Committee was considering Atlanta as a possible host city, Andy, who was the mayor at the time, insisted that the African delegation visit the King Center and meet with me. Andy told me that they were moved by their visit. When the vote was taken in 1990, the IOC chose Atlanta by a narrow margin. The African delegation's vote was large enough to make the difference, and Andy told me that the delegation's vote had a great deal to do with their visit with me at the King Center and the importance to them of the King legacy. It was common knowledge that Martin's legacy, with its emphasis on goodwill and diversity and its reputation for racial harmony, was among Atlanta's most powerful magnets, drawing strong global support to Atlanta from the Olympic board. The city motto, "The City Too Busy to Hate," reminded many of Martin's immemorial words on hate, a way of thinking and living often driven home by Daddy King as well. Moreover, the King Center was one of Atlanta's top tourist sites, bringing millions of dollars annually into the city treasuries.

Starting in the early 1990s, the King Center's board and I had been discussing how to finance necessary repairs throughout the King Center campus and expand the Center's exhibition space in preparation for the Olympics. It turned out that the National Park Service was also looking for funds for a new visitor center. In initial meetings between me, the Park Service, Ebenezer, and officials from the City of Atlanta, I understood that the Park Service was seeking twelve million dollars from the federal government to build a visitor center and that the King Center could share in that allocation of funds for our repairs. Also, I believed that the King Center would be given control over the exhibits at the new NPS visitor center to ensure the integrity of the narrative, and that there would be space in that center for black businesses to sell their wares during the Olympics.

But when the dust had cleared, the King Center did not benefit from any largesse emanating from the Olympics. The Park Service gained precious land and properties, Ebenezer Church received land for a new church as well as significant funds, the city's community center was entirely torn down, and the King Center received nothing at all. In fact, the Center lost ground. Dexter once said that the Park Service came in and took everything, just like the government had taken from the Native Americans. While that was not a particularly diplomatic statement, can you blame him for saying it?

Before the Olympics, the King District included the community center, a natatorium, Martin's birth home, a few other historic homes, a nursing home, Fire Station No. 6 (where Martin chased fire trucks as a boy), and Ebenezer Baptist Church, which for decades remained the center of worship for King family members. The district also included the King Center—its administration program and archives building, Freedom Hall Complex with its auditorium, meeting rooms, bookstore, screening room, International Chapel of All Faiths, and Martin's crypt, set in the middle of the reflecting pool near the eternal flame.

I had lobbied the city and the U.S. Congress for the creation of the Martin Luther King Historic Site and Preservation District. I had raised millions in public and private funds and worked with the City of Atlanta to restore housing in the same block as Martin's birth home. Then, in 1980, at my invitation, the Park Service became involved with the management of the historic district. Because of the nearly a million people who visit our site annually, it was impossible for the King Center to be the sole entity responsible for the District's maintenance. We continued to manage and operate the King Center, while the Park Service managed the birth home, the No. 6 Fire Station, and, eventually, the Ebenezer historic sanctuary and the new visitors' center.

From the beginning, I had envisioned including all the iconic spiritual institutions in the District, such as Wheat Street Baptist Church and Bethel AME as well as Ebenezer, along with the Atlanta Life Insurance building and the SCLC headquarters, but because of insufficient resources we could not expand. My hope was that others would be inspired to complete the venture.

I started our planning for the Olympics with no knowledge of the National Park Service's true agenda, which was hidden from us until it was too late to make a difference. Much of the conflict that bloomed in advance of the 1996 Olympics centered on the community center across the street from the King Center headquarters and Ebenezer. I had raised about $3.5 million to build that center, with the city providing matching funds. I was happy to raise the money because the community center served the Auburn community. It housed a "gymnatory" (a gymnasium that could also serve as an auditorium that would seat about a thousand people), the King Center's Early Learning Center, a library, community social services, as well as multipurpose rooms for activities such as tutoring, and it was just steps away from the natatorium, the beautiful Olympic-size pool. I saw this center as the city's and the community's portion of the King memorial. The King Center and the City of Atlanta had agreed that the city would manage the community center, and that it would be open for all to use. Initially, the National Park Service had a small office space in a neighborhood home near Martin's birth home. We thought the Park Service would support the community building and development we had already started and would also help by conducting interpretive tours and communicating the mission of the King Center.

But what the Park Service really wanted was to purchase the choice land the community center sat on so it could build the Park Service visitors' center, with exhibition space, there. In addition, the Park Service wanted control of historic Ebenezer, where Rev. Joseph Roberts was pastor. The Park Service proposed a land swap by which it would get control of the historic church site adjacent to the King Center through a long-term lease. Rev. Roberts would get cash plus land across the street to build a new church.

Dexter and I fought the deal to tear down the community center to make way for the Park Service's visitors' center. We went to Congress. We went to the U.S. Department of Housing and Urban Development. We tried to get the White House involved.

I was also excited about Dexter's plan for a high-tech museum named the Dream Center, which he wanted to build on the grounds of the community center. Using the latest technology, this museum would offer the type of sensory effects that allow visitors to feel as if they have been transported back to the major civil rights battlefields and victory celebrations, such as the victory of the 1955 Montgomery Bus Boycott. For example, in an installation showcasing the Birmingham campaign you would actually hear the police dogs barking. The centerpiece would show Martin delivering his "I Have a Dream" speech at the Lincoln Memorial via holograph, making the whole experience come alive anew.

Meanwhile, hoping to win our support for the land swap and the visitors' center, the Park Service was initially very friendly. They began a "wining and dining" process in their attempt to solicit my support. Top officials flew me in a private plane to the Lyndon Johnson Library near Austin, Texas, where I met with Lady Bird Johnson, the former first lady and a Park Service advisory board member. She talked passionately about how the Park Service had helped make the Johnson properties one of the nation's most popular tourist sites. The National Park Service had even more aggressive ambitions. The discussions quickly moved to acquiring the land that held my husband's crypt. "That's nonnegotiable" was my rather curt reply. Then they talked about acquiring Martin's birth home. Again, I told them emphatically, "That, too, is nonnegotiable. We own it. We're going to keep it." I felt, and still feel, that black people have lost too much land to white people already and that we certainly should not give up anything else. What I gleaned from these conversations, all in all, was that the Park Service wanted to buy the King Center. That too, of course, was not negotiable.

Without my knowledge, the Park Service had talked with Reverend Roberts at Ebenezer and with City Hall officials, and had also enlisted the help of Rep. John Lewis to push through legislation for funds to tear down the community center. I was disappointed that John Lewis, a movement friend, was not properly briefed on the matter. He later informed us that the Park Service had told his offices that I was on board with the changes, which of course was not true.

In the end, after intense negotiations, the City of Atlanta donated the community center property to the Park Service, so the Park Service got the land for its visitors' center which would house Park Service offices and exhibits by the Park Service, and the Park Service worked out a deal with Reverend Roberts for a long-term lease on the Ebenezer sanctuary in exchange for funds and land to build a new church.

The Ebenezer sanctuary had sacred and historic value. Visitors from all over the world came there to share in a spiritual and historic experience. Four generations of Kings had worshipped or preached there. Mama King was murdered there. Martin and A.D. co-pastored and preached at Ebenezer, and their funerals were held there. The idea of ceasing worship services at the original Ebenezer Church was very painful to me.

It might have been all right for the Park Service to take that sanctuary years hence, when Christine, Naomi, and I were no longer around and when our children were on their last legs, but to discontinue operating that church in my time when we had first-generation living heirs—I mean, it is still very painful. This is the first time I have said this publicly.

The promises I'd believed the Park Service had made to the King Center to share in the twelve-million-dollar allocation from Congress evaporated into thin air. Like other entities in the District, the King Center really could have used a face-lift, but it did not receive one dollar for improvements.

The community center was gone. Black businesses who had bought inventory thinking they could exhibit their wares at what was going to be our exhibition site during the Olympics lost their money. Some went into bankruptcy.

In future years, the Park Service and my heirs may strike up a better relationship. But what happened then was that Dexter, seeing an injustice being done, tried to rectify it and got maligned, especially in the press. The National Park Service took its concerns to the Atlanta press, which then distorted our intentions. Dexter said he had funders ready to invest the seventy-five to one hundred million dollars necessary to build the interactive Dream Center. At the time, nothing like that had been done to convey the history of the civil rights movement. But the flap with the Park Service—along with Dexter's consistent statements that James Earl Ray had not killed Martin (which I'll talk more about later on)— created such controversy that the funders backed away. When people read negative articles, it creates a climate of hostility and ill will, which dampened some of the support the Center should have received. Cynthia Tucker, the editorial page editor for the *Atlanta Journal-Constitution*, consistently wrote editorials attacking me as well as Dexter and his endeavors regarding the Dream Center. She did it for so long that I sometimes imagined she had some kind of personal problem with us, or that she was being used by others for a broader agenda. I believe also that the funders Dexter had in place were pressured to back away.

I suppose that when you become older and wiser, you are more cautious in terms of what you say and the way you say it. I cautioned Dexter about speaking so directly on certain subjects, but he and Bernice have their father's directness.

As I shifted into semiretirement from the Center, Dexter and his business partner, Phil Jones, took on the challenge of safeguarding Martin's intellectual property. Their job was to protect his words, ideas, name, and image from literary and commercial exploitation.

In one of Dexter's first meetings as head of the King Center, he emphasized the theme of ownership—not just of land, but of ideas and writings, too. As he emphasized in his book, *Growing Up King*, "The King Center is the spiritual and institutional guardian of the King legacy. Our main goal is to educate the public about, and to perpetuate and promote, my father's message of nonviolence around the world. To achieve this goal, the Estate of Martin Luther King Jr., Inc., must protect Martin's intellectual property: the name, images, writing, and speeches that embody his message.

"Land is the real estate of the past," Dexter said. "Intellectual property is the real estate of the now. If you stand back and let others steal Dad's material, then you are affecting every minority writer, every songwriter, every composer, every artist, every storyteller, every creative person."

It's well known that Martin did not live a lavish lifestyle. He gave away much of what he earned in his lifetime, including the fifty-four thousand dollars he received in connection with the Nobel Peace Prize. He left hardly any inheritance. It was our family friend Harry Belafonte who took out an insurance policy on Martin and helped obtain other contributions that aided our family in the years after Martin's death.

However, Martin did make a clear distinction between the income he derived from his work as head of the SCLC and that from his personal efforts as a private citizen. He believed that his spiritual message belonged to the world, but his copyrighted words belonged to him legally in life and to his children and me after his death. This is why, as early as 1955, he began copyrighting his speeches and writings, including his 1963 "I Have a Dream" speech, and doing so under *his name*, rather than under the names of the organizations he represented. With no land or material possessions to leave to his heirs, Martin knew that all he had to leave behind was his intellectual property.

Soon after he delivered "I Have a Dream," which is widely considered one of the most important speeches of the twentieth century, 20th Century Fox Records started mass distribution of the piece in its entirety, without Martin's permission. At that time, many people had not heard the whole speech, and 20th Century Fox took advantage of this fact, selling and profiting from Martin's words without paying him a dime. Martin sued to stop distribution of the record on the grounds of copyright infringement, and won.

In the twentieth century, millions of acres of land, especially in the South, were stolen from blacks, leaving their heirs impoverished. History repeated itself when record companies sold lyrics blacks had penned and/or sung, while giving them little or no compensation. Why should ideas and land alike be lost to blacks while the great wealth they create goes to enrich others? This historical understanding is no doubt why Martin gave the rights to distribute his "I Have a Dream" speech to Berry Gordy, founder of Motown Records.

In 1999, the Estate of Martin Luther King Jr., Inc., sued CBS News on virtually the same issue that his father had advanced with regard to 20th Century Fox: copyright infringement. The network had included footage of virtually the entire "Dream" speech, along with several of Martin's other most revered speeches, in a five-part series, and then sold the footage on home videos. They did not give the series away; they sold it for profit. They used my husband's words, name, image, and speeches to make this money, but Martin's heirs received nothing. It was unfair, and a court of law upheld this conclusion, ruling that the copyright laws protected Martin's speeches. Spending millions fighting copyright infringement was something we had to do to protect the integrity of Martin's legacy for future generations, not to make ourselves richer.

While we won in the courts, CBS's venerable *60 Minutes* program tried to sully our reputation by running a critical piece entitled "Selling the Dream." It basically accused our family of using intellectual property as a means of profiteering from Martin's work. Its argument did not make sense in court; nor did it make sense in the court of public opinion. My son also appropriately pointed out in his book, *Growing Up King*, that during the trial it was revealed that the network charged schools and nonprofits a thousand dollars per minute to use its footage of the "I Have a Dream" speech.

In cases large or small, we must safeguard Martin's legacy—his name, image, and words—for future generations. To whom should we render this vital responsibility? Corporate America? The federal government? Once again, legal trials have brought clarity and have protected the dignity that is rightfully attached to Martin's name. In the early 1980s, for example, a novelty company began manufacturing a miniature bust of Martin, claiming it was doing so in conjunction with the King Center. This was tasteless and disrespectful, a good example of why we must protect Martin's image as well as his words. If we do not call out these violations and try to put a stop to them, our silence might be viewed as acceptance.

With this in mind, before the formation of the Estate of Martin Luther King Jr., Inc., the King Center sued the manufacturer of the bust. A Georgia court upheld our right to protect Martin's image, and stopped distribution of the sculpture. The law maintains, however, that it is the responsibility of the interested or potentially aggrieved parties to police how their intellectual property is being used, or their ability to prevent others from exploiting it will be compromised. Although the King Center brought that suit, it is now the King Estate that bears the burden of ensuring that Martin's words or images are not used pornographically, indecently, or in ways incongruous to the values he presented to the world. To carry out this mission, the King Estate frequently issues licenses to businesses and individuals who use Martin's name or likeness for profit. When the use is by nonprofit groups or schools using the material for educational purposes, there is generally not a charge, or there's a nominal charge. Yet, in both the CBS and miniature bust cases, negative publicity against the King family continues to obscure the principles for which we are fighting. Much of this negativity emanates from Atlanta, a fact of life that dogged Martin and continues to hound my family. I think perhaps this negativity will stalk the King family in perpetuity, although it is my hope and prayer that it will one day cease.

Sadly, even my husband often felt alienated in his own city, the place where he grew up. For instance, when he tried to establish a campaign around school desegregation, he called the city leadership together and outlined his proposal. But he couldn't get leadership to come together. There were about twenty potential leader types, all vying for attention. So Martin forgot about Atlanta and moved on to other campaigns.

This is the kind of situation my children and I still deal with. Too many people saw me just as Mrs. King, and assumed I was riding on the coattails of my husband's notoriety. They did not see Coretta, who had gifts, talents, and ideas, as well as a passion to carry out Martin's mission for all people. They saw Mrs. King, but not Coretta, who had four children to care for and a husband who was often looked at as the president of black America, but who depended on me as his soul mate, wife, and primary confidante. Even before Martin's death, I was asked to join just about every progressive women's group and organization of color in the United States, and expected to attend regular meetings. If I didn't, I'd face the buzz that I was too high and mighty to relate to real people.

For example, when we moved to Atlanta, Martin encouraged me to join the Links chapter there. The Links is a public service organization of mostly middle-class black women; it does many worthwhile community projects. Members are asked to call and explain their absence if they can't attend a meeting or event. When we lived in Montgomery, I belonged to the Links there and was actively involved in that chapter. When I joined the Links in Atlanta, sometimes I was so busy taking care of my kids and my husband, or I was traveling for the movement, that I just plain forgot to call in my absences. Quickly, it came back to me that I was being whispered about, referred to as "Miss It" or "Miss Hot Stuff," who thought myself too busy to call. One day, after I had rushed Martin to the airport and was trying to explain why I'd forgotten a meeting, one of the Links leaders said to me, snidely, "Well, why don't you just try to come to one meeting a year instead of two?" Stung, I decided that this was just not an organization I could be a part of. I did end up being a member of the national Links organization instead, which didn't require me to be subject to time-consuming rules or dues.

All the children seemed to have inherited specific qualities from Martin and me. Yolanda has our love of the performing arts and a sense of how to balance difficult situations. Martin has his father's name, as well as his zeal for advocacy and social justice. Bernice possesses a deeply rooted spirituality and a strong zeal for advancing God's kingdom. And Dexter has an astonishing resemblance to Martin, as well as the tenacity that Martin and I shared.

———— ❀ ————

TWENTY-TWO

I Will Count It All Joy

I n my heart, I know what killed Martin. Hate killed him, just as hate killed President John F. Kennedy and Sen. Bobby Kennedy. Only love and the sincerest pursuit of justice can heal the wounds laid bare by the assassination of three of the best and brightest among us.

For if Martin, John, and Bobby can be killed, how can we ever rest in peace? If Martin, John, and Bobby could not be saved—if causes both large and small can be settled by shadow agencies, conspiracies, and covert operations—doesn't this put our nation at terrible risk? If bullets are substituted for ballots, how can we believe that democracy in America is not in jeopardy? Such actions should be unthinkable in a country that has seen so many of its men and women shed their blood to speak noble words in aid of equally noble results.

One thing has long haunted me since April 4, 1968: I believe that James Earl Ray was not my husband's assassin and that the U.S. government had a hand in my husband's death.

On August, 27, 1998, I met with U.S. attorney general Janet Reno. I asked her to open an investigation that would finally bring all the facts about my husband's death to the forefront. There are a lot of Americans, me and my family included, who continue to believe Martin's murder was the result of a conspiracy involving the U.S. government. This is why, personally, it is hard for me to believe that President Lyndon Johnson himself was not involved somehow, either directly or indirectly.

I was so disappointed when the statement Janet Reno issued promised only a "limited investigation." How can you do a partial investigation? That is nothing. I had no illusions that anything would come from such a half effort.

I did, however, get a measure of justice. On December 8, 1999, in a civil suit I filed in Memphis on behalf of my family, a jury of six whites and six blacks implicated U.S. government agencies in the wrongful death of my husband. The extensive evidence presented during the trial convinced the jury that my husband had been the victim of assassination by a conspiracy involving the Memphis Police Department as well as local, state, and federal government agencies including military intelligence, movement insiders, and the Mafia. The jury affirmed the trial's evidence, which indentified someone else, not James Earl Ray, as the shooter, and agreed that Mr. Ray had been set up to take the blame, something we had maintained all along. We requested a mere one hundred dollars in restitution to show that we were not pursuing the case for financial gain, but for the revelation of truth.

The jury's findings and conclusion were monumental. But what is absolutely amazing to me is that no more than a handful of reporters covered this trial from start to finish. The findings of the jury should have been published in their entirety by every major news source in America; it is not an overstatement to say that this was the trial of the century, rather than that of O. J. Simpson—which, I understand, about two thousand reporters covered. The mainstream media basically ignored the sworn testimony of former law enforcement agents and other persons who were direct witnesses at the time of my husband's assassination. Most Americans do not know that a jury found that their own government was party to a conspiracy to end my husband's life.

I have had thirty years to reflect on April 4, 1968, the day I felt my heart ripped apart, and I have not talked about this in much detail. But I feel more comfortable talking about it now, after that jury decision. If such a crime and cover-up could happen to a man of my husband's stature with no consequences, it could happen again, and I want everyone to be aware of what we know.

From the witnesses who testified and the court proceedings in 1999, my son Dexter and I pieced together the following account. It stands in stark contrast to the official reports, which concluded that James Earl Ray acted alone.

Thursday, April 4, 1968, is a date that still torments Memphis detective Ed Redditt and fireman Floyd Newsum, the only two blacks assigned to provide security for my husband's stay in Memphis. According to their testimony, both Redditt and Newsum were supposed to be working out of Fire Station No. 2 that night, directly across the street from the Lorraine Motel at 422½ S. Main St., where Martin was slain. The fire station's location made it ideal for surveillance: it was built on an embankment that raised it high above the street, affording it an eye-level view of, among other things, the motel's second-floor balcony.

But after comparing notes in the aftermath of the assassination, Redditt and Newsum learned that both of them had been pulled off their detail that night, ensuring that they would be nowhere near my husband when the shot was fired.

On Wednesday night, April 3, Newsum had gone to hear my husband speak. When he returned home at 10:30 p.m., he received a message telling him not to go to Fire Station No. 2 the next day; he was directed to another location, ostensibly because of a problem with understaffing. When he reported for duty at the other station, No. 31, however, he found not understaffing, but overstaffing. In fact, his assignment there meant that another man had to be detailed out. For years, Newsum wondered if events would have taken a different turn if only he had been at Fire Station No. 2.

No doubt, Redditt similarly thought, "If only I had been there!" On April 4, Redditt was at his post, in charge of stationary security for my husband. He was invaluable to this assignment. From his years of experience in town, Redditt knew everybody, from the Invaders (a black youth group) to the Klansmen, from ministers to militants. He was also such a loyal follower of my husband that he called himself one of Martin's disciples. On the morning of April 4, Redditt was surprised to learn that the King detail had been cut from ten people to two; he and his partner were it. Redditt testified that about two hours before the shot was fired, he received a call from his boss, Frank Holloman, director of the Memphis

Police and Fire Department, telling him to report to headquarters. He
told Holloman he was reluctant to leave his post, but he had to follow
orders. When he arrived, he was taken into a conference room. Holloman identified one of the people in the room as a Secret Service agent
and told Redditt that the agent had come from Washington to Memphis
to warn Redditt that there was a contract out on his life.

Why would a Secret Service agent, whose job was primarily to guard
the president and his family, be concerned with a lowly Memphis detective? Even if there was concern, why would an agent come personally?
Redditt was told that until the danger passed, he and his family were
going to be moved to a safe location for their own protection. Redditt
strenuously objected, but was overruled. Several police officers escorted
him to his home. Once there, he heard over the radio that Dr. King
had been shot.

With Newsum and Reddit out of the way, who did see what happened? By the time the state presented its case, a man named Charles
Stephens, a resident of the rooming house from which the fatal shot was,
allegedly, fired (our family maintains that the shot came from the bushes),
had become one of the state's most important witnesses. There were no
fingerprints from James Earl Ray in the rooming house; nor was there
evidence to prove that Ray's rifle fired the bullet that struck Martin. But
there was Charles Stephens's "eyewitness" testimony. Initially he said he
saw a very short, slightly built man run past his door (though James Earl
Ray was five foot ten and well built). Meanwhile, at about 4:00 p.m. (two
hours before the shot was fired), a Yellow Cab driver was dispatched
to 422½ S. Main St. to pick up a fare, who turned out to be Charles
Stephens, who was reportedly so drunk, so intoxicated, that he couldn't
get off his bed. The cabbie refused to transport the drunken Stephens,
returned to his cab, and drove away. Shortly after the shooting, when
reporters tried to question Stephens, they found him in jail, being held
"for his own protection," according to some accounts, and to improve his
memory, according to others.

On the morning of April 3, Loyd Jowers, owner of Jim's Grill, which
was across the street from the Lorraine Motel, received from a man who
was going by the name Raul the rifle that would be used in the assassination of my husband. In the court transcripts, Jowers says he put the rifle

in a box under the counter. He said that he had been given one hundred thousand dollars by a man with Mafia connections to help provide a cover for the shooting, for which a "patsy" would be provided. A few minutes after 6:01 p.m., when Martin was shot, Jowers took the gun, which was "still smoking," from the shooter and hid it back under the counter. It was picked up the next morning by the shooter, a man Jowers went on to identify as a police officer.

In the late 1990s, Don Wilson, an FBI agent working in the Atlanta bureau, told me that immediately after the shot was fired, he watched FBI agents laugh and joke about the murder of my husband. Wilson, now retired, was the agent who searched James Earl Ray's car, which was found at an Atlanta housing project several days after Martin was assassinated. In it, he found pieces of a handwritten note with the name "Raul" written on it.

My lasting wish is that an open investigation into my husband's death will be carried out by a national commission modeled after the South African Truth and Reconciliation Commission, to break down this wall of state secrecy about my husband's murder and follow up on the evidence put forward at the civil trial. Some six hundred thousand-plus pages of government records and files relating to the surveillance and murder of Martin exist. These files must be made fully available to the public, either by being released in full without review or with the appointment of an independent civilian review board to oversee the release process. This investigation and process should provide immunity for those who are willing to come forward and finally lay out all facts pertinent to the truth of who killed my dearly beloved Martin.

"Truth crushed to earth shall rise again." My husband said that many times. My lasting wish is that this truth, too, shall rise.

TRUTH, EQUALITY, FAIRNESS, justice—these are the causes to which I've tirelessly dedicated myself. But in the thick of these pursuits, there would come a point where I had to make some serious lifestyle changes.

First, in the late 1980s and early '90s, my parents were declining and needed more attention, and this turned out to be one of the most challenging times of my life. At first Edythe, Obie, and I thought our mother was just showing ordinary signs of senility, but in 1988 we learned that she was suffering from Alzheimer's disease. On some of my visits, I recall that she would put on a sweater and get her purse and say, "I need to go home. My parents are looking for me. My parents are worried about me." I would tell her, "You are already at home. This is Coretta, your daughter," but I wasn't able to reassure her. Around 1990, I moved her from Alabama to Atlanta, to my home for a few months. Then, when she began to need more care than I could provide at the house, I moved her to a nursing home associated with Georgia Baptist Hospital near the King Center, where it would be easy for me to visit her. As her health declined, I would sometimes sleep at this facility with her. On some occasions, Laura Brown would stay in my stead. Later, I moved her to a different home, one associated with Emory University, so that she could receive the around-the-clock care she needed. Some friends helped me with the expenditures. I tried to pamper her. I threw parties for her. I visited her practically every day. Although my family provided some support, I had hired caregivers to attend to my mother 24/7. I could have been comforted even more by visits from my pastors and members of my church family, but it just didn't happen. This was a very lonely and extremely difficult time for me. It was not easy, but neither was it a burden. I was often sad as I faced the reality that I was losing my parents, but I also found joy in being there for them. They had always been there for me. My mother passed in February 1996, a few weeks after her ninety-second birthday. Dad kept on working at his general store way into his early nineties, until I decided to intervene and stop him, because he was becoming frail and not as mentally sharp. Many customers were taking advantage of his weakened state, cheating him. In 1998, after a brief stay in the hospital, he died in his sleep on the Sunday before Thanksgiving. He was ninety-nine years old.

After my parents passed, there came a point when I needed to slow down, to take care of myself and my health. Following in the footsteps of my son Dexter, I became a vegan. In those years, when I spent so much time visiting my mother at the nursing home, I started getting stiff, very stiff, in my legs and my knees. I could hardly get up and down. Dexter said, "Mother, you know your body is breaking down. You're too young to allow yourself to do that." He is a vegetarian and follows a holistic regimen, and he thought I should try it. At first I eliminated red meat, except I was still eating barbecue. But eventually, I found a nutritionist. I worked with her for a year, and she started me on a raw food diet, about 80 percent raw food. I gave up meat, and I don't miss it. Dexter also introduced me to blue-green algae, a sea vegetable packed with nutrients. Once I turned from relying on prescription drugs to using alternative medicines, a more holistic approach that includes exercise together with a vegan diet, I began to feel much better and I have a higher level of energy. I use a mini-trampoline for exercise. I raise my heels up and act like I'm jogging, but I don't go very high up off the trampoline, because that would be a little too much for me. I am also into reflexology treatments, which I get from a massage therapist. I underwent a major lifestyle adjustment, and I enjoy talking about it.

In 2004 it was finally time to leave the home I'd shared with Martin and my children. I moved into a spacious condo, more than thirty floors up, with a glorious view, morning and night, that Oprah Winfrey had obtained for me quietly, without fanfare. I enjoy being able to wake up every morning and open my blinds and look out over the city, and in the evening, I love watching the beautiful sunset.

My friendships also have nourished my soul, and been a source of comfort and delight for me throughout my life and especially in my later years. One of the highlights was my "girls' weekends" with Myrlie Evers and Betty Shabazz. We met occasionally in one of the nicer Florida health spas, on the pretext of losing weight and eating healthy. Very seldom did we achieve our goals, but oh, what fun we had together! During our outings, at least one of us would usually wear a disguise: a long wig, sunglasses.

One particular trip, in May 1997, stands out in my mind. Ingrid Jones, a close friend and then vice president at Coca-Cola, generously covered the costs, and we stayed at the Doral Country Club and Spa in Florida, near Miami Beach. Myrlie arrived first, so excited. She knew how to swim, so she stayed in the pool until Betty and I arrived. When we were together, the three of us rarely talked about our status as widows, although this was the initial bond that brought us together. Myrlie's husband, Medgar, an NAACP field director, was murdered in front of their home in Jackson, Mississippi, on June 12, 1963, reportedly by a white Klansman. A black member of the Nation of Islam murdered Betty's husband, Malcolm X, on February 21, 1965. And Martin was murdered on

April 4, 1968. Our experiences were so deeply engrained in our individual consciousness that there was no need to speak of them. To do so would have been like talking about the air inside our suite, the grass outside our door, the sky above. They were an ever-present given. So it was liberating at times to be oblivious. We were not Mrs. King, Mrs. Shabazz, or Mrs. Evers. Just Coretta, Betty, and Myrlie.

At the Doral, basketball had our attention. The Bulls were playing. We screamed, we hollered; it didn't matter who won. That wasn't what we'd come for. We came to enjoy not being in charge of anything. We came because we loved one another unconditionally, despite negative news reports about how we'd tried to upstage or jealously compete with one another over the limelight. Imagine that anyone would actually want to rise to prominence on the basis of losing the man she'd loved!

When you can relax, let your hair down, and share your secrets—that's real friendship. At the end of our trip in May 1997, we took care to schedule our next girls' getaway. None of us could have imagined that a tragic turn would upset our plans.

A week after our trip, I received a call letting me know that Betty had been the victim of a fire. She'd suffered burns on more than 80 percent of her body and was in intensive care at Jacobi Medical Center in the Bronx. I dropped everything and prepared to go the hospital, hoping and praying that even with such severe burns, Betty, my dear fun, kind, friend, would live. I could not accept the fact that something like this could happen; I kept hoping that her condition had been exaggerated.

The idea of going to the hospital seemed unbearable. I called the poet and writer Maya Angelou, another close friend, and broke the news. Maya was very emotional, but said she would meet us at Jacobi. I called Bernice, who insisted upon flying to New York with me, along with my devoted special assistant, Kelvin ("Lynn") Cothren, to see Betty.

When we reached the Jacobi Medical Center, we could tell that Betty's daughters had been crying. The visibly distraught hospital administrator and PR person drew us aside. They tried to prepare us for what we were about to experience. "You will not be able to identify her," they told us grimly. Of course, Betty's six daughters, Attallah, Ilyasah, Qubilah, Malikah, Malaak, and Gamilah, knew who she was. We all knew *who* she was, yet we could not reconcile that image with the severely injured woman we would be seeing.

Yolanda, who was already in New York, soon joined us at the hospital. Phillip Mott, my cousin who lived in New York, and Maya, Bernice, Yolanda, my assistant Lynn, and I all labored to collect ourselves before entering Betty's room. We needed strength, and I asked Bernice to pray for us. As expected, she rose to the occasion—she really is a prayer warrior. Her prayers lifted our spirits as we braced ourselves.

Before we entered Betty's room, we had to put on face masks, sterile hospital gowns, paper slippers, and head coverings. When we entered the room, with one of Betty's daughters, we found that Betty's entire body had been wrapped in a heavy, gauzelike material. Only a slit exposed her eyes and mouth. Through our tears, we all managed to talk to her, hoping she was still able to listen. We told her how much we loved her, and how we were praying God would heal her. We felt that she heard us, and left feeling sure she would make it. When we came out of the room, we felt uplifted.

Although Betty never said a word, she must have been responding in some way. The doctor, who had given her no chance, started to express hope that she would make progress after skin grafts; over the next few weeks, her doctors performed five skin replacement surgeries.

However, sadly, on June 23, 1997, Betty made her transition. She died thirty-two years and four months after Malcolm X. Losing her was so hard. If anything could have made the situation worse, it was the revelation that it was her and Malcolm's twelve-year-old grandson, Malcolm Shabazz, who had set the fire in her home in Yonkers, New York. He told police he was not trying to hurt his grandmother; that he was only trying to create a situation that would force him to be sent home to his mother, Qubilah, in Texas.

WHILE I AM speaking of personal matters such as friendship, people always want to know if I dated other men after Martin died or if I ever thought about remarrying. I've also been asked why my two daughters are thus far unmarried.

As for me, I have had dates but no serious marriage proposals. One of my very good friends since our days at Antioch, Dr. Lonnie MacDonald, a psychiatrist, and I would go see operas and plays together. When I was a UN public delegate living in New York, we would take long walks together. I also dated McHenry Boatwright, a bass baritone concert singer whom I met when we were both students at the New England Conservatory of Music. McHenry was a nice person with a beautiful voice, a great musician who also played the piano. He sang at the White House during the Carter administration. He tried his best to take me out shortly after Martin died. While I did go out with him once or twice, I did not have any strong feelings for him. And I believe it was too soon after Martin's death for me to date seriously. Eventually he married Duke Ellington's sister, Ruth. He died in 1994.

At this stage, just the thought of having someone in my bedroom when I'm in my seventies is not something to look forward to. The older you get, the harder it is to adjust to another person in your space. You have to wait on him, too. I waited on Martin hand and foot. He'd step out of his pajamas and leave them right in the middle of the floor, and I'd pick them up. I'd bring his food to him in bed if he felt like staying in bed. Can you imagine me doing all that now, at my age? Imagine two old folks together. I mean, what do you do?

Companionship is nice to have, of course, especially if it's the right kind, with no responsibility, but that's not possible. For the most part, my loneliness does not come from being without someone. It comes from being such a visible person: it's hard to go somewhere and not be reminded of who you are, hard to be able to really enjoy yourself. Oftentimes, I didn't go out because I didn't feel like dealing with being a celebrity. To that extent, I feel isolated, because I cannot always find things to do that I really can enjoy without being interrupted.

As to why my daughters have not married—perhaps the answer lies in how they saw Martin. If you believe that a man like Martin comes along once in a millennium, and you hold other men to the standard of a Martin Luther King Jr., you will not find anyone. That might be what my daughters are coping with. Maybe that's true for me as well.

But there's something else, too. Liberated, independent women intimidate some men, and my daughters inherited these traits from me.

They own their own things and there is little that a man could provide for them in that way. And many men like to feel they can provide things for you, like a home or a car. Men enjoy doing such things for women, but my girls knew Coretta, and Coretta was never a dependent woman. I had to learn to make it as a single parent at an early age. My daughters are just following the example of their mother.

How did I encourage this independence? Well, for example, I never bought my children cars; they bought cars when they could afford them. I never wanted to damage my children by letting them depend on me. My mother raised me the same way. I would remember her words: "I want you to have an education so you won't have to depend on anybody, including a man."

Similarly, I trust that my children—and my grandchildren, when they come—will remember what their parents, Martin and Coretta, taught them: to live their best lives, to forgive all quickly, to walk in faith, dignity, and love.

I HAVE LIVED a life beyond anything I ever imagined or thought possible for a child born in Nowhere, USA, into a race that was virtually disqualified from humanity and a gender condemned to silence. It is a life that, at the outset, felt like the slow, dragging gait of the mule trains that would pass my daddy's house on their way to the work site. Neither man nor beast was in a hurry. No reason to rush, nothing new to expect. Just the same old steady clippity-clop, day after day. Then, unexpectedly, I was caught up by and thrust into a whirlwind, guided by a force beyond myself and shaped to a purpose I often did not understand until I had to fulfill it.

I was not a stranger to trouble. I had been born into troubled and twisted times in the South. Our family home was burned down by white terrorists. But that persecution did not stop my father from pursuing his dreams, and maybe it also planted a seed within me, gave me the strength that prepared me for the future. I understood that I might be killed if I continued alongside Martin and served as his partner in the movement. So I prayed to God for guidance; I asked Him to give me the strength to accept His will in my life, even if it meant my death.

In my struggle, I also had to learn how to be an activist and a concert artist, a public person in her own right, while also maintaining the roles of minister's wife and mother to my four children. I hope that women can learn from both my mishaps and my successes.

Without Martin, I had to find the inner strength to go on. This is a lesson, too.

I have known great triumphs. With the help of many, I created the King Center to safeguard and champion Martin's legacy to all the nations, as a mecca for spiritual growth and activism. We created a national holiday to commemorate Martin's service and sacrifice, and to encourage others to follow in his footsteps. We spurred redevelopment in Atlanta, creating a citadel of diversity that helped attract the 1996 Summer Olympics and that continues to draw visitors from around the globe. I've met with presidents and prime ministers. I've met great spiritual leaders, including Popes Paul VI and John Paul II, and the Dalai Lama. I've put in time on picket lines in nonviolent protest campaigns for decent wages and working conditions from Memphis to South Carolina to Baltimore. I have spoken at some of the largest peace demonstrations in history, in New York City and Bonn, Germany. I participated in the miraculous transformation of an evil system of violence and bigotry that was sapping the humanity from white and black Americans alike. I stand now as a proud daughter of southern soil, a devoted citizen of the United States, an ambassador of goodwill to the world, and an architect of one of the greatest legacies known to humankind.

And along my journey, I found answers to the questions I often pondered when I was that little girl in Alabama: Who will I be? What is my purpose? The answers came little by little, crisis by crisis, trauma by trauma, like climbing Jacob's ladder—"Every rung goes higher, higher." If you have a purpose, you have to discover it. Once you discover that purpose, you must follow it. If it's in line with God's will, then I believe you will find fulfillment. When I wasn't praying or in tune with God's will and purpose, I wasn't happy. In contrast, when I was in tune with the will and purpose of God, things may not have gone well, but I still felt good about what I was doing, and about myself.

My story is one of divine preparation. I was prepared to lead. I was called, and I was chosen. Looking back, I see it so clearly: Meeting

Martin was prophetic. It was synergy. It was symphony. Our destinies fused, and we became two souls with one goal. Our union prepared both of us for something larger than either of us could ever have dreamed alone. We became agents of change and servants of one of the most enduring human rights struggles of the twentieth century and beyond.

Once I found my purpose, I was ready to die to hold on to it. I've never forgotten the motto of the first president of Antioch College, my alma mater: "Be ashamed to die until you have won some victory for humanity."

Marrying Martin and the movement perfected my journey of discovery, soothed my yearning to pour out the values and vision within my soul. The bombings, the murders, even the assassination of my husband only intensified my devotion and solidified my resolve that God had allowed me to be born at the right time in history, a time when the Spirit tracked down the willing, empowered the waiting, and magnified human outcomes far above what finite minds could conceive.

I want people to know that I was committed to leaving an eternal flame, built on love, that would never be extinguished. I wanted this flame to touch lives, communities, and nations. I wanted it to ignite and inspire. I wanted it to be an urgent call to community and public service.

Love is not a program, not a political party, not a race. It is a promise with a power all its own. The contributions of Martin and me, and of those behind and before us, are the greatest witnesses I can imagine to the power of love in action.

When it is time to end this journey, I will count it all joy.

Every heartbreak preceded a breakthrough; every thorn that pierced me positioned me for the next level of challenges. My story is a freedom song from within my soul. It is a story of struggle. It is about finding one's purpose, a guide to overcoming fear and standing up for causes bigger than one's self. It is a guide to discovery, a vision of how even the worst pain and heartaches can be channeled into human monuments, impenetrable and everlasting.

TODAY, THOUGH MANY dreams have been fulfilled down in the Valley, we have not yet reached the Mountaintop.

When all is said and done, is the vision of a Beloved Community that is part of the World House that Martin and I imagined together within reach?

Did we come close to picking up the pieces of the freedom movements scattered across a multiplicity of landscapes and building a model of sacred, special shelters for all people? Are we helping to create a foundation of help, hope, and healing?

Did we help others learn to work together to end the arms race, prevent environmental catastrophes, and dismantle systems that destroy others based on racial, sexual, or political differences? Are we closer to having a democracy infused with the values of diplomacy, trust, and respect for human life over unchecked militarism, greed, and political hegemony? Have we motivated others to become activists rather than spectators, to take on campaigns to feed the hungry, save the children, and fight poverty and economic exploitation in every nation? Have we inspired others to reach out from within their own comfort zones and build bridges of relationships across economic, political, and class lines?

While these may be the right questions, there are no easy answers. And I don't think my generation is the right one to judge. How do you assess a work when its harvest comes from the invisible, the martyred, and the nameless, people who allow those of us with names to be viewed as the leaders of our shared revolution?

All I know is that the hour is late, and there is still so much unfinished business. The Dream is a work that is very much in progress. I believe my husband's prophetic words are worth repeating and remembering as we go forward: "We have a choice today. Nonviolent coexistence or violent annihilation (within and without our nation). This may be mankind's last chance to choose between chaos and community."

I am counting on the next generation to pick up the still-broken pieces of society on humanity's Jericho Roads and continue the struggle against poverty, greed, and militarism that Martin and I gave our lives to correct, for struggle is a never-ending process and freedom is never really won. You earn it and win it in every generation.

I believe future generations will have the courage, the love, and the faith to get this done. This is my hope, and this is my prayer.

Afterwords

ANDREW YOUNG

❋

I have come to realize that much of the commitment Martin and I possessed came through our wives, both of whom grew up on the outskirts of Marion, Alabama. I grew up in New Orleans, and left for Howard University at fifteen. I was working in New York with the National Council of Churches when the sit-ins started. My wife, Jean, said to me, "It's time to go back home." I said, "We are at home." And Jean said, "No, this is not home. We have to go back South."

Now, I enjoyed my job, Jean was working on a master's degree at Queens College, and we had two babies, with another on the way. Still, she insisted that we had to leave. "How am I going to do that?" I asked. "You start by handing in your resignation to this job and we put the house up for sale," she said. I mean, that was a real show of commitment. As bad as things were, Jean was not going to abandon the South.

Coretta was not anxious to come back to the South. She had musical aspirations that were impossible to fulfill there. But after her home in Montgomery was bombed, her father and Daddy King came to take her and baby Yolanda away, and she would not budge. And Martin did not budge. If she had wavered, I doubt Martin would have stayed in Montgomery. There probably would not have been a Montgomery Bus Boycott.

Coretta was gracious, but stronger than the men around her ever wanted her to be. Remember, this was the fifties. We men thought we were going to rule the roost and our women would stay home, have babies, and bake cookies. Coretta wanted a family and a career. And she did achieve both, and excelled at both. She was a real hands-on mom, despite all the other assignments she took upon herself. I think her toughness came from her father. Her daddy, Obie, was one of the coolest men I have ever known. He was not polished, he was not articulate; he wasn't a speaker. But he was a powerful, well-respected man who built up a business, watched white residents of Heiberger, Alabama, destroy it, and still had the strength to go on and start another business and not hate anybody.

People look at Coretta and Martin and expect their kids to be like them, but that often is not the case. The children have been through so much, and they have to find their own way. I would never expect my children to carry on what I've done. I wanted them to do what God called them to do. My daddy wanted me to carry on what he was doing. He was a dentist and a baseball player, the only sport I did not play. I didn't want to go into that. That is why I've encouraged the King children to find their own identities, on their own. I told Martin III that he needed to go someplace in the backwoods of Latin America or Africa, someplace where nobody had ever heard of Martin Luther King Jr., and just get to know who he is and get in touch with his own spiritual understanding of life.

Andrew Young *is an American politician, diplomat, and pastor from Georgia who has served as mayor of Atlanta, a congressman, and a U.S. ambassador to the United Nations. He also served as president of the National Council of Churches USA, and was a supporter and friend of the Rev. Dr. Martin Luther King Jr.*

❦

I had worked for the Southern Christian Leadership Conference as Dr. King's lobbyist representative. Activist Bayard Rustin was then head of the northern office of the SCLC, and when he left, he suggested me for that position. There was a meeting of the SCLC board. A lot of people came. I told them if you want someone who has titles before or after his or her name, that's one thing, but if you want someone to get the job done, I will be your best choice. I was young. I might do the same swaggering/brash/strutting thing again, some fifty years later, but I'd do it a little less.

At any rate, I was chosen for the job, and I got to meet Mrs. King. We just liked each other from the start. I was a southern woman, and she was a southern woman. We had the same attitude toward things, like being very respectful of elderly people, even when they were boring. That is really southern black. We were proud of doing certain things that we thought were feminine. We loved to cook, to dress nicely, to sing a little bit. She felt good about being a wife, a mother, and a spokesperson.

Dr. King was killed on my birthday, April 4, 1968. I was devastated. Coretta and I grieved together, literally falling into each other's arms. And we remained that close the rest of her life. Coretta would come and stay with me occasionally at my home in Winston Salem, North Carolina. Once I shared a book with her that was written about sisters. "I have a sister and a brother that are blood relatives, but my chosen sister is Maya, who makes me laugh," she'd say. She also used to say that Martin told her she didn't laugh enough, and that she should go be around Maya.

I knew how to make her laugh. I'd sneak up on her and whisper something in her ear or tell her a joke. I couldn't enjoy myself better than to catch her off guard; she would do her best to control herself, but she'd laugh. She was very kind, too, and that's a quality I claim for myself. At least I mean to be. So we liked each other for that. Coretta was kind to those people others might look down upon, people who were uneducated or unlucky or unloved. She was serious about trying to be a good Christian. I mean acting it. Living it. Being it. Showing it. Sharing it. I will never stop missing her.

Coretta is more relevant today than ever. The fact that she married, then lost, the great love of her life, one of the most charismatic human beings in the world, a man who adored her, and was able to keep going after that and move us all to a higher level—that is courageous leadership. Coretta showed her womanliness, not just her humaneness. On one level, it's very possible to become an old female who lives long enough by managing not to get run over by a truck. Then there's a female who takes responsibility for creating something better in the time she has and the space she had to occupy. That is true greatness. And Coretta did that.

Maya Angelou *was an American poet, memoirist, and civil rights activist. The author most famously of* I Know Why the Caged Bird Sings, *she was awarded the National Medal of Arts and the Presidential Medal of Freedom, among many dozens of honors.*

JOHN CONYERS

✻

What must be understood is that Coretta King doesn't just have historical significance. She's also a role model as a leader for today. She picked up the mantle of her husband and kept pushing it forward, so that people everywhere, in all nations, people of all races, could have a living model of how to create systemic change without violence, without bloodshed, without hate.

Throughout the sixties and seventies, when she was speaking out and lobbying for the King holiday bill, civil rights groups and black lawmakers were operating in a fiercely hostile climate. There were many who were not supportive of Martin Luther King Jr.'s activism, and they did not want to honor him or commemorate him in any way. Even in the African American community, there were people who vigorously disliked King. I introduced the King holiday bill in 1968—and I continued to introduce it for fifteen years. It was not signed into law until 1983.

Despite the hostility, Coretta kept going. She became the replacement for her husband. She was his copartner while he lived, and she continued as his partner after his death. At that time in the sixties, you have to remember what a standout and stand-alone woman she was. There were few black female leaders who were respected across gender, ethnic, and political lines.

Remember, we did not have a black woman in Congress until 1968, with the election of New York congresswoman Shirley Chisholm, although we'd elected a white woman, Jeannette Rankin, in 1916. Coretta's reach was extensive, both horizontally and vertically.

The whole time, Coretta carried herself with such dignity. She was never involved in any kind of scandal. She carried great moral authority. We always felt she spoke for right at the right time. Her presence in political circles helped us men move beyond gendered traditions.

John James Conyers Jr. *is the U.S. representative for Michigan's Thirteenth Congressional District. He has been a member of Congress since 1965 and is currently its longest-serving member, making him the Dean of the House of Representatives. He is a founding member and dean of the Congressional Black Caucus, and in his more than fifty years of public service, he has been a major proponent of more than one hundred pieces of critical legislation, including the Voting Rights Act of 1965, the Violence Against Women Act of 1994, the Martin Luther King Holiday Act of 1983, the Motor Voter Act of 1993, the Alcoholic Beverage Labeling Act of 1988, and the Jazz Preservation Act of 1987. He was also the driving force behind the Help America Vote Act of 2002.*

DR. BARBARA WILLIAMS-SKINNER

❋

Coretta had a strong passion for what women were doing around the world, women such as Prime Minister Indira Gandhi of India, President Corazon Aquino of the Philippines, and Dolores Huerta, leader of the United Farm Workers Union. Mrs. King had her own following globally, way beyond the American civil rights movement.

For instance, she was very committed to the antiapartheid struggle. I went with her to Johannesburg and Soweto in the early eighties. We did small prayer groups, which was very dangerous. It was against the law for so-called Coloreds, Blacks or Indians to meet together in groups. Even the idea of doing the prayer sessions was radical; it was something not done in South Africa, but Coretta Scott King had the courage to do it anyway. Since she was such a high-ranking person, we went ahead and prayed for divine intervention to achieve racial equality. We quietly met in people's homes. We always felt the peaceful resolution there was the result of those prayers.

Most of my time with Mrs. King was really as her prayer partner. I saw that prayer was central to everything she did. I often stayed at her house, and I gave her a copy of a devotional called *My Utmost for His Highest*, by theologian Oswald Chambers. Every single morning we were together, whether we were traveling or in a hotel, we would carve out time to read from the devotional and reflect on Scripture and pray. That was her connection, that's how rooted she was, and that's how important her faith was to her.

In addition, she was very active at Ebenezer Baptist Church. The Rev. Joe Roberts was her pastor. She loved reading the Bible chapters about the prophets Amos, Joel, and Isaiah, those men who were steeped in the social justice tradition of their time. She was interested in the politics of Jesus. We talked about that a lot, how Jesus was not a blue-eyed man with soft hands like doves, not like the pictures that you see around. Jesus was a tough-as-nails leader of his time. We would go through the

Bible and read about His character, about toughness and love, those qualities that confirmed Coretta's ideal of the Beloved Community. Our time together was a very precious time.

You know, I don't think the general public ever really understood who Mrs. King was. First of all, you had a male-dominated civil rights movement that, in many ways, marginalized women. There were many extraordinary women in the movement, but they were in the background, in a way. There would have been no civil rights movement without women like Rosa Parks, Daisy Bates, or Fannie Lou Hamer. They were the backbone. There were of course the unknown women, too. At the March on Washington, only one woman got to speak, and that woman was singing: Mahalia Jackson. Dorothy Height, the head of the National Council of Negro Women, was not even allowed to speak. That was a period in which women in general were not lifted up as full partners in the movement. So it wasn't unlikely that Mrs. King would be pigeonholed. First of all, she was a wife and a mother and then a widow. She loved being a mother and a wife, but she was also exceptionally bright and had a lot of great ideas.

Here was a very outspoken woman, who said the freedom struggle is a never-ending process. Freedom is never really won; it's earned, and you win it anew in every generation. She spoke about freedom and against violence and racism in every form, every chance she got. And she was probably the most sought-after speaker of her time for that reason. So she had quite a voice on her own, but she never got over the fact that she was pigeonholed. People tried to put her in a box, and she literally refused that.

Dr. Barbara Williams-Skinner, *president of the Skinner Leadership Institute and cochair of the National African American Clergy Network, is a trusted adviser, public policy strategist, faith and community leader, author, lecturer, educator, executive coach, and mentor. She has served on the White House Faith Counsel, was the first female executive director of the Congressional Black Caucus, and continues to serve as an adviser to the CBC members and to the Congressional Black Caucus Foundation.*

MYRLIE EVERS-WILLIAMS

✻

Coretta, Betty Shabazz, and I were a threesome. The public perception, fanned by the media, was that we were jealous and competitive. In reality, we three had lost our husbands, the loves of our lives. What about that was something to be in competition over? How foolish.

People don't understand what it's like to bear the weight of being "the wife of," "the widow of." The perception is that there was no difference of opinion between you and your husband. You just went along with his views. And that was simply not so. Coretta was strong-willed. Her ability to persuade people, to bring them around to her way of thinking or to intervene behind the scenes, was tremendous. I recall, when I was chairman of the NAACP and there was much debate over whether or not I should receive the Spingarn Medal, one of their highest honors. This was in 1998. The opposition argued that since my late husband, civil rights activist Medgar Evers, had received it, I couldn't; we were in the same family, and it would break protocol. I said, "I disagree. My husband, who was the NAACP field secretary in Jackson, Mississippi, gave his life. As chairman of the national organization, I picked us up and helped us move forward. I want, deserve, and demand the Spingarn." Then I called Coretta, and she asked me what I wanted her to do. "Nothing," I said.

"I will make some calls," she told me. "Not only will you receive the Spingarn, but I'll be there to present it to you myself." A lot of people thought it wouldn't happen, but just like Coretta said, I received it, and she presented it to me.

When she and Betty and I were together, we tried not to talk about our husbands, which was hard to do—our lives had been so intertwined with theirs. If we disagreed about something, Coretta would raise a red flag. I once told her, "Coretta, you are a saint, but not much of a saint." And she laughed. Being together gave us the opportunity to be open, to ask ourselves questions, such as "Are we being too tough on or too kind to our children?" Between us, we had thirteen children. As mothers, we realized that their personas were very touchy, because of all the tragedies they'd gone through. Often, we didn't have answers, but we were support for each other on our journey.

I am the only surviving one of our threesome: Coretta and Betty are gone. I miss my sisters. I miss them terribly. We could talk to one another and be open and honest. We would laugh and tell each other truths we wouldn't share with anyone else. There were times when Coretta would call me in the middle of the night, just to talk. I knew our conversations would stay between us. I don't have that now. It's a vacuum that cannot be filled. It's amazing to me that the public can put you up on a pedestal, but at the same time, get some kind of sinister joy out of cutting you down or finding fault with you. Luckily, there are also those who accept you as you are—just human, giving it your best shot. I know Coretta shared that feeling about us. We all did.

Myrlie Evers-Williams *is an American civil rights activist and journalist who worked for more than three decades to seek justice for the murder of her civil rights activist husband, Medgar Evers. She was chairwoman of the NAACP, has published several books on civil rights, and delivered the invocation at the second inauguration of President Barack Obama.*

PATRICIA LATIMORE

❀

I was Mrs. King's assistant. I started working for her in 1965. She and Dr. King had just moved into their new home, and they were looking for a babysitter. I got the job. I was just a teenager. I worked for her off and on for forty years. I was working for her in the year she died, on January 30, 2006.

People knew about the big things she did, but few people knew about the small things that were big to the many who benefited. She loved giving family and friends cards and presents. Christmastime was huge with her. She would also collect the names of people she met and send them a Christmas card or a birthday card. She would spend two or three hours in the card store, picking out just the right card for each person. She would sign them herself. Eventually, when the list grew to three thousand, we had to stop. Her staff had to begin picking out presents around Thanksgiving to get them all out for Christmas. The gifts didn't go just to her family and friends but also to people in need, especially struggling families with children. She was also known for intervening in situations where people were hurting. For example, one of the King Center's staff member's house burned down, Mrs. King sent food, clothing, funds, and whatever else was needed. She was the kind of sweet person who would get personally involved. She would make things happen for her staff and for others whose plights were brought to her attention.

She was always giving, but one gift that was given to her that she loved was the condominium Oprah Winfrey secured for her in August 2004. Mrs. King should have left her house in Vine City years before that; the house was deteriorating, and it had been broken into several times. Actually, a water leak caused the ceiling to collapse in the hallway right outside Mrs. King's bedroom, and even though the ceiling and the leak could be fixed and were fixed, that leak signaled that it was high time for her to move out. Andy Young interceded; he had a conversation with Oprah. Mrs. King and Oprah had become friends through Maya Angelou. And

Oprah wanted to do something special for Mrs. King, so she set things in motion.

The condo was on the thirty-ninth floor, in a very nice section of Peachtree Road. I had my office there. The view was magnificent. We would walk out on the balconies and see all the way to Stone Mountain. We were so happy that Oprah arranged for her to spend her last days in such a beautiful environment.

It wasn't until we moved into the condo, however, that I knew something had gone awry with Mrs. King. I began picking up that she was sick. I took care of her bills—an easy job. But then it became more difficult because she kept losing things. At the old house, her office files ended up on top of her bed. So I chalked up some of the confusion to the move. But then she began complaining that she kept seeing a shadow over her eye. I alerted Bernice, and I made an appointment with Mrs. King's eye doctor, who referred her back to her primary care physician. It seems the eye doctor had spotted a problem in her aorta, the main artery in the body that leads to the heart. Her primary care doctor then referred her to a cardiologist. Shortly thereafter, she started having TIAs, mini-strokes, and those mini-strokes led to a minor stroke and eventually a major stroke on August 16, 2005.

I will never forget the day—January 27, 2006—when we prepared her to go off to a treatment center in Mexico. She was in a wheelchair by then. She really did not want to leave the condo. Bernice, who was accompanying her to Mexico, was there. And Martin III was there, because he was going with her and Bernice to the airport. Usually, when she would go out, she would give everyone a hug. This time she just wheeled herself to the door and waited to be taken to the van. She wouldn't give me a hug. She wouldn't even say good-bye to me.

I never saw her alive again. When she arrived at a destination, I was always the first person she called. But by this point, she could not talk. Bernice called me on Friday and again on Saturday to include me in the prayer calls. But I was in church during Sunday's prayer call, and I didn't hear anything on Monday morning. That Monday night, I happened to be on the phone with Bernice's best friend, Deleice Drane. We were just talking to each other to talk out what was happening, and Bernice called Deleice right then to tell her that Mrs. King was gone. That's how I found out. In my gut, I knew before the hurting words were spoken that I would never see Mrs. King again.

Finally I pulled myself together. When I was told her body was coming into the hangar at the Charlie Brown airport, where private planes arrive, I made up my mind I had to be there. It was 5:00 a.m. when she arrived. All of Mrs. King's children were on the plane with her. I followed the hearse to the funeral home in my car. Mrs. Farris and others met us there. When I saw the body I was upset—even more so because someone had cut her hair. I knew she would not have wanted that. I left the funeral home and went back to the condo. I could not go home. I could not think. I could not work. I could not do anything.

Even after forty years, she still sometimes seemed larger than life to me, someone I expected to always be here, to live on forever.

But in a way, if people really understand what a warm, vibrant human being she was, she will live forever.

Patricia Latimore *formerly worked in client services at Pfizer and was, for more than twenty years, a personal assistant to Coretta Scott King.*

My Mother, My Mentor

by

DR. BERNICE A. KING

I am so glad that God chose me to be Coretta Scott King's daughter. He did not make a mistake. If she had not been my mother, I would have never seen or thought there could be anyone like her. She was rare. She had this unmatched blend of character, personality, spirituality, commitment, and organization. Very few people have the capacity to balance and manage all of that. She had the ability to multitask in a way I have never seen in any other person. She had a way of managing the most complex civil and human rights problems, while at the same time paying attention to the personal needs of others. And this ability never left her. Though she was tough, she was also very tender.

Three weeks before she passed, for example, Evelyn, one of her around-the-clock caregivers, and I took Mom to the hospital for tests. After the tests, I helped her into her wheelchair and wheeled her back into the waiting area where Evelyn had been seated. Evelyn had gone into the restroom. "Evelyn, Evelyn." Mom forced the words out. When Evelyn returned, I told her that my mother had been asking about her. Evelyn put two and two together, explaining, "Your mother is saying my name because she knows I am a diabetic and she knows I have not eaten today." Hearing that, my mother began nodding her head in affirmation. Evelyn was right.

After suffering several strokes and a major heart attack and being in the last stage of ovarian cancer, Mom was gravely ill, yet her major concern at that moment was the well-being of her caregiver. Who really does that? She was the epitome of unselfishness. Caring. Considerate. Giving. That is the way she was.

She made everyone feel special, so you can only imagine how special we felt being her children. While she was helping to raise a nation, she was also raising me, my two brothers—Martin III and Dexter—and my sister, Yolanda. And we always knew she put us first.

After Daddy died, Mom kept the philosophy and strategy of nonviolence before the nation. People were discounting nonviolence. Remember, you had the rise of the Black Power movement, people like H. Rap Brown, riots across the nation. My mother really had to make a case for nonviolence, to continue raising our consciousness and get us to focus on peace, to define and perpetuate the Dr. King legacy. She was leading world leaders while attending to her own birth family, being both mother and father in one. If she sensed something was going on between her children, she'd show up and talk to us individually. She'd tell us that we really ought to call our brother or sister and work things out. She was the matriarch, the glue that held us together.

One particular memory that sticks with me was when I caught pneumonia, and was confined to the house for about three weeks. I think it was around 1995. Mom came to see me every day. She would prepare soup for me to eat: would go down to the kitchen and fix it, put it on a tray, and bring it up to me. My mother did everything first-class. She was somewhat of a perfectionist. I think I get that from her. She'd put the soup bowl on a plate and then on a tray, with a napkin and a soup spoon, and she'd arrange the crackers in a circle. Some people break the crackers or give you the package and let you open it yourself, but she wouldn't just throw things together. Then she'd sit with me, and when I was through eating, she would go back to the kitchen and bring me something to drink or more soup. What I remember is how attentive she was, how she was attuned to my feelings. She was like that with all of us, despite all the challenges pulling at her. She knew how to pick information out of us. When we became adults, she didn't just cut us loose and let us go our own way; she kept her eyes and ears tuned to us. You would think other things would have distracted her, but not so, not on the important challenges we faced.

The one thing that she could not do was attend a lot of our extracurricular activities, which disappointed us when we were little. But it's something we understood as we grew older. For example, I was into everything, and she would have driven herself crazy just trying to keep up. I played soccer, I ran track, I did the shot put, the long jump, the 100-yard dash, and the relays. In high school, I played basketball and softball; in college I played tennis and volleyball. On top of that, I played in the jazz band in high school. I'd started out with the clarinet in elementary, and then moved on to the alto sax. And of course I played the piano like my mother. As a former music teacher, she knew the basics of virtually every instrument, which helped, because each one of her children played something different. Yolanda played the violin and clarinet, Dexter played the trumpet, and Martin the trombone. Both boys played the guitar. We were quite a musical family. Music was part of our lives. Often in the morning, we'd hear Mother going "MeMeMeMe . . . Mememe. . . ." Tuning up for whatever song she'd sing—mostly to herself—that day. She made sure we went to the opera, too. When she couldn't go, she'd send us with someone, to give us that exposure. I often felt it was torture, but she wanted to introduce us to the arts, to make sure we were well rounded.

In one of the most difficult periods of my life, my mother was there for me. It was the time when I was in law school and I almost committed suicide. My roommate came downstairs in our condo and saw me with a knife in my hand. In my mind, I was trying to balance which would be the worst pain: staying alive or inflicting hurt on those I would leave behind. My roommate looked at me, sensing my desperation. "What are you doing?" she asked. I don't know what I told her, but she thought the situation was serious enough to call my mother. And Mom gathered some family members and came to see me.

As I tried to untangle my feelings, I thought about the loss of my father when I was five years old. When I was six, my uncle A.D. was found dead in his pool. They said he drowned, but he was a good swimmer, and I don't believe that's how he died. Reports showed there was no water in his lungs at the time of his death. When I was eleven, my grandmother—we affectionately called her Big Mama—Mama King, was gunned down in church. My cousin Darlene dropped dead when I was thirteen, and her brother, my cousin Al, died shortly before I started law school. They were around my age, and they died of heart problems.

That Friday evening when I was contemplating suicide, all of these memories and thoughts gushed to the forefront of my mind. It troubled me—the confusion, the questions about the deaths, especially the men in my immediate family dying so young. At that time, none had lived past thirty-nine. I just started hurting. I was grieving about the past, but I was also shaken by what had happened in law school. I'd ended up on probation after only two semesters, and I'd been told that if I did not come off of it after summer break, I was in danger of being kicked out. That was devastating. Law school was my hope. It was the thing that gave me my identity, the thing that defined who I was. I was trying to get away from the whole Daddy identity. It was too overwhelming. I needed something for Bernice.

Two months after that depressive episode lifted, something strange happened. I was told a close friend had committed suicide; just got a gun and blew her brains out. It weighed so heavily upon me. Every time I closed my eyes, I could see her shooting her brains out, even though I wasn't present. I had to go see a psychiatrist; I was prescribed sleeping pills. When I look back at that time, I know it was the Holy Spirit that ministered to me, that stopped me from killing myself. He became real to me then. In my spirit, I actually heard the Lord saying to me: "Put the knife down. You have purpose, and people are going to miss you." At that time, I was feeling unloved, thinking nobody cared about me. But my mother comforted me. She came to me. I could feel her unconditional love, and I was able to come off of probation and eventually graduate.

Always, my mother gave me unconditional love. She never argued with me about the state I was in. She just helped me move out of it.

For years after my mother's good friend Betty Shabazz died, there was a lingering sadness. I began to pray that my mother would once again have the opportunity to truly let her hair down and have fun out of the glare of the spotlight that comes with being a celebrity. I was so happy when God answered my prayers through Maya Angelou. She and Oprah developed a great friendship with my mother, the three of them. They attended parties, gatherings, and cruises together. I remember in 2004, Mom was invited to Oprah's fiftieth birthday party cruise. And boy did she have a blast. Usually when she returned from one of those events, she would be laughing, almost giddy, like a schoolgirl. Because she was with other well-known, famous people she didn't have to feel like she was on display.

The condo that Oprah secured for her in Atlanta was also right on time, such a blessing. It was clear that once she had the stroke in 2005 she could not have remained at our home in Vine City. The steps were a barrier, and it would have been extremely difficult to make the house wheelchair accessible because of the way it was built. The condo, which had an elevator, provided her a place where she could feel well cared-for and every morning, awaken to a beautiful sunrise.

About nine months after Mom passed, it hit me that the very woman I had been looking at all my life was my spiritual mentor. She was more than a mother. She lived the principles she practiced. It wasn't "Do as I say, not as I do." It was like she poured out an ethical pattern before us, a pattern of excellence and honesty. We could choose it or not choose it, but it was there in front of our faces. For years, I kept searching and searching, but I could never connect with anyone. And then it hit me— I'd already connected with my mother. Even though she was not a preacher, she was a true minister, a true servant of God, a true woman of God. When I had to preach, Mom would call me and say, "Baby, how you feeling?" I'd reply with the usual: "I don't have anything to say. I'm struggling." And she would say, "Your dad would say that too. But when you open up your mouth, God will speak through you. He will use you." Then she would pray with me. And she was right. Every time.

Bernice A. King *is the fourth and last born child of Martin Luther King Jr. and Coretta Scott King. She is a graduate of Spelman College and holds Master of Divinity and Doctor of Law degrees from Emory University. In 2012, she became CEO of the Martin Luther King Jr. Center for Nonviolent Social Change.*

The Making of Her Memoir

by

REVEREND DR. BARBARA REYNOLDS

I first met Coretta King in 1975 when I wrote a cover story about her for the *Chicago Tribune Sunday Magazine*, where I worked as a reporter. I was startled, even amazed, when she called me personally to agree to my request for a series of interviews for that story. Only seven years had passed since Dr. King's assassination. To spend time with the widow of such a man was journalistic ecstasy.

I was also puzzled that she was so amenable to being interviewed by me, because I had recently written a hard-hitting book about a former King aide, the Rev. Jesse Jackson (*Jesse Jackson: America's David*). In those days, it was virtually a sin for a black journalist to write anything but flattering pieces about black leaders, leaders who already caught so much hell from whites. Breaking the black code could mean being smeared as an Uncle Tom, a CIA agent, an FBI spy, or even a spurned lover. After I wrote that book about Jesse Jackson, I got hit with all those responses, plus death threats, plus a few influential people pressuring stores to remove my book from their shelves. I was as welcome in some black circles as a skunk at a tea party.

But notwithstanding my reputation, or maybe because of it, Mrs. King called me up. "Come to Atlanta," she said. "We are an open book here. I have nothing to hide. Just promise me you will write the truth."

We met at the Interdenominational Theological Center, a predominantly African American seminary within walking distance from Morehouse College, where Dr. King had gone to school. There she was in a small classroom, amid boxes, some waiting to be unpacked because she was moving her office into the seminary as temporary headquarters. She was beautiful, graceful, even regal, but she greeted me with down-home Magnolia Blossom charm. She didn't have a desk yet, but her vision for what would become the King Center was not encumbered by her surroundings. She showed me the blueprints for the Center, a multi-million-dollar structure that she envisioned as a kind of international West Point of nonviolence.

Pondering the enormity of her goals, I asked, "How are you going to do all that? Do you know anyone else who has done something like this? Where are you going for help?"

Looking me straight in the eye, she said, "Yes, I do know someone who will help me. The Holy Spirit will guide me."

The Holy Spirit? I was not the ordained minister or seminary profes-sor I am today. I was a "just the facts, please" kind of journalist. I wanted specifics I could sink my teeth into, not an introduction to an invisible entity I couldn't interview.

But from that encounter a thirty-year relationship began. Over the decades, I peppered her with questions, some I am now embarrassed to have asked. Here was a woman who engaged with presidents, prime min-isters, princes, and premiers on a regular basis who took time not only to answer my questions but to respond so convincingly that I came to share her values. Why nonviolence? At first, it didn't make sense to me. How was it possible to love evil, mean-spirited people? How could she say that suffering was ever redemptive? And why did blacks have to be the ones to suffer? Eventually, she became my friend, mentor, and teacher—my chief explainer and interpreter of complex ideals.

For a very long time, though, from the seventies to the nineties, I didn't know I was writing her memoir. Initially, I was covering King Cen-ter events for the newspaper. If there was an event at the Center, she'd call me and say, "Why don't you come?" Later, I traveled with her as a reporter, including her in coverage at *USA Today*, where I was an editor, in a radio broadcast I did at Radio One, and in my commentaries and columns for other media. After a while, I traveled with her as a friend, to her family reunions, to events at the Kennedy Center, and so on. During those travels, too, I would take notes, record bits and pieces of what she had said, not necessarily toward a particular piece of writing, but as a way of trying to understand the inner workings of her heart and soul. Mean-while, it turned out, she was also having an effect on me. When I was a

Nieman Fellow at Harvard, she made regular calls to see what, if anything, I was learning. Sometimes our conversation would not end until I heard a steady hum signaling that she had dozed off to sleep. On other calls, she would continue to challenge me to discard some of my not-so-Christian beliefs and to understand the principles of nonviolence. Years later, I became a minister. But before I started hanging around with Mrs. King, I wasn't much of a Christian. Once, I was traveling with her on a Sunday and when she asked if I was ready for church, I said, "Mrs. King, do I have to go?"

As friends we toured places in Alabama where only a few years before neither one of us would have been safe from racial violence. In Marion, Alabama, we relaxed on the porch with her parents, Bernice and Obie Scott. Her father was in his eighties then and still operated a one-pump gas station and a country store. The Scott family owned land that went farther than the eye could see. I've always thought that coming from landowning people contributed to Coretta's innate sense of independence. I also traveled with her to the Hippocrates, an upscale Florida spa, where we ate raw vegetables for a week and drank terrible-tasting grass smoothies. As soon as I got out of her sight at the airport, I scarfed down all the chips and cookies in my reach. When I visited Atlanta, I often stayed in the Kings' family guest room, down the hall from Coretta's bedroom, where jam-packed file folders occupied the space on the bed once reserved for her beloved Martin.

I wish I could say I knew she was grooming me for the task of working on her memoir. I didn't know. And that tells you something about who she was. She had a gentle touch, a smooth flow. She could help people and events evolve without anyone understanding the dynamics of the change until it was done. Around 1997, it just seemed natural when this woman who had become my friend and mentor turned to me to help her write her book. That is when we really got serious. We had our lawyers draw up a contract.

She had access to a condominium in a nearby Atlanta suburb. On some weekends and during my vacation time, I would meet her there. We would literally lock ourselves in, not taking calls. A chef would prepare all-vegan meals. I always packed candy and chips, so when she wasn't looking I could distance myself from her healthy eating.

Our meetings had a routine. At the start, she would pull out her Bible, *The Daily Word*, and *My Utmost for His Highest* by Oswald Chambers, an early-twentieth-century Scottish Baptist and Holiness Movement evangelist, and she would lead a discussion with me, challenging me to dig deeper into the messages in those readings. Then our other work would begin. I had an outline for each session, but Mrs. King rarely stayed on point. We would start at A, and if the spirit moved her we would hit D, forgetting about anything in between.

Our meetings were never unruly or disrespectful, but they were sometimes frustrating. Her memories were strong and detailed, but I thought she sometimes used her gifts to share material that was off the point; she criticized me for being heavy-handed and not gracious enough. She was helping me to grow internally until I could rise to the challenge of understanding the vital, utmost relationship she had as a Christian. If I did not ask her the tough, even painful questions, I would fail her as a journalist, but if I approached her journey only on a secular level, I would fail her in a different way.

Sometimes I remember asking the wrong question at the wrong time and in the wrong way. For example, one time we had just come out of Ebenezer Church. We had heard a good sermon, and Mrs. King was in good spirits. And in response to a news article, I asked her if she thought Dr. King was faithful to her marriage vows. She looked at me crestfallen, saying, "Barbara?" My abrupt question clearly deflated her momentarily. I felt bad about the timing, so I changed the subject, went into damage control, and waited for another day. I did ask her about that on another day; she gave me an answer, and that answer is in the book.

It is my feeling that she agonized over the issue of when her memoirs should be published. And I sometimes thought that, perhaps subconsciously, she was delaying the publication until after her demise. On the one hand, she wanted a document that would inspire future generations for leadership; on the other hand, she wanted people to know there is no crown without a cross to carry, no gain without pain. That meant exposing her own flaws as well as her successes. This also meant identifying people who she felt had attempted to sabotage her institution-building or even the moral underpinnings of the Dream. As someone who moved on a plane of seeing past flaws to find virtue, it felt more natural to her to resist unflattering critiques. There are some things in this book I believe she did not want said in her lifetime.

Her favorite slogan was "Be ashamed to die until you have won a victory for humanity," a quote from Horace Mann, the founding president of Antioch College, where she had been a student. She often said those words aloud. And what so amazed me is that she actually meant them. Many times she put her life on the line. When her house was bombed in 1955 during the Montgomery bus boycott, her father and Dr. King's father demanded that she take her infant and go back to Atlanta. She refused. She knew if she left, Dr. King would follow. If that had happened, there might not have been a bus boycott nor the many victories that stemmed from it. The bombings all around her, the death threats against her and her loved ones, and the government harassment didn't stop with Montgomery, but she downplayed all the dangers to keep from piling mental stress on her four children.

Her courage fascinated me because I wanted that kind of courage but just didn't have it. As a student I made my first trip down South to help register blacks to vote shortly after the passage of the 1965 voting rights bill. From my closed environs in Columbus, Ohio, where I grew up, I had never given thought to the possibility that my brown face could conjure enough angst in anybody that it would make them want to kill me. Yet it happened. In 1965 our group of students was chased by the KKK and a roadblock was set for us. We escaped, but during a protest march, the police came and ordered us to disperse. The only reason I did not run was because my arms were locked, trapping me with the others. Just that one brief encounter with Southern violence terrified me. The experience showed up in my night dreams and nightmares for years.

I'd had a taste of what courage looked like, and I didn't have it. Mrs. King did. Beyond a shadow of a doubt, she was a great American hero who was willing, at any given moment and over the long haul, to give her life to set others free.

I started taping our conversations around 1975, when I wrote that story for the *Tribune*. I remember carrying around a bulky cassette tape recorder and a blue typewriter I'd bought at Sears to transcribe my notes.

I stopped interviewing her in 2000. Over the years, I had gathered about fifty tapes of our conversations. When she passed away in 2006, it never crossed my mind to stop working on the book.

I knew the book offered history and perspectives from Mrs. King that needed to be shared. What kept Mrs. King going through the lonely days of taking the movement forward without the love of her life and with recriminations from so many around her? How did she build the King Center and organize the lobbying efforts for the Humphrey-Hawkins bill and then for the King holiday? How did she do all of this and so much more as a single mother? How could she believe that our own government had played a role in Dr. King's assassination and not become bitter, but, rather, maintain a great love for America?

My task was not merely to sort through the words she gave me and to share the story she shared with me, but to put her memories into a rhythm with the right tone. I wanted her soul to talk to us. This task was very difficult and I will have to leave it to others to judge the result.